INTERNATIONAL TRADE INSTABILITY

# International trade instability

JOSEPH D. COPPOCK
*Professor Emeritus*
*The Pennsylvania State University*

SAXON HOUSE

*Published by*

SAXON HOUSE, Teakfield Limited,
Westmead, Farnborough, Hants., England.



ISBN 0 566 00154 3
Library of Congress Catalog Card Number 76–49230
Typeset in IBM Press Roman by Preface Ltd, Salisbury, Wilts
Printed in Great Britain by Biddles Ltd of Guildford

# Contents

## List of tables

## List of figures

# Preface

In 1972, about a decade after I had completed *International Economic Instability* (1962), I decided that it would be worthwhile to re-examine the problem of international trade instability on a global basis. The present study is the result.

Among the considerations affecting my decision were the increase in the number of independent countries in the world, the great improvement in economic statistics, the waning of the economic effects of the Second World War, the continuing concern of many countries with trade instability, and my belief that I could now treat the subject more satisfactorily than I had been able to in the 1962 book. Between 1965 and 1971 I wrote two monographs and supervised three doctoral dissertations on various aspects of international trade instability, but I wanted to round out my research in this field with a major global study.

The events on the international economic scene since this study was started bear ample witness to the continuing importance of the subject. In addition, the national and international efforts to deal with the large and sudden increase in oil prices in 1973 confirm the advantages of 'cushioning' policy measures, as recommended in the 1962 book and as elaborated in this one.

The present study is in several respects an improvement on the earlier one: (a) import instability is here given approximately the same attention as export instability; (b) a simpler measure of instability is employed; (c) statistics for more countries, more variables and more years underlie the present study; (d) 'contributions' of countries to world trade instability are given more explicit treatment; and (e) the analysis of export (and import) instability, particularly the multivariate analysis, employs a more satisfactory statistical technique. Probably partly as a result of these techniques, much higher coefficients of correlation between export or import instability and other variables are obtained.

The present study resembles the previous one in certain respects: (a) the country, rather than the commodity, approach is given primary attention; (b) 'cross-section' analysis is used to identify factors associated with trade instability, although the basic concern is with changes through time; (c) eclecticism characterises both the analytical and policy parts of the book, because there do not seem to be any simple explanations of, or ways of dealing with, excessive trade instability; (d) the basic statistics, arduously assembled and calculated in many cases, are included for the benefit of other investigators in this and related fields; (e) practical national and international policies are given systematic attention; and (f) I have taken pains to avoid technical terms wherever possible, so that any interested person, and not just an econometrician, can follow what is written.

This study deals primarily with a fairly well-defined historical period: 1959–71. By 1959 most of the economic readjustments consequent upon the Second World War had been made. By 1971 the gold-exchange standard, this time based on the United States dollar, had again (and finally?) failed. Despite the monetary problems of the period, it was a time of generally low trade barriers, widespread convertibility of currencies, large capital movements, and rapidly expanding and moderately stable international trade.

This study could not have been made without the money provided by the Ford Foundation, the Lilly Endowment, Inc., and The Pennsylvania State University (Department of Economics and College of Liberal Arts). Allen T. Unsworth, now of Stockton State College (New Jersey), served conscientiously as principal research assistant. He was ably assisted by Patricia O'Connor and Ru-Chiao Wang. Roy Karaoglan, of the American University of Beirut, provided very useful comments on the manuscript.

*Joseph D. Coppock*

# 1 Introduction

Fluctuations characterise all aspects of international economic relations: trade in goods and services, financial relations (monetary relations, capital movements and unilateral transfers), migration, and interchange of knowledge related to economic activities. This study, which concentrates on the fluctuations of international trade in goods and services, falls into three parts. The first part portrays statistically the instability of the foreign trade of individual countries for the years 1946–71, with particular attention to the period 1959–71. The countries included in the study are listed in Table 2.1. The second part seeks to identify factors or variables that are associated with trade instability. The third part is concerned with government policies for reducing trade instability or for mitigating its effects.

## Ramifications of the subject

Trade fluctuations affect nations' balance-of-payments positions, capital movements, levels of employment of their productive resources, consumption levels, rates of economic growth, internal distribution of income, prices, and gains from trade – to mention just some of the major kinds of effects. Trade fluctuations have effects that occasionally spill over into the political and military spheres, just as political and military actions can affect the degree of instability of trade. There are many historical examples.

The greater the degree of involvement of nations in foreign trade, usually measured by the ratio of foreign trade to national income, the more concerned they tend to be about fluctuations in their trade. Public and governmental concern with the problem of international trade instability does, however, vary with the intensity of the instability problem for various countries, regardless of the degree of involvement in trade. Since the First World War, the problem has been one of fairly frequent concern for most countries of the world. In the period since the Second World War, most of the less developed countries of the world, including many former colonies, have considered the problem of trade instability one of their main international economic problems. For them the problem ranks along with the issues of international investment and aid, international monetary arrangements, balance-of-payments disequilibrium, and artificial barriers to international trade. The more developed countries were spared severe trade instability between the late 1940s and the early 1970s, probably because of fortunate circumstances rather than wise policies.

The problem of trade instability can and should be distinguished from that of balance-of-payments disequilibrium, even though the problems overlap to some extent. A moment's reflection reveals that there can be serious disequilibrium with minimal instability, just as there can be high instability without disequilibrium. In the former case, balance-of-payments disequilibrium can develop with gradual changes in exports and/or imports. In the latter case, exports and imports can fluctuate severely but synchronously, or autonomous capital movements can offset the disequilibrating effects of sharp changes in exports or imports.

## Reasons for the country approach

It is possible to view international trade instability primarily from a commodity (industry) standpoint, rather than a country standpoint. This has been done on a limited scale[1] and is of interest particularly for goods and services that may be considered to have world markets in a meaningful sense; but, since governments of countries are the principal policy-determining agencies affecting trade, it was decided, for the present study, to make countries the main focus of attention. Trade instability for groups of goods and services is of course, implicit, in the trade instability of individual countries. If governments exercised very little influence over trade, and if most industries operated on an international or world basis, the industry or market approach would be more appropriate. In that case, though, it would probably be inappropriate to limit the inquiry to international trade: total trade (domestic as well as international), by commodity class, would be the proper focus. Of course, there is ample room for different approaches in this wide field of study.

## Export instability or import instability?

Sharp declines in essential imports constitute the most serious external short-term threat to a national economy. Unless such import declines are cushioned by stockpiles, readily available substitutes, high domestic economic adaptability, or a great capacity for abstinence, they can affect a national economy adversely – perhaps seriously so. Declines in essential imports can result from a decrease in their availability from abroad or from a deficiency, in the importing country, of the means of purchasing the imports. The country can rarely do very much in the short run to affect availability from abroad, but it can do something about deficiency of the means of purchasing imports.

This brings us to exports and to financial arrangements for acquiring imports without current exports. If, from its exports of goods and services, a country is earning enough to buy its essential imports, it ordinarily has little cause to be concerned about import fluctuations, which presumably, represent the preferences, through time, of the economic units purchasing the imports. Hence, there is a strong tendency for governments to focus their attention on exports, even though, from a fundamental national point of view, it is imports that are more important.

Current exports are the principal means of obtaining current imports, but there are also other important means. One is to draw down holdings of monetary reserves or foreign investments that have been accumulated. Other ways are to borrow abroad, to attract foreign investment, to obtain financial grants from abroad, and to receive gifts or other transfers in kind from other countries. There are private, governmental and intergovernmental sources in these various categories. As a matter of historical fact, these supplements to exports, as means of paying for or receiving imports, have not (except briefly in only a few cases) been large enough to enable countries to acquire more than a small fraction of their imports. Of course, the exact purchasing power of foreign investments, and the exact capacity for borrowing, attracting foreign investments or obtaining aid, cannot be known in advance.

It is evident from this discussion that, despite the fundamental importance of imports for production and consumption, countries tend (understandably), especially in times of peace, to emphasise exports rather than imports when considering the problem of international trade instability. Moreover, governments become more apprehensive when export earnings decline sharply than when they rise sharply, though a sharp rise often raises the spectre of a subsequent sharp decline, with attendant dislocations. If the sharp rise in exports elicits a correspondingly sharp rise in imports, a subsequent decline in exports sends additional tremors through the economy. It is possible, however, to overemphasise export fluctuations in this context. An upsurge in imports, for whatever reason, can run down a country's international monetary reserves or credit lines, and then necessitate a curtailment of imports and/or a readjustment of production and consumption in order to expand exports. Or a downturn in imports, particularly in conjunction with an upsurge in exports, can generate conditions that will call for reversals – perhaps rather sharp reversals – in both categories.

So both export instability and import instability are important; and in this study, both will receive attention. Most studies in this field have focused primarily on export instability, mainly on the ground that, if a country can count on its export proceeds, there is little cause for concern about import fluctuations, since these are presumably a matter of choice or policy by the country in question. This view overlooks the situations in which import instability arises from conditions external to the particular country. Incidentally, this general discussion should serve to show how simplistic are the Keynesian models of the interrelations of exports, national income and imports.

## Measurement of trade instability

What exactly is meant by trade instability? And how may it be measured? Trade instability should not be understood to mean *any* deviation from a fixed level. It means 'excessive' departure from some 'normal' level. However, there is no way of determining *a priori* the meanings of 'excessive' and 'normal'. Hence, we must develop our measure of instability on a commonsense basis in the light of the facts. Observation of time series of international trade in the post-Second World War period reveals strong upward secular trends in nearly all series. To use the simple average of annual values as the norm for measuring deviations would show much greater annual variations than some sort of trend line as the norm.

We choose to measure instability of trade by calculating deviations from a trend line. Several alternative measures of trend are available: straight lines, usually determined by the method of least squares, through the actual numbers or the logarithms of the numbers; non-linear, mathematically determined trends; moving averages of various durations; and freehand lines. In this study we have elected to use the linear least-squares line through the logarithms of the actual numbers. The trend thus shows a constant percentage rate of growth or decline over the period of time. It also has the virtue of making the rates of growth of the various time series readily comparable. One can easily find or visualise time series for which the log-linear trend appears inappropriate, but every measure has its weaknesses. To use different measures for different series would tend to undermine comparability. In any case, the choice is a matter of judgement; there is no sure way of testing objectively which trend measure is the most appropriate.

Next is the problem of how to measure the deviations of the actual values from the trend line. Some sort of average of these deviations is needed if the description of instability is to be reduced to a single number that can be used for statistical analysis. One may legitimately argue against this simplifying procedure, but to do so is to argue against much modern statistical procedure. Use of the absolute deviations, whether in actual numbers or logarithms, would make comparisons of instability among different time series almost meaningless, and hence this method is ruled out. The obvious corrective is to express the deviations as a relative or percentage figure. One way to do this is to express the absolute deviations from the corresponding trend values as percentages of the trend values, and then to calculate the average of these percentages. Another way is to obtain the squares of the deviations of the actual values from the corresponding trend values, take the square root of the sum of these squares, and then express the result as a percentage of the average of the original series.

The method that the present study uses for measuring instability is to obtain the average of percentage deviations of the actual values from the trend values as shown by the linear logarithmic trend line, determined by the method of least squares through the logarithms of the annual values. This method permits comparison among different time series and it is readily understood. It seems appropriate to describe the method precisely.[2]

1 List the time periods (for example, years) in column 1 of a table.

2 Number the time periods from 1 to $N$ in column 2. These are $X$ values.

3 List the values of the $Y$ variable (for instance, export receipts, by years) in column 3.

4 Obtain the logarithms of the $Y$ values in column 3 and enter them in column 4.

5 Calculate the least-squares equation for the log $Y$ values for the time periods 1 to $N$; determine the 'estimated' (trend or normal) log $Y$ values and enter them in column 5. These are the log $Y'$ values. (Show the equation at the bottom of the table.)

6 Obtain the antilogs of the log $Y'$ values and enter them in column 6. These are the $Y'$ values.

7 Subtract the $Y'$ values in column 6 from the $Y$ values in column 3. Enter the absolute (no sign) difference ($d$) in column 7.

8 Divide the $d$ values in column 7 by the corresponding $Y'$ values in column 6. Enter the resulting ratio ($r$) in column 8.
9 Add up the $r$ values in column 8; divide the sum by $N$; multiply the dividend by 100. The result is the *instability index*.
10 To obtain the *growth rate*: obtain the antilog of the $m$ value (slope) of the least-squares equation calculated in step 5 above; subtract unity (1.0) from it; multiply the result by 100. The figure obtained is the percentage growth per period (year).

Several different measures of instability have been used in studies of international trade since the Second World War. In a 1952 study, the United Nations Secretariat used the average of year-to-year percentage changes, with the denominator for each change being the larger of the values for the pair of years.[3] The same measure was used again by the Secretariat in the 1958 *World Economic Survey* (vol. 2, chapter 1, p. 40). An International Monetary Fund study in 1963 described and compared various measures of instability and favoured the average of percentage deviations around a moving-average trend, preferably of five years.[4] A study by Ilse Mintz, for the National Bureau of Economic Research in 1966, employed the Bureau's standard method for measuring fluctuations in economic activity.[5] In 1970 Benton F. Massell used the standard error of estimate around the least-squares line (through natural numbers, not logarithms) divided by the mean.[6] I used a 'logarithmic variance' measure in three earlier studies of trade instability, and other investigators also have used it.[7] Evidently, the measure is sufficiently complicated to intrigue some statisticians, but it possesses no evident superiority over the much simpler measure chosen for the present study.[8]

## Variables used in measuring trade instability

Even within the constraints of data availability, there are several choices to be made among variables that show trade instability. Fortunately, in calculating instability according to the chosen method, it is not necessary for the basic numerical data of different series to be in the same unit, although for some calculations of interest and relevance a common currency unit is desirable. For the period of this study (principally, 1959–71) the United States dollar is the most useful unit of account for putting money values on a comparable basis.

The most general trade aggregate is the sum of the value of a country's exports and imports of goods and services for specified periods of time.

More relevant for most purposes, however, is the next lower level of aggregation – namely, the value of exports of goods and services and the value of imports of goods and services, treated separately. The earlier discussion of these variables shows the advantages of treating these two variables separately for most purposes. The next lower level of aggregation is by broad commodity classes, including services. In practice this often means using the ten broad classes of the United Nations Standard International Trade Classification (SITC) for goods, plus one class, or possibly more, for services (as given in the International Monetary Fund's *Balance of Payments Yearbook*).

For countries with a high concentration of exports in a few commodities, it is of interest to consider these commodities individually, even though there are often problems of classification. Use of the finer SITC classes would vastly increase the size of the study and would show extremely erratic trade behaviour for many commodities. A country's imports are invariably more diverse than its exports are, reflecting more specialisation in production than in consumption. A variable of much interest is the value of a country's exports of goods and services minus the value of its imports of goods and services. This may be viewed as the net trade balance, net capital movements or net foreign investment (with unilateral transfers treated as capital movements).

It is also of interest to measure the instability of the physical volume and the prices of exports and imports. In practice this usually means using indexes of export and import prices and indexes of physical volume or 'quantum'. The latter are obtained by adjusting the value aggregates for changes in the price indexes, and then expressing the adjusted value aggregates in index numbers. For a few commodities, actual physical quantities can be used meaningfully. Further, from the price and quantum indexes for exports and imports, two types of terms-of-trade indexes can be obtained and their instability calculated.

Finally, international trade may be classified according to the countries or regions of destination of exports, and source of imports. Usually only the value figures for goods are available for this breakdown, but in principle all the breakdowns described could be used to measure the trade between any pair of countries.

Which of these variables should be examined to determine the instability of international trade? Shortage of statistics limits the use of some of them; and, when statistics are available in great detail, some rules of thumb must be introduced to keep the series down to a manageable number. In this study, as in most others, primary emphasis is on total receipts for exports of goods and services and on total outlays on imports of goods and services. When statistics for services are not available, the data used are for goods alone.

## The relevant time period

In measuring instability of international trade, two questions involving time have to be dealt with. One is the question of the time period – day, week, month, quarter, year, decade, or whatever – to be used in compiling or drawing on the elementary data. The year is used in this study and in most similar studies. One reason for this is that the data for most countries are most readily available on an annual basis, although quarterly and monthly data are becoming increasingly common. Another reason is that seasonal variations can be ignored. Still another is that, for the policies governments might apply in this field, evidence of instability based on annual figures would seem to be sufficient. Governments are not concerned with every little bobble in exports or imports. However, one can imagine circumstances in which quarterly entries would be useful, despite the problem of seasonal variations.

The second question has to do with the number of time periods (years) that should be used in calculating the instability index. Given the method chose for this study, three years is the minimum number that would yield any result at all, and five or six years would seem to be the practical minimum. Over, say, 20 years, however, the observable trend would be likely to depart considerably from the log-linear path, so that the calculated instability index would be inappropriately large. In this study a 13-year period, for 1959–71 and 1946–58, is used when the data are available. Just as in the selection of a measure of instability, there is no theoretical principle to determine the appropriate number of years. As a rule of thumb, 'about a decade' would seem to be sensible in this field.[9]

For the present study, the period 1959–71 happens to have historical justification. By 1958, the currencies of the principal trading countries of the world were generally convertible into the US dollar under the revived gold-exchange standard, and many of the trade barriers associated with the Second World War and its aftermath had been dismantled or reduced. By late 1971, the United States had dropped even the formality of keeping the dollar convertible into gold, even for official foreign institutions. So the period 1959–71 constitutes something of a historical era, just as does the post-war adjustment period of 1946–58.

## Plan of study

The first task is to describe the degree of instability in the international trade of the various countries. This is done in Chapter 2 with reference to some of the categories or breakdowns described above. In some instances – for example, for instability of export prices and export quantum – it seems more enlightening to include the discussion of these variables in the analysis of determinants of the instability of exports receipts (Chapter 4). In this field of study, description and analysis often tend to merge.

Chapter 3 contains a discussion of the 'contribution' of various countries to world export and import instability. For example, the 'percentage contribution' of countries to world export instability is obtained by weighting the percentage distribution of the value of world exports by the respective country export instability indexes. A country's percentage contribution reflects both its share of world exports and its relative degree of export instability. This enables one to perceive the incidence of trade instability in the world.

The second task is to attempt to ascertain variables that are systematically associated with fluctuations of export receipts and import outlays. Numerous variables are used in the analysis. The analysis is of the cross-section type, with the elements being the values of particular variables for the various countries. Most, but not all, of the variables lend themselves to standard correlation–regression analysis. Both simple and multiple correlation–regression results are shown. In selecting 'independent' variables, the tendency is to look for variables that might be controllable by governments, either in reducing trade instability or in mitigating the effects of instability. Export instability is treated as the 'dependent' variable in Chapter 4, and import instability has the same role in Chapter 5. Table A.2 (Appendix) provides the calculated values, for all 109 countries for which they were available for the years 1959–71, of all the variables used. These statistics should be useful for a variety of inquiries.

The final part of the study (Chapter 6) is devoted to the discussion of policy issues with respect to international trade instability. The results obtained in Chapters 2–5 provide an empirical basis for the policy discussion. Chapters 2 and 3 show the incidence of the 'disease', so some judgement can be made of whether 'treatment' is called for. Chapters 4 and 5 indicate at least some of the variables that are positively or negatively related to trade instability and that might be manipulated to some degree to reduce instability. The policy discussion also takes into account other factors that might well affect the choice of policies.

## Notes

[1] For example, Joseph D. Coppock, *International Economic Instability: The Experience after World War II*, McGraw-Hill, New York, 1962, chapter 3. Hereafter, this study is referred to as *International Economic Instability*.

[2] Symbolically, the instability index is described as follows:

$$\text{instability index} = \frac{\sum_{t=1}^{N} \left| \frac{Y_t - Y'_t}{Y'_t} \right| .100}{N}$$

where $Y_t$ = the observed value of the variable in the time period $t$; $Y'_t$ = the logarithmic least-squares estimate of the trend value for time period $t$ (in natural numbers); and $N$ = the number of time periods. The computer program for this measure was developed in 1968 by Jerry L. Kingston, who used it for his *'Instability of Export Proceeds of Selected Latin American Countries, 1948–65'* (doctoral dissertation at The Pennsylvania State University, 1969). The same measure was also used by Larry D. Saiers in his *'Export Instability of Sub-Sahara Africa Countries, 1948–66'* (doctoral dissertation at The Pennsylvania State University, 1970).

[3] United Nations, *Instability in Export Markets of Under-Developed Countries*, 1952, especially p. 77.

[4] Marcus Fleming, Rudolf Rhomberg and Lorette Boissonneault, 'Export norms and their role in compensatory financing', *Staff Papers* 10, March 1963, pp. 97–146.

[5] Ilse Mintz, *Cyclical Fluctuations in the Exports of the United States Since 1879*, National Bureau of Economic Research, Columbia University Press, New York 1967, chapter 3. The method is too complicated to explain briefly.

[6] Benton K. Massell, 'Export instability and economic structure', *American Economic Review*, vol. 60, September 1970, pp. 618–30. Massell described his measure as a 'trend corrected coefficient of variation'. It is one form of the methods described in the text.

[7] *International Economic Instability: Foreign Trade of the Middle*

*East*, American University of Beirut, 1966; *Foreign Trade of Asia and the Far East*, Thammasat University, Bangkok 1974. Alan J. MacFadyen also used it in his '*Instability of Canada's Foreign Trade, 1946–65*' (doctoral dissertation at The Pennsylvania State University, 1970).

[8] In symbolic form, the log-variance measure may be described as follows:

$$\text{instability index} = 100\,(\text{antilog}\sqrt{V_{\log}} - 1)$$

where

$$V_{\log} = \frac{[(\log X_{t+1} - \log X_t) - m]^2}{N - 1}$$

and where $X_t$ is the value in year $t$, $N$ is the number of years, $m$ is the arithmetic mean of the algebraic differences between the logarithms of the successive pairs of $X$s and $V_{\log}$ is the logarithmic variance of the series. B. Ivanovic, of the Research Division of the United Nations Conference on Trade and Development, constructed a 'Rectification du coefficient d'instabilité d'une series temporelle de Coppock' in 1969, after offering cogent criticisms of the measure. Others, including my colleague Professor Owen Sauerlender at The Pennsylvania State University, and Rudolf Rhomberg of the International Monetary Fund, have offered technical criticisms of the log-variance measure. I see no point in continuing to use this measure and do not recommend it to others. In retrospect, it was unfortunate that, in adopting the log-variance measure in 1959, I yielded to what seemed the superior wisdom of technical statisticians (see *International Economic Instability*, p. 23). My preference was for the measure adopted for the present study.

Correlation coefficients for the log-variance measure and the measure using the average of percentage deviations around the log-linear trend, by country, were as follows.

Exports: 1959–71, $r = .897$; 1946–58, $r = .844$.
Imports: 1959–71, $r = .827$; 1946–58, $r = .353$.

The very low $r$ value for imports for 1946–58 was double-checked. The log-variance measure was nearly always higher, contrary to the statement in *International Economic Instability* (p. 24) that the two measures would yield approximately the same results. For the same four distributions as used for the above correlations, the following comparisons are of interest.

| | *Log variance* (1) | *Average of percentage deviations from log-linear trend* (2) | *(1)/(2)* (3) |
|---|---|---|---|
| Exports, 1959–71 | | | |
| (a) mean | 11.8 | 8.0 | 1.47 |
| (b) standard deviation | 11.3 | 8.2 | |
| (b)/(a) | 0.95 | 1.02 | 0.93 |
| Exports, 1946–58 | | | |
| (a) mean | 21.5 | 15.1 | 1.42 |
| (b) standard deviation | 11.7 | 9.7 | |
| (b)/(a) | 0.54 | 0.64 | 0.84 |
| Imports, 1959–71 | | | |
| (a) mean | 10.9 | 7.9 | 1.37 |
| (b) standard deviation | 6.3 | 4.5 | |
| (b)/(a) | 0.57 | 0.56 | 1.01 |
| Imports, 1946–58 | | | |
| (a) mean | 22.7 | 13.9 | 1.63 |
| (b) standard deviation | 9.1 | 8.2 | |
| (b)/(a) | 0.40 | 0.58 | 0.68 |

On the basis of these tests, the log-variance measure is, on average, about 50 per cent higher. For example, for exports in 1946–58, the log-variance measure was higher for 74 of the 83 countries.

[9] The use of a 13-year period is accidental. *International Economic Instability*, started in 1959, used data for 1946 (the year after the Second World War ended) to 1958, the latest year for which statistics were available. The present study, started in early 1973, uses 1971 data as the latest then available, and goes back to 1959, which was not covered in the earlier study.

# 2 Export and import instability of individual countries

This chapter provides a description of the degree of international trade instability of the various countries of the world for the periods 1959–71 and 1946–58. The trade of 109 countries is covered for 1959–71 and of 80 of the same countries for the period 1946–58.

For 84 of the 109 countries covered for 1959–71, both goods and services statistics were available; for the other 25, only goods statistics were available. The results presented in this chapter are based on both goods and services statistics when they were available, but otherwise only on goods statistics. For the 84 countries with both goods and services statistics, services amounted, as a simple average, to 27.0 per cent of the total value of exports, or to 26.5 per cent if the average is weighted by the value of exports. The corresponding averages for imports were almost the same. It is probable that nearly all of the 25 countries lacking services statistics had considerably smaller-than-average percentages of exports and imports of services. Hong Kong is the most likely exception to this statement. The 84 countries for which both goods and services figures were available accounted for 86.9 per cent of the *goods* exports of the 109 countries, so that by far the largest part of the reported international trade of the world is covered. Trade among the Communist countries is not covered, as it is not published in the standard sources.

For the period 1946–58, both goods and services statistics were available for 64 of the 80 countries. Services were estimated to account for about 20 per cent of total trade for these 64 countries in 1957. For the same year, the 80 countries accounted for about 96 per cent of world international trade in goods.

The annual data used in calculating the instability index values are shown in Table A.7 for 1946–58 and in Table A.8 for 1959–71. The instability index used in measuring the degree of instability has been explained in Chapter 1. The order of discussion in this chapter is as follows:

Export instability of individual countries, 1959–71 and 1946–58
Import instability of individual countries, 1959–71 and 1946–58

Comparison of export instability and import instability, by country, 1959–71 and 1946–58
Total trade instability, by country, 1959–71 and 1946–58
Export, import and total trade instability, by country, 1946–71

## Export instability of individual countries, 1959–71 and 1946–58

Export instability index values ranged from 1.7 (United States) to 70.0 (Mauritania) for the 109 countries for the period 1959–71. The median instability index was 6.2 and the simple mean 8.3. For the 80 countries for which statistics for both 1959–71 and 1946–58 were available, the 1946–58 range was from 3.9 (Switzerland) to 54.5 (Iran). The median was 12.3 and the mean 15.1. For these same 80 countries in 1959–71, the range was from 1.7 (United States) to 32.9 (Libya) and the median was 5.5. Individual country values are shown in Figure 2.1 and in columns (1) and (3) of Table 2.1.[1]

The most striking point about the instability indexes for these two periods is the large decline in export instability from 1946–58 to 1959–71. Of the 80 countries for which there are data for both periods, all but seven had lower instability index values for their exports in 1959–71 (Figure 2.1 and column (7) of Table 2.1.) The following tabulation provides additional comparative information.

| *Measure (for exports)* | *1946–58* (1) | *1959–71* (2) | *Ratio (2)/(1)* (3) |
|---|---|---|---|
| 1 Mean instability index (II) | 15.1 | 8.3 | 0.55 |
| 2 Median II of top third | 21.9 | 11.6 | 0.53 |
| 3 Median II of middle third | 12.3 | 6.2 | 0.50 |
| 4 Median II of bottom third | 8.0 | 3.2 | 0.40 |
| 5 Variation (2 – 4) | 13.9 | 8.4 | 0.60 |
| 6 Relative variation (5/3) | 113% | 135% | 1.27 |
| 7 Standard deviation | 9.7 | 8.2 | 0.85 |
| 8 Coefficient of variation (7/1) | 53% | 99% | 1.87 |
| 9 Range | 3.9–54.5 | 1.7–70.0 | – |
| 10 No. of countries | 80 | 109 | – |

The average decline in the degree of export instability was 45 per cent. For the median country in the bottom third of countries, the decline in export instability was 60 per cent – to the very low level of 3.2 per cent variation around the trend line. The countries with the higher instability indexes experienced a smaller percentage decline than did those with lower indexes (column (3), rows 2, 3 and 4).

However, relative variation among countries increased, whether measured by the ratio of the standard deviation to the mean (coefficient of variation) or by the ratio of the difference between the medians of the top and bottom thirds to the median of the middle third. In addition, the overall range was greater in 1959–71 (68.3) than in 1946–58 (50.6).

A precise basis for observing the change in export instability from 1946–58 to 1959–71 is provided in Table 2.1, column (7), which shows the ratio of the 1959–71 export instability index to the corresponding 1946–58 index for each country. Seventy of the 80 countries had ratios of less than 1.0; 43 of them had ratios of less than 0.05; and 24 had ratios of 0.2 or less. Export instability in thirty per cent of the countries declined by 80 per cent or more!

Despite the declines, there was not a reliable tendency for the countries to maintain their relative positions: $r$ (the Pearsonian coefficient of correlation) and $r_k$ (the Spearman coefficient of rank correlation) were both .16, neither significant at the 5 per cent level. It is impressive that, while 31 per cent of the countries had export instability indexes of less than 5.0 in 1959–71, only two, Switzerland and Ireland, fell in this class in 1946–58.

It is appropriate to ask whether, in view of the large number of countries that had low export instability index values in 1959–71, the problem of export instability still existed for these countries. Eighty-two of the 109 countries had index values of below 10.0; 40 of them had index values of below 5.0. For export instability there is no minimum percentage that governments or others accept as satisfactory. Zero instability is unattainable, except by accident, and, because of the rigidities that it would tend to imply in trade relations, would probably be considered undesirable on a regular basis. In this connection, it should be recognised that the constant percentage growth rate implicit in the trend line from which deviations are measured in order to obtain the export instability index is not necessarily the desired smooth path. For a given country, comparisons with other countries and with the country's own past experience probably provide the best indications of the severity of export instability. If one uses an export instability index of 10.0 or more as *prima facie* evidence of an export instability problem, then 27 of the 109 countries – 25 per cent – had such a problem in 1959–71. Using the same criterion, the same would have been true for 58 (63 per cent) of

Table 2.1

Export and import instability indexes, with comparisons: by country, 1959–71 and 1946–58. (Ranked in ascending order. In columns (2)–(8) ranks are shown in parentheses.)

| Rank, by col. (1) | Country | 1959–71 Export instability index (1) | 1959–71 Import instability index (2) | 1946–58 Export instability index (3) | 1946–58 Import instability index (4) | Comparisons (1)/(2) (5) | Comparisons (3)/(4) (6) | Comparisons (1)/(3) (7) | Comparisons (2)/(4) (8) | |
|---|---|---|---|---|---|---|---|---|---|---|
| 1 | United States | 1.7 | 6.5 (47) | 9.2 (20) | 7.8 (15) | 0.3 (4) | 1.2 (44) | 0.2 (23) | 0.8 (57) | 1 |
| 2 | Puerto Rico | 2.2 | 1.6 (1) | 6.7 (7) | 3.6 (22) | 1.4 (91) | 1.8 (70) | 0.3 (32) | 0.4 (28) | 2 |
| 3 | Sri Lanka (Ceylon) | 2.2 | 3.8 (19) | 10.3 (28) | 10.2 (34) | 0.6 (24) | 1.0 (35) | 0.2 (20) | 0.4 (20) | 3 |
| 4 | Italy | 2.3 | 6.3 (45) | 15.4 (56) | 8.7 (20) | 0.4 (6) | 1.8 (68) | 0.1 (2) | 0.7 (50) | 4 |
| 5 | USSR | 2.3 | 3.3 (10) | 18.3 (61) | 1.7 (1) | 0.7 (43) | 11.0 (80) | 0.1 (7) | 2.0 (80) | 5 |
| 6 | Mexico | 2.4 | 3.4 (13) | 6.8 (9) | 9.0 (21) | 0.7 (39) | 0.7 (16) | 0.4 (42) | 0.4 (23) | 6 |
| 7 | Norway | 2.4 | 3.6 (16) | 11.1 (33) | 7.4 (12) | 0.7 (42) | 1.5 (59) | 0.2 (19) | 0.5 (32) | 7 |
| 8 | South Africa | 2.4 | 5.9 (39) | 7.7 (14) | 7.2 (10) | 0.4 (7) | 1.1 (37) | 0.3 (33) | 0.8 (55) | 8 |
| 9 | Poland | 2.5 | 2.4 (2) | 25.7 (71) | 21.4 (72) | 1.0 (73) | 1.2 (48) | 0.1 (6) | 0.1 (1) | 9 |
| 10 | Trinidad–Tobago | 2.5 | 4.1 (22) | – | – | 0.6 (26) | – | – | – | 10 |
| 11 | Switzerland | 2.6 | 7.3 (62) | 3.9 (1) | 11.0 (38) | 0.4 (8) | 0.4 (3) | 0.7 (63) | 0.7 (46) | 11 |
| 12 | Hungary | 2.7 | 5.7 (38) | 15.3 (55) | 30.6 (76) | 0.5 (11) | 0.5 (5) | 0.2 (15) | 0.5 (5) | 12 |
| 13 | Greece | 2.8 | 3.4 (11) | 10.5 (30) | 16.0 (62) | 0.8 (46) | 0.6 (9) | 0.3 (30) | 0.2 (7) | 13 |
| 14 | Denmark | 2.9 | 2.8 (4) | 12.0 (39) | 11.1 (39) | 1.0 (64) | 1.2 (38) | 0.2 (9) | 0.2 (12) | 14 |
| 15 | German Dem. Rep. | 2.9 | 5.2 (30) | 17.9 (59) | 10.1 (32) | 0.6 (19) | 1.8 (67) | 0.2 (10) | 0.5 (33) | 15 |
| 16 | Australia | 3.0 | 5.4 (33) | 17.7 (58) | 19.6 (69) | 0.6 (15) | 0.9 (27) | 0.2 (8) | 0.3 (15) | 16 |
| 17 | France | 3.0 | 3.2 (8) | 14.0 (48) | 13.5 (50) | 0.9 (55) | 1.0 (36) | 0.2 (12) | 0.2 (10) | 17 |
| 18 | Pakistan | 3.1 | 9.1 (77) | 20.7 (65) | 23.9 (73) | 0.3 (2) | 0.9 (25) | 0.1 (5) | 0.2 (24) | 18 |
| 19 | Sweden | 3.2 | 3.4 (14) | 10.1 (25) | 10.5 (35) | 0.9 (59) | 1.0 (31) | 0.3 (34) | 0.3 (18) | 19 |
| 20 | Ireland | 3.3 | 3.3 (9) | 6.7 (6) | 12.1 (44) | 1.0 (69) | 0.6 (6) | 0.5 (46) | 0.3 (14) | 20 |

| | | | | | | | | | | |
|---|---|---|---|---|---|---|---|---|---|---|
| 21 | Bulgaria | 3.4 | 6.1 (41) | 7.6 (11) | 40.8 (79) | 0.6 (16) | 0.2 (1) | 0.4 (38) | 0.1 (2) | 21 |
| 22 | Czechoslovakia | 3.4 | 3.2 (7) | 11.2 (34) | 15.0 (59) | 1.1 (76) | 0.7 (13) | 0.3 (27) | 0.2 (6) | 22 |
| 23 | Israel | 3.4 | 6.0 (40) | 7.1 (10) | 8.6 (18) | 0.6 (21) | 0.8 (22) | 0.5 (47) | 0.7 (48) | 23 |
| 24 | Romania | 3.4 | 9.9 (81) | 6.7 (8) | 6.9 (6) | 0.3 (3) | 1.0 (33) | 0.5 (50) | 1.4 (74) | 24 |
| 25 | United Kingdom | 3.4 | 2.6 (3) | 10.9 (32) | 9.0 (22) | 1.3 (90) | 1.2 (49) | 0.3 (36) | 0.3 (16) | 25 |
| 26 | Uganda | 3.5 | 6.2 (43) | – | – | 0.6 (27) | – | – | – | 26 |
| 27 | Venezuela | 3.6 | 6.7 (52) | 8.9 (18) | 12.0 (43) | 0.5 (14) | 0.7 (15) | 0.4 (43) | 0.6 (37) | 27 |
| 28 | Kenya | 3.7 | 3.7 (17) | – | – | 1.0 (71) | – | – | – | 28 |
| 29 | Belgium | 3.8 | 3.0 (5) | 10.1 (23) | 7.4 (13) | 1.3 (85) | 1.4 (52) | 0.4 (37) | 0.4 (27) | 29 |
| 30 | Yugoslavia | 3.8 | 6.5 (48) | 22.5 (68) | 9.7 (25) | 0.6 (29) | 2.3 (77) | 0.2 (24) | 0.7 (47) | 30 |
| 31 | Ecuador | 3.9 | 8.5 (73) | 11.2 (35) | 9.4 (24) | 0.5 (9) | 1.2 (46) | 0.3 (28) | 0.9 (61) | 31 |
| 32 | Finland | 3.9 | 7.3 (61) | 12.9 (60) | 19.3 (68) | 0.5 (10) | 0.9 (28) | 0.2 (11) | 0.4 (22) | 32 |
| 33 | Jamaica | 4.0 | 4.0 (21) | – | – | 1.0 (70) | – | – | – | 33 |
| 34 | Malaysia* | 4.0 | 3.0 (6) | 32.1 (75) | 16.6 (63) | 1.3 (88) | 1.9 (75) | 0.1 (4) | 0.2 (4) | 34 |
| 35 | Argentina | 4.2 | 13.1 (96) | 14.3 (49) | 17.0 (65) | 0.3 (1) | 0.8 (23) | 0.3 (25) | 0.8 (54) | 35 |
| 36 | Austria | 4.2 | 4.8 (27) | 14.5 (50) | 12.2 (45) | 0.9 (50) | 1.2 (45) | 0.3 (26) | 0.4 (25) | 36 |
| 37 | India | 4.3 | 9.7 (80) | 10.4 (29) | 13.1 (48) | 0.4 (5) | 0.8 (8) | 0.4 (41) | 0.7 (52) | 37 |
| 38 | Germany, West | 4.5 | 4.5 (26) | 18.6 (62) | 9.8 (28) | 1.0 (66) | 1.9 (71) | 0.2 (13) | 0.5 (29) | 38 |
| 39 | Morocco | 4.7 | 7.7 (67) | 29.8 (74) | 37.3 (78) | 0.6 (22) | 0.8 (20) | 0.2 (17) | 0.2 (8) | 39 |
| 40 | Netherlands | 4.7 | 3.8 (18) | 24.3 (70) | 9.8 (27) | 1.2 (83) | 2.5 (79) | 0.2 (18) | 0.4 (26) | 40 |
| 41 | Iraq | 5.0 | 7.8 (68) | 22.2 (67) | 11.7 (41) | 0.6 (20) | 1.9 (73) | 0.2 (16) | 0.7 (45) | 41 |
| 42 | Hong Kong | 5.2 | 4.0 (20) | – | – | 1.3 (86) | – | – | – | 42 |
| 43 | Tanzania | 5.2 | 5.2 (31) | – | – | 1.0 (74) | – | – | – | 43 |
| 44 | Canada | 5.4 | 6.2 (42) | 5.1 (2) | 6.4 (5) | 0.9 (51) | 0.8 (17) | 1.1 (73) | 1.0 (64) | 44 |
| 45 | Japan | 5.5 | 4.2 (23) | 41.8 (78) | 17.7 (66) | 1.3 (87) | 2.4 (78) | 0.1 (3) | 0.2 (11) | 45 |
| 46 | New Zealand | 5.5 | 7.9 (70) | 10.1 (24) | 13.7 (51) | 0.7 (40) | 0.7 (4) | 0.5 (49) | 0.6 (40) | 46 |
| 47 | Costa Rica | 5.6 | 6.7 (50) | 15.0 (52) | 7.3 (11) | 0.8 (44) | 2.0 (76) | 0.4 (39) | 0.9 (62) | 47 |
| 48 | Portugal | 5.7 | 3.5 (15) | 9.3 (21) | 11.8 (42) | 1.6 (97) | 0.8 (19) | 0.6 (59) | 0.3 (17) | 48 |
| 49 | Singapore† | 5.9 | 11.0 (87) | – | – | 0.5 (12) | – | – | – | 49 |
| 50 | Spain | 5.9 | 12.3 (93) | 10.9 (31) | 8.6 (19) | 0.5 (13) | 1.3 (50) | 0.5 (51) | 1.4 (73) | 50 |
| 51 | Ethiopia | 6.0 | 6.7 (51) | 13.9 (47) | 9.3 (23) | 0.9 (23) | 1.5 (56) | 0.4 (40) | 0.7 (49) | 51 |
| 52 | Peru | 6.0 | 10.7 (84) | 6.0 (4) | 9.9 (31) | 0.6 (23) | 0.6 (8) | 1.0 (72) | 1.1 (67) | 52 |

Table 2.1 *cont.*

| Rank, by col. (1) | Country | (1) | (2) | (3) | (4) | (5) | (6) | (7) | (8) | |
|---|---|---|---|---|---|---|---|---|---|---|
| 53 | Ghana | 6.2 | 9.3 (78) | 28.1 (72) | 18.8 (67) | 0.7 (33) | 1.5 (58) | 0.2 (14) | 0.5 (31) | 53 |
| 54 | Sudan | 6.2 | 10.8 (86) | 28.4 (73) | 14.8 (58) | 0.6 (25) | 1.9 (74) | 0.2 (21) | 0.7 (51) | 54 |
| 55 | Thailand | 6.2 | 4.4 (24) | 34.1 (76) | 20.4 (71) | 1.4 (93) | 1.7 (64) | 0.2 (22) | 0.2 (79) | 55 |
| 56 | Zaire | 6.2 | 7.3 (63) | 10.1 (26) | 11.3 (40) | 0.8 (49) | 0.9 (26) | 0.6 (60) | 0.6 (44) | 56 |
| 57 | Ivory Coast | 6.3 | 3.4 (12) | – | – | 1.9 (100) | – | – | – | 57 |
| 58 | Kuwait | 6.3 | 8.5 (74) | – | – | 0.7 (37) | – | – | – | 58 |
| 59 | Paraguay | 6.3 | 6.9 (54) | 7.7 (13) | 7.1 (8) | 0.9 (57) | 1.1 (39) | 0.8 (67) | 1.0 (65) | 59 |
| 60 | Syria | 6.3 | 6.9 (56) | 12.3 (42) | 10.9 (36) | 0.9 (60) | 1.1 (41) | 0.5 (52) | 0.6 (43) | 60 |
| 61 | Turkey | 6.3 | 7.1 (60) | 11.6 (37) | 35.5 (77) | 0.9 (61) | 0.3 (2) | 0.5 (53) | 0.6 (42) | 61 |
| 62 | Panama | 6.4 | 5.6 (35) | 6.4 (5) | 3.6 (3) | 1.1 (79) | 1.8 (66) | 1.0 (71) | 1.5 (77) | 62 |
| 63 | Senegal | 6.4 | 8.0 (71) | – | – | 0.8 (48) | – | – | – | 63 |
| 64 | Egypt | 6.6 | 6.4 (46) | 19.8 (64) | 16.9 (64) | 1.0 (65) | 1.2 (43) | 0.3 (29) | 0.4 (21) | 64 |
| 65 | El Salvador | 6.6 | 9.0 (75) | 11.2 (36) | 10.2 (33) | 0.7 (32) | 1.1 (40) | 0.6 (56) | 0.9 (59) | 65 |
| 66 | Guatemala | 6.6 | 6.3 (44) | 5.5 (3) | 10.9 (37) | 1.0 (67) | 0.5 (4) | 1.2 (75) | 0.6 (39) | 66 |
| 67 | Chile | 6.7 | 6.7 (49) | 12.6 (43) | 7.0 (7) | 1.0 (63) | 1.8 (69) | 0.5 (45) | 0.9 (63) | 67 |
| 68 | China, Nat. Rep. | 7.0 | 11.3 (88) | 7.7 (12) | 7.7 (14) | 0.6 (18) | 1.0 (34) | 0.9 (68) | 1.5 (75) | 68 |
| 69 | Colombia | 7.1 | 8.1 (72) | 12.1 (41) | 14.6 (57) | 0.9 (53) | 0.8 (21) | 0.6 (55) | 0.5 (34) | 69 |
| 70 | Uruguay | 7.3 | 12.0 (92) | 16.1 (57) | 13.9 (52) | 0.6 (28) | 1.2 (42) | 0.5 (54) | 0.9 (58) | 70 |
| 71 | Lebanon | 7.6 | 6.9 (53) | 12.0 (40) | 12.4 (46) | 1.1 (77) | 1.0 (32) | 0.6 (57) | 0.6 (35) | 71 |
| 72 | Sierra Leone | 7.6 | 6.9 (55) | – | – | 1.1 (81) | – | – | – | 72 |
| 73 | Saudi Arabia | 7.7 | 5.6 (36) | – | – | 1.4 (92) | – | – | – | 73 |
| 74 | Philippines | 7.8 | 7.1 (59) | 8.6 (17) | 12.7 (47) | 1.1 (80) | 0.7 (12) | 0.9 (70) | 0.6 (36) | 74 |
| 75 | Iran | 8.1 | 11.6 (90) | 54.5 (80) | 42.3 (80) | 0.7 (35) | 1.3 (51) | 0.1 (1) | 0.3 (13) | 75 |
| 76 | Malagasy Rep. | 8.1 | 5.3 (32) | – | – | 1.5 (95) | – | – | – | 76 |
| 77 | Malawi | 8.2 | 7.5 (65) | – | – | 1.1 (78) | – | – | – | 77 |
| 78 | Bolivia | 8.4 | 5.7 (37) | 15.3 (54) | 9.9 (30) | 1.5 (94) | 1.5 (62) | 0.5 (44) | 0.6 (38) | 78 |
| 79 | Cameroon | 8.6 | 4.8 (28) | – | – | 1.8 (98) | – | – | – | 79 |

| | | | | | | | | | | |
|---|---|---|---|---|---|---|---|---|---|---|
| 80 | Honduras | 8.9 | 9.0 (76) | 11.7 (38) | 8.1 (17) | 1.0 (68) | 1.4 (54) | 0.8 (65) | 1.1 (68) | 80 |
| 81 | Chad | 9.4 | 10.7 (82) | – | – | 0.9 (52) | – | – | – | 81 |
| 82 | Algeria | 9.6 | 9.4 (79) | – | – | 1.0 (62) | – | – | – | 82 |
| 83 | Iceland | 10.0 | 11.5 (89) | 13.1 (45) | 15.3 (60) | 0.9 (56) | 0.9 (24) | 0.8 (66) | 0.7 (53) | 83 |
| 84 | Togo | 10.0 | 7.6 (66) | – | – | 1.3 (89) | – | – | – | 84 |
| 85 | Haiti | 10.1 | 14.5 (97) | 1.51 (53) | 9.9 (29) | 0.7 (34) | 1.5 (61) | 0.7 (61) | 1.5 (76) | 85 |
| 86 | Nicaragua | 10.2 | 10.7 (83) | 9.4 (22) | 7.9 (16) | 1.0 (72) | 1.2 (47) | 1.1 (74) | 1.3 (72) | 86 |
| 87 | Afghanistan | 10.6 | 15.4 (101) | – | – | 0.7 (30) | – | – | – | 87 |
| 88 | Liberia | 10.8 | 14.5 (98) | 21.6 (66) | 14.2 (54) | 0.7 (38) | 1.5 (60) | 0.5 (48) | 1.0 (66) | 88 |
| 89 | Brazil | 11.2 | 16.8 (102) | 8.3 (15) | 14.4 (55) | 0.7 (31) | 0.6 (7) | 1.3 (76) | 1.2 (71) | 89 |
| 90 | China, People's Rep. | 11.3 | 18.6 (107) | 14.7 (51) | 9.8 (26) | 0.6 (17) | 1.5 (57) | 0.8 (64) | 1.9 (79) | 90 |
| 91 | Dominican Republic | 11.4 | 15.0 (99) | 9.0 (19) | 13.2 (49) | 0.8 (45) | 0.7 (1) | 1.3 (77) | 1.1 (69) | 91 |
| 92 | Cuba | 11.8 | 5.1 (29) | 13.1 (44) | 14.0 (53) | 2.3 (102) | 0.9 (29) | 0.9 (69) | 0.4 (19) | 92 |
| 93 | Central African Rep. | 12.0 | 5.5 (34) | – | – | 2.2 (101) | – | – | – | 93 |
| 94 | Yemen, Peo. Dem. Rep. | 12.0 | 12.3 (94) | – | – | 1.0 (75) | – | – | – | 94 |
| 95 | Niger | 12.1 | 18.2 (106) | – | – | 0.7 (41) | – | – | – | 95 |
| 96 | Korea, Rep. of | 12.9 | 17.5 (103) | 18.8 (63) | 19.7 (70) | 0.7 (36) | 0.9 (30) | 0.7 (62) | 0.9 (60) | 96 |
| 97 | Tunisia | 13.7 | 4.4 (25) | 40.1 (77) | 27.8 (74) | 3.1 (109) | 1.4 (55) | 0.3 (35) | 0.2 (3) | 97 |
| 98 | Burma | 14.0 | 7.5 (64) | 10.2 (27) | 15.5 (61) | 1.9 (99) | 0.7 (10) | 1.4 (78) | 0.5 (30) | 98 |
| 99 | Indonesia | 14.5 | 18.0 (105) | 51.0 (79) | 30.0 (75) | 0.8 (47) | 1.7 (65) | 0.3 (31) | 0.6 (41) | 99 |
| 100 | Nigeria | 14.5 | 12.0 (91) | 23.0 (69) | 14.5 (56) | 1.2 (84) | 1.6 (63) | 0.6 (58) | 0.8 (56) | 100 |
| 101 | Jordan | 16.7 | 7.0 (58) | 8.3 (16) | 6.1 (4) | 2.4 (103) | 1.4 (53) | 2.0 (79) | 1.1 (70) | 101 |
| 102 | Burundi | 14.9 | 7.0 (57) | – | – | 2.6 (105) | – | – | – | 102 |
| 103 | Zambia | 19.1 | 17.6 (104) | – | – | 1.1 (82) | – | – | – | 103 |
| 104 | Upper Volta | 20.9 | 7.8 (69) | – | – | 2.7 (107) | – | – | – | 104 |
| 105 | Mali | 23.7 | 15.1 (100) | – | – | 1.6 (96) | – | – | – | 105 |
| 106 | Rwanda | 25.4 | 27.4 (109) | – | – | 0.9 (58) | – | – | – | 106 |
| 107 | Dahomey | 27.0 | 10.8 (85) | – | – | 2.5 (104) | – | – | – | 107 |
| 108 | Libya | 32.9 | 12.4 (95) | 13.4 (46) | 7.1 (95) | 2.7 (106) | 1.9 (72) | 2.5 (80) | 1.7 (72) | 108 |
| 109 | Mauritania | 70.0 | 22.8 (108) | – | – | 3.1 (108) | – | – | – | 109 |

*Malaya and Singapore for 1946–58; Singapore separate from 1959–71. Thereafter only 'Malaysia' is used.
†Included under Malaysia for 1946–58.

the 80 countries surveyed for 1946–58. This comparison, showing a decline from 63 to 25, or by 63 per cent, in the proportion of countries with export instability indexes of 10.0 or more provides another indication of the substantial and widespread decline in export instability.

For the 80 countries for which there were figures for both 1946–58 and 1959–71, only nine countries (8 per cent) had export instability indexes above 15.0 in 1959–71, while 28 of 80 (35 per cent) had indexes of this level in 1946–58. Eleven of the 80 countries had export instability indexes of 10.0 or more for both periods:

| *Country (listed by 1959–71 rank)* | *Export instability index* 1946–58 (1) | 1959–71 (2) | *Ratio (2)/(1)* (3) |
|---|---|---|---|
| Libya | 13.4 | 32.9 | 2.46 |
| Nigeria* | 23.0 | 14.5 | 0.63 |
| Indonesia* | 51.0 | 14.5 | 0.28 |
| Burma | 10.2 | 14.0 | 1.37 |
| Tunisia | 40.1 | 13.7 | 0.34 |
| Korea, Rep. of* | 18.8 | 12.9 | 0.69 |
| Cuba | 13.1 | 11.8 | 0.90 |
| China, People's Rep. | 14.7 | 11.3 | 0.77 |
| Liberia* | 21.6 | 10.8 | 0.50 |
| Haiti | 15.1 | 10.1 | 0.67 |
| Iceland* | 13.1 | 10.0 | 0.76 |

There were, however, 12 countries that had export instability indexes of 10.0 or above in 1959–71, but were not included in the 1946–58 survey (see Table 2.1). Five of the 11 countries listed above (those marked with asterisks) also had import instability indexes of above 10.0 for both periods. In comparing these index values, it may be noted that countries vary greatly in their ability to withstand export (or import) instability, and also that the ability of countries in this respect changes through time, albeit rather slowly.

**Import instability of individual countries, 1959–71 and 1946–58**

We now turn to import instability. Import instability index values for the 109 countries, for the period 1959–71, ranged from 1.6 (Puerto Rico) to

27.4 (Rwanda). For the 80 countries for which data for both 1959–71 and 1946–58 were available, the range for the period 1946–58 was from 1.7 (USSR, for imports from non-Communist countries) to 42.4 (Iran). See Figure 2.2 and Table 2.1, columns (2) and (4) for the instability index values and the rankings of individual countries.

The mean import instability index value was 13.7 in 1946–58, but only 7.9 in 1959–71 – a decline of 43 per cent. The median value fell from 11.2 to 6.9, by 39 per cent. The following tabulation brings out some of the major characteristics of the distribution of import instability index values over the two periods.

| *Measure (for imports)* | *1946–58* (1) | *1959–71* (2) | *Ratio (2)/(1)* (3) |
|---|---|---|---|
| 1 Mean instability index (II) | 13.7 | 7.9 | 0.57 |
| 2 Median II of top third | 17.7 | 12.0 | 0.67 |
| 3 Median II of middle third | 11.2 | 6.9 | 0.61 |
| 4 Median II of bottom third | 7.7 | 3.8 | 0.49 |
| 5 Variation (2 – 4) | 9.9 | 8.2 | 0.82 |
| 6 Relative variation (5/3) | 88% | 118% | 1.34 |
| 7 Standard deviation | 7.9 | 4.5 | 0.56 |
| 8 Coefficient of variation (7/1) | 58% | 56% | 0.96 |
| 9 Range | 1.7–42.4 | 1.6–27.4 | – |
| 10 No. of countries | 80 | 109 | – |

The medians of the top and bottom thirds of countries fell by 33 and 51 per cent, respectively. As with exports, the countries with the higher import instability indexes experienced smaller relative declines than did those with the lower index values (column (3), rows 2, 3 and 4). Only 15 of the 80 countries included in the calculations for both periods had index values higher in 1959–71 than in 1946–58. The USSR showed the greatest increase, approximately doubling its index value. For 32 of the 80 countries, the 1959–71 import instability indexes were less than half the 1946–58 ones. For two countries (Poland and Bulgaria) they were less than one-fifth of those for the earlier period. See Table 2.1, column (8) for a full list of the import instability index ratios (1959–71/1946–58) for the various countries.

Eighty-one of the 109 countries included in the 1959–71 survey had import instability indexes of less than 10.0 (Table 2.1, column (2) and Figure 2.2). If this value is used as a cut-off level to identify countries with an import instability problem, then only 28 countries, 25 per cent of the total, had such a problem. In 1946–58, however, this was the case for 49 (61 per cent) of the 80 countries for which data were available for both periods. By this criterion, the number of problem countries, as a proportion of the total, declined by 59 per cent.

Using an import instability index of 15.0 or more as the criterion, only 11 (10 per cent) of the 109 countries had an import instability problem in 1959–71. In 1946–58, 22 (28 per cent) of the 80 countries for which we have data for both periods had import instability indexes of more than 15.0. Here again, as with the easier criterion, the decline in problem countries was about 60 per cent. Of the 80 countries for which data were available, only two, Indonesia and the Republic of Korea, had index values of above 15.0 for both periods. Twelve countries had index values of 10.0 or more for both periods:

| *Country (listed by 1959–71 rank)* | *Import instability index* 1946–58 (1) | *Import instability index* 1959–71 (2) | *Ratio (2)/(1)* (3) |
|---|---|---|---|
| Indonesia* | 30.1 | 18.0 | 0.60 |
| Korea. Rep. of* | 19.7 | 17.5 | 0.89 |
| Brazil | 14.5 | 16.8 | 1.16 |
| Dominican Rep. | 13.2 | 15.0 | 1.14 |
| Liberia* | 14.2 | 14.5 | 1.02 |
| Argentina | 14.3 | 13.1 | 0.92 |
| Nigeria* | 14.5 | 12.0 | 0.83 |
| Uruguay | 13.9 | 12.0 | 0.86 |
| Iran | 42.4 | 11.6 | 0.27 |
| Iceland* | 15.3 | 11.5 | 0.75 |
| Sudan | 14.8 | 10.8 | 0.73 |
| Peru | 10.0 | 10.7 | 1.07 |

The five countries marked with asterisks were also on the corresponding list for exports. In addition, 10 countries that were not included in the 1946–58 survey had import instability indexes of 10 or above for the period 1959–71. (See Table 2.1, columns (2) and (4).)

Although the import instability indexes were generally lower for 1959–71 than for 1946–58, there was no marked tendency for countries to maintain their relative positions. This is shown by the value of the correlation coefficients $r$ (.14) and $r_k$ (.13), neither of which is significant at the .05 level.

**Comparison of export instability and import instability, by country, 1959–71 and 1946–58**

It is of interest, in describing international trade instability, to compare export instability and import instability by country, for both of the periods under review. The average export instability index for the period 1959–71 was 8.0, as compared with 7.9 for the corresponding index for imports; the medians were 6.2 and 6.9, respectively. Mauritania had the highest instability index for exports (70.0) and the second highest for imports (22.8). Rwanda had the highest one for imports (27.4) and the fourth highest for exports (25.4). By contrast, the United States had the lowest export instability index (1.7), but was forty-seventh from the bottom with respect to import instability (6.5). Puerto Rico, with an import instability index of 1.6, was lowest for this variable and second from lowest in export instability (2.2).

Only 39 (36 per cent) of the 109 countries had higher export than import instability indexes in 1959–71 (Table 2.1, column 5), but nine of these countries were among the top 10 with regard to export instability. At the other end of the scale, only two of the 10 countries that ranked lowest in this respect had higher export than import instability indexes. The median ratio of export to import instability indexes was 0.9.

With more than a two-country world, there is no analytically necessary relation between export and import instability, but it is of interest that, for 1959–71, the coefficient of correlation ($r$) between export and import instability for the 109 countries was .63 ($r_k$ = .64). Other points of comparison are provided in the following tabulation.

| *Measure (for 1959–71)* | *Exports* (1) | *Imports* (2) | *Ratio (1)/(2)* (3) |
|---|---|---|---|
| 1 Mean instability index (II) | 8.0 | 7.9 | 1.03 |
| 2 Median II of top third | 11.6 | 12.0 | 0.97 |
| 3 Median II of middle third | 6.2 | 6.9 | 0.90 |
| 4 Median II of bottom third | 3.2 | 3.8 | 0.84 |
| 5 Variation (2 – 4) | 8.4 | 8.2 | 1.02 |
| 6 Relative variation (5/3) | 135% | 119% | 1.13 |
| 7 Standard deviation | 8.2 | 4.5 | 1.82 |
| 8 Coefficient of variation (7/1) | 103% | 57% | 1.81 |
| 9 Range | 1.7–70.0 | 1.6–27.4 | – |
| 10 No. of countries | 109 | 109 | – |

The median instability indexes for the three thirds reveal the consistent tendency for imports to be more unstable than exports in this period. The tendency was stronger for the countries with the lower index values (column (3), rows 2, 3 and 4). If the one extremely high export instability index is excluded, the mean export instability index is 7.4 instead of 8.0, which thus accords with the pattern of the medians. The various measures of dispersion show, in contrast, that, for the period 1959–71, the index values for the 109 countries were more diverse for export than for import instability.

We now compare export and import instability for the period 1946–58 for the 80 countries covered for both periods. Export instability ranged from 3.9 (Switzerland) to 54.5 (Iran), and import instability from 1.7 (USSR) to 42.4 (Iran), a somewhat smaller interval. The mean instability index was higher for exports (15.3) than for imports (13.5), as was the median (12.3 as compared with 11.2). Other points of comparison are set out as follows.

| *Measure (for 1946–58)* | *Exports* (1) | *Imports* (2) | *Ratio (1)/(2)* (3) |
|---|---|---|---|
| 1 Mean instability index (II) | 15.3 | 13.5 | 1.10 |
| 2 Median II of top third | 21.9 | 17.7 | 1.24 |
| 3 Median II of middle third | 12.3 | 11.2 | 1.10 |
| 4 Median II of bottom third | 8.0 | 7.7 | 1.04 |
| 5 Variation (2 – 4) | 13.9 | 9.9 | 1.40 |
| 6 Relative variation (5/3) | 113% | 88% | 1.28 |
| 7 Standard deviation | 9.7 | 7.9 | 1.23 |
| 8 Coefficient of variation (7/1) | 53% | 58% | 0.91 |
| 9 Range | 3.9–54.5 | 1.7–42.4 | – |
| 10 No. of countries | 80 | 80 | – |

With the exception of the coefficient of variation, exports exceeded imports for all of these measures of central tendency and dispersion (column (3) above). Whereas in 1959–71 the three median export instability indexes were lower than the corresponding medians for imports, the opposite was true for 1946–58.

For 46 countries, 58 per cent of the 80 for which data were available for both periods, the export exceeded the import instability index in 1946–58 (column (6) of Table 2.1). In 1959–71, the corresponding percentage was only 36. There is no obvious explanation for this change, but one possibility is that, owing to the fact export instability declined sharply for many countries between 1946–58 and 1959–71, generally reflecting their more stable market opportunities and production, domestic considerations could make themselves felt in the fluctuations in imports. This hypothesis is consistent with the smaller decline in the median import instability index (39 per cent) than in the median export instability index (50 per cent) over the two periods in question.

The correlation coefficient between export and import instability for 1946–58, by country, was .58 (.64 in 1959–71); the rank correlation coefficient was .50 (.63 in 1959–71). Hence, the coefficients for the two periods did not differ very much.

In 1946–58, five (6 per cent) of the 80 countries had export/import instability ratios in excess of 2.0, as compared with nine (8 per cent) out of 109 countries in 1959–71. At the bottom end of the scale, 33 (41 per cent) out of 80 countries had export/import instability ratios of less than 1.0 in 1946–58, as compared with 61 (56 per cent) out of 109 countries in 1959–71. (See Table 2.1, columns (5) and (6), for details.)

## Total trade instability, by country, 1959–71 and 1946–58

Although it might be contended that the time series for exports and for imports, treated separately, provide sufficient aggregation of these international economic transactions, it would seem to be of some interest to show that instability of exports and imports *combined* for the various countries. This index gives some indication of the *impact* on a country of total trade fluctuations. (The trade instability index used here is the simple average of the export/import instability indexes.)

Mauritania had the highest trade instability index (46.4) and the United Kingdom the lowest (1.3) for 1959–71, while in 1946–58 the index was highest for Iran (48.4) and lowest for Panama (5.0). The following tabulation brings out some other points.

| *Measure (for trade instability)* | *1946–58* (1) | *1959–71* (2) | *Ratio (2)/(1)* (3) |
|---|---|---|---|
| 1 Mean instability index (II) | 14.5 | 8.1 | 0.56 |
| 2 Median II of top third | 22.0 | 12.3 | 0.56 |
| 3 Median II of middle third | 12.0 | 6.7 | 0.56 |
| 4 Median II of bottom third | 8.4 | 4.1 | 0.49 |
| 5 Variation (2 – 4) | 13.6 | 8.2 | 0.60 |
| 6 Relative variation (5/3) | 113% | 112% | 1.08 |
| 7 Range | 5.0–48.4 | 1.3–46.9 | – |
| 8 No. of countries | 80 | 109 | – |

The declines of 44 per cent in both the mean and the median are the most notable changes from 1946–58 to 1959–71. As is evident from column (3), the decline in trade instability was characteristic of the distribution. Only the relative variation was larger in the later period. Of the 80 countries for which there were instability index values for both periods, only nine had higher trade instability indexes for 1959–71:

| *Country (listed by 1959–71 rank)* | *Trade instability index* *1946–58* (1) | *1959–71* (2) | *Ratio (2)/(1)* (3) |
|---|---|---|---|
| Libya | 10.2 | 22.7 | 2.23 |
| China, People's Rep. | 12.2 | 15.0 | 1.23 |
| Brazil | 11.4 | 14.0 | 1.23 |
| Dominican Rep. | 11.1 | 13.2 | 1.19 |
| Jordan | 7.2 | 11.9 | 1.65 |
| Nicaragua | 8.7 | 10.5 | 1.21 |
| China, Nat. Rep. | 7.7 | 9.2 | 1.19 |
| Peru | 8.0 | 8.4 | 1.05 |
| Panama | 5.0 | 6.0 | 1.20 |

Seventy-one of the 80 countries experienced declines, several of them very large declines, absolutely and relatively: Indonesia's trade instability index fell from 40.5 in 1946–58 to 16.3 in 1959–71; Iran's, from 48.4 to 9.9; Tunisia's, from 34.0 to 9.1; Morocco's, from 33.6 to 6.2; and Japan's, from 29.7 to 4.9.

The coefficient of correlation between the trade instability indexes for 1959–71 and for 1946–58, for the 80 countries, was .16 ($r_k$ = .15), not significant at the .05 level. It is noteworthy that not a single country had a trade instability index of less than 5.0 in 1946–58, but 31 per cent did in 1959–71. At the other end of the scale, only three countries out of 109 had trade instability indexes of 20.0 or more in 1959–71, whereas 14 (19 per cent) out of 80 did in 1946–58. If we consider countries with trade instability indexes of 10.0 or above to have trade instability problems, 75 per cent of countries had them in 1946–58, but only 22 per cent did in 1959–71.

**Export, import and total trade instability, by country, 1946–71**

In this section our description is even more aggregative than it has been so far. The time span 1946–71, comprising the two periods 1946–58 and

1959–71, is used in showing the instability of exports, imports and total trade for the 80 countries for which fairly satisfactory statistics were available. Table 2.2 provides the results of the computations. The export and import instability indexes for 1946–71 are the simple averages of those for the two main periods; the trade instability indexes for 1946–71 are the simple averages of the export and import instability indexes for 1946–71.

Switzerland had the lowest export instability index (3.2) for the combined periods 1946–71, but its import instability index (9.1, thirty-sixth from the bottom) put it in eighth place for trade instability. The USSR had the lowest import instability index (2.5, for trade with non-Communist countries), but its higher export instability index (10.3, fiftieth from the bottom) put it in twelfth from lowest place for trade instability. At 3.5, Puerto Rico had the lowest trade instability index for 1946–71, its export and import instability indexes being 4.4 and 2.6.

Indonesia had the highest export instability index (32.7) for 1946–71 and was second highest for imports (24.0) and for trade (28.4). Iran was highest for both imports (26.9) and trade (29.1), and was second highest for exports (31.3). Other countries with high trade instability indexes were Tunisia (21.5), Morocco (19.9), Japan (17.3), the Republic of Korea (17.2), Libya (16.4), Thailand (16.3), Nigeria (16.0) and Ghana (15.6).

In addition to Puerto Rico, the lowest 10 for trade instability included Mexico (5.4), Panama (5.5), Canada (5.8), South Africa (5.8), Belgium (6.1), Norway (6.1), Switzerland (6.2), Israel (6.3) and the United States (6.3).

The following frequency distributions throw some additional light on export, import and total trade instability for the period 1946–71.

| *Instability index (for 1946–71)* | *Number of countries* | | |
|---|---|---|---|
| | *Exports* (1) | *Imports* (2) | *Total trade* (3) |
| 0–4.9 | 3 | 3 | 1 |
| 5–9.9 | 43 | 45 | 46 |
| 10–14.9 | 21 | 21 | 20 |
| 15–19.9 | 7 | 6 | 10 |
| 20–24.9 | 3 | 4 | 1 |
| 25–29.9 | 1 | 1 | 2 |
| 30 and over | 2 | 0 | 0 |
| Total | 80 | 80 | 80 |

It is evident from this table that if an instability index of 15.0 or more is used as the criterion, only 13 countries had trade instability problems for the period 1946–71. This is about one-sixth of the countries. The number and percentage would be somewhat larger if the newly independent countries not included in the 1946–58 calculations were added. If an instability index of 10.0 or more is used as the criterion, about 40 per cent of the countries had trade instability trouble for the period 1946–71. Further statistical calculations for 1946–71 are as follows.

| *Measure (for 1946–71)* | *Exports* (1) | *Imports* (2) | *Total trade* (3) |
|---|---|---|---|
| 1 Mean instability index | 10.70 | 10.58 | 10.64 |
| 2 Median of top third | 14.5 | 14.1 | 14.6 |
| 3 Median of middle third | 9.4 | 9.5 | 9.3 |
| 4 Median of bottom third | 6.2 | 6.9 | 6.6 |
| 5 Variation of (2 – 4) | 8.3 | 7.2 | 8.0 |
| 6 Relative variation (5/3) | 88% | 76% | 86% |
| 7 Range | 3.2–32.7 | 2.5–26.9 | 3.5–29.1 |
| 8 No. of countries | 80 | 80 | 80 |

It is evident that these measures of concentration and dispersion do not vary very much for the three variables. In all three columns the distributions are skewed toward the larger values, as indicated by the ratio of the mean to the median. The relative variation tends to be greater for export than for import instability. For the period 1946–71, export and import instability were moderately correlated: $r = .59$ and $r_k = .56$ (data from columns (1) and (2) of table 2.2).

Table 2.2

Export, import, and trade instability indexes, by country, 1946–71 (Ranked in ascending order. In columns (2)–(3) ranks are shown in parentheses.)

| Rank, by col. (1) | Country | Export instability index[a] (1) | Import instability index[b] (2) | Trade instability index[c] (3) |
|---|---|---|---|---|
| 1 | Switzerland | 3.2 | 9.1 (36) | 6.2 (8) |
| 2 | Puerto Rico | 4.4 | 2.6 (2) | 3.5 (1) |
| 3 | Mexico | 4.6 | 6.2 (7) | 5.4 (2) |

*Table 2.2 cont.*

| Rank, by col. (1) | Country | (1) | (2) | (3) |
|---|---|---|---|---|
| 4 | Ireland | 5.0 | 7.7 (24) | 6.3 (11) |
| 5 | Romania | 5.0 | 8.4 (29) | 6.7 (15) |
| 6 | South Africa | 5.0 | 6.5 (10) | 5.8 (5) |
| 7 | Canada | 5.2 | 6.3 (8) | 5.8 (4) |
| 8 | Israel | 5.2 | 7.3 (20) | 6.3 (9) |
| 9 | United States | 5.4 | 7.1 (19) | 6.3 (10) |
| 10 | Bulgaria | 5.5 | 23.4 (78) | 14.5 (67) |
| 11 | Haiti | 5.8 | 12.2 (58) | 9.0 (34) |
| 12 | Peru | 6.0 | 10.3 (49) | 8.1 (22) |
| 13 | Guatemala | 6.0 | 8.6 (32) | 7.3 (19) |
| 14 | Sri Lanka (Ceylon) | 6.2 | 7.0 (17) | 6.6 (14) |
| 15 | Venezuela | 6.2 | 9.3 (39) | 7.8 (21) |
| 16 | Panama | 6.4 | 4.6 (3) | 5.5 (3) |
| 17 | Greece | 6.6 | 9.7 (44) | 8.2 (23) |
| 18 | Sweden | 6.6 | 6.9 (14) | 6.8 (16) |
| 19 | Norway | 6.7 | 5.5 (5) | 6.1 (7) |
| 20 | Belgium | 6.9 | 5.2 (4) | 6.1 (6) |
| 21 | Paraguay | 7.0 | 7.0 (16) | 7.0 (17) |
| 22 | United Kingdom | 7.1 | 5.8 (6) | 6.5 (13) |
| 23 | Czechoslovakia | 7.3 | 9.1 (35) | 8.2 (25) |
| 24 | China, Nat. Rep. | 7.3 | 9.5 (40) | 8.4 (28) |
| 25 | India | 7.3 | 11.4 (54) | 9.4 (41) |
| 26 | Denmark | 7.4 | 6.9 (13) | 7.2 (18) |
| 27 | Portugal | 7.5 | 7.6 (23) | 7.6 (20) |
| 28 | Ecuador | 7.5 | 8.9 (34) | 8.2 (27) |
| 29 | New Zealand | 7.8 | 10.8 (51) | 9.3 (39) |
| 30 | Zaire | 8.1 | 9.3 (38) | 8.7 (31) |
| 31 | Philippines | 8.2 | 9.9 (48) | 9.0 (36) |
| 32 | Spain | 8.4 | 10.4 (50) | 9.4 (43) |
| 33 | France | 8.5 | 8.3 (28) | 8.4 (29) |
| 34 | Italy | 8.8 | 7.5 (21) | 8.2 (24) |
| 35 | El Salvador | 8.9 | 9.6 (42) | 9.2 (38) |
| 36 | Turkey | 8.9 | 21.3 (76) | 15.1 (69) |
| 37 | Hungary | 9.0 | 18.1 (74) | 13.6 (63) |
| 38 | Argentina | 9.2 | 15.0 (70) | 12.1 (56) |
| 39 | Syria | 9.3 | 8.9 (33) | 9.1 (37) |
| 40 | Austria | 9.3 | 8.5 (30) | 8.9 (32) |
| 41 | Colombia | 9.6 | 11.3 (53) | 10.5 (48) |
| 42 | Chile | 9.6 | 6.8 (12) | 8.2 (26) |
| 43 | Brazil | 9.7 | 15.6 (71) | 12.7 (61) |
| 44 | Lebanon | 9.8 | 9.6 (43) | 9.7 (46) |
| 45 | Nicaragua | 9.8 | 9.3 (37) | 9.5 (45) |

*Table 2.2 cont.*

| Rank, by col. (1) | Country | (1) | (2) | (3) |
|---|---|---|---|---|
| 46 | Ethiopia | 9.9 | 8.0 (26) | 9.0 (33) |
| 47 | Dominican Rep. | 10.2 | 14.1 (67) | 12.1 (57) |
| 48 | Costa Rica | 10.3 | 7.0 (15) | 8.6 (30) |
| 49 | Honduras | 10.3 | 8.5 (31) | 9.4 (42) |
| 50 | USSR | 10.3 | 2.5 (1) | 6.4 (12) |
| 51 | Australia | 10.3 | 12.5 (60) | 11.4 (52) |
| 52 | German Dem. Rep. | 10.4 | 7.6 (22) | 9.0 (35) |
| 53 | Finland | 10.9 | 13.3 (64) | 12.1 (55) |
| 54 | Germany, Fed. Rep. | 11.5 | 7.1 (18) | 9.3 (40) |
| 55 | Iceland | 11.5 | 13.4 (65) | 12.5 (60) |
| 56 | Uruguay | 11.7 | 12.9 (62) | 12.3 (58) |
| 57 | Bolivia | 11.8 | 7.8 (25) | 9.8 (47) |
| 58 | Pakistan | 11.9 | 15.5 (73) | 14.2 (66) |
| 59 | Burma | 12.1 | 11.5 (55) | 11.8 (54) |
| 60 | Cuba | 12.4 | 9.5 (41) | 11.0 (51) |
| 61 | Jordan | 12.5 | 6.5 (9) | 9.5 (44) |
| 62 | China, People's Rep. | 13.0 | 14.2 (68) | 13.6 (64) |
| 63 | Yugoslavia | 13.1 | 8.1 (27) | 10.6 (49) |
| 64 | Egypt | 13.2 | 11.6 (56) | 12.4 (59) |
| 65 | Iraq | 13.6 | 9.7 (45) | 11.7 (53) |
| 66 | Poland | 14.1 | 11.9 (57) | 13.0 (62) |
| 67 | Netherlands | 14.5 | 6.8 (11) | 10.6 (50) |
| 68 | Korea, Rep. of | 15.8 | 18.6 (75) | 17.2 (75) |
| 69 | Liberia | 16.2 | 14.3 (69) | 15.3 (70) |
| 70 | Ghana | 17.1 | 14.0 (66) | 15.6 (71) |
| 71 | Morocco | 17.2 | 22.5 (77) | 19.9 (77) |
| 72 | Sudan | 17.3 | 12.8 (61) | 15.0 (68) |
| 73 | Malaysia | 18.0 | 9.8 (47) | 13.9 (65) |
| 74 | Nigeria | 18.7 | 13.2 (63) | 16.0 (72) |
| 75 | Thailand | 20.1 | 12.4 (59) | 16.3 (73) |
| 76 | Libya | 23.1 | 9.7 (46) | 16.4 (74) |
| 77 | Japan | 23.6 | 10.9 (52) | 17.3 (76) |
| 78 | Tunisia | 26.9 | 16.1 (72) | 21.5 (78) |
| 79 | Iran | 31.3 | 26.9 (80) | 29.1 (80) |
| 80 | Indonesia | 32.7 | 24.0 (79) | 28.4 (79) |

[a] Simple average of values in columns (1) and (3), Table 2.1; services as well as goods included when statistics available.

[b] Simple average of values in columns (2) and (4), Table 2.1; services as well as goods included when statistics available.

[c] Simple average of values in columns (1) and (2).

**Summary**

Instability indexes for exports and imports (services as well as goods, where full statistics available) were calculated for 109 countries for the period 1959–71 and for 80 of the same countries for the period 1946–58. The resulting index values were used to calculate trade instability indexes (exports plus imports) for each of the shorter periods and for the longer period 1946–71. Some of the significant results are as follows.

| *Measure* | *1946–58* | *1959–71* | *1946–71* |
|---|---|---|---|
| Export instability index | | | |
| mean | 15.1 | 8.3 | 10.7 |
| median | 12.3 | 6.2 | 9.4 |
| range | 3.9–54.5 | 1.7–70.0 | 3.2–32.7 |
| Import instability index | | | |
| mean | 13.7 | 7.9 | 10.6 |
| median | 11.2 | 6.9 | 9.5 |
| range | 1.7–42.4 | 1.6–27.4 | 2.5–26.9 |
| Trade instability index | | | |
| mean | 14.5 | 8.1 | 10.6 |
| median | 12.0 | 6.7 | 9.3 |
| range | 5.0–48.4 | 1.3–46.9 | 3.5–29.1 |
| No. of countries | 80 | 109 | 80 |

By far the most striking fact about international trade instability over the period 1946–71 is the decline of the typical instability index values by nearly one-half from 1946–58 to 1959–71.

**Note**

[1] The instability index values differ from those shown in *International Economic Instability* for 1946–58 because in that study a different measure of instability was used. See Chapter 1, note 8.

# 3 Contributions of countries to world trade instability

In Chapter 2, the degrees of instability in the international trade of individual countries were discussed without reference to the absolute or relative importance of that trade. This chapter is concerned with the relative contributions of countries to world export, import, and trade instability.

The measure of contribution is the percentage obtained by weighting a country's percentage of world exports (imports, trade) by its export (import, trade) instability index. The reasoning underlying this measure is that, if all countries had, say, the same export instability index, then each country's percentage contribution to world export instability would be appropriately measured by its percentage of world exports; hence, by weighting the percentage distribution of world exports among countries by the corresponding export instability indexes, we obtain a measure – a 'contribution percentage' – showing each country's contribution to world export instability. (The actual computation can be done with either the money values or the percentage values for each country: the values of the various countries' exports, or whatever, are multiplied by the corresponding instability index values; the sum of the products is obtained; and the product for each country is expressed as a percentage of the sum.)

It should be noted that the percentage contributions do not reveal whether the country instability indexes are generally, or on average, high or low; the percentage contributions would be the same even if all instability indexes were 10 times as large as they actually were in a given time period. Hence, a country's contribution percentage shows only its relative share of world instability. The divergence of a country's export contribution percentage from its percentage of, say, world exports – the divergence conveniently shown as a ratio – provides an informative comparison. The divergence from unity shows the influence of a country's relative export instability.

The discussion in this chapter is organised as follows:

Contribution to world export instability, by country, 1959–71 and 1946–58

Contribution to world import instability, by country, 1959–71 and 1946–58
Comparison of contribution to world export instability and to world import instability, by country, 1959–71 and 1946–58
Contribution to world trade instability, by country, 1959–71 and 1946–58
Contribution to world export instability, world import instability, and world trade instability, by country, 1946–71
Total trade instability and contribution to world trade instability, by country, 1959–71 and 1946–58

**Contribution to world export instability, by country, 1959–71 and 1946–58**

In 1959–71, 23 of the 109 countries included in the survey contributed 1 per cent or more to world export instability (figure 3.1). West Germany contributed by far the largest percentage (11.5), followed by the United Kingdom (7.5), the United States (7.4) and Japan (6.6). The United States had the largest share of world exports (17.4 per cent), with West Germany second with 10.2 per cent; but the much lower instability index of the United States, as compared with the index for West Germany, reduced its contribution to world export instability to less than one-half of its export share.

The top nine contributors to world export instability in 1959–71 contributed about 50 per cent of the world total, as compared with their share of 58 per cent in world exports (see columns (2) and (4) of table 3.1). The 23 highest contributors to world export instability accounted for 70.8 per cent of the total, as compared with 74.5 per cent in terms of total exports.

If the contributions to world export instability had derived entirely from export shares – that is, if the export instability index had been the same for all countries – then all of the ratios in column (5) of table 3.1 would have been 1.0. The divergences from unity show that differences in export instability were also a contributing factor, to the extent indicated. For example, Libya had only 0.4 per cent of world exports, but contributed 3.3 per cent to world export instability. (The contribution percentages and related data for the 86 countries not included in table 3.1 are given in table A.4.)

In 1946–58, contributions to world export instability were more concentrated than in 1959–71: six instead of nine countries provided

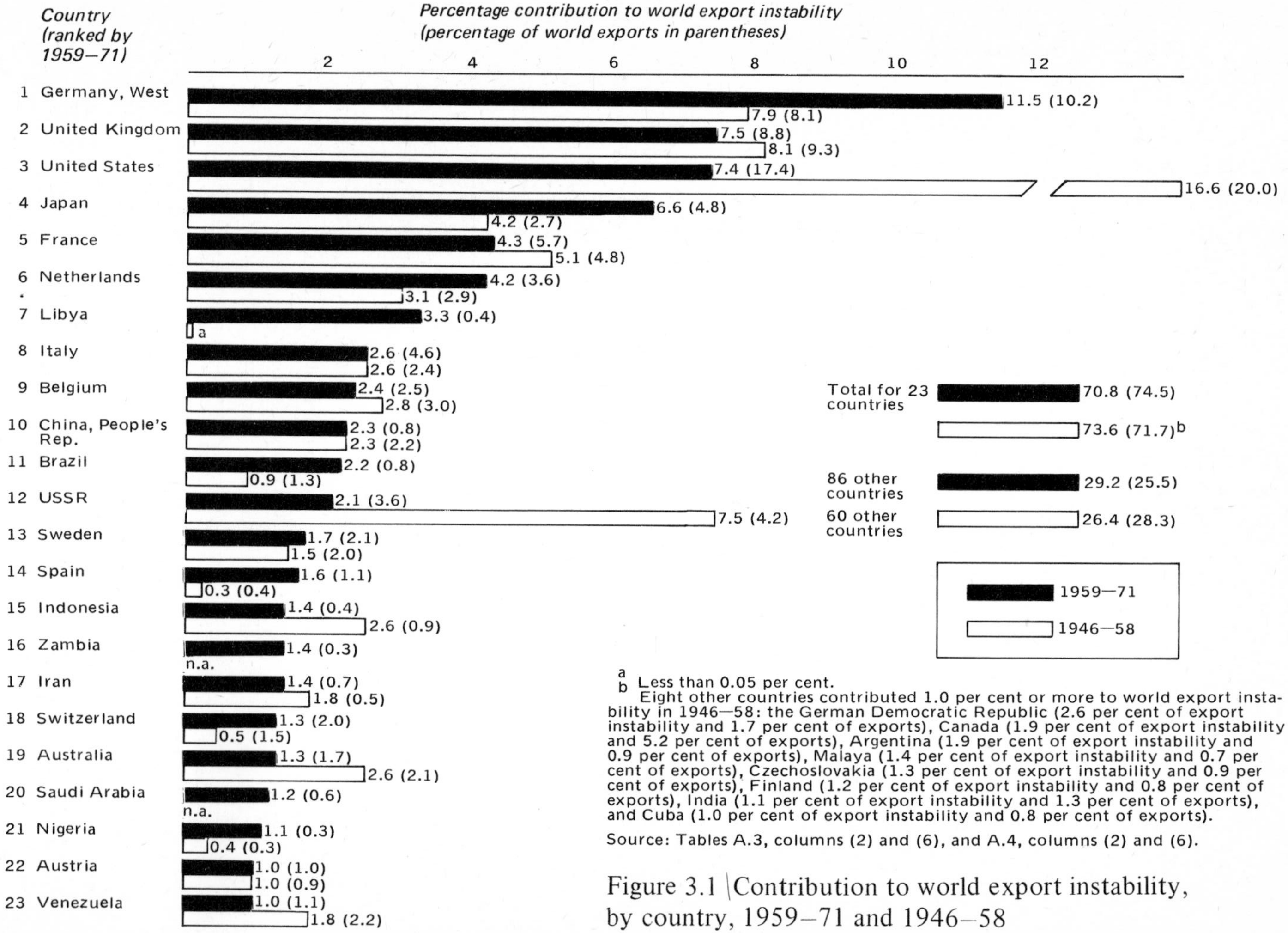


a Less than 0.05 per cent.

b Eight other countries contributed 1.0 per cent or more to world export instability in 1946–58: the German Democratic Republic (2.6 per cent of export instability and 1.7 per cent of exports), Canada (1.9 per cent of export instability and 5.2 per cent of exports), Argentina (1.9 per cent of export instability and 0.9 per cent of exports), Malaya (1.4 per cent of export instability and 0.7 per cent of exports), Czechoslovakia (1.3 per cent of export instability and 0.9 per cent of exports), Finland (1.2 per cent of export instability and 0.8 per cent of exports), India (1.1 per cent of export instability and 1.3 per cent of exports), and Cuba (1.0 per cent of export instability and 0.8 per cent of exports).

Source: Tables A.3, columns (2) and (6), and A.4, columns (2) and (6).

Figure 3.1 | Contribution to world export instability, by country, 1959–71 and 1946–58

Table 3.1

Contribution to world export instability and percentage of world exports, by country, 1959–71

| Rank, by col. (1) | Country | Percentage of world export instability | | Percentage of world exports | | |
|---|---|---|---|---|---|---|
| | | By country (1) | Cumulative (2) | By country[a] (3) | Cumulative (4) | (1)/(3) (5) |
| 1 | Germany, West | 11.5 | 11.5 | 10.2 (2) | 10.2 | 1.12 |
| 2 | United Kingdom | 7.5 | 19.0 | 8.8 (3) | 19.0 | 0.85 |
| 3 | United States | 7.4 | 26.4 | 17.4 (1) | 36.4 | 0.42 |
| 4 | Japan | 6.6 | 33.0 | 4.8 (5) | 41.2 | 1.37 |
| 5 | France | 4.3 | 37.3 | 5.7 (4) | 46.9 | 0.75 |
| 6 | Netherlands | 4.2 | 41.5 | 3.6 (7) | 50.5 | 1.16 |
| 7 | Libya[b,d] | 3.3 | 44.8 | 0.4 (41) | 50.9 | 8.25 |
| 8 | Italy | 2.6 | 47.4 | 4.6 (6) | 55.5 | 0.56 |
| 9 | Belgium | 2.4 | 49.8 | 2.5 (9) | 58.0 | 0.96 |
| 10 | China, People's Rep. | 2.3 | 52.1 | 0.8 (25) | 58.8 | 2.87 |
| 11 | Brazil[d] | 2.2 | 54.3 | 0.8 (24) | 59.6 | 2.75 |
| 12 | USSR | 2.1 | 56.4 | 3.6 (8) | 63.2 | 0.58 |
| 13 | Sweden | 1.7 | 58.1 | 2.1 (10) | 65.3 | 0.80 |
| 14 | Spain | 1.6 | 59.7 | 1.1 (18) | 66.4 | 1.45 |
| 15 | Indonesia | 1.4 | 61.1 | 0.4 (47) | 66.8 | 3.50 |
| 16 | Zambia[b,d] | 1.4 | 62.5 | 0.3 (56) | 67.1 | 4.66 |
| 17 | Iran | 1.4 | 63.9 | 0.7 (26) | 67.8 | 2.00 |
| 18 | Switzerland[d] | 1.3 | 65.2 | 2.0 (11) | 69.8 | 0.65 |
| 19 | Australia | 1.3 | 66.5 | 1.7 (12) | 71.5 | 0.76 |
| 20 | Saudia Arabia[b,d] | 1.2 | 67.7 | 0.6 (29) | 72.1 | 2.00 |
| 21 | Nigeria[b,d] | 1.1 | 68.8 | 0.3 (50) | 72.4 | 3.66 |
| 22 | Austria[b,d] | 1.0 | 69.8 | 1.0 (20) | 73.4 | 1.00 |
| 23 | Venezuela | 1.0 | 70.8 | 1.1 (19) | 74.5 | 0.90 |
| | 86 others[c] | 29.2 | 100.0 | 25.5 | 100.0 | – |
| | Total | 100.0 | 100.0 | 100.0 | 100.0 | |

[a] Rankings in parentheses.
[b] Not among top 26 in distribution of world *import* instability (Table 3.3).
[c] Five of these other countries had 1.0 per cent or more of world exports, but contributed less than 1.0 per cent to world export instability. The countries in question are Denmark (1.2 per cent of exports, 0.9 per cent of instability), Norway (1.3 per cent of exports, 0.8 per cent of instability), South Africa (1.3 per cent of exports, 0.5 per cent of instability), Czechoslovakia (1.1 per cent of exports, 0.9 per cent of instability), and the German Democratic Republic (1.3 per cent of exports, 0.9 per cent of instability).
[d] Did not contribute 1.0 per cent or more in 1946–58.
Source: Table A.4.

Table 3.2

Contribution to world export instability and percentage of world exports, by country, 1946–58

| Rank, by col. (1) | Country | Percentage of world export instability | | Percentage of world exports | | |
|---|---|---|---|---|---|---|
| | | By country (1) | Cumulative (2) | By country[a] (3) | Cumulative (4) | (1)/(3) (5) |
| 1 | United States | 16.6 | 16.6 | 20.0 (1) | 20.0 | 0.83 |
| 2 | United Kingdom | 8.1 | 24.7 | 9.3 (2) | 29.3 | 0.87 |
| 3 | Germany, West | 7.9 | 32.6 | 8.1 (3) | 37.4 | 0.97 |
| 4 | USSR | 7.5 | 40.1 | 4.2 (6) | 41.6 | 1.79 |
| 5 | France | 5.0 | 45.1 | 4.8 (5) | 46.4 | 1.05 |
| 6 | Japan | 4.2 | 49.3 | 2.7 (9) | 49.1 | 1.55 |
| 7 | Netherlands | 3.1 | 52.4 | 2.9 (8) | 52.0 | 1.08 |
| 8 | Belgium | 2.8 | 55.2 | 3.0 (7) | 55.0 | 0.93 |
| 9 | Indonesia | 2.6 | 57.8 | 0.9 (23) | 55.9 | 2.91 |
| 10 | Italy | 2.6 | 60.4 | 2.4 (10) | 58.3 | 1.08 |
| 11 | German Dem. Rep. | 2.6 | 63.0 | 1.7 (15) | 60.0 | 1.52 |
| 12 | Australia | 2.6 | 65.6 | 2.1 (13) | 62.1 | 1.22 |
| 13 | China, People's Rep. | 2.3 | 67.9 | 2.2 (12) | 64.3 | 1.04 |
| 14 | Canada | 1.9 | 69.8 | 5.2 (4) | 69.5 | 0.37 |
| 15 | Argentina[d] | 1.9 | 71.7 | 0.9 (25) | 70.4 | 2.11 |
| 16 | Venezuela | 1.8 | 73.5 | 2.2 (11) | 72.6 | 0.82 |
| 17 | Iran[b] | 1.8 | 75.3 | 0.5 (32) | 73.1 | 3.52 |
| 18 | Sweden | 1.5 | 76.8 | 2.0 (14) | 75.1 | 0.77 |
| 19 | Malaya[b,d] | 1.4 | 78.2 | 0.7 (31) | 75.8 | 2.01 |
| 20 | Czechoslovakia[b,d] | 1.3 | 79.5 | 1.3 (18) | 77.1 | 1.02 |
| 21 | Poland[d] | 1.3 | 80.8 | 0.9 (22) | 78.0 | 1.46 |
| 22 | Finland[d] | 1.3 | 82.1 | 0.8 (27) | 78.8 | 1.51 |
| 23 | India[d] | 1.1 | 83.1 | 1.3 (17) | 80.1 | 0.82 |
| 24 | Cuba[b,d] | 1.0 | 84.2 | 0.8 (28) | 80.9 | 1.30 |
| | 59 others[c] | 15.8 | 100.0 | 19.1 | 100.0 | 0.83 |
| Total | | 100.0 | 100.0 | 100.0 | 100.0 | |

[a] Rankings in parentheses.

[b] Not among the top 25 in distribution of world *import* instability (Table 3.4).

[c] Four of these countries had 1.0 per cent or more of world exports, but contributed less than 1.0 per cent to world export instability. The countries concerned are Switzerland (1.5 per cent of exports, 0.5 per cent of instability), Brazil (1.3 per cent of exports, 0.9 per cent of instability), South Africa (1.2 per cent of exports, 0.6 per cent of instability), and Denmark (1.1 per cent of exports, 0.6 per cent of instability).

[d] Did not contribute 1.0 per cent or more in 1959–71.

Source: Table A.3.

about 50 per cent of world export instability. Four countries – the United States, United Kingdom, West Germany and France – were among the largest contributors in both periods (table 3.2 for 1946–58, and table 3.1 for 1959–71). Figure 3.1 shows the contribution percentages for both 1946–58 and 1959–71 for the 23 countries with the highest contribution percentages in 1959–71. It is evident that, except for the United States and the USSR, these contribution percentages did not vary drastically from period to period. Nevertheless, there were a good many changes in the composition of the list of top contributors (1 per cent or more) from period to period, as may be seen in tables 3.1 and 3.2. Eight of the 24 countries on the 1946–58 list were not on the 1959–71 list; and seven of the 23 countries on the 1959–71 list were not on the 1946–58 list. The 16 countries that were on the list for both periods accounted for 72.3 per cent of world export instability in 1946–58 and for 59.3 per cent in 1959–71.

The degree of concentration of contributions to world export instability is indicated also by the number of countries with more than 2 per cent in either period: 13 in 1946–58, accounting for 67.9 per cent of world export instability; 12 in 1959–71, accounting for 56.4 per cent. The countries that contributed more than 2.0 per cent in both periods were the United States, the United Kingdom, West Germany, France, the USSR, Japan, the Netherlands, Belgium, Italy and the People's Republic of China. They accounted for 60.1 per cent of world export instability in 1946–58 and for 50.9 per cent in 1959–71.

It is evident from this discussion that, if world export instability were to be significantly reduced, these major contributors to instability – and to world exports – would have to be involved.

## Contribution to world import instability, by country, 1959–71 and 1946–58

The United States with 17.0 per cent, contributed the highest percentage to world import instability in 1959–71, but in 1946–58 was second to the United Kingdom (which contributed 8.4 per cent, as compared with the United States' 7.8). The percentage contributions of countries providing 1.0 per cent or more of world import instability are shown for both periods in figure 3.2. As is evident from the chart, the percentage contributions of the United Kingdom, Japan, France and the USSR declined sharply over the two periods. In the main, these changes were the

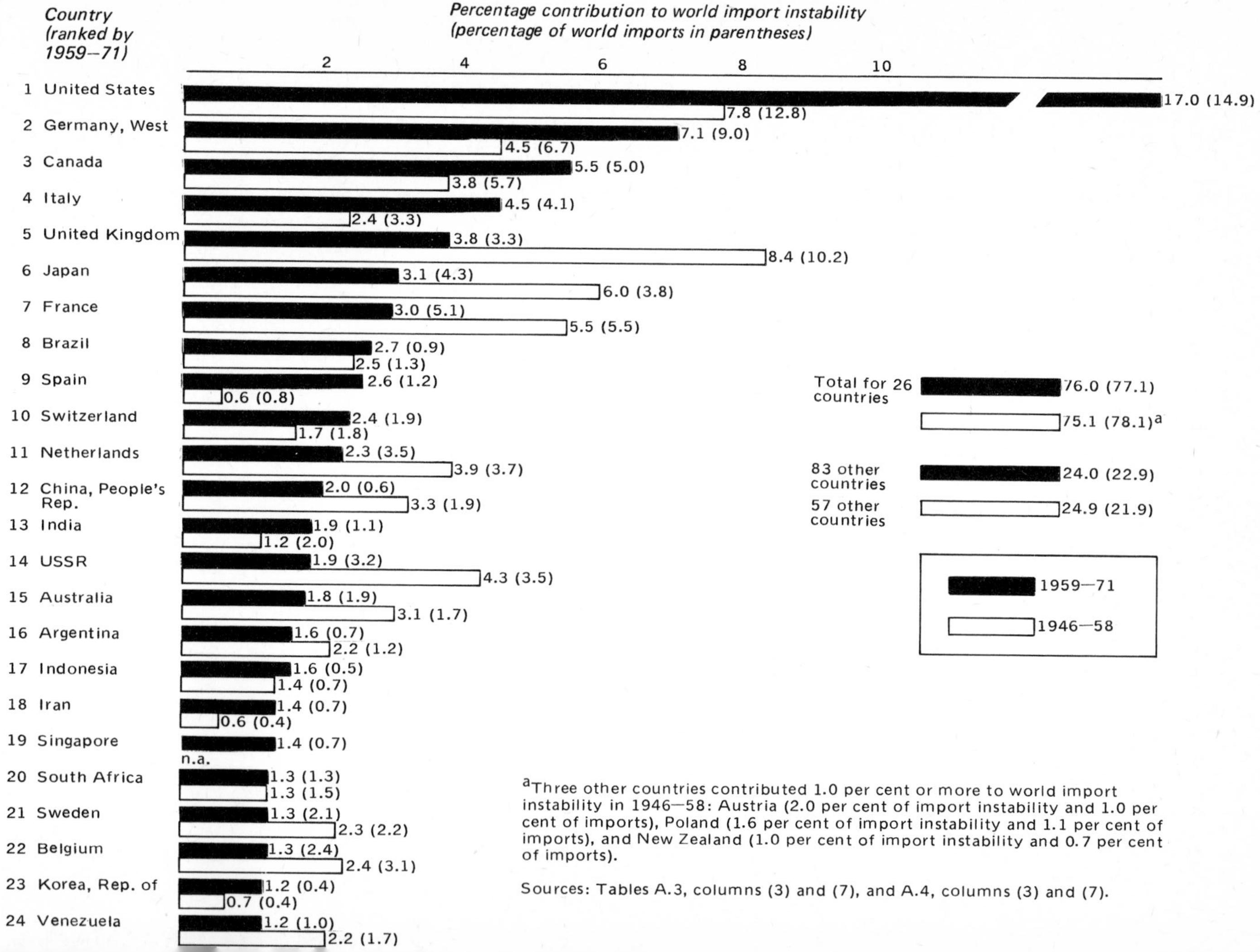


[a]Three other countries contributed 1.0 per cent or more to world import instability in 1946–58: Austria (2.0 per cent of import instability and 1.0 per cent of imports), Poland (1.6 per cent of import instability and 1.1 per cent of imports), and New Zealand (1.0 per cent of import instability and 0.7 per cent of imports).

Sources: Tables A.3, columns (3) and (7), and A.4, columns (3) and (7).

## Table 3.3

Contribution to world import instability and percentage of world imports, by country, 1959–71

| Rank, by col. (1) | Country | Percentage of world import instability | | Percentage of world imports | | |
|---|---|---|---|---|---|---|
| | | By country (1) | Cumulative (2) | By country[a] (3) | Cumulative (4) | (1)/(3) (5) |
| 1 | United States | 17.0 | 17.0 | 14.9 (1) | 14.9 | 1.14 |
| 2 | Germany, West | 7.1 | 24.1 | 9.0 (2) | 23.9 | 0.79 |
| 3 | Canada[b] | 5.5 | 29.6 | 5.0 (5) | 28.9 | 1.10 |
| 4 | Italy | 4.5 | 34.1 | 4.1 (7) | 33.0 | 1.09 |
| 5 | United Kingdom | 3.8 | 37.9 | 8.3 (3) | 41.3 | 0.45 |
| 6 | Japan | 3.1 | 41.0 | 4.3 (6) | 45.6 | 0.72 |
| 7 | France | 3.0 | 44.0 | 5.4 (4) | 51.0 | 0.55 |
| 8 | Brazil | 2.7 | 46.7 | 0.9 (24) | 51.9 | 3.00 |
| 9 | Spain[d] | 2.6 | 49.3 | 1.2 (16) | 53.1 | 2.16 |
| 10 | Switzerland | 2.4 | 51.7 | 1.9 (12) | 55.0 | 1.26 |
| 11 | Netherlands | 2.3 | 54.0 | 3.5 (8) | 58.5 | 0.65 |
| 12 | China, People's Rep. | 2.0 | 56.0 | 0.6 (34) | 59.1 | 3.33 |
| 13 | India[b] | 1.9 | 57.9 | 1.1 (18) | 60.2 | 1.72 |
| 14 | USSR | 1.9 | 59.8 | 3.2 (9) | 63.4 | 0.59 |
| 15 | Australia | 1.8 | 61.6 | 1.9 (13) | 65.3 | 0.94 |
| 16 | Argentina | 1.6 | 63.2 | 0.7 (31) | 66.0 | 2.28 |
| 17 | Indonesia | 1.6 | 64.8 | 0.5 (43) | 66.5 | 3.20 |
| 18 | Iran[d] | 1.4 | 66.2 | 0.7 (28) | 67.2 | 2.00 |
| 19 | Singapore[b,d] | 1.4 | 67.6 | 0.7 (29) | 67.9 | 2.00 |
| 20 | South Africa[b] | 1.3 | 68.9 | 1.3 (14) | 69.2 | 1.00 |
| 21 | Sweden | 1.3 | 70.2 | 2.1 (11) | 71.3 | 0.61 |
| 22 | Belgium | 1.3 | 71.5 | 2.4 (10) | 73.7 | 0.54 |
| 23 | Korea, Rep. of[d] | 1.2 | 72.7 | 0.4 (49) | 74.1 | 3.00 |
| 24 | Venezuela | 1.2 | 73.9 | 1.0 (22) | 75.1 | 1.20 |
| 25 | German Dem. Rep. | 1.1 | 75.0 | 1.2 (17) | 76.3 | 0.91 |
| 26 | Finland[b] | 1.0 | 76.0 | 0.8 (26) | 77.1 | 1.25 |
| | 83 others[c] | 24.0 | 100.0 | 22.9 | 100.0 | |
| Total | | 100.0 | 100.0 | 100.0 | 100.0 | |

[a] Rankings in parentheses.

[b] Not among the top 23 in distribution of world *export* instability (Table 3.1).

[c] Five of these countries had 1.0 per cent or more of world imports, but contributed less than 1.0 per cent to import instability. The countries concerned are Austria (1.0 per cent of imports, 0.8 per cent of instability), Norway (1.3 per cent of imports, 0.8 per cent of instability), Mexico (1.0 per cent of imports, 0.6 per cent of instability), Czechoslovakia (1.0 per cent of imports, 0.6 per cent of instability), Poland (1.0 per cent of imports, 0.4 per cent of instability).

[d] Did not contribute 1.0 per cent or more in 1946–58.

Source: Table A.4.

Table 3.4

Contribution to world import instability and percentage of world imports, by country, 1946–58

| Rank, by col. (1) | Country | Percentage of world import instability | | Percentage of world imports | | |
|---|---|---|---|---|---|---|
| | | By country (1) | Cumulative (2) | By country[a] (3) | Cumulative (4) | (1)/(3) (5) |
| 1 | United Kingdom | 8.4 | 8.4 | 10.2 (2) | 10.2 | 0.83 |
| 2 | United States | 7.8 | 16.2 | 12.8 (1) | 23.0 | 0.61 |
| 3 | Japan | 6.0 | 22.2 | 3.8 (6) | 26.8 | 1.57 |
| 4 | France | 5.5 | 27.7 | 5.5 (5) | 32.3 | 0.99 |
| 5 | Germany, West | 4.5 | 32.2 | 6.7 (3) | 39.0 | 0.68 |
| 6 | USSR | 4.3 | 36.5 | 3.5 (8) | 42.5 | 1.21 |
| 7 | Netherlands | 3.9 | 40.4 | 3.7 (7) | 46.2 | 1.07 |
| 8 | Canada | 3.8 | 44.2 | 5.7 (4) | 51.9 | 0.66 |
| 9 | China, People's Rep. | 3.3 | 47.5 | 1.9 (13) | 53.8 | 1.75 |
| 10 | Australia | 3.1 | 50.6 | 1.7 (15) | 55.5 | 1.80 |
| 11 | Brazil[b] | 2.5 | 53.1 | 1.3 (19) | 56.8 | 1.86 |
| 12 | Italy | 2.4 | 55.5 | 3.3 (9) | 60.1 | 0.74 |
| 13 | Belgium | 2.4 | 57.9 | 3.1 (10) | 63.2 | 0.77 |
| 14 | Sweden | 2.3 | 60.2 | 2.2 (11) | 65.4 | 1.05 |
| 15 | Venezuela | 2.2 | 62.4 | 1.7 (16) | 67.1 | 1.33 |
| 16 | Argentina | 2.2 | 64.6 | 1.2 (22) | 68.3 | 1.89 |
| 17 | Austria[bd] | 2.0 | 66.6 | 1.0 (26) | 69.3 | 2.02 |
| 18 | German Dem. Rep. | 1.8 | 68.4 | 1.4 (18) | 70.7 | 1.27 |
| 19 | Switzerland[b] | 1.7 | 70.1 | 1.8 (14) | 72.5 | 0.96 |
| 20 | Poland[d] | 1.6 | 71.7 | 1.1 (24) | 73.6 | 1.41 |
| 21 | Indonesia | 1.4 | 73.1 | 0.7 (31) | 74.3 | 1.97 |
| 22 | South Africa[b] | 1.3 | 74.5 | 1.5 (17) | 75.8 | 0.87 |
| 23 | Finland | 1.3 | 75.8 | 0.8 (27) | 76.6 | 1.55 |
| 24 | India | 1.2 | 77.0 | 2.0 (12) | 78.6 | 0.61 |
| 25 | New Zealand[bd] | 1.0 | 78.0 | 0.7 (30) | 79.3 | 1.35 |
| | 58 others[c] | 22.0 | 100.0 | 20.62 | 100.0 | 1.07 |
| Total | | 100.0 | 100.0 | 100.0 | 100.0 | |

[a] Rankings in parentheses.

[b] Not among the top 24 in distribution of world *export* instability (Table 3.2).

[c] Four of these countries had 1.0 per cent of world imports but contributed less than 1.0 per cent to world import instability. The countries in question are Czechoslovakia (1.2 per cent of imports, 0.8 per cent of instability), Denmark (1.2 per cent of imports, 0.7 per cent of instability), Norway (1.1 per cent of imports, 0.9 per cent of instability), and Mexico (1.0 per cent of imports, 0.8 per cent of instability).

[d] Did not contribute 1.0 per cent or more in 1959–71.

Source: Table A.3.

result of relatively large declines in these countries' import instability indexes.

In 1959–71, 26 of the 109 countries included in the study contributed 1 per cent or more to world import instability and accounted for 76.0 per cent of the total (see column (2) of table 3.3). In 1946–58, 25 of the 80 countries included in the survey contributed 1 per cent or more and accounted for 78.0 per cent of the total (see column (2) of table 3.4). Four of the 26 countries on the list in 1959–71 were not in the 1946–58 list, which included three countries not on the 1959–71 list. The remaining 20 or so countries contributed about three-fourths of world import instability in both periods.

In 1959–71, 10 countries accounted for 51.7 per cent of world import instability (and 55.0 per cent of world imports), while in 1946–58 10 countries accounted for 50.6 per cent of world import instability (and 55.5 per cent of world imports). (See columns (2) and (4) of tables 3.3 and 3.4.) Measured in this way, the degree of concentration did not change much, but there was some change in the membership of the top group. Only six countries – the United States, the United Kingdom, West Germany, Japan, France and Canada – were in this group in both periods. These six accounted for 39.5 per cent of world import instability in 1959–71 and for 36.0 per cent in 1946–58.

Looked at another way, the top 12 out of 109 countries each contributed 2.0 per cent or more to world import instability in 1959–71 and accounted for 56.0 per cent of the total (59.1 per cent of imports), while 17 out of 80 countries contributed 2.0 or more in 1946–58 and accounted for 66.6 per cent of the total (69.3 per cent of world imports). Except as regards the United States in 1959–71, with 17.0 per cent, national contributions to world import instability were quite widely diffused in both periods. Even so, the degree of concentration among the top 20 or so contributors was sufficient to mean that significant changes in world import instability must involve them.

## Comparison of contribution to world export instability and to world import instability, by country, 1959–71 and 1946–58

In this section we compare the various countries' percentage contributions to world export instability with their percentage contributions to world import instability, first for the period 1959–71 and then for 1946–58. (The statistical data for all countries are given in the Appendix, in table A.4 for 1959–71 and in table A.3 for 1946–58.)

The contribution of those countries which contributed 1.0 per cent or more to world export *or* world import instability in 1959–71 are shown on a cumulative basis in table 3.5. Interestingly, half of these countries contributed more to export than to import instability, and *vice versa* for the other half. The shares of world exports and imports are shown in parentheses in table 3.5, country by country.

Table 3.5

Contributions to world export and import instability, by principal contributors, 1959–71

| Rank, by col. (1) | Country | Percentage of world export instability[a] By country (1) | Percentage of world export instability[a] Cumulative (2) | Percentage of world import instability[b] By country (3) | Percentage of world import instability[b] Cumulative (4) | (1)/(3)[c] (5) |
|---|---|---|---|---|---|---|
| 1 | Germany, West | 11.5 (10.2) | 11.5 (11.5) | 7.1 (9.0) | 7.1 (9.0) | 1.62 (5) |
| 2 | United Kingdom | 7.5 (8.3) | 19.0 (19.0) | 3.8 (8.3) | 10.9 (17.3) | 1.97 (2) |
| 3 | United States | 7.4 (17.4) | 26.4 (36.4) | 17.0 (14.9) | 27.9 (32.2) | 0.44 (18) |
| 4 | Japan | 6.6 (4.8) | 33.0 (41.2) | 3.1 (4.3) | 31.0 (36.5) | 2.13 (1) |
| 5 | France | 4.3 (5.7) | 37.3 (46.9) | 3.0 (5.4) | 34.0 (41.9) | 1.43 (6) |
| 6 | Netherlands | 4.2 (3.6) | 41.5 (50.5) | 2.3 (3.5) | 36.3 (45.4) | 1.83 (4) |
| 7 | Italy | 2.6 (4.6) | 44.1 (55.1) | 4.5 (4.1) | 40.8 (49.5) | 0.58 (16) |
| 8 | Belgium | 2.4 (2.5) | 46.5 (57.6) | 1.3 (2.4) | 42.1 (51.9) | 1.85 (3) |
| 9 | China, People's Rep. | 2.3 (0.8) | 48.8 (58.4) | 2.0 (0.6) | 44.1 (52.5) | 1.15 (9) |
| 10 | Brazil[d] | 2.2 (0.8) | 51.0 (59.2) | 2.7 (0.9) | 46.8 (53.4) | 0.81 (13) |
| 11 | USSR | 2.1 (3.6) | 53.1 (62.8) | 1.9 (3.2) | 48.7 (56.6) | 1.11 (8) |
| 12 | Sweden | 1.7 (2.1) | 54.8 (64.9) | 1.3 (2.1) | 50.0 (58.7) | 1.31 (7) |
| 13 | Spain[d] | 1.6 (1.1) | 56.4 (66.0) | 2.6 (1.2) | 52.6 (59.9) | 0.62 (15) |
| 14 | Indonesia | 1.4 (0.4) | 57.8 (66.4) | 1.6 (0.5) | 54.2 (60.4) | 0.88 (11) |
| 15 | Iran[d] | 1.4 (0.7) | 59.6 (67.1) | 1.4 (0.7) | 55.6 (61.1) | 1.00 (10) |
| 16 | Switzerland[d] | 1.3 (2.0) | 60.5 (69.1) | 2.4 (1.9) | 58.0 (63.0) | 0.54 (17) |
| 17 | Australia | 1.3 (1.7) | 61.8 (70.8) | 1.8 (1.9) | 59.8 (64.9) | 0.72 (14) |
| 18 | Venezuela | 1.0 (1.1) | 62.8 (71.9) | 1.2 (1.0) | 61.0 (65.9) | 0.83 (12) |
| | 91 others | 37.2 (28.1) | 100.0 (100.0) | 39.0 (34.1) | 100.0 (100.0) | |
| Total | | 100.0 (100.0) | 100.0 (100.0) | 100.0 (100.0) | 100.0 (100.0) | |

[a] Figures in parentheses are percentage shares of world exports.
[b] Figures in parentheses are percentage shares of world imports.
[c] Rankings in parentheses.
[d] Not among the top contributors to export instability, 1946–58 (Table 3.6).

Source: Tables 3.1 and 3.3.

Table 3.6

Contributions to world export and import instability, by principal contributors, 1946–58

| Rank, by col. (1) | Country | Percentage of world export instability[a] | | Percentage of world import instability[b] | | |
|---|---|---|---|---|---|---|
| | | By country (1) | Cumulative (2) | By country (3) | Cumulative (4) | (1)/(3)[c] (5) |
| 1 | United States | 16.6 (20.0) | 16.6 (20.0) | 7.8 (12.8) | 7.8 (12.8) | 2.13 (1) |
| 2 | United Kingdom | 8.1 (9.3) | 24.7 (29.3) | 8.4 (10.2) | 16.2 (23.0) | 0.96 (10) |
| 3 | Germany, West | 7.9 (8.1) | 32.6 (37.4) | 4.5 (6.7) | 20.7 (29.7) | 1.76 (3) |
| 4 | USSR | 7.5 (4.2) | 40.1 (41.6) | 4.3 (3.5) | 25.0 (33.2) | 1.74 (4) |
| 5 | France | 5.0 (4.8) | 45.1 (46.4) | 5.5 (5.5) | 30.5 (38.7) | 0.91 (12) |
| 6 | Japan | 4.2 (2.7) | 49.3 (49.1) | 6.0 (3.8) | 36.5 (42.5) | 0.70 (17) |
| 7 | Netherlands | 3.1 (2.9) | 52.4 (52.0) | 3.9 (3.7) | 40.4 (46.2) | 0.79 (16) |
| 8 | Belgium | 2.8 (3.0) | 55.2 (55.0) | 2.4 (3.1) | 42.8 (49.3) | 1.17 (6) |
| 9 | Indonesia | 2.6 (0.9) | 57.8 (55.9) | 1.4 (0.7) | 44.2 (50.0) | 1.86 (2) |
| 10 | Italy | 2.6 (2.4) | 60.4 (58.3) | 2.4 (3.3) | 46.6 (53.3) | 1.08 (8) |
| 11 | German Dem. Rep.[d] | 2.6 (1.7) | 63.0 (60.0) | 1.8 (1.4) | 48.4 (54.7) | 1.44 (5) |
| 12 | Australia | 2.6 (2.1) | 65.6 (62.1) | 3.1 (1.7) | 51.5 (56.4) | 0.84 (7) |
| 13 | China, People's Rep. | 2.3 (2.2) | 67.9 (64.3) | 3.3 (1.9) | 54.8 (58.3) | 0.70 (18) |
| 14 | Canada[d] | 1.9 (5.2) | 69.8 (69.5) | 3.8 (5.7) | 58.6 (64.0) | 0.50 (20) |
| 15 | Argentina[d] | 1.9 (0.9) | 71.7 (70.4) | 2.2 (1.2) | 60.8 (65.2) | 0.86 (13) |
| 16 | Venezuela | 1.8 (2.2) | 73.5 (72.6) | 2.2 (1.7) | 63.0 (66.9) | 0.82 (15) |
| 17 | Sweden | 1.5 (2.0) | 75.0 (74.6) | 2.3 (2.2) | 65.3 (69.1) | 0.65 (19) |
| 18 | Poland[d] | 1.3 (0.9) | 76.3 (75.5) | 1.6 (1.1) | 66.9 (70.2) | 0.81 (15) |
| 19 | Finland[d] | 1.3 (0.8) | 77.6 (76.3) | 1.3 (0.8) | 68.2 (71.0) | 1.00 (9) |
| 20 | India[d] | 1.1 (1.3) | 78.7 (77.6) | 1.2 (2.0) | 69.4 (73.0) | 0.92 (11) |
| | 60 others | 21.3 (22.4) | 100.0 (100.0) | 30.6 (27.0) | 100.0 (100.0) | |
| Total | | 100.0 (100.0) | 100.0 (100.0) | 100.0 (100.0) | 100.0 (100.0) | |

[a] Figures in parentheses are percentage shares of world exports.
[b] Figures in parentheses are percentage shares of world imports.
[c] Rankings in parentheses.
[d] Not among top contributors to export instability, 1959–71 (Table 3.5).

Source: Tables 3.2 and 3.4.

One way to compare the country contributions to world export and import instability is to note the ratio of the contribution percentages. These are shown in table 3.5, column (5), with rankings. Japan's export contribution exceeded its import contribution in the ratio of 2.13 to 1. The United Kingdom (with 1.97), Belgium (with 1.85) and the Netherlands (with 1.83) were the next highest. Among the six largest trading countries, only the United States had a ratio below unity – namely, 0.44 – which was in fact the lowest for the 18 countries listed.

For the period 1946–58, table 3.6 shows the 20 countries that contributed 1.0 per cent or more to world export or import instability. Eight of the 20 countries had export contributions exceeding their import contributions; 12 the reverse. The United States had the highest ratio of export to import contributions, 2.13 to 1, as shown in column (5) of table 3.6. Oddly, this is the same ratio as the leader in 1959–71 (Japan) had; and, whereas the United States had the highest ratio in 1946–58, it had the lowest in 1959–71. Indonesia (with 1.86), West Germany (with 1.76) and the USSR (with 1.74) were next in line in 1946–58.

It is evident from tables 3.5 and 3.6 that the principal contributors to world export instability were also the principal contributors to world import instability in both periods. West Germany, the United Kingdom, the United States, Japan, France, the Netherlands, Italy, Belgium, the People's Republic of China, the USSR, Sweden, Indonesia, Australia and Venezuela were among the principal contributors in both periods. They contributed 56.3 per cent of world export instability and 51.9 per cent of world import instability in 1959–71; in 1946–58, the corresponding figures were 68.6 and 57.5 per cent.

## Contribution to world trade instability, by country, 1959–71 and 1946–58

We now describe the various countries' contributions to world *trade* (exports plus imports) instability for the two periods. Twenty-seven (25 per cent) of the 109 countries in 1959–71 had trade contribution percentages of 1.0 or more and contributed 75.5 per cent of world trade instability in this period, while 24 of these 27 countries (30 per cent of 80) contributed 77.2 per cent in 1946–58. (The contributions for all countries for both periods are shown in table A.4 for 1959–71 and in table A.3 for 1946–58.)

The United States accounted for about one-eighth of world trade instability in each period, somewhat below its trade percentage of about

Table 3.7

Contribution to world trade instability and percentage of world trade, by country, 1959–71

| Rank, by col. (1) | Country | Percentage of world trade instability | | Percentage of world trade | | |
|---|---|---|---|---|---|---|
| | | By country (1) | Cumulative (2) | By country[a] (3) | Cumulative (4) | (1)/(3) (5) |
| 1 | United States | 12.2 | 12.2 | 16.1 (1) | 16.1 | 0.76 |
| 2 | Germany, West | 9.3 | 21.5 | 9.6 (2) | 25.7 | 0.97 |
| 3 | United Kingdom | 5.7 | 27.2 | 8.6 (3) | 34.3 | 0.66 |
| 4 | Japan | 4.8 | 32.0 | 4.5 (5) | 38.8 | 1.07 |
| 5 | France | 3.7 | 35.7 | 5.6 (4) | 44.4 | 0.66 |
| 6 | Italy | 3.5 | 39.2 | 4.3 (6) | 48.7 | 0.82 |
| 7 | Netherlands | 3.3 | 42.5 | 3.6 (7) | 52.3 | 0.92 |
| 8 | Canada | 3.1 | 45.6 | 2.8 (9) | 55.1 | 1.13 |
| 9 | Brazil | 2.4 | 48.0 | 0.8 (24) | 55.9 | 2.88 |
| 10 | China, People's Rep. | 2.2 | 50.2 | 0.7 (30) | 56.6 | 3.07 |
| 11 | Libya[b] | 2.1 | 52.3 | 0.4 (46) | 57.0 | 5.25 |
| 12 | Spain[b] | 2.1 | 54.4 | 1.2 (17) | 58.2 | 1.83 |
| 13 | USSR | 2.0 | 56.4 | 3.4 (8) | 61.6 | 0.59 |
| 14 | Belgium | 1.0 | 58.3 | 2.4 (10) | 64.0 | 0.76 |
| 15 | Switzerland | 1.8 | 60.1 | 1.9 (12) | 65.9 | 0.95 |
| 16 | Australia | 1.6 | 61.7 | 1.8 (13) | 67.7 | 0.86 |
| 17 | Indonesia | 1.5 | 63.2 | 0.4 (42) | 68.1 | 3.33 |
| 18 | Sweden | 1.5 | 64.7 | 2.1 (11) | 70.2 | 0.71 |
| 19 | India | 1.4 | 66.0 | 1.0 (22) | 71.2 | 1.47 |
| 20 | Iran | 1.4 | 67.5 | 0.7 (28) | 71.9 | 2.00 |
| 21 | Argentina | 1.1 | 68.6 | 0.7 (31) | 72.6 | 1.64 |
| 22 | Singapore[b] | 1.1 | 69.8 | 0.7 (32) | 73.3 | 1.77 |
| 23 | Venezuela | 1.1 | 70.9 | 1.0 (18) | 74.3 | 1.05 |
| 24 | South Africa[b] | 1.0 | 71.9 | 1.3 (14) | 75.6 | 0.81 |
| 25 | German Dem. Rep. | 1.0 | 72.9 | 1.2 (16) | 76.8 | 0.80 |
| 26 | Zambia[b] | 1.0 | 73.9 | 0.3 (60) | 77.1 | 4.00 |
| | 83 others[c] | 26.1 | 100.0 | 22.9 | 100.0 | 1.14 |
| Total | | 100.0 | 100.0 | 100.0 | 100.0 | |

[a] Rankings in parentheses.

[b] Did not contribute 1.0 per cent or more in 1946–58.

[c] Three of these countries contributed 1.0 per cent or more to world trade, but less than 1.0 per cent to world trade instability. The countries in question are Norway (1.3 per cent of world trade, 0.8 per cent of instability), Czechoslovakia (1.1 per cent of world trade, 0.8 per cent of instability), and Austria (1.0 per cent of world trade, 0.9 per cent of instability).

Source: Table A.4.

Table 3.8

Contribution to world trade instability and percentage of world trade, by country, 1946–58

| Rank, by col. (1) | Country | Percentage of world trade instability: By country (1) | Percentage of world trade instability: Cumulative (2) | Percentage of world trade: By country[a] (3) | Percentage of world trade: Cumulative (4) | (1)/(3) (5) |
|---|---|---|---|---|---|---|
| 1 | United States | 12.2 | 12.2 | 16.4 (1) | 16.4 | 0.74 |
| 2 | United Kingdom | 8.3 | 20.5 | 9.8 (2) | 26.2 | 0.85 |
| 3 | Germany, West | 6.2 | 26.7 | 7.4 (3) | 33.6 | 0.84 |
| 4 | USSR | 5.9 | 32.6 | 3.9 (6) | 37.5 | 1.52 |
| 5 | France | 5.3 | 37.9 | 5.1 (5) | 42.6 | 1.02 |
| 6 | Japan | 5.1 | 43.0 | 3.3 (8) | 45.9 | 1.57 |
| 7 | Netherlands | 3.5 | 46.5 | 3.3 (7) | 49.2 | 1.07 |
| 8 | Canada | 2.9 | 49.4 | 5.4 (4) | 54.6 | 0.52 |
| 9 | Australia | 2.8 | 52.2 | 1.9 (14) | 56.5 | 1.48 |
| 10 | China, People's Rep. | 2.8 | 55.0 | 2.1 (12) | 58.6 | 1.37 |
| 11 | Belgium | 2.6 | 57.6 | 3.0 (9) | 61.6 | 0.85 |
| 12 | Italy | 2.5 | 60.1 | 2.8 (10) | 64.4 | 0.88 |
| 13 | German Dem. Rep. | 2.2 | 62.3 | 1.6 (17) | 66.0 | 1.41 |
| 14 | Argentina | 2.1 | 64.4 | 1.0 (22) | 67.0 | 1.98 |
| 15 | Indonesia | 2.0 | 66.4 | 0.8 (27) | 67.8 | 2.49 |
| 16 | Venezuela | 2.0 | 68.4 | 2.0 (13) | 69.8 | 1.04 |
| 17 | Sweden | 1.9 | 70.3 | 2.1 (11) | 71.9 | 0.91 |
| 18 | Brazil | 1.7 | 72.0 | 1.3 (19) | 73.2 | 1.28 |
| 19 | Austria[b] | 1.5 | 73.5 | 1.0 (25) | 74.2 | 1.58 |
| 20 | Poland[b] | 1.5 | 75.0 | 1.0 (23) | 75.2 | 1.44 |
| 21 | Finland[b] | 1.2 | 76.2 | 0.8 (28) | 76.0 | 1.54 |
| 22 | Iran | 1.2 | 77.4 | 0.4 (40) | 76.4 | 2.73 |
| 23 | India | 1.1 | 78.5 | 1.7 (15) | 78.1 | 0.69 |
| 24 | Malaya[b] | 1.1 | 79.6 | 0.6 (31) | 78.7 | 1.76 |
| 25 | Czechoslovakia[b] | 1.1 | 80.7 | 1.3 (20) | 80.0 | 0.85 |
| 26 | Switzerland | 1.1 | 81.8 | 1.6 (16) | 81.6 | 0.66 |
| | 54 others[c] | 18.2 | 100.0 | 18.4 | 100.0 | 0.99 |
| Total | | 100.0 | 100.0 | 100.0 | 100.0 | |

[a] Rankings in parentheses.

[b] Did not contribute 1.0 per cent or more in 1959–71.

[c] Two of these countries contributed 1.0 per cent or more to world trade, but less than 1.0 per cent to world trade instability. The countries in question are South Africa (1.4 per cent of world trade, 0.98 per cent of instability) and Denmark (1.1 per cent of world trade, 0.6 per cent of instability).

Source: Table A.3.

one-sixth. The most noticeable declines over the two periods were for the United Kingdom and the USSR. Their trade percentages did not change much, but, owing to reduction in their trade instability indexes, their percentage contributions declined.

In 1959–71, the top 10 contributors to world trade instability accounted for about 50 per cent of the total and for about 57 per cent of world trade (see column (2) of table 3.7). In 1946–58, the corresponding shares of the top 10 were 55 and about 58 per cent, respectively (see column (2) of table 3.8). Eight countries – the United States, West Germany, the United Kingdom, Japan, France, the Netherlands, Canada and the People's Republic of China – were among the top 10 in both periods.

As may be seen in tables 3.7 and 3.8, 26 countries contributed 1.0 per cent or more to world trade instability in both periods. Twenty-one of these countries occur in both lists, and between them accounted for 75.4 per cent of world trade instability (76.9 per cent of world trade) in 1946–58 and 66.6 per cent (73.2 per cent of world trade) in 1959–71.

It is evident from this discussion that, in both periods, about one-tenth of the countries included in the survey contributed about one-half of world trade instability, and that about one-fifth of the countries contributed about three-fourths of it. Hence, any sharp change in the distribution of world trade instability would certainly have to involve these major contributors (and traders). It should be noted once more that the contribution percentages do not reflect the general level of trade instability; they reflect only the combined influence of the relative trade and instability positions of the various countries.

## Contribution to world export, import, and trade instability, by country, 1946–71

In this section we combine the contribution results for the two periods 1946–58 and 1959–71 into those for a single period, 1946–71. Since data for only 80 countries were available for both 1946–58 and 1959–71, only 80 countries can be taken into account. The percentage contributions used are averages of those for the two 13-year periods.

Ten countries contributed just over one-half of world trade, export, and import instability for 1946–71 (columns (2), (4) and (6) of table 3.9). With one exception, the same 10 countries were at the top of all three lists. The United States was the largest contributor in all three lists, with

Table 3.9

Contribution to world trade, export, and import instability, by country, 1946–71.

| Rank, by col. (1) | Country | Percentage of world trade instability, 1946–71 | | Percentage of world export instability, 1946–71 | | Percentage of world import instability, 1946–71 | |
|---|---|---|---|---|---|---|---|
| | | By country (1) | Cumulative (2) | By country[a] (3) | Cumulative (4) | By country[a] (5) | Cumulative (6) |
| 1 | United States | 12.2 | 12.2 | 12.0 (1) | 12.0 | 12.4 (1) | 12.4 |
| 2 | Germany, West | 7.8 | 20.0 | 9.7 (2) | 21.7 | 5.8 (3) | 18.2 |
| 3 | United Kingdom | 7.0 | 27.0 | 7.8 (3) | 29.5 | 6.1 (2) | 24.3 |
| 4 | Japan | 5.0 | 32.0 | 5.4 (4) | 34.9 | 4.6 (5) | 28.9 |
| 5 | France | 4.5 | 36.5 | 4.6 (6) | 39.5 | 4.3 (6) | 33.2 |
| 6 | USSR | 4.0 | 40.5 | 4.8 (5) | 44.3 | 3.1 (8) | 36.3 |
| 7 | Netherlands | 3.4 | 43.9 | 3.6 (7) | 47.9 | 3.1 (9) | 39.4 |
| 8 | Canada | 3.0 | 46.9 | 1.3 (20) | 49.2 | 4.7 (4) | 44.1 |
| 9 | Italy | 3.0 | 49.9 | 2.6 (9) | 51.8 | 3.5 (7) | 47.6 |
| 10 | China, People's Rep. | 2.5 | 52.4 | 2.3 (10) | 54.1 | 2.7 (10) | 50.3 |
| 11 | Belgium | 2.3 | 54.7 | 2.6 (8) | 56.7 | 1.9 (15) | 52.2 |

| | | | | | | | |
|---|---|---|---|---|---|---|---|
| 12 | Australia | 2.2 | 56.9 | 1.9 (13) | 58.6 | 2.5 (12) | 54.7 |
| 13 | Brazil | 2.0 | 58.9 | 1.5 (17) | 60.1 | 2.6 (11) | 57.3 |
| 14 | Indonesia | 1.8 | 60.7 | 2.0 (12) | 62.1 | 1.5 (20) | 58.8 |
| 15 | Sweden | 1.7 | 62.4 | 1.6 (15) | 63.7 | 1.8 (16) | 60.6 |
| 16 | German Dem. Rep. | 1.6 | 64.0 | 1.7 (14) | 65.4 | 1.5 (21) | 62.1 |
| 17 | Argentina | 1.6 | 65.6 | 1.3 (19) | 66.7 | 1.9 (14) | 64.0 |
| 18 | Switzerland | 1.5 | 67.1 | 0.9 (24) | 67.6 | 2.1 (13) | 66.1 |
| 19 | Venezuela | 1.5 | 68.6 | 1.4 (18) | 69.0 | 1.7 (17) | 67.8 |
| 20 | India | 1.3 | 69.9 | 1.0 (22) | 70.0 | 1.6 (19) | 69.4 |
| 21 | Iran | 1.3 | 71.2 | 1.6 (16) | 71.6 | 1.0 (25) | 70.4 |
| 22 | Spain | 1.2 | 72.4 | 1.0 (23) | 72.6 | 1.6 (18) | 72.0 |
| 23 | Austria | 1.2 | 73.6 | 1.0 (21) | 73.6 | 1.4 (22) | 73.4 |
| 24 | Libya | 1.1 | 74.7 | 2.2 (11) | 75.8 | 0.5 (26) | 73.9 |
| 25 | Finland | 1.0 | 75.7 | 0.7 (25) | 76.5 | 1.3 (23) | 75.2 |
| 26 | South Africa | 1.0 | 76.7 | 0.7 (26) | 77.2 | 1.3 (24) | 76.5 |
| | 54 others | 23.3 | 100.0 | 22.8 | 100.0 | 23.5 | 100.0 |
| Total | | 100.0 | 100.0 | 100.0 | 100.0 | 100.0 | 100.0 |

[a] Rankings in parentheses.

Source: For columns (1), (3) and (5), columns (1), (2) and (3), respectively, of Tables A.3 and A.4.

Table 3.10a

Countries grouped in thirds with respect to international trade instability (ITI) index and percentage contribution to world trade instability (WTI), 1959–71

| | Bottom third by percentage contribution to WTI | | | Middle third by percentage contribution to WTI | | | Top third by percentage contribution to WTI | | |
|---|---|---|---|---|---|---|---|---|---|
| | Country | ITI index | WTI (% cont.) | Country | ITI index | WTI (% cont.) | Country | ITI index | WTI (% cont.) |
| Bottom third by ITI index | Sri Lanka (Ceylon) | 3.0 | 0.15 | Puerto Rico | 1.9 | 0.25 | United Kingdom | 1.3 | 5.65 |
| | Trinidad–Tobago | 3.3 | 0.15 | Poland | 2.4 | 0.50 | USSR | 2.8 | 2.00 |
| | Kenya | 3.7 | 0.15 | Denmark | 2.8 | 0.55 | Norway | 3.0 | 3.65 |
| | Jamaica | 4.0 | 0.15 | Mexico | 2.9 | 0.55 | France | 3.1 | 3.65 |
| | Uganda | 4.8 | 0.10 | Greece | 3.1 | 0.25 | Czechoslovakia | 3.0 | 0.75 |
| | | | | Ireland | 3.3 | 0.30 | Sweden | 3.3 | 1.50 |
| | | | | Malaysia | 3.5 | 0.45 | Belgium | 3.4 | 1.85 |
| | | | | Hungary | 4.2 | 0.50 | German Dem. Rep. | 4.0 | 1.00 |
| | | | | Hong Kong | 4.6 | 0.65 | | | |
| | | | | Portugal | 4.6 | 0.45 | United States | 4.1 | 12.20 |
| | | | | Israel | 4.7 | 0.45 | South Africa | 4.1 | 1.05 |
| | | | | Bulgaria | 4.7 | 0.45 | Australia | 4.2 | 1.55 |
| | | | | Ivory Coast | 4.8 | 0.20 | Netherlands | 4.2 | 3.35 |
| | | | | | | | Italy | 4.3 | 3.55 |
| | | | | | | | Austria | 4.5 | 0.90 |
| | | | | | | | Germany, West | 4.5 | 9.30 |
| | | | | | | | Japan | 4.8 | 4.85 |
| | | | | | | | Switzerland | 4.9 | 1.85 |
| | | | | | | | Venezuela | 5.1 | 1.10 |

| | | | | | | | | | |
|---|---|---|---|---|---|---|---|---|---|
| by ITI index | Panama | 6.0 | 0.15 | Pakistan | 6.1 | 0.40 | Finland | 5.6 | 0.80 |
| | Costa Rica | 6.1 | 0.10 | Morocco | 6.2 | 0.30 | Canada | 5.8 | 3.10 |
| | Ecuador | 6.2 | 0.15 | Iraq | 6.4 | 0.55 | Romania | 6.6 | 0.65 |
| | Ethiopia | 6.3 | 0.10 | Egypt | 6.5 | 0.50 | Saudi Arabia | 6.6 | 0.85 |
| | Guatemala | 6.4 | 0.15 | Chile | 6.7 | 0.45 | India | 7.0 | 1.40 |
| | Paraguay | 6.6 | – | New Zealand | 6.7 | 0.55 | | | |
| | Syria | 6.6 | 0.15 | Turkey | 6.7 | 0.45 | | | |
| | Cameroon | 6.7 | 0.15 | Zaire | 6.7 | 0.30 | | | |
| | Malagasy Rep. | 6.7 | 0.05 | Lebanon | 7.2 | 0.30 | | | |
| | Bolivia | 7.0 | 0.15 | Kuwait | 7.4 | 0.60 | | | |
| | Senegal | 7.2 | 0.15 | Philippines | 7.4 | 0.65 | | | |
| | Sierra Leone | 7.2 | 0.05 | Colombia | 7.6 | 0.45 | | | |
| | El Salvador | 7.8 | 0.20 | Ghana | 7.7 | 0.25 | | | |
| | Malawi | 7.8 | 0.05 | Peru | 7.8 | 0.50 | | | |
| | | | | Cuba | 8.4 | 0.45 | | | |
| Top third by ITI index | Central African Rep. | 8.7 | – | Sudan | 8.5 | 0.20 | Singapore | 8.4 | 1.15 |
| | Togo | 8.8 | – | Tunisia | 9.0 | 0.20 | Argentina | 8.6 | 1.15 |
| | Honduras | 8.9 | 0.20 | China, Nat. Rep. | 9.1 | 0.55 | Spain | 9.1 | 2.10 |
| | Chad | 10.0 | – | Uruguay | 9.6 | 0.20 | Algeria | 9.5 | 0.85 |
| | Burma | 10.7 | 0.20 | Nicaragua | 10.4 | 0.25 | Iran | 9.8 | 1.40 |
| | Jordan | 11.8 | 0.05 | Iceland | 10.7 | 0.20 | Nigeria | 13.2 | 0.95 |
| | Haiti | 12.3 | – | Yemen, Peo. Dem. Rep. | 12.1 | 0.25 | Brazil | 14.0 | 2.45 |
| | Burundi | 12.4 | – | Dominican Rep. | 13.2 | 0.30 | China, People's Rep. | 14.9 | 2.15 |
| | Liberia | 12.6 | 0.15 | | | | Korea, Rep. of | 15.2 | 0.90 |
| | Afghanistan | 13.0 | 0.15 | | | | Indonesia | 16.2 | 1.50 |
| | Upper Volta | 14.3 | – | | | | | | |
| | Niger | 15.1 | – | | | | | | |
| | Dahomey | 18.9 | – | | | | | | |
| | Mali | 19.4 | – | | | | | | |
| | Mauritania | 46.4 | – | | | | | | |

Note: A dash (–) means less than 0.005 per cent.
Source: Table A.4, columns (1) and (4).

about one-eighth of world trade, export, and import instability. West Germany and the United Kingdom shared second and third places.

Twenty-six countries each contributed 1.0 per cent or more to world trade instability, and accounted for 76.7 per cent of the total. The percentages for world export import instability were similar.

## Total trade instability and contribution to world trade instability, by country, 1959–71 and 1946–58

In this section we show the distribution of countries with reference to two variables: the trade instability index and the contribution to world trade instability ('trade' being exports and imports combined). The two periods 1959–71 and 1946–58 are treated separately.

For convenience the countries are grouped by thirds with respect to each of the two variables (tables 3.10a and 3.10b for 1959–71). The countries in the bottom third with respect to both trade instability and percentage contribution to world trade instability in 1959–71 included Sri Lanka (Ceylon), Trinidad–Tobago, Kenya, Jamaica and Uganda, which obviously had very stable trade and made minimal contributions (amounting to no more than 0.7 per cent overall) to world trade instability in this period. By contrast, the 12 countries in the top third for both variables accounted for 17.7 per cent of world trade instability. One interesting point that may be observed from table 3.10a is that the largest contributors to world trade instability had relatively small trade instability indexes. A summary of the data in table 3.10a is provided in table 3.10b.

Tables 3.11a and 3.11b provide the corresponding information for 1946–58. The 11 countries in the bottom third with respect to both variables accounted for only 1.03 per cent of world trade instability and their median trade instability index was only two-thirds of that for the entire list of countries. In contrast, the 10 countries in the top third with respect to both variables contributed 26.7 per cent of world trade instability and had a median trade instability index of 21.1, nearly double the general median. As in 1959–71, the largest contribution to world trade instability was made by the countries (nine of them) with the lowest trade instability indexes and the highest percentage contributions. They contributed 37.7 per cent of world trade instability, and their median instability index was two-thirds of that for all countries.

From tables 3.10a and 3.11a it is possible to see which countries were most (or least) involved in international trade instability. This is one way of portraying the incidence and relative importance, among countries, of international trade instability.

Table 3.10b

Summary of Table 3.10a (1959–71)

| | Bottom third by WTI, % cont. | Middle third by WTI, % cont. | Top third by WTI, % cont. | Overall |
|---|---|---|---|---|
| *Bottom third by ITI index* | | | | |
| No. of countries | 5 | 13 | 18 | 36 |
| WTI, % cont. | | | | |
| sum | 0.70 | 5.55 | 56.80 | 63.05 |
| median | 0.15 | 0.45 | 1.85 | 0.70 |
| range | 0.10–0.15 | 0.20–0.65 | 0.75–12.20 | 0.10–12.20 |
| ITI index | | | | |
| median | 3.70 | 3.50 | 4.13 | 4.03 |
| range | 3.00–4.85 | 1.90–4.85 | 1.30–5.15 | 1.30–5.15 |
| *Middle third by ITI index* | | | | |
| No. of countries | 15 | 16 | 6 | 37 |
| WTI, % cont. | | | | |
| sum | 1.70 | 7.10 | 7.55 | 16.35 |
| median | 0.15 | 0.45 | 0.83 | 0.30 |
| range | *x*–0.20 | 0.25–0.65 | 0.65–3.10 | *x*–3.10 |
| ITI index | | | | |
| median | 6.60 | 6.73 | 6.23 | 6.70 |
| range | 5.20–7.75 | 5.30–8.45 | 5.15–7.00 | 5.15–8.45 |
| *Top third by ITI index* | | | | |
| No. of countries | 16 | 8 | 12 | 36 |
| WTI, % cont. | | | | |
| sum | 0.75 | 2.15 | 17.70 | 20.60 |
| median | *x* | 0.23 | 1.28 | 0.20 |
| range | *x*–0.20 | 0.20–0.55 | 0.85–2.45 | *x*–2.45 |
| ITI index | | | | |
| median | 12.55 | 10.05 | 13.63 | 12.23 |
| range | 8.75–46.40 | 8.50–13.70 | 8.45–22.65 | 8.45–46.40 |
| *Overall* | | | | |
| No. of countries | 36 | 37 | 36 | 109 |
| WTI, % cont. | | | | |
| sum | 3.15 | 14.80 | 82.05 | 100.00 |
| median | 0.10 | 0.45 | 1.45 | 6.70 |
| range | *x*–0.20 | 0.20–0.65 | 0.65–12.20 | *x*–12.20 |
| ITI index | | | | |
| median | 7.53 | 6.70 | 5.15 | 6.70 |
| range | 3.00–46.40 | 1.90–13.20 | 1.30–22.65 | 1.30–46.40 |

Note: An italic x (*x*) indicates less than 0.005 per cent.
Source: Table 3.10a.

Table 3.11a

Countries grouped in thirds with respect to international trade instability (ITI) index and percentage contribution to world trade instability (WTI), 1946–58

| | Bottom third by percentage contribution to WTI | | | Middle third by percentage contribution to WTI | | | Top third by percentage contribution to WTI | | |
|---|---|---|---|---|---|---|---|---|---|
| | Country | ITI index | WTI (% cont.) | Country | ITI index | WTI (% cont.) | Country | ITI index | WTI (% cont.) |
| Bottom third by ITI index | Panama | 5.02 | 0.05 | Puerto Rico | 5.16 | 0.29 | Canada | 5.77 | 2.85 |
| | Romania | 6.80 | 0.18 | Israel | 7.83 | 0.48 | Switzerland | 7.43 | 1.08 |
| | Jordan | 7.19 | 0.03 | Mexico | 7.91 | 0.58 | South Africa | 7.45 | 0.97 |
| | Paraguay | 7.38 | 0.03 | Peru | 7.97 | 0.33 | United States | 8.51 | 12.20 |
| | China, Nat. Rep. | 7.72 | 0.17 | Norway | 9.23 | 0.79 | Belgium | 8.74 | 2.58 |
| | Guatemala | 8.20 | 0.08 | Ireland | 9.37 | 0.31 | United Kingdom | 9.97 | 8.27 |
| | Nicaragua | 8.67 | 0.04 | Spain | 9.77 | 0.41 | USSR | 9.98 | 5.88 |
| | Honduras | 9.92 | 0.05 | Chile | 9.81 | 0.38 | Sweden | 10.31 | 1.90 |
| | Libya | 10.24 | 0.04 | | | | Venezuela | 10.43 | 2.01 |
| | Ceylon (now Sri Lanka) | 10.27 | 0.23 | | | | | | |
| | Ecuador | 10.33 | 0.13 | | | | | | |

| | | | | | | | | | |
|---|---|---|---|---|---|---|---|---|---|
| Middle third by ITI index | Portugal | 10.56 | 0.26 | Philippines | 10.64 | 0.65 | Brazil | 11.37 | 1.69 |
| | El Salvador | 10.69 | 0.09 | Belgian Congo (Zaire) | 10.71 | 0.38 | India | 11.74 | 1.14 |
| | Cambodia | 10.76 | 0.07 | | | | Italy | 12.03 | 2.51 |
| | Dominican Rep. | 11.10 | 0.16 | Denmark | 11.54 | 0.62 | China, People's Rep. | 12.23 | 2.82 |
| | Costa Rica | 11.16 | 0.06 | New Zealand | 11.89 | 0.77 | | | |
| | Syria | 11.59 | 0.13 | Lebanon | 12.18 | 0.31 | Czechoslovakia | 13.12 | 1.07 |
| | Ethiopia | 11.62 | 0.08 | Burma | 12.83 | 0.36 | Austria | 13.33 | 1.52 |
| | Haiti | 12.48 | 0.04 | Colombia | 13.36 | 0.38 | Cuba | 13.55 | 0.95 |
| | Bolivia | 12.61 | 0.10 | Rhodesia–Nyasaland | 13.99 | 0.33 | France | 13.77 | 5.26 |
| | Greece | 13.27 | 0.27 | | | | German Dem. Rep. | 13.98 | 2.21 |
| Top third by ITI index | Iceland | 14.20 | 0.06 | Yugoslavia | 16.09 | 0.80 | Germany, West | 14.21 | 6.20 |
| | Uruguay | 15.01 | 0.22 | Iraq | 16.94 | 0.35 | Argentina | 15.63 | 2.06 |
| | Liberia | 17.89 | 0.06 | Egypt | 18.35 | 0.48 | Netherlands | 17.05 | 3.53 |
| | Sudan | 21.59 | 0.25 | Nigeria | 18.74 | 0.33 | Finland | 18.61 | 1.22 |
| | Vietnam, South | 23.30 | 0.26 | Korea, Rep. of | 19.25 | 0.37 | Australia | 18.64 | 0.28 |
| | Bulgaria | 24.22 | 0.25 | Pakistan | 22.31 | 0.70 | Poland | 23.57 | 1.44 |
| | Tunisia | 33.96 | 0.21 | Hungary | 22.97 | 0.47 | Malaya | 24.34 | 1.09 |
| | | | | Ghana | 23.44 | 0.31 | Japan | 29.73 | 5.10 |
| | | | | Turkey | 23.57 | 0.54 | Indonesia | 40.52 | 2.02 |
| | | | | Thailand | 27.27 | 0.51 | Iran | 48.42 | 1.20 |
| | | | | Morocco | 33.55 | 0.54 | | | |

Source: Table A.3, columns (1) and (4).

Table 3.11b

Summary of Table 3.11a (1946–58)

| | Bottom third by WTI, % cont. | Middle third by WTI, % cont. | Top third by WTI, % cont. | Overall |
|---|---|---|---|---|
| *Bottom third by ITI index* | | | | |
| No. of countries | 11 | 8 | 9 | 28 |
| WTI, % cont. | | | | |
| sum | 1.03 | 3.57 | 37.74 | 42.34 |
| median | 0.05 | 0.40 | 2.57 | 3.55 |
| range | 0.03–0.23 | 0.29–0.79 | 0.97–12.20 | 0.03–12.20 |
| ITI index | | | | |
| median | 8.20 | 8.60 | 8.74 | 8.59 |
| range | 5.02–10.33 | 5.16–9.81 | 5.77–10.43 | 5.02–10.43 |
| *Middle third by ITI index* | | | | |
| No. of countries | 10 | 8 | 9 | 27 |
| WTI, % cont. | | | | |
| sum | 1.26 | 3.80 | 19.17 | 24.23 |
| median | 0.10 | 0.38 | 1.69 | 0.38 |
| range | 0.04–0.27 | 0.31–0.77 | 0.95–5.26 | 0.04–5.26 |
| ITI index | | | | |
| median | 11.37 | 12.03 | 13.12 | 12.03 |
| range | 10.56–13.37 | 10.64–13.99 | 11.37–13.98 | 10.56–13.99 |
| *Top third by ITI index* | | | | |
| No. of countries | 7 | 11 | 10 | 28 |
| WTI, % cont. | | | | |
| sum | 1.32 | 5.40 | 26.71 | 33.43 |
| median | 0.22 | 0.47 | 2.03 | 0.52 |
| range | 0.06–0.26 | 0.31–0.80 | 1.09–6.20 | 0.06–6.20 |
| ITI index | | | | |
| median | 21.59 | 22.35 | 21.15 | 21.95 |
| range | 14.20–33.96 | 16.09–33.55 | 14.21–48.42 | 14.20–48.42 |
| *Overall* | | | | |
| No. of countries | 28 | 27 | 28 | 83 |
| WTI, % cont. | | | | |
| sum | 3.61 | 12.77 | 83.62 | 100.00 |
| median | 0.09 | 0.41 | 2.03 | 0.41 |
| range | 0.03–0.26 | 0.29–0.80 | 0.95–12.20 | 0.03–12.20 |
| ITI index | | | | |
| median | 10.93 | 12.83 | 13.22 | 12.03 |
| range | 5.02–33.96 | 5.16–33.55 | 5.77–48.42 | 5.02–48.42 |

Source: Table 3.11a, which gives data for 83 countries, as opposed to 80 for some other tables.

## Summary

In this chapter we have described the contribution to world trade instability – for exports, imports, and total trade – of the various countries of the world for the periods 1959–71 and 1946–58. The measure of contribution was the percentage distribution (of exports, imports or trade) weighted by the corresponding instability index. It is important to note that the general level of instability may be high or low, regardless of countries' percentage contributions.

There is no easy way to summarise this intentionally detailed descriptive material. However, the following tabulations bring out some of the most interesting points (FRG = West Germany).

| | *1959–71* | *1946–58* | *1946–71* |
|---|---|---|---|
| Top contributors to world trade instability | US (12.2%)<br>FRG (9.3%)<br>UK (5.7%) | US (12.2%)<br>UK (8.3%)<br>FRG (6.2%) | US (12.2%)<br>FRG (7.8%)<br>UK (7.0%) |
| Percentage of world trade instability, 10 top contributors | 50.2% | 55.0% | 52.4% |
| Percentage of world trade instability, countries contributing 1% or more | 73.9% (26 of 109 countries) | 81.8% (26 of 80 countries) | 76.7% (26 of 80 countries) |

| *Country groups by trade instability index* | *Country groups by percentage contribution to world trade instability* | | | |
|---|---|---|---|---|
| | *Bottom third* | *Middle third* | *Top third* | *Total* |
| Bottom third | | | | |
| 1959–71 | 0.7 | 5.5 | 56.8 | 63.0 |
| 1946–58 | 1.0 | 3.6 | 37.7 | 42.3 |
| Middle third | | | | |
| 1959–71 | 1.7 | 7.1 | 7.5 | 16.3 |
| 1946–58 | 1.3 | 3.8 | 19.2 | 24.3 |
| Top third | | | | |
| 1959–71 | 0.8 | 2.2 | 17.7 | 20.7 |
| 1946–58 | 1.3 | 5.4 | 26.7 | 33.4 |
| Total | | | | |
| 1959–71 | 3.2 | 14.8 | 82.0 | 100.0 |
| 1946–58 | 3.6 | 12.8 | 83.6 | 100.0 |

World trade instability was determined more by the relative shares of countries in world trade than by their trade instability indexes. The same was true for exports and imports considered separately. With minor variations, the countries contributing most to world trade instability in 1959–71 were the same as in 1946–58. The obvious policy implication of this fact is that policies designed to reduce world trade instability will have to involve the principal trading countries, not just the countries that have high trade instability indexes.

# 4 Analysis of export instability

In this chapter we attempt to ascertain which of several variables are closely related to export instability, and to measure the functional relations between export instability and other variables. The dependent variable is the instability index of export receipts, explained in Chapter 1. The independent variables are various characteristics of countries. The method used is mainly standard statistical correlation–regression analysis, simple and multiple.

Although we are basically interested in what happens to export proceeds through time, the system of analysis is of the 'cross-section' type.[1] Nearly all of the variables used are for the 13-year period 1959–71. Strictly interpreted, our statistical results show only how the various independent variables are statistically related to the index of export receipts instability for that period. Additional assumptions have to be made to apply the results to other periods or to apply them to any one country. For example, even though our calculations might show a strong positive relation between the instability and the growth rate of receipts from exports for the 109 countries for the years 1959–71, this statistical relation may not be applicable to country *x* for the 1970s or 1980s.

How were the independent variables selected? It would be pretentious to say that they were selected on the basis of a well-formulated theory, for there is no such theory in this field. Probably the best general statement that can be made is that the variables were selected on the basis of, first, considerable knowledge of the economic processes involved; and, second, a wide acquaintance with (mainly speculative) writings on the subject. All of the variables should strike even casually informed persons as intuitively relevant to some degree. The approach taken is deliberately eclectic. It would be a considerable achievement if this study could narrow down the number of closely related variables.

The questions of cause, effect and interdependence naturally arise, and, in considering them in connection with particular variables, it is necessary to take into account the economic processes involved. The statistical results are of no help in this respect. Frequently the line of causation can plausibly be said to run either way. For example, it can plausibly be said that exports sometimes vary because of changes in national product; but it is also plausible to say that national product sometimes varies because exports vary (in the Keynesian vein). In the single-independent-variable analysis that follows, it is usually possible to give a plausible rationale; but to do so becomes almost impossible when many independent variables are employed. However, nothing is methodologically wrong in trying to find an economic explanation *post hoc* for a relation that turns up from the statistical calculations.

In framing hypotheses, one tends to think of the economic processes through time, but our statistical exercises relate to a cross-section of cases (countries) for a particular period. Also, we are dealing here with macro-variables, which are one or more steps removed from the actual 'micro-behaviour' of individual economic units with respect to particular prices and quantities of specified commodities in particular short periods of time. Hence, if the relations among the macro-variables should turn out to be very close, one should suspect tautologies or errors.

So far, the discussion here applies, *mutatis mutandis*, to imports, which are discussed in the next chapter.

Part (A) of this chapter deals with single independent variables in relation to instability of receipts from exports. Part (B) contains the multi-variable analysis. Part (C) employs various non-quantitative characteristics of countries.

## (A) SINGLE-VARIABLE ANALYSIS

The dependent variable, $X_{100}$, is the country instability index of the value of exports of goods and services, or of goods only if statistics for services are not available. In the regression equations, $Y_c$ is the computed value of this variable. Values for $X_{100}$ and for all other variables are given in the Appendix (table A.2; definitions as in table A.1). Table A.5 gives the regression equations and correlation coefficients for $X_{100}$ and the independent variables in the analysis.

The variables are discussed under the following headings. The order is only for expository convenience. Frequently more than one variable is considered under a particular heading.

Instability of export price indexes and export quantum indexes
Size and growth of exports
Terms of trade
Relative importance of foreign trade
Direction of exports
Degree of bilateralism
Commodity composition of exports

Size of national economy
Importance of agriculture
Real income per capita
National income
Price levels
Balance of trade
Monetary reserves

For the reader wanting only a digest of the results, without discussion, table 4.1 shows the correlation coefficients and the regression equations for which the regression coefficients were significant at the 0.01 level or better. The complete results are given in table A.5.

Table 4.1

Correlation coefficients and regression equations significant at the 0.01 level with export value instability ($X_{100}$) as the dependent variable, for countries, 1959–71

| Rank | Independent variable[a] No. | Independent variable[a] Name | $r$ (1)[b] | $r^2$ (2)[b] | No. of countries (3) | Regression equation[c] (4) |
|---|---|---|---|---|---|---|
| 1 | 115 | Instability index (II), import value | .612 | .374 | 109 | $Y_c = -0.690 + 1.089\ X_{115}$ (−0.55) (8.10) |
| 2 | 118 | II, real GDP per capita | .602 | .363 | 87 | $Y_c = 1.913 + 2.000\ X_{118}$ (2.58) (7.07) |
| 3 | 200 | Percentage growth, export value | .590 | .348 | 109 | $Y_c = 1.607 + 0.683\ X_{200}$ (1.52) (7.66) |
| 4 | 114 | II, real GDP | .529 | .280 | 86 | $Y_c = 2.525 + 1.578\ X_{114}$ (3.26) (5.83) |
| 5 | 108 | II, export quantum | .458 | .210 | 81 | $Y_c = 3.203 + 0.542\ X_{108}$ (4.01) (4.72) |
| 6 | 214 | Percentage growth, real GDP | .431 | .186 | 86 | $Y_c = 2.249 + 0.717\ X_{214}$ (2.23) (4.52) |
| 7 | 352 | Bilateralism percentage | −.416 | .173 | 109 | $Y_c = 23.139 - 0.231\ X_{352}$ (7.28) (4.86) |
| 8 | 310 | Concentration of exports by SITC classes | .400 | .160 | 91 | $Y_c = -7.440 + 0.248\ X_{310}$ (−0.192 (4.27) |
| 9 | 117 | II, foreign trade as a percentage of GDP | .378 | .143 | 96 | $Y_c = 4.100 + 0.492\ X_{117}$ (4.95) (4.10) |
| 10 | 110 | II, import quantum | .352 | .124 | 64 | $Y_c = 3.280 + 0.302\ X_{110}$ (4.6) (3.1) |
| 11 | 365 | Energy consumption per capita | −.332 | .110 | 108 | $Y_c = 10.118 - 0.002\ X_{365}$ (11.03) (3.77) |

*Table 4.1 cont.*

| Rank | | Independent variable | (1) | (2) | (3) | (4) |
|---|---|---|---|---|---|---|
| 12 | 331 | Service imports as a percentage of total imports | .327 | .107 | 84 | $Y_c = 2.270 + 0.168 X_{331}$ (1.56) (3.31) |
| 13 | 112 | II, quantum terms of trade | .313 | .098 | 63 | $Y_c = 3.532 + 0.223 X_{112}$ (4.84) (2.78) |
| 14 | 120 | II, monetary reserves as a percentage of imports | .307 | .094 | 97 | $Y_c = 4.998 + 0.148 X_{120}$ (3.77) (3.30) |
| 15 | 113 | II, GDP | .305 | .093 | 96 | $Y_c = 5.334 + 0.317 X_{113}$ (7.82) (3.27) |
| 16 | 364 | Percentage of GDP from agriculture | .300 | .090 | 97 | $Y_c = 4.337 + 0.095 X_{364}$ (4.70) (3.24) |
| 17 | 349 | GDP per capita | −.297 | .088 | 97 | $Y_c = 8.176 - 0.002 X_{349}$ (12.61) (3.21) |
| 18 | 325 | Percentage of exports in primary goods | .295 | .087 | 102 | $Y_c = 2.007 + 0.085 X_{325}$ (1.01) (3.24) |
| 19 | 321 | Percentage of exports to EEC | .281 | .079 | 106 | $Y_c = 4.589 + 0.117 X_{321}$ (3.41) (3.16) |
| 20 | 218 | Percentage growth, real GDP per capita | .243 | .059 | 87 | $Y_c = 4.842 + 0.447 X_{218}$ (6.25) (2.52) |
| 21 | 315 | Average value, imports | −.200 | .040 | 109 | $Y_c = 8.905 - 0.000 X_{315}$ (10.56) (2.34) |

[a] Full descriptions of variables are given in Table A.1. Results for all variables tested appear in Table A.5. A few variables with results significant at the .01 level have been omitted here owing to the fact that they are essentially duplicative of some that have been included.

[b] The $r^2$ and $r$ values are corrected for size of sample. Uncorrected values are shown in Table A.5.

[c] The $t$ value is in parentheses. $Y_c$ is the computed or trend value of the export value instability index ($X_{100}$).

## Instability of export price and quantum indexes

The average price of a particular kind of export from a country, multiplied by the total quantity of such exports for a year, gives the annual value of such exports. Price and quantity are thus the necessary proximate determinants of value. However, export price and quantum instability indexes, the variables with which we have to work in this aggregative analysis, are *not* the necessary determinants of export value (receipts) instability. A brief discussion should make this clear. If the instability index of the export price index were zero for the specified period of time, then the export value and export quantum instability indexes would be identical in value. If the instability index of the export quantum index were zero over the period in question, then the export value-instability index and the instability index of the export price index would be identical. For all other combinations of values of the price and quantum instability indexes, anything can happen: they can reinforce each other and cause an even higher instability index of value; or they can compensate each other in varying degrees – even to the point of perfectly offsetting each other and leaving the value instability index at zero. Hence, there is no deductive relation between the price and quantum instability indexes, on the one hand, and the instability index of value, on the other. This discussion applies to imports as well as exports.

The coefficient of correlation ($r$) between export price and export value instability, for the period 1959–71, was only –.114.[2] Only goods exports were included, since indexes of service export prices were not available. The degree of correlation is negligible – a very surprising result, utterly at variance with widely-held opinions that export price instability is a major source of export value instability. Country data for 79 countries are given in table A.2, columns 100 and 107. The regression equation, with $Y_c$ the normal or computed instability index value for export value, was as follows, with $t$ values in parentheses.[3]

$$Y_c = \underset{(12.12)}{6.402} + \underset{(.110)}{0.005}\, X_{107} \quad (r^2 = .013\text{; not significant at the .05 level})$$

Now consider instability of export quantum as the independent variable. Export quantum is obtained by dividing export value figures by the index of export prices; it is usually expressed as an index number rather than in monetary terms. The coefficient of correlation between the export quantum and export value instability indexes turned out to be .458. The equation was

$$Y_c = \underset{(4.01)}{3.203} + \underset{(4.72)}{0.542}\, X_{108} \quad (r^2 = .210\text{; significant at the .01 level})$$

Country data for 81 countries given in table A.2, columns 100 and 108.

According to the usual interpretation, 21 per cent of the variation in the export value instability index is accounted for by the export quantum instability index. Even though this is not a high percentage, it is evident that, by this analysis, the instability index for export quantum is much more important than that for export price as a determinant of the export value instability index.

## Size and growth of exports

What, for period 1959–71, is the statistical relation between the average money value of exports and the instability of export receipts? On the presumption that more markets are involved when exports are larger, and that export receipts are more likely to go up in some markets when they go down in others, rather than move in the same way in all markets, larger export receipts should be associated with lower export instability. The sign of the correlation coefficient is indeed negative, but the $r$ value is low: –.184. The regression equation was

$$Y_c = 8.773 - 0.003\, X_{300}\ (r^2 = .034;\ \text{significant at .05 level})$$

Country data for 109 countries are given in table A.2, columns 100 and 300.

What is a plausible hypothesis about the relation between the rate of growth of exports and the instability of export receipts? The rapid economic growth that has taken place in the past century or so has been accompanied by sizable fluctuations; so, on the basis of this historical generalisation, it seems plausible to expect that the growth rate and instability of exports are positively correlated. The correlation calculation supported the historical generalisation: $r = .590$. The rather high correlation coefficient for the growth rate of export receipts ($X_{200}$) and of export quantum ($X_{208}$) – namely, .73 ($r^2 = .53$) – shows one of the main sources of this relation. (See Table 4.2 for intercorrelations.) The equation was

$$\underset{(1.52)}{Y_c = 1.607} + \underset{(7.66)}{0.683}\, X_{200}\ (r^2 = .348;\ \text{significant at the .01 level})$$

Country data for 109 countries are given in table A.2, columns 100 and 200.

## Imports

On the theory that countries spend quite promptly on imports of goods and services all they earn from exports, it can be argued that receipts from exports and outlays on imports vary together rather closely. Or the line of causation can run the other way, meaning that countries must import in order to provide their trading partners with the means of purchasing their exports. Of course, both of these speculations leave out of account the lack of equality, or proportionality, in a given time period, of exports and imports financed by other means.

For 109 countries in 1959–71, the computer run showed an $r$ value of .612 for the correlation between export and import value instability. This was the highest $r$ value obtained. Whichever theory one prefers, this value indicates a fairly close relation. The equation was

$$Y_c = -0.690 + 1.089\, X_{115} \quad (r^2 = .374;\ \text{significant at the .01 level})$$
$$(-.55) \quad (8.10)$$

Country data are given in table A.2, columns 100 and 115. Goods and services statistics were available for 84 countries; for the other 25, only goods statistics were available.

Where the average value of imports ($X_{315}$) was the independent variable, $r$ was equal to –.20 (details in table A.5).

**Terms of trade**

Instability of terms of trade is often cited, along with instability of export prices alone, as a major cause of fluctuations in export receipts. In this section, attention is primarily focused on the concept of terms of trade calculated by dividing the export price index by the import price index. (Similar results were obtained by using the gross-barter terms-of-trade index, for which the import quantum index is divided by the export quantum index. See under $X_{112}$ in table A.5.) The coefficient of correlation between instability of terms of trade and of export receipts was .266. The regression equation was

$$Y_c = 4.283 + 0.290\, X_{111} \quad (r^2 = .071;\ \text{significant at the .05 level})$$
$$(7.21) \quad (2.41)$$

Country data for 64 countries are given in table A.2, columns 100 and 111. According to this test, only about 7 per cent of the variance in export value instability is explained by terms-of-trade instability. This result should surprise academicians and government officials who emphasise changes in terms of trade as a major cause of instability of export receipts.

Is the *trend* of terms-of-trade instability a significant factor? No, according to the correlation test: $r = .03$ with $X_{211}$ and –.12 with $X_{112}$ (quantum terms of trade instability) as independent variables. Details are given in table A.5.

## Relative importance of foreign trade

What sensible hypothesis can be formulated about the relation between foreign trade, as a percentage of national income, and export value instability? (The percentages are highly correlated, whether one uses exports, imports, or total trade as a percentage of national income or a similar aggregate. Our 'foreign-trade percentage' was calculated with the value of exports and imports – including services when available – in the numerator, and gross domestic product in the denominator.) A high foreign-trade percentage would seem to imply involvement in numerous markets, so that export instability would be lower the greater the involvement. On the other hand, high dependence on foreign markets, which, particularly when the number of export commodities is small, is subject to various kinds of disruptions, would seem to point to a positive relation. The calculations showed no relation: $r$ = .063. One could say that the forces indicated in the two hypotheses cancelled each other out. The regression equation was

$$Y_c = \underset{(6.09)}{6.318} + \underset{(0.61)}{0.011}\, X_{346} \quad (r^2 = .004;\ \text{not significant at the .05 level})$$

Country data for 76 countries are given in table A.2, columns 100 and 346.

Instability of the foreign-trade percentage and of export receipts showed an $r$ value of .378. This relatively high correlation is probably partly the result of including export value variations as part of the numerator of the foreign-trade percentage; and partly the result of the relatively high correlation between import and export instability (.612), discussed earlier. The equation was

$$Y_c = \underset{(4.95)}{4.100} + \underset{(4.10)}{0.492}\, X_{117} \quad (r^2 = .143;\ \text{significant at the .01 level})$$

Country data for 96 countries are given in table A.2, columns 100 and 117.

There was no relation between the trend of the foreign-trade percentage ($X_{217}$) and export receipts instability, although one might easily hypothesise a negative relation, based on the idea of the stabilising influence of larger markets. The $r$ value was .055 ($r^2$ = .003), which was not significant (details in table A.5).

## Direction of exports

Now we consider the influence that concentration of exports by countries of destination has on the instability of export receipts. It is possible to make a very detailed analysis, showing the instability index values for each country's exports to each of its customer countries; but a more aggregative approach is used here. The first independent variable explored is the Hirschman concentration index of (goods) exports, by country of destination, for each of 107 countries in 1963–67.[4] Again on the presumption that wider markets are more stable than narrower markets, the hypothesis is that high export instability accompanies high concentration by country of destination. The hypothesis is supported, though weakly, by an $r$ value of .190. The equation was

$$Y_c = \underset{(1.54)}{3.416} + \underset{(2.23)}{0.110}\, X_{316} \quad (r^2 = .036\text{; significant at the .05 level})$$

Country data are given in table A.2, columns 100 and 316.

The next test looks at the relation between export instability and the percentage of a country's goods exports going to the United States in 1963–67. Historical evidence, particularly for the interwar years, shows US imports to be quite unstable, so countries with a high ratio of exports to the United States would presumably show relatively high export instability index values. Moreover, the view is widely held that US import fluctuations are a major factor in the export instability of many countries. However, no significant relation emerged from the correlation calculations, which gave $r = .100$. The equation was

$$Y_c = \underset{(8.22)}{8.80} - \underset{(1.0)}{0.042}\, X_{320} \quad (r^2 = .01\text{; not significant at the .05 level})$$

Country data for 106 countries are given in table A.2, columns 100 and 320.

The next test is similar, but relates to the percentage of a country's exports going to the six members of the European Economic Community in 1963–67. The 106 countries used in the computation included the EEC countries themselves. The hypothesis here is similar to that for the United States, since the more industrialised countries are presumably more likely to initiate cyclical fluctuations. The statistical results support the hypothesis: $r = .281$. The equation was

$$Y_c = 4.589 + 0.117\ X_{321}\ (r^2 = .079;\ \text{significant at the .01 level})$$
$$(3.41)\quad (3.16)$$

Country data are given in table A.2, columns 100 and 321.

Thus, on the basis of the three tests used here, it can be stated that there is some support for the view that export receipts will be less, not more, unstable the greater the number of 'baskets' holding the 'eggs'.

## Degree of bilateralism

The hypothesis advanced here is that the higher the degree of bilateral balancing of trade by pairs of countries, the lower will be the degree of year-to-year export instability. The key point in this hypothesis is that when the degree of bilateral balancing is high, fewer balance-of-payments adjustments are called for, and, thus, trade relations tend to be maintained on a relatively steady basis from year to year.

The following formula was devised to calculate the 'bilateralism percentage' of a country:

$$B = 100(2\Sigma F)/(\Sigma X + \Sigma M)$$

where $B$ is the bilateralism percentage, $X$ is the value of exports, $M$ is the value of imports, and $F$ is the amount of 'offset' (that is, for trade between the 'home' country and a partner country, the smaller of $X$ and $M$, treated as a positive number).[5]

The correlation results supported the hypothesis rather impressively: $r = .416$. The equation was

$$Y_c = 23.139 - 0.231\ X_{352}\ (r^2 = .173;\ \text{significant at the .01 level})$$
$$(7.28)\quad (4.86)$$

Country data for 109 countries are given in table A.2, columns 100 and 352.

## Commodity composition of exports

Another version of the diversification thesis is that, the more diversified a country's exports of goods and services, the lower the export value instability index tends to be. This proposition was tested in various ways.

The first test took as the independent variable the percentage share of services in total exports of goods and services. The higher this percentage, the lower the export instability index tends to be: $r = -.197$. The hypothesis was moderately supported. The equation was

$$Y_c = 7.270 - 0.001\ X_{305}\ (r^2\ -.039;\ \text{significant at the .05 level})$$
$$(12.7)\qquad (2.1)$$

Country data for 84 countries are given in table A.2, columns 100 and 305.

The second test used as the independent variable the percentage of goods exports consisting of primary commodities (Standard International Trade Classification classes 0, 1, 2, 3 and 4 for the years 1964–67). The hypothesis was again supported: the higher the degree of concentration, the higher the export instability index. The $r$ value was .295. The equation was

$$Y_c = 2.007 + 0.085\ X_{325}\ (r^2 = .087;\ \text{significant at .01 level})$$

Country data for 102 countries are given in table A.2, columns 100 and 325.

The final test of commodity composition of exports employed, for 91 countries in 1964–67, the Hirschman concentration index for the 10 main SITC classes. Again the hypothesis was supported, and relatively strongly: $r = .400$. The equation was

$$Y_c = -7.44 + 0.248\ X_{310}\ (r^2 = .160;\ \text{significant at the .01 level})$$
$$(-.197)(4.27)$$

Country data are given in table A.2, columns 100 and 310.

## Size of national economy

Do economically large countries have higher or lower export instability than smaller countries have? On the presumption that larger countries tend to have larger exports (in money terms) than smaller countries do, one can invoke the principle that larger markets tend to be more stable than smaller ones. Also, economically larger countries tend to be richer, per capita, than economically small countries, and therefore tend to have a greater capacity to adapt their exports to changing conditions.[6] Hence, our hypothesis is that, as a rule, larger countries have lower export instability indexes than smaller countries have.

The variable used for economic size was average gross domestic product (where available) for 1964–66 in current US dollars. The correlation results just barely supported the hypothesis: $r = -.161$. The equation was

$$Y_c = 7.078 - 0.001\ X_{348} \quad (r^2 = .026;\ \text{significant at the .05 level})$$
$$(13.43) \quad (1.89)$$

Country data for 97 countries are given in table A.2, columns 100 and 348.

A cruder measure of economic size, population ($X_{350}$), showed no significant relation to export receipts instability (table A.5).

## Importance of agriculture

Since agricultural products are subject to variations in supply resulting froms natural causes that do not affect other products, and since the demand for them is usually considered to be relatively inelastic with respect to price, it seems plausible to argue that countries for which agriculture contributes a relatively large share of the national product should have relatively unstable export receipts. This hypothesis was supported by the correlation analysis: $r = .300$. The equation was

$$Y_c = 4.337 + 0.095\ X_{364} \quad (r^2 = .090;\ \text{significant at the .01 level})$$
$$(4.70) \quad (3.24)$$

Country data for 97 countries are given in table A.2, columns 100 and 364.

## Real income per capita

Do countries with higher per capita incomes have higher or lower export instability than countries with lower per capita incomes have? Presumably, countries in which per capita incomes are higher have more economic adaptability; so the hypothesis is that income per capita and export instability are negatively related.

Per capita income of the various countries was expressed in US dollars for the years 1964–66, adjusted for price changes. Of necessity, the per capita dollar figures are, in many cases, based on rough estimates of gross domestic product and population, as well as on many rather arbitrary exchange rates. Moreover, these figures are extremely crude indications of comparative levels of living, as is usually pointed out by compilers, but ignored by users, of such numbers. The hypothesis received even stronger support than did that involving total gross domestic product: $r = -.297$.

The equation was

$$Y_c = 8.176 - 0.002\ X_{349}\ (r^2 = .088;\ \text{significant at the .01 level})$$
$$(12.61)\quad (3.21)$$

Country data for 97 countries are given in table A.2, columns 100 and 349.

Another indicator of the relative per capita level of living is energy consumption per capita ($X_{365}$). (The correlation coefficient between $X_{349}$ and $X_{365}$ was .91.) Not surprisingly, the correlation results with energy consumption per capita as the independent variable resembled those obtained with real income per capita: $r = -.332$. The equation was

$$Y_c = 10.118 - 0.002\ X_{365}\ (r^2 = .110;\ \text{significant at the .01 level})$$
$$(11.03)\quad (3.77)$$

Country data for 108 countries are given in table A.2, columns 100 and 365.

It is quite clear, from both these tests, that poorer countries tend to have higher export instability than richer countries have.

In considering the *growth* of per capita real income, the hypothesis is the same as before – namely, that countries with rapid rates of growth tend to have relatively unstable economies. In the present case, our surmise is that export instability is positively associated with the growth of real gross domestic product per capita. The calculations supported the hypothesis: $r = .243$. The equation was

$$Y_c = 4.842 + 0.447\ X_{218}\ (r^2 = .059;\ \text{significant at the .01 level})$$
$$(6.25)\quad (2.52)$$

Country data for 87 countries are given in table A.2, columns 100 and 218.

Finally, let us consider the relation between the *instability* of per capita real gross domestic product and export value instability. The hypothesis we advance is that they are positively correlated. The rationale is derived from business-cycle history: that real income per capita and exports tend to vary together. The simple correlation coefficient was one of the highest obtained: $r = .602$. The regression equation was

$$Y_c = 1.913 + 2.000\ X_{118}\ (r^2 = .363;\ \text{significant at the .01 level})$$
$$(2.58)\quad (7.07)$$

Country data for 87 countries are given in table A.2, columns 100 and 118.

## National income

We now test, albeit roughly, the hypothesis that national income and exports tend to move together. The statistical calculations give support to the hypothesis: $r$ = .305. The equation was

$$Y_c = 5.334 + 0.317\ X_{1\,1\,3}\ (r^2 = .093;\ \text{significant at the .01 level})$$
$$(7.82)\quad (3.27)$$

Country data for 87 countries are given in table A.2, columns 100 and 113.

Hence, by the usual interpretation, this cross-section test shows that nearly 10 per cent of export instability is accounted for by national income instability, or *vice versa*. The result falls far short of what might be expected, in view of the numerous economists who repeat the exercises of the foreign-trade multiplier in illustrative form, without reference to any facts. (As noted below, instability of the net balance – exports minus imports – showed no significant relation.)

What hypothesis seems plausible for the relation between export instability and *growth* of gross domestic product (in current prices)? If we invoke once again the positive historical association of economic growth and instability, it would seem that high instability of exports should be associated with a high growth rate of income. This relation is supported, but with a very low degree of correlation: $r$ = .148. The regression equation was

$$Y_c = 4.75 + 0.265\ X_{2\,1\,3}\ (r^2 = .022;\ \text{significant at the .05 level})$$
$$(3.58)\ (1.77)$$

Country data for 95 countries are given in table A.2, columns 100 and 213.

Despite the long term historical association between economic growth and economic instability, the relation between the growth and instability of national income for the period 1959–71 is not supported by the correlation analysis: $r$ = –.11, not significant at the .05 level.

## Price levels

On the hypothesis that export price instability is positively associated with export value instability – not supported by the statistical evidence – and that domestic price level instability (measured by instability of the consumer price index) and export price instability tend to be associated (although $r$ = only .14), we suggest that export value instability should be positively associated with consumer price index instability. According to our test, we are wrong: $r$ = .084. The equation was

$$Y_c = \underset{(8.23)}{7.704} + \underset{(.79)}{0.066}\, X_{121} \quad (r^2 = .007; \text{not significant at the .05 level})$$

Country data for 92 countries are given in table A.2, columns 100 and 121.

Does the rate of inflation have any influence on export value instability? On the theory that, the higher the rate of inflation, the more disruptive an influence it becomes, we hypothesise a positive relation. Two measures of inflation were available, the rate of growth of consumer prices and the rate of growth of the export price index.

Surprisingly, the correlation coefficient between export instability and the growth rate of the consumer price index is statistically insignificant: $r$ = .078. The regression equation was

$$Y_c = \underset{(0.95)}{7.684} + \underset{(0.05)}{0.041}\, X_{221} \quad (r^2 = .006; \text{not significant at the .05 level})$$

Country data for 92 countries are given in table A.2, columns 100 and 221.

The growth rate of the export price index did not show a statistically significant relation either, but the $r$ value was a little higher: .130. The equation was

$$Y_c = \underset{(9.44)}{5.837} + \underset{(1.55)}{0.326}\, X_{207} \quad (r^2 = .017; \text{not significant at the .05 level})$$

Country data for 78 countries are given in table A.2, columns 100 and 207.

## Balance of trade

The fact that export and import instability were closely associated ($r$ = .612) leads one to hypothesise no significant relation between export instability and instability of the net balance of trade (that is, value of exports minus value of imports). The surmise was supported by the correlation result: $r$ = .077. The equation was

$$Y_c = \underset{(4.74)}{9.519} - \underset{(0.81)}{2.303}\, X_{122} \quad (r^2 = .006; \text{not significant at the .05 level})$$

Country data for 107 countries are given in table A.2, columns 100 and 122. The measure of instability used was $1-r^2$, owing to the fact that some negative numbers were involved. The growth of the net balance, $X_{222}$ (in this case the slope of the least-squares line through the annual net balance figures), also showed no significant relation to export value instability ($r = .032$; $r^2 = .001$); and the average net balance of payments as a percentage of average imports, $X_{347}$, showed no relation to it whatsoever ($r = .000$).

The correlation results in this section may seem somewhat surprising in showing no statistical relation between export instability and the 'basic' balance of payments (exports minus imports). The fairly high correlation between export and import instability ($r = .612$) provides only a partial explanation.

## Monetary reserves

One would expect instability of monetary reserves, particularly as a percentage of imports, to be positively correlated with instability of export receipts, barring parallel import value instability. The expectation was confirmed to some degree by the correlation coefficient, .307. The equation was

$$Y_c = 4.998 + 0.148\ X_{120} \quad (r^2 = .094; \text{significant at the .01 level})$$

Country data for 97 countries are given in table A.2, columns 100 and 120.

The growth rate of monetary reserves as a percentage of imports ($X_{220}$) was not significantly correlated with export value instability ($r = .095$; $r^2 = .009$). Neither was average monetary reserves as a percentage of imports ($r = .045$; $r^2 = .002$). (See table A.5.)

In view of the widely-held opinion that countries with highly unstable export receipts are particularly prone to balance-of-payments difficulties, it is surprising that only one of the variables discussed in this and the preceding section – namely, instability of monetary reserves as a percentage of imports – should show any significant degree of correlation with export value instability. (Exchange rate instability was not measured, since, during the period used, 1959–71, there were very few floating currencies. The variations around par values permitted by the International Monetary Fund, or by national governments, were too small to be important for our purposes, and many countries known to be experiencing balance-of-payments disequilibrium were employing exchange controls rather than changing their exchange rates.)

## (B) MULTI-VARIABLE ANALYSIS

We now take up multiple regression analysis for several different combinations of independent variables, with export value instability ($X_{100}$) as the dependent variable. In the equations, $Y_c$ is the computed value for $X_{100}$ and the $t$ values are given in parentheses under the regression coefficients.

### Results of step-wise procedure

The principal regression program involved a 'step-wise' procedure, whereby an initially large number of variables – 38 for 55 countries in the principal runs – were eliminated one by one until all of those remaining had regression coefficients with $t$ values exceeding a predetermined minimum level.

In the first run, the minimum acceptable $t$ value was set at 2.4, so that all retained variables would have statistical significance at the .01 level. Eight variables remained:

$X_{107}$ export price instability ($r^2$ = .013)
$X_{108}$ export quantum instability ($r^2$ = .210)
$X_{117}$ instability of foreign trade as a percentage of GDP ($r^2$ = .143)
$X_{200}$ growth rate of export value ($r^2$ = .348)
$X_{207}$ growth rate of export price index ($r^2$ = .017)
$X_{215}$ growth rate of import value ($r^2$ = .008)
$X_{330}$ goods imports as a percentage of total imports ($r^2$ = .107)
$X_{347}$ average net balance of payments as a percentage of average imports ($r^2$ = .000)

The coefficient of multiple determination ($R^2$) was .610 ($F$ = 11.54). The regression equation was

$$\begin{aligned} Y_c = \underset{(3.92)}{12.360} - \underset{(4.03)}{0.504}\, X_{107} + \underset{(3.03)}{0.320}\, X_{108} + \underset{(4.67)}{0.485}\, X_{117} + \underset{(3.15)}{0.553}\, X_{200} \\ - \underset{(2.82)}{0.373}\, X_{207} - \underset{(3.16)}{0.721}\, X_{215} - \underset{(2.80)}{0.098}\, X_{330} - \underset{(3.22)}{0.062}\, X_{347} \end{aligned} \qquad (4.1)$$

This equation still held when the minimum $t$ value was as high as 2.58, thus increasing confidence in the results.

In the second run, the minimum acceptable $t$ value was lowered to 1.66, with a significance level of .05. Again, there were 38 variables for 55 countries at the start of the process. As would be expected, the coefficient of multiple determinations ($R^2$) was higher than in the first run: .673 ($F = 11.11$). Eleven variables, including the eight from the first run, appeared in the regression equation. The three new ones were

$X_{109}$ import price instability index ($r^2$ = .006)
$X_{209}$ growth rate of import price index ($r^2$ = .000)
$X_{364}$ percentage of GDP from agriculture ($r^2$ = .090)

The regression equation was

$$\begin{aligned} Y_c = {} & \underset{(4.97)}{14.99} - \underset{(4.90)}{0.629\,X_{107}} + \underset{(2.20)}{0.224\,X_{108}} + \underset{(2.41)}{0.457\,X_{109}} + \underset{(4.26)}{0.429\,X_{117}} \\ & + \underset{(3.66)}{0.592\,X_{200}} - \underset{(2.48)}{0.358\,X_{207}} - \underset{(2.52)}{0.476\,X_{209}} - \underset{(3.40)}{0.718\,X_{215}} \\ & - \underset{(4.13)}{0.143X_{330}} - \underset{(2.93)}{0.056X_{347}} + \underset{(2.08)}{0.047X_{364}} \end{aligned} \tag{4.2}$$

Several variables that had very low simple coefficients of determination ($r^2$) had some influence in the multiple regression analysis, and several variables with relatively high $r^2$ values did not show up at all in equations (4.1) and (4.2). In fact, of the 21 highest $r$ values shown in table 4.1, only variables $X_{200}$ (growth rate of export value), $X_{108}$ (instability of export quantum), $X_{117}$ (instability of foreign trade as a percentage of GDP), $X_{331}$ (services imports as a percentage of total imports; the complement of $X_{330}$), and $X_{113}$ (instability of GDP) appeared in any way among the 11 independent variables in equation (4.2). Of these five variables, only two appeared among the eight significant variables when the .01 significance test was applied. Faced with these lists of variables, one can only register mild surprise, while recognising, of course, that they are statistically possible. Even the intercorrelations among the independent variables (some shown in table 4.2) do not do much to explain the results. How much faith should one have in the multiple regression technique?

A third run was made, using the same 38 variables for 55 countries, to obtain the highest possible $R^2$ value. This value turned out to be .694 ($F = 6.85$). Twenty-one independent variables were in the equation (not reproduced), but the regression coefficients of 10 of them were not significant at the .05 level ($t$ = 1.7 or less); four were significant at the .05 level; and seven were significant at the .01 level or better ($t$ = 2.4 or more).

Hence, by increasing the number of variables from eight to 11, the (corrected) $R^2$ value was raised from .610 to .673; and, by increasing the number of variables from 11 to 21 – to obtain the maximum $R^2$ value – the $R^2$ value was increased only from .673 to .695. Of course, the reliability of the results decreased with addition of more variables, as indicated by the lower $t$ values. My preference is for the eight-variable equation involving the .01 significance test.

As a further test, another computer program was employed. This again involved the step-wise procedure, but in this case all 109 countries were represented and the average values of variables were substituted for the blanks (i.e. where values were required for countries not among the original 55). An $R^2$ value of .906 was obtained with eight variables, with all coefficients significant at the .05 level or better. The variables were

$X_{108}$ export quantum instability index
$X_{110}$ import quantum instability index*
$X_{115}$ import value instability index*
$X_{200}$ growth rate, export value
$X_{208}$ growth rate, export quantum*
$X_{215}$ growth rate, import value
$X_{352}$ bilateralism percentage*
$X_{364}$ percentage of GDP from agriculture

The asterisked variables did not appear in equations (4.1) and (4.2). The regression equation was

$$Y_c = 8.302 + 0.337\,X_{108} - 0.694\,X_{110} + 0.740\,X_{115} + 1.112\,X_{200}$$
$$- 0.822X_{215} - 0.443X_{208} - 0.087X_{352} - 0.070X_{364} \qquad (4.3)$$

Although the replacement of blanks with somewhat arbitrary (average) values seems questionable, particularly given the large number of variables and countries for which this was done (38 and 55 respectively), the $R^2$ of .906 is certainly impressive. It is probable that the actual values, were they available, would diverge considerably from the average values used in the calculations. Even so, the results seem worth reporting.[7]

## Intercorrelations

In considering the variables that turned out to be closely associated with export value instability, one naturally wonders whether the variables are essentially duplicative, either definitionally or functionally. Table 4.2

Table 4.2

Correlation coefficients ($r$) for pairs of independent variables significant in multiple regression analysis of export instability

| | $X_{107}$ | $X_{108}$ | $X_{109}$ | $X_{110}$ | $X_{115}$ | $X_{117}$ | $X_{200}$ | $X_{207}$ | $X_{208}$ | $X_{209}$ | $X_{215}$ | $X_{330}$ | $X_{347}$ | $X_{352}$ |
|---|---|---|---|---|---|---|---|---|---|---|---|---|---|---|
| $X_{108}$ | .37 | | | | | | | | | | | | | |
| $X_{109}$ | .53 | .16 | | | | | | | | | | | | |
| $X_{110}$ | .27 | .47 | .11 | | | | | | | | | | | |
| $X_{115}$ | .27 | .41 | .11 | *.74* | | | | | | | | | | |
| $X_{117}$ | .42 | .33 | .12 | .49 | *.71* | | | | | | | | | |
| $X_{200}$ | −.28 | −.07 | −.27 | .07 | .19 | .15 | | | | | | | | |
| $X_{207}$ | .13 | −.06 | .41 | .20 | .08 | .18 | .14 | | | | | | | |
| $X_{208}$ | −.23 | −.14 | −.27 | .04 | .18 | .06 | *.85* | −.04 | | | | | | |
| $X_{209}$ | .19 | −.11 | .56 | −.04 | −.08 | .01 | −.13 | .41 | −.08 | | | | | |
| $X_{215}$ | −.40 | −.03 | −.33 | .03 | .10 | .04 | *.94* | .07 | *.78* | −.17 | | | | |
| $X_{330}$ | −.20 | .01 | −.10 | .01 | −.07 | −.17 | .06 | −.33 | .08 | .21 | .04 | | | |
| $X_{347}$ | −.29 | −.25 | −.17 | −.43 | −.33 | −.38 | −.10 | −.13 | −.11 | −.15 | −.07 | −.14 | | |
| $X_{352}$ | −.14 | −.26 | .08 | −.44 | −.23 | −.15 | −.19 | −.15 | −.21 | .11 | −.13 | −.06 | .45 | |
| $X_{364}$ | .33 | .41 | .19 | .38 | .37 | .37 | −.21 | −.20 | −.14 | .07 | −.25 | .30 | −.47 | .27 |

Note: The (corrected) $r$ values in this table were obtained by using data for only the 55 countries used in the principal multiple regression runs. Another table (Table A.9, which is available from the author on request) shows the $r$ values obtained by using the maximum number of countries available for each pair of variables.

The names of the variables employed here are given in the text and in Table A.1. Intercorrelations were obtained for 49 variables for Table A.9.

Address: Joseph D. Coppock, Department of Economics, Pennsylvania State University, University Park, Pennsylvania 16802, USA.

presents the simple coefficients of correlation for all the 15 independent variables included in equations (4.1), (4.2) and (4.3). For only five pairs of variables out of the total of 105 was the coefficient of correlation above .60 (indicated by italics in table 4.2):

.94 $X_{200}$ (growth rate, export value); $X_{215}$ (growth rate, import value)

.85* $X_{200}$ (growth rate, export value); $X_{208}$ (growth rate, export quantum)

.78 $X_{208}$ (growth rate, export quantum); $X_{215}$ (growth rate, import value)

.74* $X_{110}$ (import quantum instability index); $X_{115}$ (import value instability index)

.71* $X_{115}$ (import value instability index); $X_{117}$ (instability index, foreign trade as percentage of GDP)

For the three pairs indicated by asterisks, there is some degree of overlap in the definitions of the variables of each pair. For the other two pairs, an economic rationale can be provided for the association. The growth rate of exports ($X_{200}$) and of imports ($X_{215}$), the only pair that appeared in equations (4.1) and (4.2), are sufficiently highly correlated ($r$ = .94) to make either variable redundant in the regression equation. In view of the large number of pairs of variables with relatively low $r$ values (98 of 105 have values below .50), it appears that the multiple regression equations do not involve a significant degree of multicollinearity.

## Comparisons with the 1946–58 period

It is of interest to discover whether the variables closely associated with export value instability in the 1946–58 period were the same as in 1959–71. Table 4.3 shows the $r$ values for the independent variables used both for 1959–71 and for the study of export instability in 1946–58.

Comparisons between the two periods, for the 25 variables for which there are measures for both periods, show that there is some degree of uniformity in the relation between export value instability and some other variables. The highest simple correlation coefficients did not differ greatly: .61 for the import value instability index for 1959–71, and .58 for the export quantum instability index for 1946–58. The import value instability index, with the highest $r$ value in 1959–71, was second highest in 1946–58. The second highest $r$ value in 1959–71 was for instability of per capita real income (.60), but this variable was ninth of 25 in the earlier

Table 4.3

Correlation coefficients (*r*) between export value instability and other variables, for countries, 1959–71 and 1946–58

| Rank, 1959–71 | Independent variable[a] No. | Independent variable[a] Name | *r* value 1959–71 | *r* value 1946–58[b] |
|---|---|---|---|---|
| 1 | 115 | II, import value | .61 | .43 (2) |
| 2 | 118 | II, real GDP per capita | .60 | –.15 (9) |
| 3 | 200 | Percentage growth, export value | .59 | .23 (6) |
| 4 | 108 | II, export quantum | .46 | .58 (1) |
| 5 | 214 | Percentage, real GDP | .43 | –.01 (25) |
| 6 | 310 | Concentration of exports by SITC classes | .40 | .03 (21) |
| 7 | 365 | Energy consumption per capita | –.33 | –.16 (8) |
| 8 | 120 | II, monetary reserves as a percentage of imports | .31 | .02 (23) |
| 9 | 113 | II, GDP | .31 | .07 (17) |
| 10 | 349 | GDP per capita | –.30 | –.04 (20) |
| 11 | 325 | Percentage of exports in primary goods | .30 | .11 (14) |
| 12 | 111 | II, price terms of trade | .27 | .38 (3) |
| 13 | 218 | Percentage growth, real GDP per capita | .24 | –.15 (10) |
| 14 | 315 | Average value, imports | –.20 | –.10 (15) |
| 15 | 316 | Concentration of exports by country | .19 | –.20 (7) |
| 16 | 300 | Average value, exports | –.18 | –.10 (16) |
| 17 | 348 | Average real GDP | –.16 | .01 (24) |
| 18 | 107 | II, export prices | .11 | .13 (13) |
| 19 | 320 | Percentage of exports to US | –.10 | –.27 (5) |
| 20 | 109 | II, import prices | .08 | .13 (12) |
| 21 | 122 | II, net trade balance | –.08 | .06 (19) |
| 22 | 221 | Percentage growth, consumer prices | .08 | .14 (11) |
| 23 | 346 | Foreign trade as a percentage of GDP | .06 | –.30 (4) |
| 24 | 350 | Population | –.06 | .06 (18) |
| 25 | 361 | Monetary reserves as a percentage of imports | .05 | .02 (22) |

[a] Full descriptions in Table A.1.
[b] Rankings in parentheses.

Sources: Table A.5 and *International Economic Instability*, pp. 119–22.

period (–.15; though it should be noted that the relevant statistics in this case were very poor). The third highest $r$ value for 1959–71 was for the rate of growth of export proceeds (.59); this variable was sixth of 25 for the earlier period (.23). The export quantum instability index, which had the highest $r$ value in the earlier period, was fourth highest in the later period (.47). Obviously, there was considerable continuity in the influence of several of the independent variables over the two periods: the top four in 1959–71 were among the top nine in 1946–58.

Since the number of countries for which data were available was higher for 1959–71 (a maximum of 109 countries) than for 1946–58 (maximum 83), and since, for most countries, the statistical data were much more complete in the later period than in the earlier, it seems sensible to place more reliance on the $r$ values for 1959–71. A different measure of instability was used for each period; but, as discussed in Chapter 1, the two measures were usually highly correlated, so that this should not affect the comparisons appreciably.

The multiple correlation coefficients were not as high for 1946–58 as for 1959–71. This was perhaps the result of using different combinations of independent variables. The highest $R$ value obtained in the earlier period was .668 ($R^2$ = .446), with four independent variables: import value instability, foreign trade percentage of GDP, export quantum instability, and GDP per capita. For several other combinations, involving two, three or four independent variables, results were obtained that approximated this $R$ value. In 1959–71, similar – relatively unsystematic – runs yielded almost identical maximum results: $R$ = .667 ($R^2$ = .445), as noted earlier. Two of the variables in the four-variable tests were the same in both periods: instability of import value and of export quantum. Thus, over the two periods, there was some degree of consistency in the multivariate analysis. It is possible, of course, that the step-wise regression technique, with more variables and with the same instability index, would have yielded for 1946–58 an $R^2$ value approximating those in the .6–.7 range that were obtained for 1959–71.

## (C) NON-QUANTITATIVE VARIABLES

We now consider export instability with reference to some non-quantitative characteristics of countries. For several of these comparisons it is convenient to use some classifications employed by the International Monetary Fund.[8] Results for both 1959–71 and 1946–58 are shown in table 4.4. The averages used are simple (unweighted) means.[9]

Consider first the 'developed' and the 'less developed' countries (other than those of the 'Soviet Area') as designated by the IMF.[10]

| | *Average export instability index* | | *Median export instability index* | |
|---|---|---|---|---|
| | *1959–71* | *1946–58* | *1959–71* | *1946–58* |
| Developed | 4.1 | 13.6 | 3.8 | 11.1 |
| Less developed | 7.3 | 16.5 | 7.2 | 12.2 |

Clearly, the less developed countries typically had higher export instability indexes than did the more developed countries (table 4.4, rows

Table 4.4

Average export value instability indexes of countries, by region of world, 1959–71 and 1946–58

| | Region(s), etc. | No. of countries (1) | Average export instability index (2) | Median export instability index (3) | Range (4) |
|---|---|---|---|---|---|
| 1 | Industrial[a] | | | | |
| | 1959–71 | 14 | 3.5 | 3.6 | 1.7–5.5 |
| | 1946–58 | 14 | 14.4 | 11.5 | 3.9–41.8 |
| 2 | Other developed[b] | | | | |
| | 1959–71 | 11 | 4.8 | 3.9 | 2.4–10.0 |
| | 1946–58 | 11 | 12.5 | 10.9 | 6.7–22.5 |
| 3 | Rows 1 and 2 inclusive | | | | |
| | 1959–71 | 25 | 4.1 | 3.8 | 1.7–10.0 |
| | 1946–58 | 25 | 13.6 | 11.1 | 3.9–41.8 |
| 4 | Latin America | | | | |
| | 1959–71 | 22 | 6.4 | 6.6 | 2.2–11.4 |
| | 1946–58 | 21 | 10.6 | 11.2 | 5.5–16.1 |
| 5 | Middle East[c] | | | | |
| | 1959–71 | 10 | 8.0 | 7.1 | 3.4–16.7 |
| | 1946–58 | 7 | 19.5 | 12.3 | 7.1–54.5 |
| 6 | Asia[d] | | | | |
| | 1959–71 | 13 | 7.2 | 6.2 | 2.2–14.5 |
| | 1946–58 | 11 | 19.9 | 14.7 | 10.3–51.0 |
| 7 | Africa[e] | | | | |
| | 1959–71 | 30 | 7.8 | 9.4 | 3.5–7.0 |
| | 1946–58 | 9 | 23.2 | 23.0 | 10.1–40.1 |

*Table 4.4 cont.*

| | Region(s), etc. | (1) | (2) | (3) | (4) |
|---|---|---|---|---|---|
| 8 | Rows 4–7 inclusive | | | | |
| | 1959–71 | 75 | 7.3 | 7.2 | 2.2–70.0 |
| | 1946–58 | 46 | 16.5 | 12.2 | 5.5–54.5 |
| 9 | Rows 3 and 8 inclusive | | | | |
| | 1959–71 | 100 | 6.5 | 6.3 | 2.0–70.0 |
| | 1946–58 | 71 | 15.8 | 12.0 | 3.9–54.5 |
| 10 | Soviet Area[f] | | | | |
| | 1959–71 | 9 | 4.9 | 3.4 | 2.3–11.8 |
| | 1946–58 | 9 | 14.5 | 14.7 | 6.7–25.7 |
| 11 | All countries | | | | |
| | 1959–71 | 109 | 8.1 | 6.2 | 1.7–70.0 |
| | 1946–58 | 80 | 15.3 | 12.1 | 3.9–54.5 |

[a] Industrial continental Western Europe, plus the United Kingdom, United States, Canada and Japan.

[b] Other 'developed' 14 countries in Western Europe, plus Australia, New Zealand and South Africa.

[c] Includes Iran and Egypt; excludes Turkey.

[d] Excludes China (People's Republic) and Middle East.

[e] Excludes Egypt and South Africa.

[f] Includes China (People's Republic) and Cuba; no intra-Soviet Area trade.

Source: Table 2.1. Classification from *International Financial Statistics.*

3 and 8). Although the values were much smaller for the later period for both groups, the relative difference was much larger (78 per cent in 1959–71, compared with 21 per cent in 1946–58, for the average instability index).

If the Soviet Area countries, which here include Cuba and the People's Republic of China, as well as the East European members of the Communist group (excluding Yugoslavia), are compared with other countries of the world included in this study, the results are as follows (from table 4.4, rows 10 and 9).

| | *Average export instability index* | | *Median export instability index* | |
|---|---|---|---|---|
| | *1959–71* | *1946–58* | *1959–71* | *1946–58* |
| Soviet Area | 4.9 | 14.5 | 3.4 | 14.7 |
| Other countries | 6.5 | 15.8 | 6.3 | 12.0 |

In the later period the Soviet Area countries clearly tended to have lower export instability than other countries had, but the evidence is mixed for the earlier period. The data for the Soviet Area were only for trade with countries outside the area, probably less than half the Communist countries' foreign trade.

When Soviet Area export instability is compared with that for the 'developed' and 'less developed' countries, some more differences emerge (table 4.4, rows 3, 8 and 10).

| | *Average export instability index* | | *Median export instability index* | |
|---|---|---|---|---|
| | *1959–71* | *1946–58* | *1959–71* | *1946–58* |
| Developed | 4.1 (1) | 13.6 (1) | 3.8 (2) | 11.1 (1) |
| Less developed | 7.3 (3) | 16.5 (3) | 7.2 (3) | 12.2 (2) |
| Soviet Area | 4.9 (2) | 14.5 (2) | 3.4 (1) | 14.7 (3) |

With the exception of the 1959–71 median, all the measures show the developed countries as having the lowest typical export instability indexes. And, except for the 1946–58 median, the less developed countries had the highest typical export instability. The Soviet Area countries tended to be in between. It is also of interest that, from the earlier to the later period, the measures of central tendency dropped by two-thirds or more for the developed and the Soviet Area countries, but by only about one-half for the less developed countries.

A breakdown of the less developed countries by region of the world also shows some variations (table 4.4, rows 4, 5, 6 and 7).

| | *Average export instability index* | | *Median export instability index* | |
|---|---|---|---|---|
| | *1959–71* | *1946–58* | *1959–71* | *1946–58* |
| Latin America | 6.4 (1) | 10.6 (1) | 6.6 (2) | 11.2 (1) |
| Asia | 7.2 (2) | 19.9 (3) | 6.2 (1) | 14.7 (3) |
| Africa | 7.8 (3) | 23.2 (4) | 9.4 (4) | 23.0 (4) |
| Middle East | 8.0 (4) | 19.5 (2) | 7.1 (3) | 12.3 (2) |

Latin America clearly tends to be the most stable, and Africa the least stable, region among those listed. In fact, Latin American export instability is only a little greater than that for the more developed countries and the Soviet Area. Asia and the Middle East do not differ much from each other. From 1946–58 to 1959–71, the typical indexes declined by nearly two-thirds for Asia, Africa and the Middle East, but by only two-fifths for Latin America, where the index was already relatively low.

A division of the 25 developed countries into 'industrial' and 'other', again following the IMF classification, is also of interest. The comparisons are as follows (table 4.4, rows 1 and 2).

| | *Average export instability index* | | *Median export instability index* | |
|---|---|---|---|---|
| | *1959–71* | *1946–58* | *1959–71* | *1946–58* |
| Industrial | 3.5 | 14.4 | 3.6 | 11.5 |
| Other developed | 4.8 | 12.5 | 3.9 | 10.9 |

From the earlier to the later period, the ranking was reversed, although the differences in each period were not large. Also, the declines from 1946–58 to 1959–71 were similar, with the industrial countries' instability index dropping by over two-thirds, and that for the other developed countries dropping by somewhat less than two-thirds.

Table 4.5 shows several other groupings of countries and brings out further differences in typical export instability indexes. We shall compare the results for each grouping with only one other set of results, although it is clear that numerous comparisons can be made. Since the medians were very close to the means, though usually a little smaller, only the means are discussed in the text. The ranges, shown in table 4.2, indicate considerable dispersion of instability index values among countries.

The principal oil exporting countries had much higher export instability indexes than did their principal customer countries, the members of the Organisation for Economic Co-operation and Development (OECD) (table 4.5, rows 1 and 5).

| | *Average export instability index* | |
|---|---|---|
| | *1959–71* | *1946–58* |
| Oil countries | 11.3 | 28.8 |
| OECD countries | 4.2 | 13.2 |

Table 4.5

Average export value instability indexes of countries, by various groupings of countries, 1959–71 and 1946–58

| | Group | No. of countries (1) | Average export instability index (2) | Median export instability index (3) | Range (4) |
|---|---|---|---|---|---|
| 1 | Oil exporters | | | | |
| | 1959–71 | 9 | 11.3 | 8.1 | 5.0–32.9 |
| | 1946–58 | 6 | 28.8 | 18.2 | 8.9–54.5 |
| 2 | Arab states | | | | |
| | 1959–71 | 13 | 10.4 | 7.6 | 4.7–32.9 |
| | 1946–58 | 9 | 20.7 | 19.8 | 8.3–40.1 |
| 3 | EEC | | | | |
| | 1959–71 | 5 | 3.7 | 3.8 | 3.0–4.7 |
| | 1946–58 | 5 | 16.5 | 15.4 | 10.1–24.3 |
| 4 | EFTA | | | | |
| | 1959–71 | 7 | 3.5 | 3.2 | 2.4–5.7 |
| | 1946–58 | 7 | 10.3 | 10.9 | 3.9–14.5 |
| 5 | OECD | | | | |
| | 1959–71 | 20 | 4.2 | 3.6 | 1.7–10.0 |
| | 1946–58 | 20 | 13.2 | 11.0 | 3.9–41.8 |
| 6 | NATO | | | | |
| | 1959–71 | 13 | 3.8 | 3.4 | 1.7–6.3 |
| | 1946–58 | 13 | 12.3 | 11.1 | 5.1–24.3 |
| 7 | Warsaw Pact | | | | |
| | 1959–71 | 7 | 2.9 | 2.9 | 2.3–3.4 |
| | 1946–58 | 7 | 14.7 | 15.3 | 6.7–25.7 |
| 8 | Newly independent | | | | |
| | 1959–71 | 48 | 11.1 | 8.0 | 2.2–70.0 |
| | 1946–58 | 22 | 16.0 | 13.2 | 7.1–51.0 |
| 9 | All countries | | | | |
| | 1959–71 | 109 | 8.1 | 6.2 | 1.7–70.0 |
| | 1946–58 | 80 | 15.3 | 12.1 | 3.9–54.5 |

Source: Table 2.1.

Not only were the index values more than double for the oil countries; in addition, they showed a smaller percentage decline than did the values for the OECD countries (70 per cent as against the oil countries' 60).

A comparison between the Arab states (in the Middle East and North Africa) and all countries yields the following results (table 4.5, rows 2 and 9).

| | *Average export instability index* | |
|---|---|---|
| | *1959–71* | *1946–58* |
| Arab states | 10.4 | 20.7 |
| All countries | 8.1 | 15.3 |

The Arab states tended to have higher-than-average export instability for both periods. The decline from 1946–58 to 1959–71 was about the same – about 50 per cent – for both groups.

A similar comparison for the European Economic Community (EEC) countries shows the following (table 4.5, rows 3 and 9).

| | *Average export instability index* | |
|---|---|---|
| | *1959–71* | *1946–58* |
| EEC | 3.7 | 16.5 |
| All countries | 8.1 | 15.3 |

In the earlier period the EEC countries tended to have higher than average export instability, but in the later period their typical instability index was less than one-half of that for all countries. Moreover, the drop in instability was, on average, nearly 80 per cent, as compared with a 50 per cent decline overall. In 1959–71, the range for the five components – France, West Germany, Italy, the Netherlands and Belgium – Luxembourg – was only from 3.0 to 4.7. This is an extremely low degree of export instability.

The situation was similar for the European Free Trade Association (EFTA), although in 1946–58 EFTA's average export instability index was much lower thansthe EEC's. The comparison with all countries is as follows (from table 4.5, rows 4 and 9).

| | *Average export instability index* | |
|---|---|---|
| | *1959–71* | *1946–58* |
| EFTA | 3.5 | 10.3 |
| All countries | 8.1 | 15.3 |

The EFTA average was only two-thirds of the general average in the earlier period and was well under half of it in the later period. EFTA's average export instability index declined by a full two-thirds, compared with the overall average decline of not quite 50 per cent.

The OECD export instability index is of particular interest, because this group includes the world's main industrial countries. Its members are the United States, Canada, Japan, the EEC and EFTA countries, and four other West European countries. It is illuminating to compare the OECD countries with the less developed countries of the world (table 4.5, row 5 and table 4.4, row 8).

| | *Average export instability index* | |
|---|---|---|
| | *1959–71* | *1946–58* |
| OECD | 4.2 | 13.2 |
| Less developed | 7.3 | 16.5 |

The OECD countries clearly had lower export instability in both periods, especially in 1959–71. The decline in the average instability index for the OECD was 70 per cent, as compared with just over 50 per cent for the less developed countries.

The next comparison is between the principal military groupings of the post-war era, the countries of the North Atlantic Treaty Organisation (NATO) and the members of the Warsaw Pact (table 4.5, rows 6 and 7).

| | *Average export instability index* | |
|---|---|---|
| | *1959–71* | *1946–58* |
| NATO | 3.8 | 12.3 |
| Warsaw Pact | 2.9 | 14.7 |

NATO had a slightly lower average instability index in the earlier period, but a slightly higher one in the later. The decline was dramatic for both groups: by four-fifths for the Warsaw Pact countries and by 70 per cent for the NATO countries. It should be noted that the instability indexes for the Warsaw Pact countries were based on their trade with non-Communist countries only.

The final comparison involves the numerous countries that have been politically independent only since the Second World War. The comparison is with the OECD countries, with which many of the newly independent countries have had strong economic links (table 4.5, rows 8 and 5).

| | *Average export instability index* | |
|---|---|---|
| | *1959–71* | *1946–58* |
| Newly independent | 11.1 | 16.0 |
| OECD | 4.2 | 13.2 |

The newly independent countries' tendency toward higher export instability is evident. Moreover, whereas the OECD countries' typical instability index was reduced by 70 per cent from 1946–58 to 1959–71, the newly independent countries' index was lowered by only 30 per cent. It should be noted, however, that less than one-half of the 48 newly independent countries included in the calculation for 1959–71 were included in the 1946–58 calculation. It would be interesting to compare export instability for these countries for periods before and after independence.

Although these various groupings involving non-quantitative independent variables overlap to some extent, there are noticeable differences in nearly all cases.

On the grounds that political instability and involvement in military activity nearly always affect the instability of international trade, an attempt was made to classify countries with reference to the degree to which they experienced such influences. The attempt was, however, unsuccessful. It also proved impossible to obtain enough data on tariffs and other trade barriers to test these factors for their effect on trade instability. The exploratory investigation substantiated, however, our guess that political instability, military involvement, and relatively high trade barriers are positively related to export (and import) instability.

## Summary

In this chapter, an attempt has been made to identify the country characteristics that were significantly correlated, positively or negatively, with export receipts instability, and to obtain reasonably reliable regression equations with the export instability index as the dependent variable. For 1959–71, the highest simple coefficients of correlation between export receipts instability and the selected independent variables were

instability of import value ($r = .61$; $r^2 = .37$)
instability of real GDP per capita ($r = .60$; $r^2 = .36$)
growth rate of export receipts ($r = .59$; $r^2 = .35$)
instability of real GDP ($r = .53$; $r^2 = .28$)
instability of export quantum ($r = .46$; $r^2 = .21$)

Mutiple regression analysis yielded an $R^2$ value of .610, with all regression coefficients of the (eight) variables in the equation significant at the .01 level. When the signficance level was changed to .05, $R^2$ equalled .673, with 11 variables.

Comparisons between the correlation results for 1959–71 and for 1946–58 indicated some degree of consistency. The maximum simple correlation coefficients were similar: .61 and .58. Three of the six variables most highly correlated with export instability were the same for both periods: import instability, growth rate of export receipts, and instability of export quantum.

Higher coefficients of multiple determination were obtained for 1959–71 than for 1946–58, but the variables and methods were not the same for both periods. With 11 independent variables and with regression coefficients all significant at the .05 level, an $R^2$ of .673 was obtained for 1959–71. The highest $R^2$ for 1946–58 was .446, with four independent variables. The elaborate computer program used for the regression analysis for 1959–71 undoubtedly accounted for part of the difference.

So far as I know the $R^2$ value of .673 is the highest statistically reliable value that has been obtained in studies of export instability.

For the non-quantifiable characteristics of countries, the oil exporting countries were in both periods the grouping with the highest average export instability index: 11.3 for 1959–71 and 28.8 for 1946–58. The lowest average in 1959–71 was for the Warsaw Pact countries (2.9; for exports to non-Communist countries), and in 1946–58 for the EFTA countries (10.3). In both periods, the export instability index was higher for the less developed countries (7.3 in 1959–71 and 16.5 in 1946–58) than for the developed countries (4.1 in 1959–71 and 13.6 in 1946–58).

## Notes

[1] Another approach would be to use different time periods instead of different countries. This approach will be used only for countries for which data were available for several decades.

[2] 'Corrected' $r$ values and $r^2$ values (for number of cases) are used throughout, although bar notation ($\bar{r}$) is not used. The corrected values are in nearly all cases only slightly lower than the uncorrected values, as may be seen from table A.5, which shows both.

[3] The $t$ values should not be less than about 2.0 (depending on the number of observations) for the $r$ value to be significant at the 5 per cent (.05) level; they should be nearly 3.0 or more to be significant at the 1 per cent (.01) level. (Significance at, say, the .01 level means that the chances of the result occurring on a random basis are only one in 100. Hence, the degree of association represented by the regression equation and the $r$ value can be considered statistically reliable to that degree.) These remarks are applicable throughout this chapter and chapter 5.

[4] This measure of concentration is the square root of the sum of the squares of the percentage shares of a distribution. The source of the measure is Albert O. Hirschman, *National Power and the Structure of Foreign Trade*, University of California Press, Berkeley, Calif., 1945, Appendix A.

[5] The author devised this measure in connection with his *Foreign Trade of Asia and the Far East* (Thammasat University Press, Bangkok, 1974), and subsequently discovered that others had devised the same or similar measures. See M. Michaely, *American Economic Review,* September 1962; F. L. Pryor, *The Communist Foreign Trade System*, 1963; P. Lloyd, unpublished manuscript, Australian National University; M. Finger, Ph.D. thesis, University of North Carolina; and P. Wiles, *Communist International Economics*, 1968. Since the calculation of the bilateralism percentage is somewhat complicated, the following illustration is offered. Suppose that, for a given time period, country A's exports to and imports from various other countries are as shown in columns $X$ and $M$ below ($X$, $M$ and $F$ are exports, imports and 'offset', respectively).

| *Trading partner country* | *X* | *M* | *F (smaller of X and M)* |
|---|---|---|---|
| A | $157 | $ 77 | $ 77 |
| B | 13 | 29 | 13 |
| C | 414 | 329 | 329 |
| D | 44 | 41 | 41 |
| E | 56 | 7 | 7 |
| F | 33 | 25 | 25 |
| G | 48 | 169 | 48 |

| *Trading partner country* | *X* | *M* | *F* |
|---|---|---|---|
| H | 23 | 6 | 6 |
| I | 28 | 7 | 7 |
| J | 94 | 135 | 94 |
| Total | 910 | 825 | 647 |

A sold \$157 worth of goods to B and bought \$77 worth, so \$77 of exports were offset by imports and \$77 of imports were offset by exports. A exported only \$48 worth to G, but bought \$169 worth, so \$48 worth of exports were offset by imports and \$48 worth of imports were offset by exports. Likewise with the other countries. The sum of the exports is \$910, \$647 of which were offset by imports, so that the bilateralism percentage for exports was 100(647/910) or 71.1. Similarly, for imports, the bilateralism percentage was 100(647/825) or 78.4. The combined or trade bilateralism percentage was thus 100(647 + 647)/(910 + 825) or 74.6. In formula terms, this becomes $B = 100(2F)/(X + M)$, as shown in the text. In our calculations, we included partners until 75 per cent of the trade was covered or until all countries with 5 per cent or more of exports or imports had been included, whichever gave the higher result. We used a five-year period in order to avoid unusual annual figures. A computer program was devised.

[6] The coefficient of correlation ($r$) between GDP ($X_{348}$) and GDP per capita ($X_{349}$) was .45.

[7] As a matter of curiosity, a few multiple regression runs were made using as independent variables those that yielded the highest simple $r$ values. The highest $R$ value obtained by this unsystematic method was .667 ($R^2 = .445$), not much higher than the highest simple $r$ value, .612 ($X_{115}$, import value instability index).

[8] *International Financial Statistics* (monthly), various tables.

[9] Weighted means would imply an interest in particular regions, rather than in the typical behaviour of the countries. Data for calculating weighted averages are, however, provided in table A.2, columns 100 and 300.

[10] 'Developed', 'less developed' and similar terms are not easily defined. In statistical studies, there is a strong tendency to use per capita income, expressed in US dollars, as the measure of *level* of development, despite the weaknesses of this measure. The *growth rate* of per capita

income, in national currencies and adjusted for price changes, is usually used as an index of the rate of economic development or growth through time. The values for these variables for 1959–71 are given in table A.2, columns 349 and 218.

# 5 Analysis of import instability

In Chapter 2 (figure 2.2 and table 2.1) it was very apparent that import value instability varied greatly from country to country. The value of the import instability index ranged from 1.6 to 27.4 in 1959–71 and from 1.7 to 42.4 in 1946–58. Why?

This chapter seeks to provide something of an answer to this question. Neither economic theory nor common knowledge provide good explanations, but they do give us some clues in seeking out relevant variables. As with export instability, we shall generally look for causal factors; but, when interdependence or reverse dependence seem the relationships to expect, we shall take note of them. The general discussion at the start of Chapter 4 – on export instability as a variable derived from the highly aggregative variable of export receipts – applies, *mutatis mutandis*, to import instability.

On the basis of one's knowledge or sense of economic processes, import fluctuations can be associated with numerous factors: knowledge and availability of foreign goods and services; availability of foreign-exchange or credit arrangements acceptable to foreign sellers; the need or desire of domestic producers or consumers for foreign goods and services; the level and distribution of national income; prices of imports (including freight, insurance, tariffs, etc.) compared with prices of domestic substitutes; government controls over imports; emergency buying; foreign investment in the home country; foreign aid; etc. Changes in one or more of these factors – and in others that may be noted – can affect the level of import outlays.

Although import prices and the respective import quantities are the logically necessary proximate determinants of import outlays, import value instability cannot be calculated directly from import price instability and import quantum instability, as explained in some detail at the start of Chapter 4, in connection with exports.

Most of the variables considered in this chapter are quantifiable, although often in forms that fall far short of the 'real' variables. There are no satisfactory measures of, or proxies for, some of the obviously relevant variables mentioned above. Some non-quantifiable characteristics of countries are taken into account toward the end of the chapter. As with exports, an eclectic approach was used in searching for key variables.

The dependent variable throughout this chapter is the instability index of import outlays – outlays on goods and (where data were available) services – for the 13 years 1959–71. In some instances, comparisons with import instability experience in 1946–58 are made.

Part (A) of this chapter deals individually with the various independent variables. Standard statistical correlation–regression analysis is the usual tool. Part (B) involves multi-variable analysis of the standard sort. Part (C) uses non-quantitative characteristics of countries.

## (A) SINGLE-VARIABLE ANALYSIS

The variables considered in relation to import value instability are grouped for expository convenience into several classes. The order has no significance, but similar variables are discussed together.

- Growth of imports
- Import and export quantum
- Import and export prices
- Terms of trade
- Export proceeds
- Commodity concentration
- Geographic concentration
- Bilateralism
- Size of foreign trade
- Net balance of trade
- Monetary reserves
- Size of economy
- Income per capita
- Changes in national income
- Importance of agriculture
- Consumer prices

Table 5.1 shows the simple correlation coefficients and the regression equations for which the regression coefficients were significant at the .01 level or better. Table A.6 gives the complete results.

### Growth of imports

On the basis of the historical generalisation that economic instability tends to be associated with economic growth, we should expect relatively high import instability to be positively correlated with relatively high

Table 5.1

Correlation coefficients and regression equations significant at the .01 level with import value instability ($X_{115}$) as the dependent variable: for countries, 1959–71

| | Independent variable[a] | | $r$ | $r^2$ | No. of countries | Regression equation[c] |
|---|---|---|---|---|---|---|
| Rank | No. | Name | (1)[b] | (2)[b] | (3) | (4) |
| 1 | 110 | Instability index (II), import quantum | .756 | .572 | 64 | $Y_c = 1.682 + 0.739\ X_{110}$ (2.80) (9.23) |
| 2 | 117 | II, foreign trade as a percentage of GDP | .653 | .426 | 96 | $Y_c = 3.908 + 0.602\ X_{117}$ (7.93) (8.45) |
| 3 | 112 | II, quantum terms of trade | .615 | .378 | 63 | $Y_c = 2.792 + 0.483\ X_{112}$ (3.95) (6.21) |
| 4 | 100 | II, export value | .612 | .374 | 109 | $Y_c = 5.232 + 0.349\ X_{100}$ (10.60) (8.10) |
| 5 | 113 | II, GDP in current prices | .575 | .331 | 96 | $Y_c = 5.262 + 0.418\ X_{113}$ (12.35) (6.93) |
| 6 | 114 | II, GDP in constant prices | .519 | .269 | 86 | $Y_c = 3.986 + 1.327\ X_{114}$ (5.95) (5.68) |
| 7 | 365 | Energy consumption per capita | –.370 | .137 | 108 | $Y_c = 9.319 - 0.001\ X_{365}$ (18.21) (4.24) |
| 8 | 310 | Concentration of exports, SITC classes | .326 | .106 | 91 | $Y_c = 1.123 + 0.109\ X_{310}$ (.54) (3.41) |
| 9 | 120 | II, monetary reserves as a percentage of imports | .318 | .101 | 97 | $Y_c = 6.319 + 0.082\ X_{120}$ (8.93) (3.43) |
| 10 | 353 | Bilateralism index | –.307 | .094 | 109 | $Y_c = 14.468 - 0.098\ X_{352}$ (7.68) (3.49) |

| | | | | | | |
|---|---|---|---|---|---|---|
| 11 | 200 | Percentage growth, exports | .305 | .093 | 109 | $Y_c = 6.088 + 0.207\,X_{200}$ (8.65) (3.48) |
| 12 | 108 | II, export quantum | .305 | .093 | 81 | $Y_c = 5.179 + 0.390\,X_{108}$ (5.80) (3.04) |
| 13 | 221 | Percentage growth, consumer price index | .302 | .091 | 92 | $Y_c = 7.322 + 0.090\,X_{221}$ (14.72) (3.19) |
| 14 | 325 | Percentage of goods exports in primary goods | .295 | .087 | 102 | $Y_c = 4.656 + 0.046\,X_{325}$ (4.32) (3.26) |
| 15 | 121 | II, consumer price index | .279 | .078 | 92 | $Y_c = 7.424 + 0.130\,X_{121}$ (15.05) (2.96) |
| 16 | 308 | Service exports as a percentage of total exports | −.268 | .072 | 84 | $Y_c = 9.383 - 0.076\,X_{308}$ (12.11) (3.41) |
| 17 | 364 | Percentage of GDP from agriculture | .263 | .069 | 97 | $Y_c = 5.731 + 0.062\,X_{364}$ (8.31) (2.84) |
| 18 | 111 | II, price terms of trade | .261 | .068 | 64 | $Y_c = 5.473 + 0.335\,X_{111}$ (7.82) (2.36) |
| 19 | 349 | GDP per capita | −.259 | .067 | 97 | $Y_c = 8.183 - 0.001\,X_{349}$ (17.18) (2.80) |
| 20 | 107 | II, export price index | .253 | .064 | 78 | $Y_c = 5.716 + 0.399\,X_{107}$ (6.59) (2.50) |
| 21 | 315 | Average value of imports | −.219 | .048 | 109 | $Y_c = 8.554 - 0.000\,X_{315}$ (17.99) (2.52) |
| 22 | 300 | Average value of exports | −.202 | .041 | 109 | $Y_c = 8.479 - 0.000\,X_{300}$ (18.09) (2.38) |

[a] Full descriptions of variables are given in Table A.1. Results for all variables tested appear in Table A.6. A few variables with results significant at the .01 level have been omitted here owing to the fact that they are duplicative of some that have been included.

[b] The $r^2$ and $r$ values are corrected for size of sample. Uncorrected values are shown in Table A.6.

[c] The $t$ value is in parentheses. $Y_c$ is the computed or trend value of the import instability index ($X_{115}$).

growth of imports, and *vice versa*. The expectation is not realised for the 109 countries for 1959–71: $r = .125$.[1] The regression equation for the relation, with $Y_c$ as the trend value, or computed value for import instability, was [2]

$$Y_c = 6.511 + 0.171 X_{215} \quad (r^2 = .023; \text{not significant at the .05 level})$$
$$(7.04) \quad (1.89)$$

Country data are given in table A.2, columns 115 and 215.

## Import and export quantum

Import quantum index numbers were obtained by dividing the annual import value figures by the corresponding annual index numbers for import prices, and then expressing the deflated import value figures as index numbers. This variable is likely to show a close relation to import value instability when price instability is not high, as was the case in the 1960s. So it is no surprise to find an $r$ value of .756. This was the highest simple correlation coefficient obtained in the analysis of import instability. The equation was

$$Y_c = 1.682 + 0.739\, X_{110} \quad (r^2 = .572; \text{significant at the .01 level})$$
$$(2.80) \quad (9.23)$$

Country data for 64 countries are given in table A.2, columns 115 and 110.

Instability of *export* quantum showed a much weaker relation to import value instability: $r = .305$. (It is of some interest that the coefficient of correlation between instability of import quantum and export quantum instability was .49.) The equation was

$$Y_c = 5.179 + 0.390\, X_{108} \quad (r^2 = .093; \text{significant at the .01 level})$$
$$(5.80) \quad (3.04)$$

Country data for 81 countries are given in table A.2, columns 115 and 108.

Neither the import nor the export quantum growth rate ($X_{210}$ and $X_{208}$, respectively) was significantly related to import value instability: $r = .071$ and $-.032$, respectively.

## Import and export prices

It seems plausible, in view of the frequent claims of countries that price instability affects the stability of their outlays on imports, that the indexes of import price instability and import outlays should be rather highly correlated, despite the analytical demonstration that there need not be a high correlation. The results were indeed surprising: $r = .032$, obviously not a statistically significant result. The equation was

$$Y_c = \underset{(8.72)}{6.681} + \underset{(0.21)}{0.045}\, X_{109} \quad (r^2 = .001;\ \text{not significant at the .05 level})$$

Country data for 65 countries are given in table A.2, columns 115 and 109.

There was a much closer relation between import outlay instability and *export* price instability: $r = .253$. One line of explanation is that export price changes may affect export receipts, which in turn affect import outlays. The equation was

$$Y_c = \underset{(6.59)}{5.716} + \underset{(2.50)}{0.399}\, X_{107} \quad (r^2 = .064;\ \text{significant at the .01 level})$$

Country data for 78 countries are given in table A.2, columns 115 and 107.

Neither the growth rate of import prices ($X_{209}$) nor that of export prices ($X_{207}$) was significantly correlated with instability of import outlays: $r = -.055$ and $.126$, respectively.

## Terms of trade

If a country's export prices decline relative to its import prices, and if the quantity of exports does not increase enough to compensate for the decline in revenue per unit of exports, export receipts will decline and there is a strong likelihood that import outlays will also do so. Hence, there is a possible, perhaps plausible, connection between the instability of the price terms of trade ($P_x/P_m$) and the instability of import outlays. The statistical analysis modestly supported the hypothesis: $r = .261$. The equation was

$$Y_c = \underset{(7.82)}{5.473} + \underset{(2.36)}{0.335}\, X_{111} \quad (r^2 = .068;\ \text{significant at the .05 level})$$

Country data for 64 countries are given in table A.2, columns 115 and 111.

An even stronger relation was found between the instability of the quantum (gross-barter) terms of trade ($Q_m/Q_x$) and the instability of import outlays: $r = .615$, one of the highest simple correlation coefficients obtained. This meaning of this result, as compared with that obtained for the price (commodity) terms of trade, is that the relative quantities of exports and imports, as measured by the quantum indexes, underwent much greater year-to-year change than did relative prices. Various combinations of elasticities and shifts of demand and supply curves could elicit this result. The equation was

$$Y_c = \underset{(3.95)}{2.792} + \underset{(6.21)}{0.483}\, X_{112} \quad (r^2 = .378;\ \text{significant at the .01 level})$$

Country data for 63 countries are given in table A.2, columns 115 and 112.

Neither the growth rate of the price terms of trade ($X_{211}$) nor that of the quantum terms of trade ($X_{212}$) was significantly related to import instability: $r = .078$ and $-.141$, respectively.

## Export receipts

With instability of export receipts treated as the independent variable and instability of import outlays as the dependent variable, the $r$ value was .612. The equation was

$$Y_c = \underset{(10.60)}{5.232} + \underset{(8.10)}{0.349}\, X_{100} \quad (r^2 = .374;\ \text{significant at the .01 level})$$

Country data for 109 countries are given in table A.2, columns 115 and 100.

As noted in the discussion of export instability, this was one of the highest $r$ values obtained. The hypothesis that underlies the relation is usually understood to be that import outlays depend to a large extent on export receipts, so that, if export receipts fluctuate, import outlays tend to do the same. This hypothesis seems reasonable for most countries most of the time; but in at least one case, that of the United States shortly after the Second World War, exports were limited by imports. In the case cited, however, this tendency was weakened by the willingness of the United States to finance foreigners' imports from the country.

The instability of import outlays was also positively correlated with the growth rate of export receipts: $r = .305$. The equation was

$$Y_c = \underset{(8.65)}{6.088} + \underset{(3.48)}{0.207}\, X_{200} \quad (r^2 = .093; \text{significant at the .01 level})$$

Country data for 109 countries are given in table A.2, columns 115 and 200.

### Commodity concentration

With the percentage of imports that consist of services rather than goods as the independent variable ($X_{331}$), the correlation with import outlay instability was only .138, not significant at the .05 level (details in table A.6).

Curiously, when services *exports* as a percentage of total exports was used as the independent variable, the $r$ value was $-.268$. The equation was

$$Y_c = \underset{(12.11)}{9.383} - \underset{(3.41)}{0.076}\, X_{308} \quad (r^2 = .072; \text{significant at the .01 level})$$

Country data for 84 countries are given in table A.2, columns 115 and 308.

This means that, as the percentage of services exports increases, the instability of import outlays tends to decrease. One explanation is that fluctuations in receipts from services exports tend to compensate for fluctuations in receipts from goods exports, thereby decreasing the instability of export receipts and having a similar effect on import outlays.

The next breakdown considered is that between primary goods exports (Standard International Trade Classification classes 0, 1, 2, 3, 4) and non-primary goods exports (SITC classes 5, 6, 7, 8 and 9). Services were omitted. Imports were not broken down in this fashion, as nearly all countries import a wide variety of items, and the differences in the concentration indexes would therefore be quite small. The coefficient of correlation between the percentage of primary goods exports and import outlay instability was .295. The rationalisation is that receipts from exports of primary goods tend to be more unstable than receipts from exports of other goods; and, because of this, the instability of export receipts is in turn reflected in import outlays. Obviously, this does not have to be the case. The equation was

$$Y_c = \underset{(4.32)}{4.656} + \underset{(3.26)}{0.046}\, X_{325} \quad (r^2 = .087; \text{significant at the .01 level})$$

Country data for 102 countries are given in table A.2, columns 115 and 325.

When the Hirschman concentration index for goods *exports*, by the 10 main SITC classes, was used as the independent variable, the $r$ value was .326. The equation was

$$Y_c = \underset{(0.54)}{1.123} + \underset{(3.41)}{0.109}\ X_{221} \quad (r^2 = .106;\ \text{significant at the .01 level})$$

Country data for 91 countries are given in table A.2, columns 115 and 310. The rationale in this case is based on the statistically significant relation between export receipts instability and concentration of exports ($r = .41$), with import instability accompanying export instability.

## Geographical concentration

The Hirschman concentration index, applied to exports by country of destination, is now used as the independent variable. The hypothesis is similar to the preceding one – namely, that geographical concentration, like commodity concentration, makes for instability of export receipts, which in turn is transmitted to imports. The influence showed up weakly, however: $r = .164$. The equation was

$$Y_c = \underset{(4.63)}{5.637} + \underset{(1.98)}{0.054}\ X_{316} \quad (r^2 = .027;\ \text{significant at the .05 level})$$

Country data for 107 countries are given in table A.2, columns 115 and 316.

What of the relationship between import instability of countries and the percentage of their exports going to the United States ($X_{320}$)? There was no significant relation ($r = .032$). However, when the percentage of exports going to the EEC was used as the independent variable, $r$ was equal to .195. The equation was

$$Y_c = \underset{(9.76)}{6.558} + \underset{(2.27)}{0.047}\ X_{321} \quad (r^2 = .038;\ \text{significant at the .05 level})$$

Country data for 106 countries are given in table A.2, columns 115 and 321. Evidently some import instability was transmitted through exports: the $r$ value for export value instability and the percentage of exports to the EEC was .28 (table 4.1).

## Bilateralism

How does the degree of bilateralism – the extent to which a country's exports to and imports from each trading partner are balanced – affect the instability of imports? On the basis of essentially the same reasoning as was suggested in connection with exports, there is a presumption that bilateralism tends to reduce instability. There is nothing necessary about this suggested relation, unless there are long-term agreements that call for approximate bilateral balancing and only gradual changes from year to year. Even in the absence of such agreements, there are often governmental pressures, usually related to balance-of-payments difficulties, that make for more bilateralism than would otherwise exist. The correlation coefficient supports the hypothesis: $r = -.307$. The regression equation was

$$Y_c = \underset{(7.68)}{14.468} - \underset{(3.49)}{0.98}\, X_{352} \quad (r^2 = .094;\ \text{significant at the .01 level})$$

Country data for 109 countries are given in table A.2, columns 115 and 352. See chapter 4 for an explanation of how bilateralism is measured.

## Size of foreign trade

Our hypothesis here is that, the larger the money value of a country's imports, the lower its import instability index is. The reasoning is that diversification by commodity and by country of source is likely to be greater with larger outlays, and that broader markets make for less instability. The hypothesis received modest support: $r = -.219$. The equation was

$$Y_c = \underset{(17.99)}{8.554} - \underset{(2.52)}{0.0002}\, X_{315} \quad (r^2 = .048;\ \text{significant at the .01 level})$$

Country data for 109 countries are given in table A.2, columns 115 and 315. The coefficient of correlation between average export value ($X_{300}$) and import value instability was almost identical (–.202).

With the value of foreign trade as a percentage of gross domestic product ($X_{346}$) as the independent variable, the hypothesis is essentially the same as for the previous variable: import instability is expected to fall as the ratio of trade to GDP rises, even though this ratio tends to decline as the money value of imports rises ($X_{346}$ and $X_{315}$ in table 5.3). The hypothesis is not supported with a correlation coefficient significant at the .05 level, although the $t$ value is very close: $r = -.095$ ($r^2 = .009$). (See table A.6 line 346, for the equation.)

On the other hand, the instability index of the foreign-trade percentage of GDP showed the second highest simple correlation coefficient with import value instability as the dependent variable: $r = .653$. The reason for this would seem to be that GDP is not as rapidly changing a variable as trade (or exports or imports alone), so that there is a degree of tautology reflected in this relatively high $r$ value. The equation was

$$Y_c = \underset{(7.93)}{3.908} + \underset{(8.45)}{0.602}\, X_{117} \quad (r^2 = .426\text{; significant at the .01 level})$$

Country data for 96 countries are given in table A.2, columns 115 and 117. The growth rate of the foreign-trade percentage ($X_{217}$) showed no connection with import value instability: $r = .071$ (table A.6).

## Net balance of trade

The value of a country's exports of goods and services, minus the value of its imports of goods and services for the same period may be viewed as the net balance of trade or as net capital movements. A positive sign for this net value indicates net capital exports; a negative sign net capital imports. The method of financing the difference – whether by formal loans, direct investments, gifts or otherwise – is of no concern here. One can easily imagine a stable net balance with highly unstable exports and imports, provided that exports and imports move pretty much together. Although there is a tendency for export and import instability to move together ($r = .61$), there is ample variance to allow for other influences. Our hypothesis is that, as imports rise, the net balance tends to fall; and, as imports fall, the net balance tends to rise. Hence, we posit a negative relation between instability of the net balance ($X_{122}$) and import value instability. The $r$ value turned out to be insignificant: .032. (Instability of the net balance was measured by $1 - r^2$, since some negative values were involved.)

Three other related variables show statistically insignificant results: $X_{222}$, the growth rate of the net balance ($r = -.089$); $X_{345}$, the average net balance ($r = -.077$); and $X_{347}$, the average net balance as a percentage of imports ($r \equiv -.055$). (See table A.6.)

The implications of this inconclusive result – that fluctuations in the net balance on the goods and services account are not significantly connected with fluctuations in imports – are interesting. The same weak relation was found between export instability and net balance instability ($r = .08$). Possibly the cross-section analysis used in this study does not bring out a plausible relation.

## Monetary reserves

Monetary reserves – gold, convertible foreign exchange, and funds available through special drawing rights with the International Monetary Fund – would seem likely to vary inversely with the instability of imports: as imports rise, reserves fall, *ceteris paribus*. To facilitate comparisons among countries, the independent variable used here was instability of monetary reserves as a percentage of annual imports ($X_{120}$). Surprisingly, the $r$ value obtained was a *positive* .318. Obviously, the other factors affecting monetary reserves have an overriding influence. The equation was

$$Y_c = \underset{(15.05)}{6.319} + \underset{(2.96)}{0.082}\, X_{120} \quad (r^2 = .101\text{; significant at the .01 level})$$

Country data for 97 countries are given in table A.2, columns 115 and 120. The relation between the average of this percentage ($X_{361}$) and import value instability was insignificant: $r = -.089$ (see table A.6).

The trend or growth rate of monetary reserves as a percentage of imports ($X_{220}$) showed a negative relation with import instability: $r = -.170$ ($r^2 = .029$), significant at the .05 level (Table A.6). This inverse relation seems plausible on the ground that, as the monetary reserve percentage rises, monetary reserves exercise a decreasing restraint on imports.

## Size of economy

Do economically large countries have higher or lower import instability than economically small countries do? On the 'larger market' theory, employed several times already, we should expect an inverse relation. With gross domestic product as the independent variable, the minus sign appeared, but the $r$ value was not significant at the .05 level: $r = -.071$. For the relevant equation, see table A.6; country data are given in table A.2, column 348.

Oddly, when population ($X_{350}$) was used as the size variable, $r$ was equal to .138, higher than for GDP and of opposite sign. The equation was

$$Y_c = 7.789 + 0.009\ X_{350}\ (r^2 = .019;\ \text{significant at the .05 level})$$
$$(16.84)\quad (1.77)$$

Country data for 109 countries are given in table A.2, columns 115 and 350. The fact that a few countries with large populations had high import instability indexes is sufficient to explain the positive slope of the regression line. (See table A.2, especially the values of $X_{115}$ and $X_{350}$, and related rankings, for India, the People's Republic of China, Indonesia and Pakistan.)

**Income per capita**

How is the level of per capita income (calculated as gross domestic product per capita) related to import instability? A hypothesis concerning this relation would seem to depend upon one or more empirical generalisations. If we assume that per capita income in low-income countries is more volatile than in high-income countries (supported by the correlation results), and if we assume that import value instability is positively associated with national income instability (total or per capita), we may then hypothesise that import value instability is inversely correlated with the per capita level of income. Our surmise was supported: $r = -.259$. The equation was

$$Y_c = 8.183 - 0.011\ X_{349}\ (r^2 = 0.67;\ \text{significant at the .01 level})$$
$$(17.18)\quad (2.80)$$

Country data for 97 countries are given in table A.2, columns 115 and 349.

Another measure of the level of living, uncomplicated by currency conversions, is energy consumption per capita, which we would expect to be related to import instability in a way similar to that just described. In fact, the relevant $r$ value, which we should have expected to be much the same as that obtained with per capita income as the independent variable, was higher: $-.370$. There could, no doubt, be other rationalisations of these results. The equation was

$$Y_c = 9.319 - 0.001\ X_{365}\ (r^2 = .137;\ \text{significant at the .01 level})$$
$$(15.21)\quad (4.24)$$

Country data for 108 countries are given in table A.2, columns 115 and 365.

### Changes in national income

The independent variables considered here in relation to import instability are the instability and growth of national income (gross domestic product), aggregate and per capita, in current and real terms.

The most popular theory of import instability is that associated with Keynesian or macroeconomic analysis; namely, that changes in national income give rise to changes in a country's imports. For this relation to hold firmly, the country must have a constant marginal propensity to import (ratio of an increment of imports to an increment of national income). This theory was devised with successive time periods in mind, usually with a lag in the response of imports to changes in national income. Our test of this theory uses cross-section data, but the test should result in the expected relation. GDP was expressed in current prices. The results were reassuring: $r = .575$ ($r^2 = .331$), significant at the .01 level, of course. This was the fifth highest simple $r$ value obtained for import instability. About one-third of the variance of import instability is explained by this variable, according to the usual interpretation. The equation was

$$Y_c = 5.262 + 0.418\ X_{113} \quad (r^2 = .331;\ \text{significant at the .01 level})$$
$$(12.35) \quad (6.93)$$

Country data for 96 countries are given in table A.2, columns 115 and 113.

Curiously, the correlation analysis showed no relation whatsoever between import instability and the growth rate of national income ($X_{213}$): $r = .000$.

When GDP was adjusted for price changes and used for calculating the instability indexes and growth rates for countries, the results were similar. The coefficient of correlation between instability of GDP in constant prices and import instability was .519. The equation was

$$Y_c = 3.986 + 1.327\ X_{114} \quad (r^2 = .269;\ \text{significant at the .01 level})$$
$$(5.95) \quad (5.68)$$

Country data for 86 countries are given in table A.2, columns 115 and 114. The $r$ value was only an insignificant .071 when the growth rate of real national income ($X_{214}$) was used as the independent variable.

As might be expected from the results reported above, instability of income per capita and growth rate per capita yielded similar respective results, because the population divisor did not change very much from year to year. The $r$ value with instability of real income per capita ($X_{118}$)

as the independent variable was .53 ($r^2$ = .281), as compared with an insignificant −.055 for the growth rate of real income per capita ($X_{218}$). (See table A.6 for details.)

## Importance of agriculture

It is often stated that the national income of countries highly dependent on agricultural production is particularly susceptible to variations, which in turn give rise to variations in exports and imports. This empirical generalisation – although the first part of it is not supported by the coefficient of correlation between $X_{364}$ and $X_{113}$ or $X_{114}$ – provides our hypothesis that import instability increases as the share of a country's national income coming from agriculture increases. There are two supporting lines of thought. One is that, as exports vary, so do imports (indicated by an $r$ of .61). The other is that, as national income varies, so do imports ($r$ = .58). The results for the correlation of import instability and the percentage of GDP from agriculture were in accord with this line of reasoning, but not strong: $r$ = .263. The equation was

$$Y_c = \underset{(8.31)}{5.731} + \underset{(2.84)}{0.062}\, X_{364} \quad (r^2 = .069;\ \text{significant at the .01 level})$$

Country data for 97 countries are given in table A.2 columns 115 and 364.

## Consumer prices

One would expect a positive relation between domestic price instability (instability index of the consumer price index) and import value instability, on the grounds that (all other things being equal), as domestic prices rise, imports of substitutes increase, and *vice versa*. Of course, this assumes that the elasticity of demand for imports, with respect to the relative price of imports ($P_m/P_d$), is greater than unity for changes in the $P_m/P_d$ ratio ($m$ = imported goods; $d$ = domestic goods). The statistical test confirmed the hypothesis: $r$ = .279. The equation was

$$Y_c = \underset{(15.05)}{7.424} + \underset{(2.96)}{0.130}\, X_{121} \quad (r^2 = .078;\ \text{significant at the .01 level})$$

Country data for 92 countries are given in table A.2 columns 115 and 121.

The rate of domestic inflation was also positively correlated with import value instability: $r = .302$. One possible rationalisation of this result is that, as domestic inflation increases, domestic buyers turn more and more to imports, but sporadically. Perhaps a stronger reason is that domestic price instability and the domestic rate of inflation are highly correlated ($r = .98$), so that import instability is affected by domestic price instability, which in turn is positively associated with domestic inflation. The equation was

$$Y_c = \underset{(14.72)}{7.322} + \underset{(3.19)}{0.090}\, X_{221} \quad (r^2 = .091;\ \text{significant at the .01 level})$$

Country data for 92 countries are given in table A.2, columns 115 and 221.

## Comparison of 1959–71 and 1946–58 correlations

Table 5.2 shows the available simple coefficients of correlation between import value instability and other variables for the period 1946–58 and

Table 5.2

Correlation coefficients ($r$) between import value instability and other variables, for countries, 1959–71 and 1946–58

| Rank, 1959–71 | Independent variable[a] No. | Name | $r$ value 1959–71 | 1946–58[b] |
|---|---|---|---|---|
| 1 | 100 | II, export value | .612 | .417 (1) |
| 2 | 113 | II, GDP in current prices | .575 | .219 (4) |
| 3 | 310 | Concentration of exports, by SITC classes | .326 | –.112 (9) |
| 4 | 108 | II, export, quantum | .305 | .264 (2) |
| 5 | 200 | Growth rate, export value | .305 | .080 (12) |
| 6 | 349 | GDP per capita | –.259 | –.115 (8) |
| 7 | 107 | II, export price index | .253 | .093 (11) |
| 8 | 315 | Average value, imports | –.219 | –.172 (7) |
| 9 | 316 | Concentration of exports, by country | .164 | –.184 (6) |
| 10 | 346 | Foreign trade as a percentage GDP | –.095 | –.264 (3) |
| 11 | 348 | GDP | –.071 | –.112 (10) |
| 12 | 320 | Percentage of exports to US | –.032 | –.226 (5) |

[a] Full descriptions in Table A.1.
[b] Rankings (without reference to sign) in parentheses.

Sources: Table A.6 (for 1959–71) and *International Economic Instability*, p. 129 (for 1946–58).

(with slight variations in some of the variables employed) for 1959–71. The measures of instability were different for the two periods, but they were usually highly correlated, as noted in Chapter 1. Also, data for more countries were included in the 1959–71 runs.

The variable most closely correlated with import value was the same in both periods: export value instability, with $r$ = .612 in 1959–71 and .417 in 1946–58. Instability of national income was second highest in 1959–71 and fourth highest in 1946–58. In eight of the 12 cases the $r$ values for 1959–71 were larger than those for 1946–58 – much larger in six cases. For 10 of the 12 variables, the signs were the same in both periods, the exceptions being the variables for export concentration, by commodity and by country or region of destination. Five of the 12 1946–58 $r$ values were too low to be significant at the .05 level, whereas only three were that low for 1959–71.

Probably the most notable point to emerge from this comparison is that three of the four highest independent variables were the same in both periods; the instability indexes of export value, national income (GDP), export quantum.

## (B) MULTI-VARIABLE ANALYSIS

The use of more than one independent variable in the analysis of import instability should considerably increase the value of the correlation coefficient and make for a more reliable regression equation. This section gives the results of the multiple regression-correlation analysis. The approach used roughly parallels that employed in the multivariate analysis of export instability; again, a 'step-wise' system (as described at the beginning of part (B) of Chapter 4) was employed. The values of 38 variables for 55 countries provided the basic data. (In this case no use was made of the computer program in which, by using the average values of variables to fill the blank cells for countries not among the original 55, all 109 countries were represented.)

The first run involved the elimination of all variables for which the regression coefficients did not have $t$ values of 2.583 or more. This requirement was even more demanding than that for significance at the .01 level. Only five independent variables were left and they yielded a (corrected) multiple determination coefficient ($R^2$) of .777, with an $F$ value of 38.6. The five variables, ranked in descending order of $r$ values, were

$X_{110}$ import quantum instability ($r^2$ = .572)

$X_{117}$ instability of foreign trade as a percentage of GDP ($r^2$ = .426)
$X_{200}$ growth rate of export value ($r^2$ = .093)
$X_{217}$ growth rate of foreign trade as a percentage of GDP (negative) ($r^2$ = .005)
$X_{218}$ growth rate of real GDP per capita (negative) ($r^2$ = .003)

According to the standard interpretation, these five variables accounted for 77.7 per cent of the variance in import value instability – and with a high degree of reliability. The equation ($t$ values in parentheses) was

$$\begin{aligned} Y_c = & -0.446 + 0.539\,X_{110} + 0.391\,X_{117} + 0.487\,X_{200} \\ & \;(-0.55)\quad (7.32) \qquad\quad (4.31) \qquad\quad (4.58) \\ & -0.449\,X_{217} - 0.750\,X_{218} \\ & \;(3.81) \qquad\quad (3.34) \end{aligned} \tag{5.1}$$

For the next run, the criterion for the $t$ value was reduced to 2.4, so that all regression coefficients that survived the step-wise process would be significant at the .01 level or better. The effect was to raise the $R^2$ value by .033, to .810, with $F = 33.9$. Two variables were added to the five listed above:

$X_{316}$ concentration index of goods exports by country of destination ($r_2$ = .027)
$X_{350}$ Population ($r^2$ = .019)

The equation was

$$\begin{aligned} Y_c = & -2.786 + 0.544\,X_{110} + 0.387\,X_{117} + 0.514\,X_{200} - 0.519\,X_{217} \\ & \;(-2.46)\quad (7.86) \qquad\quad (4.60) \qquad\quad (5.22) \qquad\quad (4.59) \\ & -0.699\,X_{218} + 0.047\,X_{316} + 0.007\,X_{350} \\ & \;(3.36) \qquad\quad (2.56) \qquad\quad (2.43) \end{aligned} \tag{5.2}$$

A third run isolated the independent variables for which the regression coefficients were significant at the .05 level or better ($t$ = 1.7 or more). A corrected $R^2$ value of .877 was obtained, with an $F$ value of 26.78. Fifteen variables were involved, including the seven in equation (5.2). The eight additional variables were

$X_{100}$ instability of export value ($r^2$ = .374)
$X_{120}$ instability of monetary reserves as a percentage of imports (negative) ($r^2$ = .101)
$X_{315}$ average value of imports ($r^2$ = .048)
$X_{321}$ percentage of exports going to the EEC ($r^2$ = .038)
$X_{325}$ percentage of exports in primary goods ($r^2$ = .087)

Table 5.3

Correlation coefficients ($r$) for pairs of independent variables significant in multiple regression analysis of import instability

| | $X_{100}$ | $X_{110}$ | $X_{117}$ | $X_{120}$ | $X_{200}$ | $X_{217}$ | $X_{218}$ | $X_{315}$ | $X_{316}$ | $X_{321}$ | $X_{325}$ | $X_{346}$ | $X_{347}$ | $X_{349}$ |
|---|---|---|---|---|---|---|---|---|---|---|---|---|---|---|
| $X_{110}$ | .34 | | | | | | | | | | | | | |
| $X_{117}$ | .05 | *.49* | | | | | | | | | | | | |
| $X_{120}$ | .32 | .24 | .45 | | | | | | | | | | | |
| $X_{200}$ | .19 | .07 | .15 | .05 | | | | | | | | | | |
| $X_{217}$ | .23 | .14 | .20 | –.21 | *.79* | | | | | | | | | |
| $X_{218}$ | –.13 | –.08 | –.17 | .23 | *.76* | .47 | | | | | | | | |
| $X_{315}$ | –.32 | –.29 | –.36 | –.19 | .11 | .07 | .14 | | | | | | | |
| $X_{316}$ | .33 | –.06 | .10 | .07 | .03 | .21 | –.10 | –.30 | | | | | | |
| $X_{321}$ | .05 | –.09 | –.04 | .18 | .05 | .14 | –.04 | .04 | –.16 | | | | | |
| $X_{325}$ | .34 | .30 | .27 | .13 | *–.50* | –.37 | *–.50* | *–.53* | .38 | –.26 | | | | |
| $X_{346}$ | –.09 | –.43 | –.19 | –.33 | –.07 | –.02 | –.01 | –.28 | .30 | .10 | .06 | | | |
| $X_{347}$ | –.40 | –.43 | –.38 | –.19 | –.10 | –.16 | .03 | *.56* | –.15 | .09 | –.32 | .15 | | |
| $X_{349}$ | –.41 | –.44 | –.41 | –.24 | .10 | .02 | .15 | *.68* | –.20 | .07 | *–.49* | .09 | .45 | |
| $X_{350}$ | –.07 | .10 | –.03 | .09 | –.10 | –.09 | –.08 | .32 | –.19 | –.18 | –.18 | *–.49* | .07 | .01 |

Note: The (corrected) $r$ values in this table were obtained by using data for only the 55 countries used in the principal multiple regression runs. See note to Table 4.2 about another table showing $r$ values obtained by using the maximum number of countries available for each pair of variables.

The names of the variables employed here are given in the text and in Table A.1.

$X_{346}$ foreign trade as a percentage of GDP (negative) ($r^2$ = .000)
$X_{347}$ average net trade balance as a percentage of average imports ($r^2$ = .000)
$X_{349}$ GDP per capita ($r^2$ = .067)

The equation was as follows (variables in order of subscripts):

$$
\begin{aligned}
Y_c = & -4.536 + 0.158\,X_{100} + 0.520\,X_{110} + 0.449\,X_{117} \\
& (-2.77) \quad (1.75) \qquad (7.74) \qquad (5.08) \\
& -0.063\,X_{120} + 0.447\,X_{200} - 0.488\,X_{217} - 0.384\,X_{218} \\
& (3.28) \qquad (5.52) \qquad (5.00) \qquad (2.15) \\
& -0.000\,X_{315} + 0.052\,X_{316} + 0.040\,X_{321} + 0.025\,X_{325} \\
& (1.86) \qquad (2.78) \qquad (3.15) \qquad (2.49) \\
& -0.033\,X_{346} + 0.045\,X_{347} + 0.001\,X_{349} + 0.012\,X_{350} \\
& (2.59) \qquad (2.78) \qquad (2.90) \qquad (3.80)
\end{aligned} \qquad (5.3)
$$

Thus, about 88 per cent of the variance in import instability was accounted for by the 15 variables with regression coefficients significant at the .05 level or better. As noted earlier, 81 per cent of the variance was explained with seven variables, with all coefficients significant at the .01 level or better; and 78 per cent was explained by only five variables, the coefficients of which were significant at an even more demanding level. These results are about as high as one can expect to obtain in trying to identify the variables associated with fluctuations in an aggregate such as imports. I know of no study with which these results may be compared.

## Intercorrelations

We now try to discover whether there was a significant degree of overlap or redundancy among the variables that turned up in multiple regression equations (5.1), (5.2) and (5.3). Table 5.3 shows the simple correlation coefficients for all pairings of the variables contained in those equations. Very high $r$ values (italicised in the table) would imply overlap or redundancy. The pairs with $r$ values of .60 or more were

.79 $X_{217}$ (growth rate of foreign trade as a percentage of GDP); $X_{200}$ (growth rate of export value)
.76 $X_{200}$ (growth rate of export value); $X_{218}$ (growth rate of real GDP per capita)
.68 $X_{315}$ (average value of imports); $X_{349}$ (GDP per capita)

In addition, seven pairs had *r* values of between .49, and .56 so only 10 of the 105 pairs could be considered to be moderately high correlated. Variables $X_{217}$ and $X_{200}$, the pair with the highest *r* value, overlap to some degree, as export value is a component of the numerator of the foreign-trade ratio of GDP.

It appears therefore, that the results of the multivariate analysis of import instability are not impaired by a significant degree of redundancy or intercorrelation among the variables.[3]

## (C) NON-QUANTITATIVE VARIABLES

Furthering our analysis of variations in import value instability among countries, we now consider several non-quantitative characteristics: level of economic development, type of political–economic system, geographical location, political affiliations, and so on. The discussion roughly parallels the discussion of non-quantitative variables in relation to export instability (part (C) of Chapter 4).

The comparisons are all summarised in tables 5.4 and 5.5, the data for which were drawn from Table 2.1. Both periods, 1959–71 and 1946–58, are covered. Usually the comparisons are made with reference to the average instability index for the particular groups. The median import value instability index is generally a bit lower than the average, because of the skewness to the right of nearly all of the distributions; but it would serve just as well for comparisons. The simple, rather than the weighted, average is used because it is the behaviour of the typical country of the group, not of the group as an aggregate, that interests us here. The data for calculating weighted averages, should they be desired, are given in Table A.2, columns 115 and 315.

We consider first the difference between the 'developed' and the 'less developed' countries, as classified by the International Monetary Fund in *International Financial Statistics*. The 'Soviet Area' is excluded from this comparison. Data are taken from table 5.4, rows 3 and 8.

| | *Average import instability index* | |
|---|---|---|
| | *1959–71* | *1946–58* |
| Developed | 5.5 | 12.4 |
| Less developed | 9.1 | 14.3 |

Table 5.4

Average import value instability indexes of countries, by region of world, 1959–71 and 1946–58

| | Region(s), etc | No. of countries (1) | Average import instability index (2) | Median import instability index (3) | Range (4) |
|---|---|---|---|---|---|
| 1 | Industrial | | | | |
| | 1959–71 | 14 | 4.4 | 4.0 | 2.6–7.3 |
| | 1946–58 | 14 | 10.2 | 9.8 | 6.4–17.7 |
| 2 | Other developed | | | | |
| | 1959–71 | 11 | 6.7 | 6.5 | 2.6–12.3 |
| | 1946–58 | 11 | 15.3 | 13.7 | 7.2–35.5 |
| 3 | Rows 1 and 2 inclusive | | | | |
| | 1959–71 | 25 | 5.5 | 4.8 | 2.6–12.3 |
| | 1946–58 | 25 | 12.4 | 11.0 | 6.4–35.5 |
| 4 | Latin America | | | | |
| | 1959–71 | 22 | 8.4 | 7.5 | 1.6–16.8 |
| | 1946–58 | 21 | 10.1 | 9.9 | 3.6–17.0 |
| 5 | Middle East | | | | |
| | 1959–71 | 10 | 7.9 | 6.9 | 5.6–12.3 |
| | 1946–58 | 7 | 15.6 | 11.7 | 6.1–42.3 |
| 6 | Asia | | | | |
| | 1959–71 | 13 | 9.4 | 9.7 | 3.0–18.0 |
| | 1946–58 | 11 | 16.3 | 15.5 | 7.7–30.0 |
| 7 | Africa | | | | |
| | 1959–71 | 30 | 9.9 | 7.7 | 3.4–27.4 |
| | 1946–58 | 9 | 17.2 | 14.5 | 7.1–37.3 |
| 8 | Rows 4–7 inclusive | | | | |
| | 1959–71 | 75 | 9.1 | 7.6 | 1.6–27.4 |
| | 1946–58 | 46 | 14.3 | 11.8 | 3.6–42.3 |
| 9 | Rows 3 and 8 combined | | | | |
| | 1959–71 | 100 | 8.2 | 7.0 | 1.6–27.4 |
| | 1946–58 | 71 | 13.6 | 11.7 | 3.6–42.3 |
| 10 | Soviet Area | | | | |
| | 1959–71 | 9 | 7.0 | 5.2 | 3.2–18.6 |
| | 1946–58 | 9 | 16.7 | 14.0 | 1.7–42.3 |
| 11 | All countries | | | | |
| | 1959–71 | 109 | 8.1 | 6.9 | 1.6–27.4 |
| | 1946–58 | 80 | 13.7 | 11.5 | 1.7–42.3 |

Source: Table 2.1. See footnotes to Table 4.1 for countries in regions or groups.

Table 5.5

Average import value instability indexes of countries, by various groupings of countries, 1959–71 and 1946–58

| Group | No. of countries (1) | Average import instability index (2) | Median import instability index (3) | Range (4) |
|---|---|---|---|---|
| 1 Oil exporters | | | | |
| 1959–71 | 9 | 10.4 | 10.7 | 5.6–18.0 |
| 1946–58 | 6 | 19.6 | 13.3 | 7.1–42.3 |
| 2 Arab states | | | | |
| 1959–71 | 13 | 8.3 | 7.7 | 4.4–12.4 |
| 1946–58 | 9 | 16.1 | 12.4 | 6.1–37.3 |
| 3 EEC | | | | |
| 1959–71 | 5 | 4.2 | 3.8 | 3.0–6.3 |
| 1946–58 | 5 | 9.8 | 9.8 | 7.4–13.5 |
| 4 EFTA | | | | |
| 1959–71 | 7 | 4.0 | 3.5 | 2.6–7.3 |
| 1946–58 | 7 | 10.4 | 11.0 | 7.4–12.2 |
| 5 OECD | | | | |
| 1959–71 | 20 | 5.3 | 4.0 | 2.6–12.3 |
| 1946–58 | 20 | 12.1 | 10.7 | 6.4–35.5 |
| 6 NATO | | | | |
| 1959–71 | 13 | 4.3 | 3.6 | 2.6–7.1 |
| 1946–58 | 13 | 11.9 | 9.8 | 6.4–35.5 |
| 7 Warsaw Pact | | | | |
| 1959–71 | 7 | 5.6 | 5.2 | 3.2–9.9 |
| 1946–58 | 7 | 18.1 | 15.0 | 1.7–40.8 |
| 8 Newly independent | | | | |
| 1959–71 | 48 | 9.1 | 7.0 | 3.0–27.4 |
| 1946–58 | 22 | 18.9 | 14.6 | 6.1–37.3 |
| 9 All countries | | | | |
| 1959–71 | 109 | 8.1 | 6.9 | 1.6–27.4 |
| 1946–58 | 80 | 13.7 | 11.5 | 1.7–42.3 |

Source: Table 2.1.

The developed countries typically had lower import instability in both periods. The average import instability index declined, from 1946–58 to 1959–71, by nearly 60 per cent for the developed countries and by just over one-third for the less developed. For 1959–71, the results were consistent with those obtained through standard correlation analysis, with per capita income ($X_{349}$) and energy consumption per capita ($X_{365}$) as the independent variables.

The next comparison is between the countries of the Soviet Area – most of the Communist countries – and the rest of the countries of the world for which data were available (see table 5.4, rows 9 and 10).

| | *Average import instability index* | |
|---|---|---|
| | *1959–71* | *1946–58* |
| Soviet Area | 7.0 | 16.7 |
| Other countries | 8.2 | 13.6 |

Data for Soviet Area trade were limited to trade with non-Soviet Area countries, which probably accounts for less than half the total foreign trade of the countries in question. In 1946–58, Soviet Area imports were more unstable than those of other countries, but in 1959–71 the reverse was the case. The decline in the average import instability index was much greater for the Soviet Area (63 per cent) than for other countries (40 per cent).

It is perhaps more informative to compare Soviet Area import instability with that of the 'developed' and 'less developed' groups, considered separately (table 5.4, rows 3, 8 and 10).

| | *Average import instability index* | |
|---|---|---|
| | *1959–71* | *1946–58* |
| Developed | 5.5 (1) | 12.5 (1) |
| Less developed | 9.1 (3) | 14.3 (2) |
| Soviet Area | 7.0 (2) | 16.7 (3) |

The developed-country average was clearly lower than the Soviet average in both periods, but the average for the less developed countries was lower than the Soviet average in the earlier period and higher in the later. The decline in import instability was very nearly the same for the developed countries and the Soviet Area (56 and 58 per cent, respectively), but for the less developed countries it was only about one-third. The medians showed similar changes (column (3) of table 5.4).

Let us now compare the various less developed countries by geographical region (table 5.4, rows 4–7).

| | *Average import instability index* | |
|---|---|---|
| | *1959–71* | *1946–58* |
| Middle East | 7.9 (1) | 15.6 (2) |
| Latin America | 8.4 (2) | 10.1 (1) |
| Asia | 9.4 (3) | 16.3 (3) |
| Africa | 9.9 (4) | 17.2 (4) |

Except as regards Latin America and the Middle East, whose positions were reversed, the ranking was the same for both periods. The range between the highest and lowest averages was quite small (2.0) in 1959–71, but quite large (7.1) in 1946–58. The decline in import instability was greatest for the Middle East (about 50 per cent) and smallest for Latin America (17 per cent).

When the 25 developed countries were divided into 'industrial' and 'other developed' – again, following the IMF classification – the following was the result (table 5.4, rows 1 and 2).

| | *Average import instability index* | |
|---|---|---|
| | *1959–71* | *1946–58* |
| Industrial | 4.4 | 10.2 |
| Other developed | 6.7 | 15.3 |

The most industrialised countries typically showed lower import instability indexes than did the next most developed group: about a third lower in both periods. For both groups the decline in the import instability index was well over 50 per cent.

The main oil exporting countries are now compared with the developed countries belonging to the OECD (table 5.5, rows 1 and 5).

| | *Average import instability index* | |
|---|---|---|
| | *1959–71* | *1946–58* |
| Oil exporting countries | 10.4 | 19.6 |
| OECD countries | 5.2 | 12.1 |

Clearly, the oil exporting countries had much higher import instability in both periods. The average import instability index declined by nearly three-fifths for the OECD countries and by 45 per cent for the oil exporting countries (whose median, however, declined by only 20 per cent).

The following figures compare the average import instability index for all countries with that of the Arab states of the Middle East and North Africa for which statistics were available (table 5.5, rows 2 and 9).

| | *Average import instability index* | |
|---|---|---|
| | *1959–71* | *1946–58* |
| Arab states | 8.3 | 16.1 |
| All countries | 8.1 | 13.7 |

The comparison showed no significant difference between the two groups in 1959–71, but the index was noticeably higher for the Arab countries in 1946–58. The average declined by 50 per cent for the Arab states, as against only 40 per cent for all countries.

It is interesting to note the effect that the establishment of the EEC (which came into existence on 1 January 1958) evidently had on the import instability of the countries involved (table 5.5, rows 3 and 9).

| | *Average import instability index* | |
|---|---|---|
| | *1959–71* | *1946–58* |
| EEC | 4.2 | 9.8 |
| All countries | 8.1 | 13.7 |

The average import instability index was decidedly lower for the EEC countries, for which it declined by 60 per cent. The decline was the same as for the OECD group (to which the EEC countries belong), though the EEC group had lower import instability indexes in both periods.

A similar comparison was made for the EFTA countries (table 5.5, rows 4 and 9), whose experience was very similar to that of the EEC countries.

| | *Average import instability index* | |
|---|---|---|
| | *1959–71* | *1946–58* |
| EFTA | 4.0 | 10.4 |
| All countries | 8.1 | 13.7 |

The EFTA average was lower in both periods and declined by over three-fifths (as against two-fifths for all countries).

For the OECD countries, perhaps the most interesting comparison that can be made is that with the less developed countries (table 5.5, rows 5 and 8).

| | *Average import instability index* | |
|---|---|---|
| | *1959–71* | *1946–58* |
| OECD | 5.2 | 12.1 |
| Less developed | 8.2 | 13.6 |

In both periods the OECD countries had the smaller average import instability index, though only by a small margin in 1946–58. The average declined by about three-fifths for the OECD, but by only two-fifths for the less developed countries.

We now compare the NATO and Warsaw Pact countries as regards import instability (table 5.5, rows 6 and 7).

| | *Average import instability index* | |
|---|---|---|
| | *1959–71* | *1946–58* |
| NATO | 4.3 | 11.9 |
| Warsaw Pact | 5.6 | 18.1 |

As can be seen, the NATO countries had the lower average in both periods, though the percentage decline in the average import instability index was a little higher for the Warsaw Pact countries (70 per cent, as against 64 per cent for NATO). The medians showed similar changes.

Finally, we compare the OECD countries and the states that have become independent since the Second World War (table 5.5, rows 5 and 8).

| | *Average import instability index* | |
|---|---|---|
| | *1959–71* | *1946–58* |
| Newly independent | 9.1 | 18.9 |
| OECD | 5.2 | 12.1 |

While the OECD countries had the lower average import instability index in both periods, the index declined only slightly more for the OECD countries (58 per cent) than for the newly independent states (53 per cent).

These comparisons with respect to non-quantitative variables throw some additional light on the incidence of import instability. Other comparisons can be made from tables 5.4 and 5.5, and the data supplied in table 2.1 can easily be used to make comparisons between other groupings of countries. As noted in chapter 4 in connection with export instability, it was not possible, on the basis of the data available, to discover precisely what effect political instability and military involvement have on trade instability. However, judging by the countries that suffer from a high level of trade instability, it seems clear that there is some relationship between the two.

## Summary

This chapter has attempted to identify variables associated with import instability and to measure the degree of association by means of correlation and regression techniques. The analysis for the years 1959–71 was based on a maximum of 50 quantifiable variables, with data available for a maximum of 109 countries. There were a few comparisons with the period 1946–58.

Seven simple coefficients of correlation between the import value instability index and various independent variables were over .50. The independent variables concerned were as follows.

| | *Independent variable* | $r$ | $r^2$ |
|---|---|---|---|
| $X_{110}$ | Instability index of import quantum | .756 | .572 |
| $X_{117}$ | Instability index of foreign trade as a percentage of GDP | .653 | .426 |
| $X_{112}$ | Instability index of quantum terms of trade | .615 | .378 |

| | | | |
|---|---|---|---|
| $X_{100}$ | Instability index of export value | .612 | .374 |
| $X_{113}$ | Instability index of GDP in current prices | .575 | .331 |
| $X_{118}$ | Instability index of GDP per capita in constant prices | .530 | .281 |
| $X_{114}$ | Instability index of GDP in constant prices | .519 | .269 |

It is evident that there is some conceptual overlapping among these variables. Three pairs had $r$ values above .70: $X_{100}$ and $X_{112}$; $X_{113}$ and $X_{117}$; and $X_{114}$ and $X_{118}$.

Instability of import quantum, with an $r$ of .756 ($r^2$ = .572), presumably explains nearly three-fifths of the variance of the import value instability index. Similar inferences may be drawn for the other variables.

Twenty-three of the 50 independent variables tested against import instability had correlation coefficients significant at the .01 level or better; five more were significant at the .01 to .05 level; and the remaining 22 were not significant at the .05 level.

As regards non-quantitative characteristics, the greatest difference in average import instability in 1959–71 was that between the EFTA countries (average 4.0) and the oil exporting countries (average 10.4). For 1946–58, the greatest difference was that between the EEC countries (average 9.8) and the oil exporting countries (19.6).

The most interesting coefficient of multiple determination – $R^2$ = .777 – was obtained with only five independent variables, all significant at considerably better than the .01 level. The variables concerned were instability of import quantum ($X_{110}$), instability of the foreign-trade percentage ($X_{117}$), growth rate of export proceeds ($X_{200}$), growth rate of the foreign-trade percentage ($X_{217}$), and growth rate of real GDP per capita ($X_{218}$). The absence of national income instability ($X_{113}$) is notable. Even higher $R^2$s, involving more independent variables, were obtained where weaker significance tests were applied. These results were gratifying in view of the obviously large number of factors connected with import instability. According to the standard interpretation, over three-fourths of the variance of the import instability index was accounted for by the five variables listed above.

## Notes

[1] Throughout the chapter the $r$ values and $r^2$ values are corrected for the number of observations, but bar notation ($\bar{r}$) is not used. Table A.6

shows both the corrected and uncorrected values, as well as the regression equations, for all simple correlation–regression calculations.

[2] The numbers in parentheses under the equation are $t$ values, the basis for the significance levels. See note 3, Chapter 4, for a discussion.

[3] For the 1946–58 period, there are no multiple correlation results with import instability as the dependent variable.

# 6 Summary and policy observations

This study has three main aims: (1) to describe, for the periods 1959–71 and 1946–58, the instability of the exports and imports of the various countries of the world; (2) to discover the country characteristics that are associated with various degrees of export and import instability; and (3) to suggest policies, national and international, for reducing, or mitigating the undesirable effects of, export and import instability. The first two aims have been served in the preceding chapters, which are summarised in part (A) below. Part (B) deals with policies.

## (A) SUMMARY

### The problem

It has for a long time been widely recognized that 'excessive' international trade instability has undesirable effects. 'Excessive' instability does not have a precise meaning, but comparisons with other countries and with other time periods can make the concept useful for individual countries. Primarily because of the differences in their effects on the balance of payments, large increases in exports and large decreases in imports are usually viewed with less apprehension than large decreases in exports and large increases in imports are; but other effects on national economies, short-term and long-term, can also be important. (See chapter 1.)

### Method of measuring instability

How international trade instability is measured is to a considerable extent a matter of choice. In this study the year has been chosen as the basic unit of time, and the money value of exports and imports has been the focus of attention. A 13-year period has been used, but this has no particular significance. Since there has been a strong growth trend in international trade since the Second World War, the measure of trade instability should in some way measure the fluctuations around the trend, rather than include the trend changes as part of the instability. From numerous possibilities a very simple measure was chosen: the average of percentage deviations of the actual annual values from the trend values, as shown by the linear least-squares line through the logarithms of the actual annual values. This measure is usually highly correlated with other measures, including the logarithmic variance measure.[1] To the extent that the log-linear trend does not characterise the time series, this measure is inappropriate. In the process of calculating this measure, one also obtains the average growth rate per year for the time series. (See chapter 1.)

### Countries included

The countries included were selected mainly on the basis of the size of their trade and the availability of statistics. For 1959–71, the period that was the main focus of attention, data for 109 countries were used. For 1946–58, data related to a maximum of 83 (usually 80) countries. Statistics on exports and imports of services (as well as of goods) were available for 84 out of 109 countries for 1959–71, and for 64 out of 83 for 1946–58. No data were available for trade among the Communist countries or for their trade in services with non-Communist countries. (See chapter 2.)

### Instability index values

The values of the export and import instability indexes varied considerably among countries.

| | *1959–71* | *1946–58* |
|---|---|---|
| Export instability index | | |
| range | 1.7–70.0 | 3.9–54.5 |
| mean | 8.1 | 15.3 |
| median | 6.2 | 12.1 |
| coefficient of variation | 99% | 53% |
| Import instability index | | |
| range | 1.6–27.4 | 1.7–42.4 |
| mean | 7.9 | 13.7 |
| median | 6.9 | 11.2 |
| coefficient of variation | 56% | 58% |

From 1946–58 to 1959–71, the typical export instability index declined by about 50 per cent and the typical import instability index by about 40 per cent. Nearly all countries shared in the decline, but, according to the correlation tests, the rankings of their index values were by no means the same in both periods. In 1959–71, only 27 (25 per cent) of the 109 countries had export instability indexes of over 10.0, whereas in 1946–58 58 (63 per cent) of 80 countries had had export instability indexes of this level. (See figure 2.1 for index values.) Import instability indexes of over 10.0 had been shared by 28 (25 per cent) of 109 countries in 1959–71, and by 49 (61 per cent) of 80 in 1946–58. (See figure 2.3 for index values.) Crude as this type of comparison is, it is evident that the problem of trade instability was much smaller and less widespread in the later than in the earlier period.

Average export and import instability indexes were about the same in 1959–71, but export instability tended to be higher than import instability in 1946–58. For both periods combined, the mean export instability index was 10.7 and the mean import instability index was 10.6. The medians also were similar: 9.4 and 9.5, respectively. (See chapter 2.)

## Contribution of countries to world trade instability

If the highly unstable traders did not represent a large percentage of world trade, world trade instability could be quite low, even if many countries continued to have high export and/or import instability indexes. In order to determine the 'contribution' of individual countries to world trade (and export and import) instability, the percentage distribution of trade (and exports and imports) among countries was weighted by the corresponding instability indexes.

In 1959–71, West Germany, the United Kingdom and the United States contributed 26.4 per cent of world export instability; in 1946–58, the same three countries contributed 32.0 per cent. (See figure 3.1 for the other principal contributors.)

As regards world import instability, the three largest contributors in 1959–71 were the United States, West Germany and Canada which together contributed 29.6 per cent of the total; and in 1946–58, the United Kingdom, the United States and Japan, which together contributed 22.2 per cent. (See figure 3.2 for the other main contributors.)

The principal contributors to world trade instability in 1946–71 (the average of percentage contribution to export and import instability in 1959–71 and 1946–58) were the United States (12.2), West Germany

(7.8), the United Kingdom (7.0), Japan (5.0), France (4.5), the USSR (4.0), the Netherlands (3.4), Canada (3.0) and Italy (3.0), which together contributed nearly 50 per cent of the total (see table 3.9). It should be noted that the contribution percentages do not reveal whether the average level of trade instability is high or low. (See chapter 3.)

## Variables correlated with export instability

On the basis of country data for the 1959–71 period, the quantitative variables most highly correlated with export value instability were, import value instability ($r = .61$; $r^2 = .37$), instability of real GDP per capita ($r = .60$; $r^2 = .36$), growth rate of export receipts ($r = .59$; $r^2 = .35$), and export quantum instability ($r = .46$; $r^2 = .21$). All except instability of real GDP per capita were among the four highest $r$ values for 1946–58, with export quantum instability in first place ($r = .58$; $r^2 = .34$), import value instability in second place ($r = .43$; $r^2 = .18$), and growth rate of export receipts in fourth place ($r = .23$; $r^2 = .05$). This represents an impressive degree of consistency over the two periods. If the data on national income (GDP) had been better for 1946–58, instability of real GDP per capita might also have had one of the four highest $r$ values in that period.

The highest multiple correlation coefficient obtained for 1959–71, with export receipts instability as the dependent variable, and with all variables significant at the .01 level, was .781 ($R^2 = .610$; $F = 11.54$), with eight independent variables. These variables thus explain over three-fifths of the variance in export value instability. The regression equation, equation (4.1), and the relevant variables for this result were

$$\underset{(3.92)}{Y = 12.360} - \underset{(4.03)}{0.504\,X_{107}} + \underset{(3.03)}{0.320\,X_{108}} + \underset{(4.67)}{0.485\,X_{117}} + \underset{(3.15)}{0.553\,X_{200}}$$

$$- \underset{(3.16)}{0.721\,X_{215}} - \underset{(2.82)}{0.373\,X_{207}} - \underset{(2.80)}{0.098\,X_{330}} - \underset{(3.22)}{0.062\,X_{347}}$$

($t$ values in parentheses; $F = 11.54$)

The variables, with their simple coefficients of determination ($r^2$), were as follows:

$X_{107}$: export price instability ($r^2 = .013$)
$X_{108}$: export quantum instability ($r^2 = .210$)
$X_{117}$: instability of foreign trade as a percentage of GDP ($r^2 = .143$)
$X_{200}$: growth rate of export value ($r^2 = .348$)

$X_{215}$: growth rate of import value ($r^2$ = .008)
$X_{207}$: growth rate of export price index ($r^2$ = .017)
$X_{330}$: goods imports as percentage of total imports ($r^2$ = .107)
$X_{347}$: average net balance of trade as percentage of average imports ($r^2$ = .000)

The highest $R$ value for 1946–58 was .668 ($R^2$ = .449), but it was not obtained from the same computer program as gave the highest result for 1959–71. There were four independent variables in the equation concerned.

When the countries were grouped according to various non-quantitative criteria, the principal oil producing countries showed the highest average export instability for both periods, while the countries of the EEC had the lowest average in 1959–71, and those that later formed EFTA had the lowest for 1946–58. (See chapter 4.)

### Variables correlated with import instability

The variables that were most highly correlated with import value instability, by country, for the period 1959–71 were

instability index of import quantum ($r$ = .756; $r^2$ = .572)
instability of foreign trade as a percentage of GDP ($r$ = .653; $r^2$ = .426)
instability of quantum terms of trade index ($r$ = .615; $r^2$ = .378)
instability of export value ($r$ = .612; $r^2$ = .374)
instability of GDP in current prices ($r$ = .575; $r^2$ = .331)

For 1946–58 the top five simple correlation coefficients were[2]

export value instability ($r$ = .417; $r^2$ = .174)
export quantum instability ($r$ = .264; $r^2$ = .070)
foreign trade as a percentage of GDP ($r$ = –.264; $r^2$ = .070)
instability of GDP in current prices ($r$ = .219; $r^2$ = .018)
percentage of exports to the United States ($r$ = –.226; $r^2$ = .051)

Although the $r$ values for the two periods were quite different, two variables – export value instability and instability of GDP in current prices – were among the top five in both periods.

For 1959–71, the coefficient of multiple correlation reached an impressive .881 ($R^2$ = .777; $F$ = 38.61) with only five independent variables, all with regression coefficients significant at better than the .01

level. The regression equation was as follows:

$$Y_c = -0.446 + 0.539\,X_{110} + 0.391\,X_{117} + 0.487\,X_{200} - 0.449\,X_{217}$$
$$(-.55)\quad(7.32)\qquad(4.31)\qquad(4.58)\qquad(3.81)$$
$$-0.750\,X_{218}$$
$$(3.34)$$

($t$ values in parentheses; $t = 2.4$ for significance at .01 level; $F = 38.61$). The variables, with their simple coefficients of determination, were:

$X_{110}$ import quantum instability ($r^2 = .572$)
$X_{117}$ instability of foreign trade as a percentage of GDP ($r^2 = .426$)
$X_{200}$ growth rate of export value ($r^2 = .093$)
$X_{217}$ growth rate of foreign trade as a percentage of GDP ($r^2 = .005$)
$X_{218}$ growth rate of real GDP per capita ($r^2 = .003$)

The five variables accounted for over three-fourths of the variance in the import instability index. With less severe reliability standards (minimum $t$ values of 1.7, significant at the .05 level), $R^2$ rose to .877 ($F = 26.78$), with 15 independent variables. It is interesting that higher coefficients were obtained with fewer independent variables in the case of import instability than in the case of export instability.

For the non-quantitative characteristics tested, it was found that the oil exporting countries, as a group, had the highest average import instability index for both periods, while the countries of EFTA had the lowest average in 1959–71 and the countries later to become the EEC had the lowest average in 1946–58.

## (B) POLICY OBSERVATIONS

We now undertake a general discussion of policies for dealing with export and/or import instability. The discussion must be general, since actual policies must necessarily depend on the situations of particular countries at particular times. Even so, many relevant and useful things can be said about policies in this field.

### Importance of facts

First, it is necessary for a government to decide whether it has a problem of export and/or import instability. Broadly speaking, there would be *prima facie* evidence of a problem when export receipts or import outlays deviated more than typically from the projected trend line based on several years' statistics. For example, if a country's customary export or import instability index is 10.0 – that is, 10 per cent above or below the trend line – and the receipts or outlays for the most recent year or two are 20 per cent off the trend line, there would be some evidence of a problem. Of course, a government is more likely to see such deviations as a problem if the export receipts are down and the import outlays are up, for it may than have not only a trade instability problem but also the problem of a deficit disequilibrium in its balance of payments.

If the problems connected with trade instability were only those involving balance-of-payments disequilibrium, deficit or surplus, the policy questions could be discussed within the very familiar framework of how to rectify disequilibrium in the balance of payments. The task we have set ourselves, however, is that of determining policies for reducing trade instability, or for mitigating its undesirable effects, whether or not a serious balance-of-payments problem is involved. The diverse effects of trade instability on national economies warrant this special attention, since it is quite possible to have an international monetary system and balance-of-payments adjustment policies that achieve approximate balance-of-payments equilibrium and still leave undesirable international trade instability. We emphasise this point because of the tendency of some people to confuse the two broad and important problems.

In pursuit of the facts, a government must go below the global aggregates of the country's exports and imports to the breakdowns (a) by country of destination and source, (b) by commodity (and service) group, and (c) by (a) and (b) combined. Moreover, detailed price and quantity figures or indexes, as well as values, should be obtained for each class or 'cell'. Trends based on this factual information provide a firm basis for measuring the relative instability of the various country–commodity combinations. Such information can be provided only by government statistical bureaus.

### *Statistical criteria of instability*

In trying to determine whether it has a trade instability problem or not, a government can be guided by the country's past experience and/or the experience of other countries. In comparing the country's experience with that of other countries, it will, of course, be necessary to use the same instability measure. If the country is in, say, the fourth or fifth highest place with respect to export and/or import instability, it may have a problem. (It would be much more efficient if, instead of individual governments doing the work, a United Nations agency assembled the national statistics and calculated the instability indexes on a regular basis.) In looking at the country's own past experience, the government can use various measures of instability, and can make use of the statistical record to discover how the country weathered earlier periods of sharp instability. In this way the government can reach a conclusion about what may reasonably be deemed to be the country's 'warning' level of trade instability. There is no reason to believe that the instability index value that is considered unacceptable should be the same for every country.

*A temporary problem?*

As posed here, the trade instability problem is a fairly long-range one, and this should be borne in mind when considering it. Certainly the reduction in trade instability from the 1946–58 to the 1959–71 period would support the view that for many countries there has been a tendency for the problem to disappear, at least for the principal trade aggregates. Hence, before a government decides it has a problem, it should examine the trend of its trade instability, with due attention to country–commodity details.

*Capacity to bear trade instability*

Obviously, a country with only moderate dependence on foreign trade and with a diversified and flexible economy can stand a higher degree of trade instability than can a country that is highly dependent on foreign trade and has a highly specialised and inflexible production pattern. Rich countries are likely to find it easier to bear high instability than poor countries. Whatever characteristics are involved, it is evident that countries vary in their capacity to bear trade instability. Hence, in deciding on what level of trade instability calls for some kind of action, a government needs to have some idea about how much trade instability the country's economy can bear.

*Types of policies*

For purposes of discussion, policies for dealing with trade instability may conveniently be divided into two broad categories. With some policies, the main object is to cushion the undesirable effects of trade instability, or to ease the adjustments necessitated by it. With others, the main intention is to reduce the instability. A few policies do not fit this classification easily.

The two types of policies need not be in conflict with each other, so it is possible for both types to be employed simultaneously.

*Policy agencies*

Policies can be administered by national governments acting separately, by national governments working together, or by co-operative intergovernmental arrangements involving temporary or permanent international organisations. Some measures could, of course, be administered by non-government agencies, or by them in co-operation with governments. The policies of national and international agencies might or might not be inconsistent with each other.

*Criteria for judging policies*

The first test of any policy in this field is whether it can be expected to be reasonably effective in reducing undesirable trade instability and/or cushioning the economy against the negative effects of instability. A second test is whether the policy is administratively feasible at reasonable cost. A third test is the financial requirements, if any, of the policy, aside from administrative costs. A fourth test – or set of tests – has to do with spillover or side effects. For example, would the policy hamper or help desirable changes in trade or in national income? How might it affect national defence? Would it impede or facilitate adjustments in the balance of payments? Would it elicit retaliation by other countries? Other considerations would come to mind in considering specific policies at specific times for specific countries.

In the following discussion, the policies that will be considered are (a) those that would be administered independently by particular national governments, and (b) international policies. For both types, both the cushioning and the instability-reducing kinds of policies will be discussed.

## National policies

*Cushioning policies*

These policies are considered with reference to sharp changes in exports and in imports, as revealed by statistics. It is assumed that a government has decided that it has a problem and that it wants to do something about it.

Consider export instability first. A rapid upswing of exports is not likely to evoke demands for government action unless prices rise sharply and supplies cannot be increased rapidly. What sort of cushioning policies should a government be prepared to adopt in these circumstances? Obviously, to increase supplies and/or reduce demand would be in order. If the government has a stockpile of the scarce items, it could sell some. Subsidies could be provided if these would elicit increased supplies. The government could decrease its own demand for the commodities involved and mount an advertising campaign to try to persuade users of the commodities to reduce their use of them or to shift to more abundant substitutes. In extreme cases, rationing could be introduced. The government could ask other governments to take some measures to reduce imports. If the export increase put firms out of business or workers out of jobs, programmes aimed at redirecting productive resources could be instituted. Retraining and relocation may be required.

More likely to evoke calls for government aid are sharp declines in exports. The most direct cushioning measure that can be used here is for the government to step into the market to bolster the demand for the commodities experiencing reduced foreign demand. If the government is a regular user of the commodities, and if the commodities are storable, the main effect would be to redistribute government purchases through time. If the government is not a regular user, it then has to deal with the problem of surplus acquisitions. If the goods are storable, or stocks can be rotated, they could be held (in the fashion of a buffer stock or ever-normal-granary scheme) to meet a possible strong export demand in the future. Alternatively, the government could sell the goods at bargain prices, or give them away, to people who would not be regular demanders. Obviously, non-storable commodities and services present more difficult problems than storable ones do. Some governments have had considerable experience with programmes for the disposal of domestic surpluses.

Another policy that a government in this situation could adopt is that of trying to promote new markets, at home or abroad, for the export commodities involved in the decline. Alternatively, it could promote reductions in supply by helping producers shift to more advantageous industries, or it could maintain these firms on a stand-by basis if there is strong assurance of a resumption of export sales. Information, technical assistance, loan funds and perhaps outright subsidies would be involved here.

If the export decline is large enough and long enough significantly to reduce the availability of foreign exchange, the government could arrange foreign loans, investments or aid so as to allow imports into the country to be maintained. Measures of this sort verge on the international type, so we shall not discuss them further in this section.

It is evident from this discussion that, without resorting to direct controls on foreign trade or to international measures, a government can do many things to soften the impact of export instability. Actual situations always generate ingenious ideas about the measures that should be taken, but it is useful to have a kit of policies available so that the requisite policies do not have to be reinvented every time the need arises.

Let us now consider import instability. A sharp increase in imports may have severe effects on competing domestic producers, and further multiplier effects on the economy. What cushioning policies can the government pursue? On the demand side, the government can enter the market for the products of the competing domestic producers and cut down its demand, if any, for the foreign goods. This policy of acquisition raises all of the problems of subsequent disposal discussed in connection with export policies. The government can subsidise other buyers, of course, and take steps to promote the sale of domestic products.

On the supply side, the government can help the competing domestic industries to adjust so that they can compete more successfully with foreign suppliers. If there is little that can be done in this direction, the government can assist the transference of productive resources to other industries. If the increase in imports is large enough in relation to exports to cause a sizable deficit in the balance of payments, one or more of the various standard adjustment measures could be employed.

A sharp decrease in imports presents a different situation. If there are not ample quantities of domestic substitutes at prices only moderately higher than those of the imports, the government will be under pressure to do something. On the demand side, it may be able to reduce or postpone its own demand or to persuade domestic users of the imports to curtail their use of them or turn to domestic substitutes. If necessary, the commodities involved could be rationed. On the supply side, the government could offer for sale some of its reserve stocks, if it has any, and it could take measures designed to increase the supply, both at home and abroad. The domestic measures it could take would tend to involve technical assistance, financing and perhaps subsidies; but the measures it could take on its own with respect to increasing supplies from abroad would usually be of limited effectiveness. (Possible international measures are discussed in the next section.) Related balance-of-payments problems, if any, would have to be dealt with in the standard ways.

Obviously, the policies undertaken to deal with the shortage of imports would have to take into account the circumstances that led to it. If the shortage seriously crippled, or threatened to cripple, the national economy, there would be a tendency for strong measures to be taken to acquire more imports from abroad, increase domestic supplies, conserve available supplies, develop substitutes, and reorganise the economy to deal with the emergency. Governments usually face problems of this sort in times of war, but the embargo on oil exports by some oil producing countries in 1973 presented many oil importing countries with an unusual peacetime problem of this type.

In conclusion, it should be emphasised that there are several things a government can do on its own to reduce the undesirable effects of trade instability without introducing new measures to restrict or expand trade.

*Policies for reducing trade instability*

We now turn from cushioning policies to policies aimed at reducing trade instability, directly or indirectly. We are still concerned with what can be done by a government acting unilaterally.

It is in this context that consideration of the factors associated with trade instability (discussed in detail in Chapters 4 and 5) may have some utility for policy purposes. If the variables that our analysis has (at least tentatively) identified as causes of export or import instability could be manipulated by a government, presumably this would enable such instability to be reduced. This is an *indirect* approach to the reduction of instability. Examination of the variables that our simple and multiple regression analyses have shown to be the most closely associated with export and import instability reveals that nearly all of the variables concerned are related to foreign trade. The exceptions are those involving gross domestic product.

Let us now consider trying to use at least some of these variables to reduce export or import instability. If the line of causation is assumed to run from instability of gross domestic product to instability of import outlays, reduction of GDP instability by, say, 10 index points would reduce import instability by about four points, according to our statistical results. It is hard to imagine a government trying to reduce GDP instability just in order to reduce import instability, even if it were capable of doing so. Of course, if the government wanted to reduce GDP instability primarily for domestic reasons, the measures taken could help, incidentally, to reduce import instability.

Consider now the relation between export instability and GDP instability, which are positively correlated. The line of causation can plausibly be argued to run either way. As in the type of case just discussed, governments would be very unlikely to make efforts to reduce GDP instability just in order to reduce export instability; but, if there were good reasons for trying to reduce GDP instability, any associated reduction in export instability (estimated at about one-third) would be a desirable side-effect. For countries for which export fluctuations have an important bearing on fluctuations in GDP, this approach would make little sense.

The growth rate of exports is another variable positively related statistically with instability of export receipts and of import outlays. Should a government attempt to reduce the rate of growth of its exports by, say, 10 index points in order to reduce export instability by (according to our analysis) about seven points? To ask the question is to answer it, for most governments in most situations. Even if a government is administratively able to curtail the growth rate of export receipts (and, implicitly, the growth rate of import outlays), it is difficult to imagine that it will be willing to give up export growth for a partial stabilisation of export receipts.

According to our analysis, instability of export quantum is closely associated with instability of export receipts, and instability of import quantum is closely associated with instability of import outlays. (Price instability did not turn out be an important variable in either case.) If a government could decrease quantum instability by, say, 10 index points, it could, according to our results, reduce export receipts instability by about five points and import outlay instability by about seven points. Control of physical quantities is probably more feasible for imports than for exports, since imports usually depend mainly on the home country's willingness to buy, while exports depend mainly on foreign countries' willingness to buy. However, it would be simpler to deal with instability of export receipts and import outlays directly than to try to control them by controlling quantity instability.

This discussion should have demonstrated that the variables that are most closely associated with instability of export receipts and import outlays are not satisfactory control variables. However, one can say, on the basis of the statistical analysis, that a reduction in the instability of one or more of these variables is likely to spread to the others, so that a variety of measures tending in the same direction would be likely to have cumulative results.

Why, it may be asked, did we not choose for our analysis variables that have a greater potential as control variables? We tried about 50, but this approach obviously did not succeed. In some respects this is a disappointing conclusion, but it should not be entirely surprising. To discover the cause of a disease is not always, *ipso facto*, to discover its cure. And, of course, we did not really identify causes. In addition, the fact that the analysis revealed many factors at work tells governments, if they care to learn, that manipulation of one or a few variables is not likely to reduce trade instability very much. If this lesson is taken to heart, many costly errors of policy may be avoided.

If a government cannot reduce trade instability by policies that *indirectly* affect trade instability, what can it do unilaterally by means of *direct* measures? Let us first consider exports. A government's principal policy tools are subsidies, taxes, quantitative controls, price controls, and foreign-exchange controls. If a government wishes to curtail exports, it can tax them, reduce subsidies on them, apply restrictive quantitative controls, set lower official export prices, or (in an exchange-control system) reduce the amount of foreign exchange that exporters are permitted to retain. For all of these measures, strong administration is required. If the government wishes to expand exports, it can subsidise them, lower export taxes, raise official export prices, relax quantitative controls, or increase the amount of foreign exchange that exporters are permitted to keep. Obviously, a government's power to curtail exports is greater than its power to expand them, unless export demand is very strong. Moreover, the effects on export receipts will vary with the elasticity of demand, an unknown figure in practice. Essentially the same situation would prevail whether the government were dealing with private traders or itself conducting foreign trade. The reactions of other governments to these measures cannot be predicted, although the tendency to retaliate is strong.

Now consider direct measures with respect to imports. The policy tools are the same as with exports. If a government wishes to reduce outlays on imports, it can raise taxes, reduce subsidies, apply quantitative restrictions, raise prices (including foreign-exchange rates), or restrict allotments of foreign exchange. If it wishes to raise outlays, it can do the reverse. In both cases, the effect on outlays will depend on the domestic demand for imports. The government is more likely to be effective in reducing outlays (which it is better placed to do) than in increasing them, and must take into account the possibility of retaliation by foreign governments. As with exports, the situation is essentially the same whether the government deals with private traders or itself manages trade.

The seemingly unavoidable conclusion is that taxes, subsidies, quantitative controls and price fixing are not policy tools that can be counted on to reduce trade instability. Of the tools discussed in this section, tight foreign-exchange controls – very hard to enforce – seem to be the most effective for reducing instability, but their disadvantages are numerous. Measures designed to affect the flow of trade may be taken by governments for several different reasons; so it is very unlikely that they would be consistently applied to the object of achieving trade stabilisation, even if they were technically capable of attaining it.

## International policies

Because of the deficiencies of national policies for dealing with international trade instability, governments have naturally turned to (or, at least, have considered) international measures. We follow the same pattern as before in considering cushioning measures first and control measures second.

### *Cushioning policies*

For many years, the aspect of trade instability that has attracted the most international attention has been a sharp decline in export receipts. What can be done internationally to cushion the effects of such declines? The most obvious thing is to have a pool of money that governments can draw on, so that imports can, if desired, be maintained when exports decline sharply. The International Monetary Fund (IMF) provides such a pool – perhaps not as large as some governments would like, but still sizable and capable of expansion. There are, of course, other sources of foreign funds for countries temporarily short of foreign exchange. In addition to their international monetary reserves, governments usually have some credit lines available, access to some foreign aid, and some saleable assets. There is no reason why additional arrangements should not be made by groups of countries acting together.

The problems related to this type of international facility are of three sorts: (1) the funds might not be sufficient; (2) they might not be as readily available, on acceptable terms, as the demanders would like; and (3), while enabling countries to maintain their imports at higher levels than would otherwise be possible, this type of facility does nothing directly for the depressed export industries. It is conceivable, but unlikely, that the maintenance or restoration of imports by one country would help sustain the national incomes of other countries and thus indirectly help to maintain or restore the original country's exports.

Despite the problems related to it, however, the availability of foreign exchange in times of export decline is a major factor in policies for dealing with export and import instability.

What cushioning measures can be taken internationally when the exports of some countries *increase* sharply? If the countries experiencing the increases formerly drew foreign currencies from the IMF or other institutions, they could be called on to pay them back. If they are not so indebted, they could be asked to deposit with the IMF or other institutions some of the additional money earned from exports. In both cases, the tendency to expand imports in response to the sharp – and presumably temporary – expansion of exports would be damped and a contribution made to reducing international trade instability. It is unlikely, however, that such international measures for dealing with export expansion would be as successful as those for dealing with export contraction. Governments may be reluctant to repay loans ahead of time or to sterilise their foreign funds. But, even in the case of export contraction, there would be no guarantee that the funds drawn from the IMF or other institutions would be used to maintain imports.

Let us now turn to the policy possibilities from the point of view of import instability. If a country's imports decline sharply without there being a corresponding decline in its exports, there must be a decline in the exports of some other countries. Presumably the country reducing its imports would have no need to draw on international funds to maintain its desired imports, but the countries with reduced exports may need to do so.

On the other hand, if a country's imports rise sharply and its exports remain unchanged, the country may well demand funds from the IMF or other institutions. Should such agencies respond to this demand, even though doing so would increase trade instability? Obviously, if reduction of trade instability were the only policy goal of the agencies concerned, they would respond reluctantly, if at all. However, international institutions such as the IMF have other purposes as well, and thus would find it difficult to resist a demand of the type described. This illustrates how the availability of an international 'cushion' may increase rather than decrease trade instability.

### *Control measures for reducing trade instability*

Measures for reducing trade instability by international action tend to be direct control measures. In order to highlight their nature, we first examine an extreme form of international trade stabilisation policy. Suppose that all countries enter into a multi-commodity agreement covering all commodities (including services) for a considerable period of time, with prices and quantities all specified, and the inter-country flows of every commodity specified. This elaborate matrix could provide for bilateral balancing, for multilateral balancing, or for international capital movements to handle the net country export–import discrepancies, Such complete planning of international trade is, of course, politically impossible, administratively beyond realisation, and economically wasteful, but it could reduce international trade instability drastically – to zero in the limiting case.

Feasible policies for reducing trade instability by control measures are very far removed from this 'perfect' model. One approach is to reduce (even to one) the number of commodities involved in any agreement, but to include all countries. Another approach is to reduce (even to two) the number of countries, but to include all commodities. Between the extremes are many possible combinations, as illustrated by Figure 6.1.

Point 16 in Figure 6.1 represents the case of complete control of all international trade. Point 13 represents the case of a single-commodity agreement participated in by all countries. Point 4 represents the bilateral trading agreement covering all trade between two countries. Point 1 represents the case of a bilateral agreement covering only one commodity. All other points, representing many more possibilities than the points shown, are for the intermediate cases.

There are other possible variations. For example, either sellers or buyers, but not both, could be involved in an agreement. Also, the agreement could relate to prices, quantities or values. The duration of the agreements could vary.

Where, in this large field of possible international co-operation with respect to trade (in the present context, with respect to reducing trade instability), are the practical policies? Concluding an agreement should be

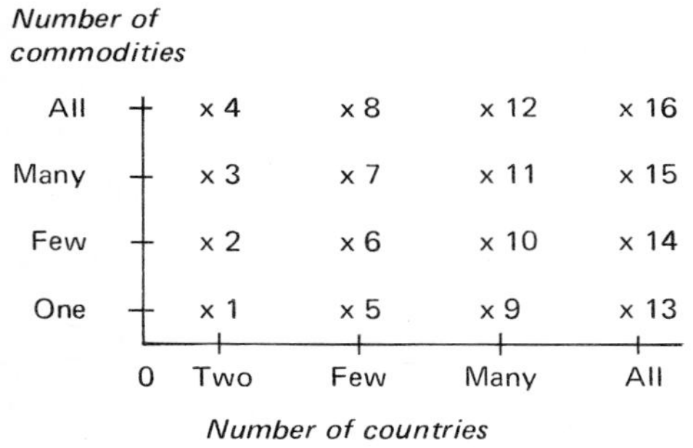


Figure 6.1 Classification of types of international trade control agreements, by number of commodities and number of countries

easier the fewer the countries and commodities involved. Hence, a bilateral agreement for one commodity should be the easiest of all to conclude, though it would make only an extremely small contribution to the reduction of international trade instability. Numerous such agreements could be operated, of course, but there would be little certainty about their overall effect. Next easiest, it would seem, would be the number of countries participating, particularly if only seller countries are involved. This is the international cartel approach. Stabilisation of export receipts has, however, been only one of several objects of agreements of this sort. Participation by importing countries would be likely to make reduction of trade instability relatively more important as a policy aim.

Bilateral agreements covering all, or nearly all, trade between two countries are fairly easy to arrange and have been used widely, particularly by the Communist countries. They tend to involve bilateral balancing and to take away some of the advantages of international trade, but they ease balance-of-payments problems and appear to help reduce trade instability. In Chapter 4 it was shown that export instability tended to be lower the higher the degree of bilateralism – although bilateralism does not necessarily involve formal bilateral trade-balancing agreements. The periodic renegotiation or break-up of such agreements could make for high trade instability, as has been exemplified by a number of cases in the last several decades; but there seems to be a tendency not to alter them drastically from year to year. In addition, as compared with normal multilateral trade, reshipments of goods acquired under bilateral agreements tend to reduce economic losses. Hence, we conclude that bilateral trade agreements involving many commodities do offer a workable technique for reducing trade instability, though their effectiveness in this respect depends on how highly the reduction of such instability ranks as a policy aim. As strong administrative control is required, agreements of this type are more likely to succeed where they are concluded between governments that are in sole charge of their countries' foreign trade.

It seems that the many possibilities involving more than two countries and more than one commodity – most of the situations depicted in figure 6.1 – offer few opportunities for practical policies. Historically, most multi-commodity multi-country proposals have focused on food, minerals and agricultural raw materials. Even if all international trade in primary commodities were covered by such agreements, only about one-fourth of international trade in goods and services would be covered. Hence, without going into the numerous problems connected with multi-commodity multi-country agreements, it can be stated that the problems of negotiating and administering them are too great for it to be possible to view them as practical means for reducing trade instability, even if they could be held to that objective.

### *Buffer stocks*

A type of international arrangement that has some cushioning and some control elements is the buffer-stock scheme. The essence of it is that an international authority in possession of money and a stock of a storable standard commodity buys the commodity when the price drops to a specified lower limit and sells it when the price rises to a specified higher limit. More than one commodity can be included in the scheme. If the specified price range is smaller than the price range that would apply otherwise, price fluctuations are reduced.

The buffer-stock concept is of the same family of economic arrangements as the gold standard, the bimetallic (or symetallic) monetary system, open-market operations of central banks, and some agricultural price-support and control schemes. World currency proposals calling for close links between money and a considerable number of storable primary commodities are also closely related.[3] There are also buffer-stock elements in the Food and Agriculture Organisation's *Proposals for a World Food Board* (1946) and the proposals of the United Nations Conference on Trade and Development (1974). Arrangements for buying up storable goods in times of relative surplus and selling them in times of relative shortage have been widely proposed. Various purposes are specified: preventing distress among producers; raising or lowering prices; maintaining an emergency stock of important commodities; providing commodities to preferred buyers at discount prices; and so on. Reducing the instability of export receipts or import outlays is just one of the objectives of most plans of this sort. Sometimes, as in the case of the International Tin Agreement, the characteristics of a buffer-stock scheme and commodity control agreement are combined.

The buffer-stock system has an appealing simplicity because it does not require the use of direct government controls. The administering authority simply buys, stores and sells in accordance with the established rules.

With regard to the problem of reducing the instability of countries' export receipts and import outlays, several points of difficulty arise. One is that storable, standard, widely-traded commodities constitute no more than 10–20 per cent of world trade. The percentage varies according to the extent to which commodities that are expensive to store are included. Under the most optimistic arrangements, only a modest fraction of world trade would be covered. A second point is that reduction of price instability does not necessarily reduce instability of export receipts or import outlays. For this to happen, price elasticities approximating unity are required, and there is little evidence of such elasticities. Our statistical exercises showed, for both imports and exports, a very weak relation between price and value instability. Third, the price ceilings and floors for particular commodities would have to be set at levels that would not involve vast accumulations or exhaustion of stocks. Sellers would want high floors; buyers would want low ceilings. Fourth, for the stocks to be acquired, a large amount of money – impossible to determine precisely, but running into many thousands of millions of dollars – would be required. However, under a multi-commodity scheme, there may be some saving if the prices of various commodities do not rise or fall more or less together. Fifth, expenses (interest, storage costs, general administration, and so on) would tend to be high, and there would be a risk of some loss of capital, since speculation in the commodity markets is an inherent part of such schemes. If the scheme provided for discount sales to preferred buyers, losses would be almost certain. Sixth, adjustment of floor and ceiling prices to avoid large accumulations or large sales would tend to defeat the price stabilisation objective. Seventh, the benefits would be very unequally shared among countries and it would be very difficult to assign costs even roughly according to benefits. Eighth, the scheme would have to be negotiated and kept in existence by governments having diverse and often conflicting interests. There are other problems, of course, but these are sufficient to dampen one's enthusiasm for the buffer-stock idea.

There has been hardly any experience with pure buffer stocks. The few attempts at keeping prices within a set range, or even one that is modified from time to time, have been accompanied by export controls and/or import commitments, often supplemented by attempts at production controls. If a buffer-stock scheme were established, it would probably tend to be modified in the direction of a commodity control agreement or cartel, since the influence of exporters would tend to be dominant. This influence would make for higher and higher floor prices, which would stimulate production, accumulation of stocks, increased investment and, eventually, trade and production controls, if not collapse of the scheme. Excess production capacity would tempt exporters to drop out of the scheme and benefit from larger exports even at slightly lower prices. If a commodity control agreement is desired, it is better to set it up as precisely that than to drift into it through the weakening of a buffer-stock system. It is not hard to see how the objective of reducing the instability of export receipts and import outlays could be subordinated to other aims.

*Other international measures*

Would international trade be more stable for most countries if tariffs and other trade restrictions were lowered, or raised? Our attempt to get a statistical answer to this question failed, because data on tariff levels were not available for enough countries; resort must therefore be had to general economic reasoning. Lower trade restrictions would increase the opportunities for advantageous trade (except in a few unlikely circumstances); so, if the elasticities of demand and supply are relatively high, there would be enlarged trade. Wider markets and a larger volume of trade over a number of years would seem to make for less instability rather than more. Governments are not likely to negotiate reductions in trade barriers primarily to reduce trade instability, but the results should be favourable. Looked at the other way, additional trade barriers, along with the retaliations they usually evoke, are almost certain to increase trade instability. Of course, barriers high enough to eliminate trade would eliminate the trade instability!

International monetary and financial arrangements that facilitate trade and long-term capital movements should, in general, contribute to international trade stability. Large and frequent movements of short-term capital tend, however, to disturb trade, because governments tend to impose controls to protect their balances of payments and internal monetary policies. The International Monetary Fund and the International Bank for Reconstruction and Development, along with other financial organisations operating internationally, are the principal instruments available in this field. The main thing they can do is to take into account the desirability of reducing trade instability.

Co-ordination of national monetary and fiscal policies (in so far as this is possible) can help maintain high levels of economic activity in different countries and thus contribute to the maintenance of moderately stable international trade. Fortunately, there are other and stronger reasons for pursuing policies to promote domestic economic stability and growth; and, with these in mind, the countries carrying about two-thirds of world trade have consultation procedures within the framework of the Organisation for Economic Co-operation and Development. There are also other international forums, in many of which most countries can participate.

## Information on trade instability

One of the hindrances to appropriate policies in this field has been the lack of systematically organised information on the instability of exports and imports. In order that problems of trade instability may be examined promptly against a background of facts, it would be very useful if a United Nations agency – one thinks of the United Nations Conference on Trade and Development, with headquarters at Geneva, Switzerland – would collect and publish at regular intervals instability indexes for several international-trade time series. The most obvious candidates for inclusion would be instability indexes for export receipts and import outlays, by country; but it would also be desirable to have instability indexes for subdividions of these aggregates, by commodity groups and by direction of trade. Price and quantity instability indexes would also be very useful. The underlying data could be grouped in various ways, according to interest and experience. It would be very much cheaper for the countries of the world to have this task performed by a United Nations agency than to do it for themselves.

Owing to its simplicity and the fact that it also provides growth rates, measure of instability used in this study – the average of absolute percentage deviations from the log-linear trend line – would be an appropriate one to use, though any standard measure would do. If the indexes were published annually, it would perhaps prove sensible to base the calculations on time series for moving 10-year periods. Past 10-year periods, perhaps starting with 1948, would provide a basis for comparisons through time and by country. In cases where detailed breakdowns are desired, the agency responsible could also prepare special analyses for individual countries or groups of countries.

## General conclusions on policy

The problem of trade instability is not going to disappear and will continue to affect countries at different times and in different ways. Because of this, it is important that policies for dealing with it should be those that can be applied by governments when and where the problem becomes important.

National measures can usually be applied more promptly and can be more closely adapted to national economic conditions than international measures can. However, international measures can bring more resources to bear on the problem, and can deal with aspects of the problem that cannot be dealt with by a national government acting alone.

Cushioning measures, national and international, are generally more practical, because they do not involve direct controls on trade. Financial assistance, provided by a national government or by an international agency such as the International Monetary Fund, is the principal cushioning tool.

Attempts to reduce trade instability by direct or indirect control measures have several disadvantages: they are likely to reduce the gains from trade; they might slow down the rate of economic growth; they are difficult to enforce; they tend to be expensive; and they tend to break down. Of the trade control measures, bilateral balancing is the one most likely to bring reduced trade instability, even though it may well violate the principle of comparative advantage. It may, however, be doubted whether the gains in reduced instability would be worth the losses from less advantageous trade patterns. Commodity agreements could be used for a few commodities, but the negotiation and enforcement of them are notoriously difficult. Moreover, such agreements usually emphasise more goals than just that of reducing instability of export receipts and import outlays. Buffer-stock schemes are not very promising as an effective means for reducing trade instability, but they could be tried for a few commodities.

Evidently the world is going to have to live with a considerable amount of trade instability, even if some of the policies suggested here are successfully applied. However, if, public knowledge of the details of international trade instability is increased, through information provided on a systematic and continuing basis by a United Nations agency, better national and international policies in this field may well be the result.

## Notes

[1] Used by the author in *International Economic Instability* (1962). That measure tended to be about 50 per cent higher than the one used here.

[2] *International Economic Instability*, p. 129. Only 13 variables were tested for import instability for the period 1946–58.

[3] *International Commodity Stockpiling* (M. K. Bennett et al., Stanford University Press, 1949) is an analysis of the proposals of Benjamin Graham, probably the most widely-known advocate of a commodity reserve currency. Many others have also written on the subject. See, for example, Albert G. Hart, Nicholas Kaldor, and Jan Tinbergen, *The Case for an International Commodity Reserve Currency*, Contributed Paper no. 7, United Nations Conference on Trade and Development, 1964.

# Appendix

## Table A.1

### Definitions and sources of variables

*General note.* The variables used in this study are divided into three broad categories: variables numbered 100–199 are instability indexes; variables numbered 200–299 are percentage growth rates per year; variables numbered in the 300s are all others. The definition of each variable and the source(s) of data for it are given below. Since the underlying data for the 200-series variables are the same as for the corresponding 100-series variables, definitions and sources for the former are not given, except for variable 222.

*Sources*

International Monetary Fund: *Balance of Payments Yearbook (BPY)*, vols 12–24, 1959–71; *Direction of Trade Annual (DT)*, 1963–67; *International Financial Statistics (IFS)*, *Supplement*, 1972, and various monthly issues.

United Nations: *Demographic Yearbook (DY)*, 1967; *Monthly Bulletin of Statistics (MBS)*, various issues; *Statistical Yearbook (SY)*, 1969; *Yearbook of International Trade Statistics (YITS)*, 1967–71; *Yearbook of National Accounts Statistics (YNAS)*, 1968 and 1972.

| *Variable number* | *Description and source* |
|---|---|
| 100 | Instability index of receipts from exports, 1959–71. Exports include exports of services as well as of goods for countries for which data were available; otherwise, they are restricted to exports of goods only. Sources: *BPY*, vols 12–24, 1959–71; *IFS Supplement*, 1972, and various monthly issues; *YITS*, 1967 and 1971 (historical series). |
| 101 | Instability index of receipts from exports of goods. Sources: see variable 100. |
| 102 | Instability index of receipts from exports of services. The relevant data were available for 84 out of 109 countries. Source: *BPY*, vols 12–24, 1959–71. |
| 103 | Instability index of receipts from exports of goods and services. Source: see variable 102. |
| 104 | Instability index of outlays on imports of goods, 1959–71. Sources: *BPY*, vols 12–24, 1959–71; *IFS Supplement*, 1972 and various monthly issues; *YITS*, 1967 and 1971 (historical series). |
| 105 | Instability index of outlays on import of services. Source: see variable 102. |
| 106 | Instability index of outlays on imports of goods and services. Source: see variable 102. |
| 107 | Instability index of export price index ($P_x$; calculated as described in the |

| *Variable number* | *Description and source* |
|---|---|
| | introduction to any recent issue of *YITS*). Sources: *IFS Supplement*, 1972, country tables; *YITS*, 1967 and 1971 (historical series). |
| 108 | Instability index of export quantum index ($Q_x$; calculated as described in the introduction to any recent issue of *YITS*). Sources: see variable 107. |
| 109 | Instability index of import price index ($P_m$; calculated as described in the introduction to any recent issue of *YITS*). Sources: *IFS Supplement*, 1972, country tables; *YITS*, 1967 and 1971 (historical series). |
| 110 | Instability index of import quantum index ($Q_m$; calculated as described in the introduction to any recent issue of *YITS*). Sources: see variable 109. |
| 111 | Instability index of price terms of trade ($P_x/P_m$). |
| 112 | Instability index of quantum terms of trade ($Q_m/Q_x$). |
| 113 | Instability index of gross domestic product (GDP) in current prices. For this variable and all others involving GDP, gross national product at factor cost was used if GDP was not available. For Soviet Area countries, net material product (NMP) was used. Sources: *YNAS*, 1968 and 1972; *MBS*, various issues; *IFS Supplement*, 1972. |
| 114 | Instability index of GDP in constant prices. For countries for which only GDP in current prices was available, but for which the consumer price index (CPI) was available, GDP in current prices was deflated by the CPI. Sources: *YNAS*, 1968 and 1972; *MBS*, various issues; *IFS Supplement*, 1972 and various monthly issues of *IFS* (country tables); *SY*, 1969. |
| 115 | Instability index of outlays on imports, 1959–71. Imports include imports of services as well as of goods for countries for which data were available; otherwise, they are restricted to imports of goods only. Sources: see variable 100. |
| 117 | Instability index of foreign-trade percentage. Foreign trade percentage = 100 (exports + imports)/GDP. Goods and services were used when available; otherwise, goods only. Sources: for exports and imports, see variable 100; for GDP, see variable 113. |
| 118 | Instability index of GDP per capita in constant prices. Sources: for 'real' GDP, see variable 114; for population, *DY*, 1967. See also *IFS Supplement*, 1972. |
| 120 | Instability index of monetary reserves as a percentage of imports. Imports include goods and services where statistics for the latter were available; otherwise, goods only. Reserves are gold and foreign-exchange holdings. Sources: for monetary reserves, *IFS Supplement*, 1972 (world table); for imports, see variable 115. |
| 121 | Instability of consumer price index. Sources: *IFS Supplement*, 1972; *IFS*, various monthly issues (country tables); *SY*, 1969. |
| 122 | Instability index of net balance on goods and services account, or instability of goods balance when services not available. Since the regular instability index cannot be computed when negative numbers are involved, $1 - r^2$ was used as a measure of instability. The coefficient of correlation ($r$) is for the net balance ($y$) on time ($x$). Sources: see variables 100 and 115. |

| *Variable number* | *Description and source* |
|---|---|
| 200 | Average annual growth rate of receipts from exports (of goods and services where data available; otherwise, of goods only). |
| 201 | Average annual growth rate of receipts from exports of goods. |
| 202 | Average annual growth rate of receipts from exports of services. |
| 203 | Average annual growth rate of receipts from exports of goods and services. |
| 204 | Average annual growth rate of outlays on imports of goods. |
| 205 | Average annual growth rate of outlays on imports of services. |
| 206 | Average annual growth rate of outlays on imports of goods and services. |
| 207 | Average annual growth rate of export price index ($P_x$). |
| 208 | Average annual growth rate of export quantum index ($Q_x$). |
| 209 | Average annual growth rate of import price index ($P_m$). |
| 210 | Average annual growth rate of import quantum index ($Q_m$). |
| 211 | Average annual growth rate of price terms of trade ($P_x/P_m$). |
| 212 | Average annual growth rate of quantum terms of trade ($Q_m/Q_x$). |
| 213 | Average annual growth rate of GDP in current prices. |
| 214 | Average annual growth rate of GDP in constant prices. |
| 215 | Average annual growth rate of outlays on imports (of goods and services where data available; otherwise, of goods only). |
| 217 | Average annual growth rate of foreign-trade percentage. |
| 218 | Average annual growth rate of GDP per capita in constant prices. |
| 220 | Average annual growth rate of monetary reserves as a percentage of annual imports. |
| 221 | Average annual growth rate of consumer price index. |
| 222 | Average annual growth rate – in money, not percentage – of net balance on goods and services account (or goods only when data for services not available). |
| 300 | Average annual value of exports of goods and (where data available) services, 1959–71. Sources: *BPY*, vols 12–24, 1959–71; *IFS Supplement*, 1972; *YITS*, 1967 and 1971. |
| 301 | Average annual value of exports of goods, 1959–71. Sources: see variable 300. |
| 302 | Average annual value of exports of services, 1959–71. Source: *BPY*, vols 12–24, 1959–71. |
| 303 | Average annual value of exports of goods and services, 1959–71. Source: see variable 302. |
| 304 | Average annual value of imports of goods, 1959–71. Sources: *BPY*, vols 12–24, 1959–71; *IFS Supplement*, 1972 (country tables); *YITS*, 1967 and 1971 (historical series). |
| 305 | Average annual value of imports of services, 1959–71. Source: *BPY*, vols 12–24, 1959–71. |
| 306 | Average annual value of imports of goods and services, 1959–71. Source: see variable 305. |
| 307 | Exports of goods as a percentage of exports of goods and services, 1959–71 (average). Source: *BPY*, vols 12–24, 1959–71. |

| *Variable number* | *Description and source* |
|---|---|
| 308 | Exports of services as a percentage of goods and services, 1959–71 (average). Source: see variable 307. |
| 310 | Hirschman concentration index for exports of goods by SITC classes, average 1964–67. Source: *YITS*, 1971. For Hirschman index, see p. 91. |
| 315 | Average annual value of imports of goods and (where data available) services, 1959–71. Sources: see variable 304. |
| 316 | Hirschman concentration index for exports of goods by country of destination, average 1963–67. Source: *DT*, 1963–67. |
| 320 | Percentage of goods exported to the US, average 1963–67. Source: *DT*, 1963–67. |
| 321 | Percentage of exports of goods to the EEC, average 1963–67. Source; *DT*, 1963–67. |
| 325 | Percentage of exports of goods in primary goods (SITC classes 0, 1, 2, 3, 4), average 1964–67. Source: *YITS*, 1967. |
| 330 | Imports of goods as a percentage of imports of goods and services, average 1959–71. Source: *BPY*, vols 12–24, 1959–71. |
| 331 | Imports of services as a percentage of imports of goods and services, average 1959–71. Sources: see variable 330. |
| 345 | Average net balance on goods and (where data available) services account 1959–71. Sources: see variables 100 and 115. |
| 346 | Average foreign-trade percentage, 1959–71. See variable 117 for definition and sources. |
| 347 | Average net balance as a percentage of average imports of goods and (where data available) services, 1959–71. Sources: see variables 100 and 115. |
| 348 | Average real GDP in US dollars, 1964–66. Sources: *YNAS*, 1968, 1972; *MPS*, various issues; *IFS Supplement*, 1972. Exchange rates used in converting to dollars are taken from *IFS Supplement*, 1972; *BPY*, various issues; *YITS*, 1967; *MBS*, various issues. |
| 349 | Average real GDP per capita in US dollars, 1964–66. Sources: for GDP and exchange rates, see variable 348; for population, *IFS Supplement*, 1972. |
| 350 | Population, average 1964–67. Sources: *DY*, 1967; *IFS Supplement*, 1972. |
| 352 | Bilateralism index, average 1963–67. For definition, see p. 91. Source: *DT*, 1963–67. |
| 361 | Average monetary reserves as percentage of average imports of goods and (where data available) services, 1959–71. Sources: for monetary reserves, see variable 120; for imports, see variable 115. |
| 364 | Percentage of GDP from agriculture, 1965. Sources: *SY*, 1969; *YNAS*, 1972. |
| 365 | Energy consumption per capita (in kilowatt hours), 1965. Source: *SY*, 1969. |

## Table A.2

Values of variables used in analysing instability of exports and imports, for 109 countries, 1959–71 (variables as described in Table A.1; countries listed by region and ranked, in ascending order, as shown in parentheses)

(a) Variables 100–118

| | Country, etc. | 100 | 101 | 102 | 103 | 104 | 105 | 106 | 107 | 108 | 109 | 110 | 111 | 112 | 113 | 114 | 115 | 117 | 118 | |
|---|---|---|---|---|---|---|---|---|---|---|---|---|---|---|---|---|---|---|---|---|
| 1 | United States | 1.7 | 2.7 | 9.4 | 1.7 | 7.1 | 5.5 | 6.5 | 2.2 | 2.3 | 3.2 | 5.4 | 1.3 | 6.4 | 1.7 | 2.0 | 6.5 | 1.7 | 1.9 | 1 |
| | | (1) | (8) | (49) | (1) | (52) | (25) | (36) | (14) | (5) | (41) | (27) | (12) | (25) | (15) | (45) | (45) | (8) | (43) | |
| 2 | United Kingdom | 3.4 | 3.3 | 3.7 | 3.4 | 2.5 | 3.2 | 2.6 | 3.1 | 3.1 | 3.5 | 2.2 | 1.6 | 3.0 | 3.2 | 1.3 | 2.6 | 4.3 | 0.9 | 2 |
| | | (22) | (18) | (7) | (17) | (3) | (4) | (2) | (26) | (21) | (46) | (2) | (15) | (6) | (50) | (22) | (3) | (39) | (7) | |
| 3 | Austria | 4.2 | 6.6 | 5.5 | 4.2 | 5.4 | 5.1 | 4.8 | 2.7 | 4.1 | 3.6 | 2.6 | 1.9 | 4.3 | 2.1 | 1.2 | 4.8 | 3.3 | 1.4 | 3 |
| | | (35) | (56) | (20) | (28) | (30) | (17) | (23) | (21) | (29) | (48) | (6) | (22) | (13) | (33) | (15) | (28) | (30) | (27) | |
| 4 | Belgium–Luxembourg | 3.8 | 3.8 | 6.3 | 3.8 | 2.7 | 5.3 | 3.0 | 1.6 | 3.0 | 1.5 | 2.3 | 1.2 | 1.0 | 2.1 | 1.7 | 3.0 | 2.4 | 1.0 | 4 |
| | | (29) | (27) | (26) | (23) | (4) | (23) | (5) | (8) | (18) | (10) | (3) | (9) | (1) | (32) | (37) | (6) | (19) | (9) | |
| 5 | Denmark | 2.9 | 3.1 | 3.4 | 2.9 | 3.2 | 3.4 | 2.8 | 2.3 | 1.5 | 2.7 | 3.5 | 1.8 | 3.0 | 1.7 | 1.3 | 2.8 | 2.0 | 1.4 | 5 |
| | | (15) | (14) | (5) | (11) | (5) | (7) | (3) | (16) | (2) | (37) | (10) | (19) | (7) | (13) | (19) | (4) | (12) | (26) | |
| 6 | France | 3.0 | 3.3 | 6.7 | 3.0 | 4.2 | 6.1 | 3.2 | 3.0 | 4.4 | 3.3 | 7.1 | 0.6 | 10.4 | 1.8 | 0.8 | 3.2 | 2.7 | 0.7 | 6 |
| | | (16) | (16) | (31) | (13) | (18) | (31) | (6) | (25) | (32) | (43) | (40) | (2) | (49) | (21) | (4) | (8) | (22) | (6) | |
| 7 | West Germany | 4.5 | 4.2 | 6.3 | 4.5 | 5.0 | 5.6 | 4.5 | 0.9 | 2.9 | 1.5 | 3.7 | 1.5 | 5.1 | 4.7 | 1.6 | 4.5 | 2.4 | 1.6 | 7 |
| | | (38) | (35) | (27) | (31) | (22) | (26) | (22) | (1) | (17) | (9) | (12) | (14) | (18) | (66) | (31) | (26) | (18) | (35) | |
| 8 | Italy | 2.3 | 2.5 | 2.1 | 2.3 | 7.4 | 3.9 | 6.3 | 2.3 | 3.7 | 2.4 | 7.1 | 2.1 | 7.1 | 1.9 | 1.7 | 6.3 | 3.1 | 1.3 | 8 |
| | | (4) | (4) | (1) | (4) | (56) | (13) | (33) | (17) | (26) | (34) | (39) | (25) | (27) | (23) | (36) | (44) | (26) | (22) | |
| 9 | Netherlands | 4.7 | 5.2 | 3.6 | 4.7 | 4.3 | 2.3 | 3.8 | 1.6 | 5.1 | 2.2 | 2.9 | 1.1 | 3.5 | 1.9 | 1.3 | 3.8 | 2.7 | 1.1 | 9 |
| | | (39) | (40) | (6) | (32) | (19) | (2) | (15) | (9) | (44) | (29) | (8) | (7) | (9) | (22) | (20) | (18) | (23) | (11) | |
| 10 | Norway | 2.4 | 2.6 | 2.9 | 2.4 | 3.6 | 3.7 | 3.6 | 2.7 | 2.4 | 2.3 | 2.6 | 1.1 | 3.4 | 2.0 | 0.6 | 3.6 | 1.3 | 0.7 | 10 |
| | | (6) | (7) | (3) | (5) | (11) | (10) | (13) | (20) | (6) | (32) | (5) | (6) | (8) | (30) | (2) | (16) | (3) | (5) | |

*Table A.2a cont.*

| | Country, etc. | 100 | 101 | 102 | 103 | 104 | 105 | 106 | 107 | 108 | 109 | 110 | 111 | 112 | 113 | 114 | 115 | 117 | 118 | |
|---|---|---|---|---|---|---|---|---|---|---|---|---|---|---|---|---|---|---|---|---|
| 11 | Sweden | 3.2 | 3.2 | 4.5 | 3.2 | 3.3 | 6.5 | 3.4 | 2.5 | 1.7 | 1.8 | 4.0 | 1.1 | 3.0 | 1.1 | 1.3 | 3.4 | 3.3 | 1.1 | 11 |
| | | (19) | (15) | (9) | (15) | (8) | (35) | (10) | (18) | (4) | (19) | (16) | (8) | (5) | (5) | (18) | (13) | (31) | (13) | |
| 12 | Switzerland | 2.6 | 2.8 | 2.5 | 2.6 | 6.8 | 12.2 | 7.3 | 1.0 | 2.8 | 1.4 | 4.8 | 1.2 | 5.5 | 2.8 | 1.8 | 7.3 | 3.5 | 1.3 | 12 |
| | | (11) | (11) | (2) | (9) | (46) | (63) | (51) | (3) | (15) | (8) | (20) | (10) | (20) | (45) | (42) | (63) | (33) | (23) | |
| 13 | Canada | 5.4 | 5.7 | 6.2 | 5.4 | 6.7 | 7.5 | 6.2 | 1.1 | 2.7 | 1.4 | 5.8 | 2.1 | 4.2 | 5.1 | 1.7 | 6.2 | 1.3 | 1.8 | 13 |
| | | (44) | (46) | (25) | (36) | (44) | (42) | (32) | (5) | (13) | (7) | (32) | (23) | (12) | (69) | (34) | (43) | (4) | (38) | |
| 14 | Japan | 5.5 | 5.3 | 9.1 | 5.5 | 5.0 | 2.7 | 4.2 | 3.7 | 3.7 | 1.3 | 4.6 | 3.6 | 8.1 | 2.4 | 2.4 | 4.2 | 3.1 | 2.3 | 14 |
| | | (46) | (42) | (46) | (38) | (23) | (3) | (19) | (34) | (27) | (6) | (19) | (29) | (34) | (37) | (57) | (23) | (28) | (52) | |
| 15 | Finland | 3.9 | 4.2 | 5.4 | 3.9 | 7.5 | 6.8 | 7.3 | 5.4 | 4.1 | 5.9 | 5.8 | 1.6 | 5.4 | 4.6 | 2.0 | 7.3 | 5.8 | 2.0 | 15 |
| | | (31) | (34) | (19) | (24) | (59) | (37) | (50) | (54) | (30) | (57) | (33) | (16) | (19) | (64) | (43) | (62) | (59) | (46) | |
| 16 | Greece | 2.8 | 4.0 | 4.6 | 2.8 | 4.2 | 9.6 | 3.4 | 3.4 | 5.2 | 1.7 | 4.0 | 3.9 | 8.8 | 1.4 | 1.2 | 3.4 | 1.8 | 1.7 | 16 |
| | | (13) | (29) | (11) | (10) | (17) | (53) | (11) | (30) | (46) | (17) | (15) | (32) | (36) | (7) | (13) | (14) | (10) | (37) | |
| 17 | Iceland | 10.0 | 14.3 | 6.6 | 10.0 | 12.2 | 10.9 | 11.5 | 8.7 | 10.4 | 5.9 | 9.1 | 5.9 | 9.7 | 18.0 | 5.5 | 11.5 | 12.2 | 5.2 | 17 |
| | | (84) | (96) | (30) | (71) | (90) | (59) | (71) | (71) | (71) | (58) | (53) | (48) | (46) | (93) | (82) | (89) | (89) | (83) | |
| 18 | Ireland | 3.3 | 3.7 | 4.7 | 3.3 | 3.2 | 7.0 | 3.3 | 3.6 | 3.4 | 3.1 | 2.8 | 1.3 | 4.2 | 2.9 | 1.7 | 3.3 | 2.7 | 1.8 | 18 |
| | | (20) | (25) | (13) | (16) | (6) | (38) | (7) | (33) | (23) | (40) | (7) | (11) | (11) | (47) | (38) | (10) | (24) | (39) | |
| 19 | Portugal | 5.7 | 3.4 | 17.8 | 5.7 | 3.9 | 12.2 | 3.5 | 2.7 | 3.0 | 4.4 | 5.1 | 6.6 | 7.7 | 2.6 | 0.8 | 3.5 | 5.7 | 0.6 | 19 |
| | | (48) | (23) | (67) | (40) | (14) | (64) | (12) | (19) | (19) | (52) | (24) | (53) | (32) | (40) | (5) | (15) | (58) | (4) | |
| 20 | Spain | 5.9 | 7.9 | 13.5 | 5.9 | 13.9 | 5.9 | 12.3 | 2.7 | 11.2 | 4.0 | 15.0 | 4.4 | 25.8 | 5.0 | 1.8 | 12.3 | 3.8 | 2.5 | 20 |
| | | (50) | (64) | (59) | (42) | (94) | (30) | (75) | (22) | (75) | (51) | (62) | (38) | (63) | (68) | (40) | (94) | (37) | (61) | |
| 21 | Turkey | 6.3 | 4.1 | 12.6 | 6.3 | 8.6 | 16.0 | 7.1 | 4.9 | | 5.5 | | 8.9 | | 2.6 | 1.5 | 7.1 | 4.7 | 2.1 | 21 |
| | | (59) | (31) | (58) | (52) | (68) | (73) | (48) | (49) | | (55) | | (63) | | (42) | (29) | (60) | (44) | (50) | |
| 22 | Yugoslavia | 3.8 | 4.6 | 4.6 | 3.8 | 7.0 | 6.1 | 6.5 | 2.2 | 4.6 | 1.8 | 5.3 | 0.9 | 7.5 | 7.4 | 2.4 | 6.5 | 7.1 | 2.3 | 22 |
| | | (30) | (36) | (12) | (22) | (48) | (32) | (37) | (15) | (37) | (21) | (26) | (5) | (30) | (80) | (56) | (48) | (76) | (56) | |
| 23 | Australia | 3.0 | 3.3 | 5.1 | 3.0 | 6.2 | 5.3 | 5.4 | 3.8 | 4.4 | 1.5 | 5.2 | 4.5 | 7.3 | 2.6 | 1.4 | 5.4 | 3.4 | 1.4 | 23 |
| | | (17) | (17) | (15) | (12) | (37) | (22) | (25) | (37) | (33) | (11) | (25) | (39) | (29) | (39) | (23) | (33) | (32) | (28) | |

| | | | | | | | | | | | | | | | | | | | | |
|---|---|---|---|---|---|---|---|---|---|---|---|---|---|---|---|---|---|---|---|---|
| 24 | New Zealand | 5.5 (45) | 5.7 (47) | 8.8 (44) | 5.5 (37) | 9.6 (72) | 5.1 (18) | 7.9 (56) | 4.4 (44) | 3.6 (25) | 6.0 (59) | 7.9 (47) | 6.6 (54) | 10.5 (51) | 5.6 (71) | 1.8 (41) | 7.9 (70) | 3.2 (29) | 1.8 (40) | 24 |
| 25 | South Africa | 2.4 (7) | 2.2 (1) | 10.4 (52) | 2.4 (7) | 7.5 (58) | 6.4 (34) | 5.9 (29) | 1.7 (10) | 4.6 (36) | 1.9 (24) | 6.5 (36) | 2.1 (24) | 9.4 (43) | 1.9 (25) | 1.3 (21) | 5.9 (39) | 1.5 (6) | 1.4 (25) | 25 |
| 26 | Argentina | 4.2 (36) | 6.5 (55) | 22.8 (76) | 4.2 (29) | 15.4 (97) | 15.7 (70) | 13.1 (77) | 4.1 (39) | 7.0 (55) | 1.5 (14) | 11.8 (58) | 4.2 (36) | 15.0 (60) | 9.9 (87) | 2.8 (62) | 13.1 (96) | 9.0 (85) | 2.4 (60) | 26 |
| 27 | Bolivia | 8.4 (78) | 9.3 (80) | 25.1 (80) | 8.4 (68) | 6.7 (45) | 10.5 (58) | 5.7 (28) | 8.2 (70) | 4.1 (31) | | | | | 1.5 (11) | 1.5 (26) | 5.7 (38) | 6.2 (64) | 1.1 (14) | 27 |
| 28 | Brazil | 11.2 (89) | 9.3 (81) | 30.0 (82) | 11.2 (74) | 17.1 (103) | 18.5 (78) | 16.8 (81) | 4.8 (48) | 4.7 (38) | 2.2 (28) | 9.9 (55) | 6.2 (51) | 9.9 (47) | 10.8 (89) | 4.6 (77) | 16.8 (102) | 13.3 (92) | 2.5 (63) | 28 |
| 29 | Chile | 6.7 (67) | 8.1 (68) | 10.6 (54) | 6.7 (58) | 6.6 (42) | 9.4 (51) | 6.7 (41) | 6.2 (62) | 4.9 (41) | 3.2 (42) | 7.7 (45) | 6.7 (55) | 10.4 (50) | 7.2 (79) | 1.5 (25) | 6.7 (52) | 7.1 (75) | 1.2 (19) | 29 |
| 30 | Colombia | 7.1 (69) | 7.9 (66) | 7.4 (37) | 7.1 (60) | 10.5 (80) | 5.0 (15) | 8.1 (57) | 5.9 (59) | 2.8 (16) | 2.4 (33) | 9.9 (56) | 6.9 (56) | 12.0 (55) | 6.8 (77) | 0.9 (6) | 8.1 (72) | 6.5 (67) | 1.1 (15) | 30 |
| 31 | Costa Rica | 5.6 (47) | 5.4 (43) | 7.2 (34) | 5.6 (39) | 8.0 (65) | 5.2 (20) | 6.7 (38) | 4.1 (38) | 9.4 (68) | 2.2 (30) | 6.4 (35) | 5.4 (45) | 9.0 (39) | 6.1 (74) | | 6.7 (49) | 2.7 (21) | | 31 |
| 32 | Dominican Rep. | 11.4 (91) | 11.8 (90) | 13.5 (60) | 11.4 (75) | 16.8 (101) | 13.7 (68) | 15.0 (79) | 5.2 (53) | 11.8 (77) | | | | | 6.3 (75) | 3.5 (68) | 15.0 (99) | 6.5 (70) | 3.6 (76) | 32 |
| 33 | Ecuador | 3.9 (32) | 4.6 (37) | 10.6 (53) | 3.9 (25) | 6.5 (41) | 12.2 (65) | 8.5 (59) | 5.4 (55) | 5.8 (47) | | | | | 6.4 (76) | 2.2 (51) | 8.5 (74) | 6.1 (62) | 2.3 (55) | 33 |
| 34 | El Salvador | 6.6 (65) | 6.8 (59) | 9.1 (47) | 6.6 (55) | 10.8 (83) | 8.7 (49) | 9.0 (60) | 6.2 (63) | 9.7 (69) | 2.4 (35) | 8.6 (49) | 6.4 (52) | 13.3 (58) | 1.9 (26) | 2.1 (50) | 9.0 (75) | 6.0 (61) | 2.0 (47) | 34 |
| 35 | Guatemala | 6.6 (64) | 5.9 (50) | 11.7 (56) | 6.6 (56) | 5.9 (33) | 9.4 (50) | 6.3 (34) | | | 3.0 (50) | | | | 2.4 (38) | 1.0 (8) | 6.3 (45) | 6.5 (68) | 1.0 (10) | 35 |
| 36 | Haiti | 10.1 (85) | 11.3 (89) | 25.9 (81) | 10.1 (72) | 10.7 (81) | 17.4 (77) | 14.5 (78) | 5.5 (56) | 7.6 (62) | | | | | | | 14.5 (97) | | 1.6 (34) | 36 |
| 37 | Honduras | 8.9 (80) | 8.9 (76) | 14.0 (62) | 8.9 (69) | 6.8 (47) | 23.6 (81) | 9.0 (61) | 2.1 (13) | 10.5 (72) | 3.5 (47) | 5.6 (28) | 4.6 (40) | 9.3 (40) | 1.8 (20) | 2.2 (53) | 9.0 (76) | 7.0 (74) | 2.0 (48) | 37 |
| 38 | Mexico | 2.4 (8) | 3.8 (26) | 5.8 (21) | 2.4 (6) | 4.0 (15) | 3.4 (6) | 3.4 (8) | | | | | | | 1.4 (8) | 4.5 (76) | 3.4 (11) | 1.8 (11) | 1.5 (30) | 38 |

*Table A.2a cont.*

| | Country, etc. | 100 | 101 | 102 | 103 | 104 | 105 | 106 | 107 | 108 | 109 | 110 | 111 | 112 | 113 | 114 | 115 | 117 | 118 | |
|---|---|---|---|---|---|---|---|---|---|---|---|---|---|---|---|---|---|---|---|---|
| 39 | Nicaragua | 10.2 | 10.7 | 7.8 | 10.2 | 11.5 | 10.2 | 10.7 | 3.4 | 12.7 | 2.7 | 11.8 | 4.8 | 7.6 | 1.8 | 2.8 | 10.7 | 8.9 | 3.1 | 39 |
| | | (86) | (86) | (39) | (73) | (88) | (55) | (67) | (31) | (76) | (38) | (59) | (42) | (31) | (19) | (63) | (84) | (84) | (69) | |
| 40 | Panama | 6.4 | 15.7 | 4.5 | 6.4 | 5.3 | 8.5 | 5.6 | 5.0 | 10.8 | 2.2 | 3.6 | 6.2 | 9.6 | 1.2 | 0.9 | 5.6 | 4.7 | 1.2 | 40 |
| | | (62) | (101) | (10) | (54) | (27) | (48) | (27) | (51) | (74) | (31) | (11) | (50) | (45) | (6) | (7) | (36) | (43) | (17) | |
| 41 | Paraguay | 6.3 | 7.3 | 24.1 | 6.3 | 7.9 | 5.7 | 6.9 | | 8.4 | | | | | 3.9 | 1.1 | 6.9 | 8.0 | 0.9 | 41 |
| | | (58) | (62) | (77) | (53) | (64) | (27) | (42) | | (64) | | | | | (58) | (12) | (53) | (79) | (8) | |
| 42 | Peru | 6.0 | 7.3 | 6.5 | 6.0 | 13.2 | 8.5 | 10.7 | 3.1 | 7.2 | 2.9 | 12.4 | 3.8 | 9.5 | 7.1 | 3.5 | 10.7 | 4.4 | 3.4 | 42 |
| | | (52) | (61) | (28) | (43) | (92) | (47) | (66) | (28) | (59) | (39) | (60) | (30) | (44) | (78) | (69) | (83) | (41) | (72) | |
| 43 | Uruguay | 7.3 | 4.1 | 3.9 | 7.3 | 14.2 | 7.8 | 12.0 | 5.2 | 8.5 | | | | | 25.2 | 2.2 | 12.0 | 21.0 | 1.8 | 43 |
| | | (70) | (32) | (8) | (61) | (95) | (44) | (73) | (52) | (65) | | | | | (95) | (52) | (91) | (95) | (42) | |
| 44 | Venezuela | 3.6 | 3.4 | 18.9 | 3.6 | 10.1 | 5.2 | 6.7 | 6.4 | 1.4 | 2.2 | 7.9 | 5.6 | 8.0 | 5.4 | 2.4 | 6.7 | 4.8 | 2.4 | 44 |
| | | (27) | (22) | (69) | (20) | (76) | (21) | (39) | (64) | (1) | (27) | (46) | (46) | (33) | (70) | (55) | (50) | (48) | (58) | |
| 45 | Jamaica | 4.0 | 5.7 | 5.2 | 4.0 | 5.4 | 5.9 | 4.0 | 4.8 | 5.0 | 1.5 | 4.4 | 4.2 | 8.8 | 3.3 | 2.0 | 4.0 | 3.6 | 2.4 | 45 |
| | | (34) | (45) | (16) | (26) | (29) | (29) | (17) | (47) | (42) | (12) | (17) | (33) | (37) | (51) | (47) | (21) | (35) | (57) | |
| 46 | Trinidad–Tobago | 2.5 | 3.0 | 6.2 | 2.5 | 6.5 | 10.4 | 4.1 | | | | | | | 2.7 | | 4.1 | 6.3 | | 46 |
| | | (9) | (13) | (23) | (8) | (40) | (57) | (18) | | | | | | | (44) | | (22) | (66) | | |
| 47 | Puerto Rico | 2.2 | 2.4 | 2.9 | 2.2 | 2.2 | 1.9 | 1.6 | | | | | | | 0.4 | 5.1 | 1.6 | 1.2 | 0.5 | 47 |
| | | (2) | (3) | (4) | (2) | (1) | (1) | (1) | | | | | | | (1) | (79) | (1) | (2) | (2) | |
| 48 | Iran | 8.1 | 8.4 | 18.9 | 8.1 | 13.5 | 10.2 | 11.6 | 1.0 | | 1.2 | | 1.7 | | 2.9 | 3.0 | 11.6 | 5.1 | 2.8 | 48 |
| | | (76) | (72) | (70) | (66) | (93) | (54) | (72) | (4) | | (4) | | (17) | | (48) | (65) | (90) | (53) | (68) | |
| 49 | Iraq | 5.0 | 5.5 | 10.1 | 5.0 | 10.4 | 6.2 | 7.8 | 5.7 | 4.5 | | | | | 2.2 | 3.2 | 7.8 | 3.7 | 3.5 | 49 |
| | | (41) | (44) | (50) | (34) | (78) | (33) | (55) | (58) | (35) | | | | | (36) | (67) | (69) | (36) | (74) | |
| 50 | Israel | 3.4 | 2.5 | 8.0 | 3.4 | 7.3 | 6.8 | 6.0 | 9.2 | 2.7 | 7.9 | 7.5 | 7.5 | 1.6 | 8.7 | 2.9 | 6.0 | 10.7 | 2.1 | 50 |
| | | (24) | (6) | (41) | (18) | (54) | (36) | (30) | (73) | (14) | (63) | (44) | (60) | (2) | (86) | (64) | (40) | (87) | (51) | |
| 51 | Jordan | 16.7 | 15.5 | 19.1 | 16.7 | 6.1 | 22.9 | 7.0 | 11.0 | 17.3 | | | | | 4.6 | | 7.0 | 6.7 | | 51 |
| | | (101) | (99) | (71) | (81) | (35) | (80) | (46) | (77) | (80) | | | | | (65) | | (58) | (71) | | |

| | | | | | | | | | | | | | | | | | | | | |
|---|---|---|---|---|---|---|---|---|---|---|---|---|---|---|---|---|---|---|---|---|
| 52 | Kuwait | 6.3 (57) | 6.4 (53) | 8.1 (43) | 6.3 (51) | 8.4 (67) | 12.1 (61) | 8.5 (58) | | | | | | | 1.7 (16) | | 8.5 (7.3) | 2.1 (14) | | 52 |
| 53 | Lebanon | 7.6 (71) | 12.3 (95) | 9.2 (48) | 7.6 (63) | 7.4 (57) | 29.5 (84) | 6.9 (45) | | | | | | | 1.6 (12) | | 6.9 (56) | 1.8 (9) | | 53 |
| 54 | Saudi Arabia | 7.7 (73) | 9.2 (78) | 25.0 (79) | 7.7 (64) | 7.3 (55) | 8.0 (45) | 5.6 (26) | | | | | | | 2.1 (34) | 1.5 (27) | 5.6 (35) | 4.9 (50) | 1.4 (29) | 54 |
| 55 | Yemen, Peo. Dem. Rep. | 12.0 (94) | 12.0 (93) | | | 12.3 (91) | | | | | | | | | | | 12.3 (93) | | | 55 |
| 56 | Syria | 6.3 (61) | 9.3 (79) | 7.4 (38) | 6.3 (50) | 7.6 (60) | 15.9 (71) | 6.9 (44) | 1.7 (11) | 6.8 (53) | 1.5 (13) | 9.0 (51) | 2.9 (26) | 3.7 (10) | 3.4 (53) | 4.0 (71) | 6.9 (55) | 6.1 (63) | 5.4 (84) | 56 |
| 57 | Egypt | 6.6 (66) | 7.9 (65) | 21.9 (75) | 6.6 (57) | 7.0 (49) | 5.5 (24) | 6.4 (35) | 4.3 (41) | 4.8 (40) | 1.7 (16) | 9.1 (52) | 1.8 (21) | 9.4 (42) | 4.3 (62) | 2.1 (48) | 6.4 (46) | 6.8 (73) | 3.6 (77) | 57 |
| 58 | Afghanistan | 10.6 (87) | 10.6 (85) | | | 15.4 (98) | | | | | | | | | | | 15.4 (101) | | | 58 |
| 59 | Burma | 14.0 (98) | 15.2 (97) | 4.8 (14) | 14.0 (78) | 8.9 (70) | 10.3 (56) | 7.5 (53) | 7.0 (67) | 15.6 (79) | | | | | 3.3 (52) | 3.0 (66) | 7.5 (65) | 13.2 (91) | 3.1 (70) | 59 |
| 60 | Sri Lanka (Ceylon) | 2.2 (3) | 2.8 (10) | 5.4 (18) | 2.2 (3) | 3.4 (10) | 16.1 (74) | 3.8 (16) | 4.5 (45) | 3.9 (28) | 7.0 (62) | 8.8 (50) | 3.3 (28) | 11.8 (54) | 2.2 (35) | 1.5 (28) | 3.8 (19) | 2.0 (13) | 1.9 (44) | 60 |
| 61 | China, Nat. Rep. | 7.0 (68) | 9.0 (77) | 17.7 (66) | 7.0 (59) | 10.4 (79) | 16.9 (75) | 11.3 (70) | 6.6 (65) | 7.1 (57) | 2.0 (26) | 9.3 (54) | 7.6 (61) | 9.3 (41) | 1.9 (24) | 1.6 (32) | 11.3 (88) | 8.1 (80) | 1.8 (41) | 61 |
| 62 | Hong Kong | 5.2 (42) | 5.2 (41) | | | 4.0 (16) | | | | | | | | | | | 4.0 (20) | | | 62 |
| 63 | India | 4.3 (37) | 3.9 (28) | 7.3 (35) | 4.3 (30) | 11.0 (86) | 9.5 (52) | 9.7 (65) | 9.2 (74) | 4.7 (39) | 9.1 (64) | 8.3 (48) | 1.8 (20) | 10.7 (52) | 8.5 (84) | 2.1 (49) | 9.7 (80) | 4.9 (51) | 1.9 (45) | 63 |
| 64 | Indonesia | 14.5 (100) | 15.4 (98) | 74.5 (84) | 14.5 (80) | 17.0 (102) | 20.0 (79) | 18.0 (84) | | 3.7 (25) | | | | | 31.4 (94) | 6.2 (83) | 18.0 (105) | 26.3 (96) | 2.6 (65) | 64 |
| 65 | Korea, Rep. of | 12.9 (96) | 5.9 (51) | 20.9 (72) | 12.9 (76) | 16.6 (100) | 24.6 (82) | 17.5 (82) | 3.4 (32) | 3.0 (20) | 1.1 (3) | 16.2 (63) | 3.8 (31) | 17.2 (62) | 23.0 (94) | 5.3 (81) | 17.5 (103) | 12.3 (90) | 6.1 (85) | 65 |
| 66 | Malaysia | 4.0 (33) | 4.7 (39) | 7.4 (36) | 4.0 (27) | 3.8 (13) | 3.9 (12) | 3.0 (4) | 6.2 (61) | 6.2 (51) | 3.3 (44) | 7.0 (38) | 7.3 (58) | 4.7 (15) | 1.5 (10) | 1.1 (10) | 3.0 (5) | 2.8 (25) | 1.1 (12) | 66 |

*Table A.2a cont.*

| | Country, etc. | 100 | 101 | 102 | 103 | 104 | 105 | 106 | 107 | 108 | 109 | 110 | 111 | 112 | 113 | 114 | 115 | 117 | 118 | |
|---|---|---|---|---|---|---|---|---|---|---|---|---|---|---|---|---|---|---|---|---|
| 67 | Pakistan | 3.1 (18) | 3.6 (24) | 7.9 (40) | 3.1 (14) | 9.3 (71) | 14.1 (69) | 9.1 (62) | 7.4 (68) | 9.2 (67) | 1.5 (15) | 17.2 (64) | 7.3 (59) | 16.7 (61) | 2.7 (43) | 2.3 (54) | 9.1 (77) | 6.2 (65) | 2.7 (66) | 67 |
| 68 | Philippines | 7.8 (74) | 6.3 (52) | 24.9 (78) | 7.8 (65) | 6.2 (38) | 12.1 (62) | 7.1 (47) | 3.7 (35) | 5.9 (48) | 1.7 (18) | 6.9 (37) | 4.4 (37) | 11.4 (53) | 15.0 (92) | 4.8 (78) | 7.1 (59) | 13.5 (93) | 1.4 (24) | 68 |
| 69 | Singapore | 5.9 (49) | 8.7 (75) | 5.8 (22) | 5.9 (41) | 11.0 (87) | 10.9 (60) | 11.0 (69) | | | | | | | 4.9 (67) | | 11.0 (87) | 4.9 (49) | | 69 |
| 70 | Thailand | 6.2 (53) | 6.6 (57) | 16.8 (65) | 6.2 (48) | 4.8 (20) | 3.3 (5) | 4.4 (20) | 2.0 (12) | 7.1 (56) | 3.3 (45) | 7.3 (43) | 4.2 (34) | 12.1 (56) | 3.1 (49) | 1.7 (39) | 4.4 (24) | 3.1 (27) | 1.2 (16) | 70 |
| 71 | Algeria | 9.6 (82) | 9.5 (83) | 11.8 (57) | 9.6 (70) | 11.6 (89) | 7.7 (43) | 9.4 (64) | | | | | | | 1.9 (29) | | 9.4 (79) | 7.4 (77) | | 71 |
| 72 | Burundi | 17.9 (102) | 17.9 (102) | | | 7.0 (51) | | | | | | | | | | | 7.0 (57) | | | 72 |
| 73 | Cameroon | 8.6 (79) | 8.6 (73) | | | 4.8 (21) | | | 10.2 (75) | 6.9 (54) | 9.1 (65) | 5.7 (31) | 6.1 (49) | 5.9 (21) | 1.7 (14) | 4.2 (74) | 4.8 (17) | 4.3 (40) | 4.5 (81) | 73 |
| 74 | Central African Rep. | 12.0 (93) | 12.0 (92) | | | 5.5 (31) | | | | | | | | | | | 5.5 (34) | | | 74 |
| 75 | Chad | 9.4 (81) | 9.4 (82) | | | 10.7 (82) | | | 2.8 (24) | 18.9 (81) | | | | | | | 10.7 (82) | | | 75 |
| 76 | Zaire | 6.2 (56) | 5.9 (49) | 10.2 (51) | 6.2 (45) | 9.7 (73) | 3.8 (11) | 7.3 (49) | 4.9 (50) | 7.5 (60) | 6.0 (60) | 10.4 (57) | 7.7 (62) | 8.8 (38) | 13.0 (90) | 4.2 (73) | 7.3 (61) | 6.7 (72) | 4.3 (80) | 76 |
| 77 | Dahomey | 27.0 (107) | 27.0 (107) | | | 10.8 (84) | | | | | | | | | 1.0 (4) | | 10.8 (85) | 10.8 (88) | | 77 |
| 78 | Ethiopia | 6.0 (51) | 5.7 (48) | 13.7 (61) | 6.0 (44) | 7.1 (53) | 8.1 (46) | 6.7 (40) | 6.7 (66) | 8.6 (66) | 1.8 (22) | | 6.9 (57) | | 3.5 (57) | 0.6 (3) | 6.7 (51) | 3.9 (38) | 0.5 (3) | 78 |
| 79 | Ghana | 6.2 (55) | 7.8 (63) | 11.4 (55) | 6.2 (46) | 10.2 (77) | 7.2 (40) | 9.3 (63) | 18.8 (78) | 11.5 (76) | 6.5 (61) | 7.1 (41) | 17.2 (64) | 13.7 (59) | 7.4 (81) | 2.0 (44) | 9.3 (78) | 8.7 (83) | 2.5 (62) | 79 |

| | | | | | | | | | | | | | | | | | | | | |
|---|---|---|---|---|---|---|---|---|---|---|---|---|---|---|---|---|---|---|---|---|
| 80 | Ivory Coast | 6.3 (60) | 6.7 (58) | 6.6 (29) | 6.3 (49) | 3.7 (12) | 3.6 (9) | 3.4 (9) | 8.8 (72) | 7.5 (61) | | | | | 3.4 (54) | 4.4 (75) | 3.4 (12) | 2.2 (16) | 3.2 (71) | 80 |
| 81 | Kenya | 3.7 (28) | 4.2 (33) | 6.2 (24) | 3.7 (21) | 5.1 (24) | 4.4 (14) | 3.7 (14) | 2.8 (23) | 2.4 (7) | 1.8 (20) | 5.0 (22) | 1.7 (18) | 4.9 (17) | 2.0 (31) | 1.1 (11) | 3.7 (17) | 2.5 (20) | 1.3 (21) | 81 |
| 82 | Liberia | 10.8 (88) | 10.8 (87) | | | 14.5 (96) | | | | | | | | | | | 14.5 (98) | | | 82 |
| 83 | Libya | 32.9 (108) | 71.1 (109) | 35.0 (83) | 32.9 (84) | 7.7 (62) | 25.1 (83) | 12.4 (76) | | | | | | | 14.6 (91) | 7.1 (86) | 12.4 (95) | 3.5 (84) | 7.2 (87) | 83 |
| 84 | Malagasy Rep. | 8.1 (75) | 8.1 (69) | | | 5.3 (28) | | | 3.8 (36) | 6.4 (52) | 2.0 (25) | 3.7 (13) | 3.2 (27) | 7.2 (28) | 1.8 (18) | 2.6 (59) | 5.3 (32) | 1.2 (1) | 2.8 (67) | 84 |
| 85 | Malawi | 8.2 (77) | 8.1 (70) | 8.9 (45) | 8.2 (67) | 9.9 (74) | 3.6 (8) | 7.5 (52) | 4.4 (43) | 5.9 (49) | | | | | 7.7 (83) | 1.3 (17) | 7.5 (64) | 5.5 (57) | 3.4 (73) | 85 |
| 86 | Mali | 23.7 (105) | 25.7 (106) | 18.5 (68) | 23.7 (83) | 17.8 (104) | 13.3 (67) | 15.1 (80) | | | | | | | | | 15.1 (100) | | | 86 |
| 87 | Mauritania | 70.0 (109) | 70.0 (108) | | | 22.8 (108) | | | | | | | | | | | 22.8 (108) | | | 87 |
| 88 | Morocco | 4.7 (40) | 4.6 (38) | 14.2 (63) | 4.7 (33) | 8.7 (69) | 5.0 (16) | 7.7 (54) | 4.7 (46) | 4.5 (34) | 5.7 (56) | 7.2 (42) | 4.7 (41) | 8.3 (35) | 3.6 (56) | 4.0 (70) | 7.7 (67) | 5.2 (54) | 3.9 (78) | 88 |
| 89 | Niger | 12.1 (95) | 12.1 (94) | | | 18.2 (105) | | | | | | | | | 4.1 (60) | 5.2 (80) | 18.2 (106) | 13.9 (94) | 5.1 (82) | 89 |
| 90 | Nigeria | 14.5 (99) | 15.6 (100) | 6.9 (33) | 14.5 (79) | 15.7 (99) | 13.0 (66) | 12.0 (74) | 3.1 (29) | 3.3 (22) | 1.9 (23) | 5.7 (29) | 1.4 (13) | 6.8 (26) | 6.1 (73) | 1.7 (35) | 12.0 (92) | 8.1 (81) | 1.5 (33) | 90 |
| 91 | Rwanda | 25.4 (106) | 25.4 (105) | | | 27.4 (109) | | | 7.7 (69) | 8.3 (63) | | | | | | | 27.4 (109) | | | 91 |
| 92 | Senegal | 6.4 (63) | 6.4 (54) | | | 8.0 (66) | | | | | | | | | 4.1 (59) | 2.4 (58) | 8.0 (71) | 5.1 (52) | 2.3 (53) | 92 |
| 93 | Sierra Leone | 7.6 (72) | 8.4 (71) | 8.0 (42) | 7.6 (62) | 7.0 (50) | 7.1 (39) | 6.9 (43) | | | | | | | 2.8 (46) | 1.6 (33) | 6.9 (54) | 5.9 (60) | 1.6 (36) | 93 |
| 94 | Sudan | 6.2 (54) | 8.1 (67) | 16.3 (64) | 6.2 (47) | 10.9 (85) | 16.0 (72) | 10.8 (68) | 5.6 (57) | 10.1 (70) | 4.6 (53) | 13.5 (61) | 5.1 (43) | 13.2 (57) | 2.6 (41) | 2.7 (61) | 10.8 (86) | 6.5 (69) | 2.4 (59) | 94 |

*Table A.2a cont.*

| | Country, etc. | 100 | 101 | 102 | 103 | 104 | 105 | 106 | 107 | 108 | 109 | 110 | 111 | 112 | 113 | 114 | 115 | 117 | 118 | |
|---|---|---|---|---|---|---|---|---|---|---|---|---|---|---|---|---|---|---|---|---|
| 95 | Tanzania | 5.2 | 7.0 | 6.8 | 5.2 | 6.0 | 7.5 | 5.2 | 4.2 | 5.1 | 3.9 | 6.2 | 5.8 | 6.1 | 4.1 | 1.2 | 5.2 | 4.8 | 1.2 | 95 |
| | | (43) | (60) | (32) | (35) | (34) | (41) | (24) | (40) | (45) | (49) | (34) | (47) | (23) | (61) | (16) | (31) | (47) | (18) | |
| 96 | Togo | 10.0 | 10.0 | | | 7.6 | | | 6.0 | 10.6 | | | | | 1.4 | | 7.6 | 8.4 | | 96 |
| | | (83) | (84) | | | (61) | | | (60) | (73) | | | | | (9) | | (66) | (82) | | |
| 97 | Tunisia | 13.7 | 8.6 | 21.2 | 13.7 | 6.4 | 5.8 | 4.4 | 3.1 | 7.2 | 4.9 | 5.7 | 5.2 | 10.1 | 4.4 | 1.5 | 4.4 | 5.4 | 2.3 | 97 |
| | | (97) | (74) | (73) | (77) | (39) | (28) | (21) | (27) | (58) | (54) | (30) | (44) | (48) | (63) | (24) | (25) | (56) | (54) | |
| 98 | Uganda | 3.5 | 4.0 | 5.3 | 3.5 | 6.7 | 5.1 | 6.2 | 4.4 | 6.1 | 2.5 | 5.0 | 4.2 | 6.2 | 8.5 | 6.6 | 6.2 | 4.7 | 3.6 | 98 |
| | | (26) | (30) | (17) | (19) | (43) | (19) | (31) | (42) | (50) | (36) | (23) | (34) | (24) | (85) | (85) | (42) | (46) | (75) | |
| 99 | Upper Volta | 20.9 | 20.9 | | | 7.8 | | | | | | | | | 1.9 | | 7.8 | 5.3 | | 99 |
| | | (104) | (104) | | | (63) | | | | | | | | | (28) | | (68) | (55) | | |
| 100 | Zambia | 19.1 | 19.7 | 21.8 | 19.1 | 18.8 | 17.1 | 17.6 | 10.6 | 5.0 | | | | | 9.9 | 6.5 | 17.6 | 7.9 | 6.3 | 100 |
| | | (103) | (103) | (74) | (82) | (107) | (76) | (83) | (76) | (43) | | | | | (88) | (84) | (104) | (78) | (86) | |
| 101 | Bulgaria | 3.4 | 3.4 | | | 6.1 | | | | 2.7 | | 4.5 | | 6.0 | 1.7 | 2.0 | 6.1 | 4.6 | 2.1 | 101 |
| | | (23) | (20) | | | (36) | | | | (12) | | (18) | | (22) | (17) | (46 | (41) | (42) | (49) | |
| 102 | China, People's Rep. | 11.3 | 11.3 | | | 18.6 | | | | | | | | | | | 18.6 | | | 102 |
| | | (90) | (88) | | | (106) | | | | | | | | | | | (107) | | | |
| 103 | Cuba | 11.8 | 11.8 | | | 5.1 | | | | | | | | | 5.9 | 2.7 | 5.1 | 1.4 | 2.6 | 103 |
| | | (92) | (91) | | | (25) | | | | | | | | | (72) | (60) | (29) | (5) | (64) | |
| 104 | Czechoslovakia | 3.4 | 3.4 | | | 3.2 | | | | 2.5 | | 3.1 | | 2.8 | 7.7 | 4.2 | 3.2 | 9.0 | 4.2 | 104 |
| | | (25) | (21) | | | (7) | | | | (8) | | (9) | | (4) | (82) | (72) | (7) | (86) | (79) | |
| 105 | German Dem. Rep. | 2.9 | 2.9 | | | 5.2 | | | 0.9 | 1.6 | 1.3 | 3.9 | 0.6 | 4.8 | 0.9 | 0.2 | 5.2 | 1.6 | 0.3 | 105 |
| | | (14) | (12) | | | (26) | | | (2) | (3) | (5) | (14) | (1) | (16) | (3) | (1) | (30) | (7) | (1) | |
| 106 | Hungary | 2.7 | 2.7 | | | 5.7 | | | 1.2 | 2.6 | 0.9 | 5.0 | 0.8 | 4.6 | 3.5 | 1.5 | 5.7 | 4.7 | 1.5 | 106 |
| | | (12) | (9) | | | (32) | | | (7) | (11) | (2) | (21) | (3) | (14) | (55) | (30) | (37) | (45) | (32) | |
| 107 | Poland | 2.5 | 2.5 | | | 2.4 | | | 1.2 | 2.5 | 0.7 | 2.0 | 0.9 | 2.7 | 0.9 | 1.1 | 2.4 | 2.1 | 1.3 | 107 |
| | | (10) | (5) | | | (2) | | | (6) | (9) | (1) | (1) | (4) | (3) | (2) | (9) | (2) | (15) | (20) | |
| 108 | Romania | 3.4 | 3.4 | | | 9.9 | | | | | | | | | | | 9.9 | | | 108 |
| | | (21) | (19) | | | (75) | | | | | | | | | | | (81) | | | |

| | | | | | | | | | | | | | | | | | | | |
|---|---|---|---|---|---|---|---|---|---|---|---|---|---|---|---|---|---|---|---|
| 109 USSR | 2.3 (5) | 2.3 (2) | | | 3.3 (9) | | | | 2.6 (10) | | 2.4 (4) | | | 1.9 (27) | 1.2 (14) | 3.3 (9) | 2.3 (17) | 1.5 (31) | 109 |
| Number of countries | 109 | 109 | 84 | 84 | 109 | 84 | 84 | 78 | 81 | 65 | 64 | 64 | 63 | 96 | 86 | 109 | 96 | 87 | |
| Range | 1.7 to 70.0 | 2.2 to 71.1 | 2.1 to 74.5 | 1.7 to 32.9 | 2.2 to 27.4 | 1.9 to 29.5 | 1.6 to 18.0 | 0.9 to 18.8 | 1.4 to 18.9 | 0.7 to 9.1 | 2.0 to 17.2 | 0.6 to 17.2 | 1.0 to 25.8 | 0.4 to 31.4 | 0.2 to 7.1 | 1.6 to 27.4 | 1.2 to 26.3 | 0.3 to 7.2 | |
| Median | 6.2 | 6.5 | 8.1 | 6.0 | 7.3 | 7.6 | 6.9 | 4.2 | 4.9 | 2.4 | 5.8 | 4.1 | 7.7 | 3.0 | 2.0 | 6.9 | 4.9 | 1.9 | |
| Mean | 8.1 | 8.8 | 11.7 | 6.8 | 8.6 | 9.4 | 7.6 | 4.6 | 6.0 | 3.1 | 6.7 | 4.0 | 8.1 | 4.9 | 2.4 | 8.1 | 5.6 | 2.2 | |
| Standard deviation | 8.2 | 9.9 | 10.0 | 4.9 | 4.7 | 5.9 | 3.8 | 2.9 | 3.6 | 2.0 | 3.4 | 2.8 | 4.3 | 5.1 | 1.5 | 4.6 | 4.0 | 1.4 | |
| Cofficient of variation | 100 | 110 | 85 | 72 | 54 | 62 | 50 | 63 | 60 | 64 | 51 | 70 | 53 | 110 | 63 | 57 | 72 | 61 | |

(b) Variables 120–214

| Country, etc. | 120 | 121 | 122 | 200 | 201 | 202 | 203 | 204 | 205 | 206 | 207 | 208 | 209 | 210 | 211 | 212 | 213 | 214 | |
|---|---|---|---|---|---|---|---|---|---|---|---|---|---|---|---|---|---|---|---|
| 1 United States | 5.3 | 2.8 | 0.9 | 8.6 | 8.2 | 10.7 | 8.6 | 10.7 | 9.1 | 10.1 | 2.0 | 6.2 | 1.6 | 8.7 | 0.4 | 2.3 | 7.1 | 4.3 | 1 |
| | (5) | (63) | (85) | (50) | (52) | (46) | (40) | (80) | (30) | (56) | (53) | (39) | (34) | (40) | (42) | (55) | (37) | (15) | |
| 2 United Kingdom | 24.5 | 2.0 | 0.6 | 6.2 | 6.0 | 6.6 | 6.2 | 5.6 | 5.9 | 5.7 | 3.3 | 4.8 | 2.6 | 5.0 | 0.6 | 0.2 | 5.3 | 2.8 | 2 |
| | (62) | (42) | (51) | (29) | (33) | (19) | (25) | (27) | (13) | (18) | (64) | (30) | (53) | (19) | (47) | (33) | (17) | (7) | |
| 3 Austria | 9.5 | 0.5 | 0.7 | 10.5 | 9.3 | 13.6 | 10.5 | 10.0 | 15.8 | 11.0 | −0.2 | 9.7 | −0.2 | 10.1 | 0.1 | 0.4 | 8.8 | 4.7 | 3 |
| | (18) | (1) | (53) | (73) | (60) | (68) | (58) | (73) | (70) | (60) | (9) | (64) | (11) | (51) | (27) | (35) | (60) | (26) | |
| 4 Belgium–Luxembourg | 9.0 | 1.5 | 0.7 | 11.1 | 10.8 | 12.2 | 11.1 | 10.3 | 12.6 | 10.8 | 0.9 | 10.7 | 0.6 | 10.4 | 0.3 | −0.3 | 8.6 | 4.7 | 4 |
| | (16) | (27) | (54) | (85) | (81) | (59) | (67) | (76) | (58) | (59) | (25) | (71) | (14) | (54) | (36) | (26) | (56) | (27) | |
| 5 Denmark | 20.7 | 1.6 | 0.3 | 8.8 | 8.4 | 10.1 | 8.8 | 9.1 | 10.8 | 9.4 | 1.9 | 7.0 | 1.8 | 7.9 | 0.1 | 0.8 | 10.0 | 4.6 | 5 |
| | (55) | (31) | (12) | (52) | (54) | (40) | (41) | (55) | (39) | (42) | (47) | (49) | (36) | (36) | (29) | (43) | (72) | (23) | |
| 6 France | 27.8 | 1.3 | 1.0 | 13.2 | 13.3 | 13.0 | 13.2 | 13.8 | 15.0 | 14.1 | 2.4 | 8.7 | 1.5 | 5.8 | 0.9 | −2.7 | 9.5 | 5.7 | 6 |
| | (68) | (19) | (91) | (94) | (96) | (66) | (74) | (100) | (67) | (78) | (56) | (58) | (31) | (25) | (52) | (8) | (67) | (53) | |
| 7 Germany, West | 12.9 | 0.8 | 0.5 | 11.3 | 11.7 | 9.7 | 11.3 | 11.4 | 11.2 | 11.4 | 0.6 | 9.9 | −0.3 | 10.3 | 0.9 | 0.4 | 9.5 | 4.8 | 7 |
| | (32) | (3) | (37) | (86) | (89) | (34) | (68) | (89) | (43) | (63) | (19) | (66) | (9) | (53) | (53) | (36) | (68) | (29) | |

*Table A.2b cont.*

| | Country, etc. | 120 | 121 | 122 | 200 | 201 | 202 | 203 | 204 | 205 | 206 | 207 | 208 | 209 | 210 | 211 | 212 | 213 | 214 | |
|---|---|---|---|---|---|---|---|---|---|---|---|---|---|---|---|---|---|---|---|---|
| 8 | Italy | 12.8 | 1.7 | 0.5 | 13.7 | 14.4 | 12.2 | 13.7 | 12.1 | 14.9 | 12.8 | 1.0 | 13.0 | 1.2 | 11.0 | −0.2 | −1.8 | 10.1 | 5.4 | 8 |
| | | (29) | (33) | (38) | (96) | (100) | (60) | (75) | (92) | (66) | (71) | (33) | (76) | (24) | (56) | (23) | (12) | (75) | (46) | |
| 9 | Netherlands | 5.2 | 2.0 | 1.0 | 10.9 | 10.9 | 10.9 | 10.9 | 10.9 | 14.2 | 11.5 | 0.7 | 10.2 | 0.8 | 9.8 | −0.1 | −0.3 | 11.1 | 5.5 | 9 |
| | | (4) | (40) | (97) | (82) | (83) | (48) | (65) | (82) | (64) | (64) | (21) | (68) | (21) | (50) | (26) | (27) | (83) | (48) | |
| 10 | Norway | 6.9 | 1.8 | 1.0 | 9.7 | 11.0 | 8.6 | 9.7 | 9.6 | 8.2 | 9.2 | 1.0 | 8.6 | 0.7 | 9.4 | 0.4 | 0.7 | 9.6 | 4.9 | 10 |
| | | (7) | (37) | (99) | (61) | (85) | (29) | (50) | (61) | (23) | (39) | (34) | (57) | (20) | (46) | (40) | (41) | (69) | (32) | |
| 11 | Sweden | 17.6 | 1.3 | 1.0 | 9.5 | 10.0 | 7.9 | 9.5 | 9.1 | 11.3 | 9.5 | 2.0 | 7.9 | 2.0 | 6.8 | 0.1 | −0.1 | 9.2 | 4.7 | 11 |
| | | (46) | (22) | (103) | (58) | (68) | (23) | (47) | (56) | (44) | (48) | (52) | (52) | (45) | (29) | (33) | (20) | (64) | (28) | |
| 12 | Switzerland | 4.0 | 0.9 | 0.5 | 10.5 | 10.4 | 11.0 | 10.5 | 9.9 | 6.5 | 9.4 | 3.1 | 8.7 | 1.9 | 9.1 | 1.1 | 0.3 | 9.2 | 4.4 | 12 |
| | | (2) | (8) | (41) | (74) | (75) | (50) | (59) | (71) | (18) | (45) | (63) | (59) | (42) | (45) | (56) | (34) | (65) | (19) | |
| 13 | Canada | 14.7 | 2.0 | 0.5 | 11.0 | 11.2 | 9.9 | 11.0 | 9.9 | 8.3 | 9.5 | 2.1 | 9.6 | 1.9 | 8.2 | 0.2 | −1.3 | 8.4 | 5.4 | 13 |
| | | (37) | (39) | (34) | (84) | (86) | (38) | (66) | (66) | (24) | (46) | (54) | (63) | (40) | (38) | (34) | (16) | (54) | (47) | |
| 14 | Japan | 39.1 | 0.9 | 0.5 | 17.1 | 17.4 | 15.6 | 17.1 | 14.3 | 17.9 | 15.2 | 0.4 | 16.8 | 0.6 | 13.9 | −0.2 | −2.5 | 16.4 | 10.9 | 14 |
| | | (87) | (6) | (39) | (104) | (104) | (74) | (81) | (101) | (75) | (79) | (15) | (79) | (17) | (61) | (24) | (9) | (93) | (85) | |
| 15 | Finland | 20.8 | 1.7 | 0.8 | 9.0 | 8.5 | 11.6 | 9.0 | 9.0 | 11.7 | 9.4 | 4.4 | 6.9 | 4.1 | 7.7 | 0.3 | 0.7 | 7.6 | 4.8 | 15 |
| | | (56) | (32) | (62) | (55) | (55) | (55) | (44) | (54) | (47) | (44) | (70) | (47) | (61) | (34) | (37) | (40) | (41) | (30) | |
| 16 | Greece | 12.9 | 1.2 | 0.1 | 11.6 | 10.5 | 12.7 | 11.6 | 12.6 | 13.7 | 12.7 | 1.2 | 10.0 | 0.6 | 10.9 | 0.6 | 0.8 | 10.2 | 7.3 | 16 |
| | | (33) | (13) | (2) | (89) | (76) | (63) | (70) | (96) | (63) | (70) | (37) | (67) | (15) | (55) | (45) | (44) | (77) | (71) | |
| 17 | Iceland | 27.2 | 4.0 | 0.8 | 7.7 | 6.1 | 10.2 | 7.7 | 6.7 | 13.3 | 8.7 | 2.5 | 2.9 | −0.5 | 7.5 | 2.9 | 4.5 | 9.8 | 4.8 | 17 |
| | | (66) | (75) | (64) | (43) | (34) | (41) | (34) | (36) | (62) | (36) | (57) | (16) | (7) | (33) | (60) | (60) | (70) | (31) | |
| 18 | Ireland | 8.6 | 2.4 | 0.4 | 9.3 | 10.7 | 6.6 | 9.3 | 9.6 | 9.1 | 9.5 | 3.0 | 7.7 | 2.3 | 8.1 | 0.6 | 0.4 | 8.1 | 4.2 | 18 |
| | | (15) | (54) | (27) | (56) | (79) | (18) | (45) | (60) | (29) | (47) | (61) | (50) | (48) | (37) | (46) | (37) | (49) | (13) | |
| 19 | Portugal | 8.0 | 4.0 | 0.3 | 12.5 | 9.9 | 18.7 | 12.5 | 12.5 | 16.2 | 13.1 | 1.9 | 9.7 | 1.8 | 12.1 | 0.1 | 2.3 | 9.8 | 6.3 | 19 |
| | | (10) | (76) | (19) | (91) | (64) | (78) | (72) | (95) | (72) | (74) | (50) | (65) | (39) | (58) | (32) | (54) | (71) | (65) | |
| 20 | Spain | 23.3 | 3.0 | 0.8 | 16.2 | 14.1 | 19.1 | 16.2 | 17.2 | 20.5 | 17.8 | 3.0 | 12.7 | 2.1 | 17.1 | 1.0 | 3.9 | 11.6 | 7.1 | 20 |
| | | (60) | (67) | (68) | (102) | (98) | (79) | (80) | (105) | (81) | (81) | (62) | (75) | (46) | (63) | (55) | (59) | (88) | (69) | |

| | | | | | | | | | | | | | | | | | | | | |
|---|---|---|---|---|---|---|---|---|---|---|---|---|---|---|---|---|---|---|---|---|
| 21 | Turkey | 33.2 | 3.7 | 1.0 | 8.9 | 5.3 | 16.8 | 8.9 | 6.7 | 6.0 | 7.2 | 1.1 | | 2.9 | | −1.8 | | 10.4 | 6.0 | 21 |
| | | (79) | (73) | (105) | (54) | (32) | (75) | (43) | (37) | (14) | (25) | (36) | | (56) | | (8) | | (79) | (58) | |
| 22 | Yugoslavia | 35.6 | 6.3 | 0.8 | 15.2 | 11.6 | 23.8 | 15.2 | 12.7 | 18.9 | 13.5 | 3.3 | 7.9 | 2.7 | 8.7 | 0.6 | 0.8 | 12.2 | 6.1 | 22 |
| | | (82) | (87) | (70) | (100) | (88) | (81) | (78) | (97) | (78) | (76) | (65) | (53) | (55) | (41) | (48) | (46) | (90) | (60) | |
| 23 | Australia | 23.8 | 1.9 | 0.6 | 9.4 | 8.6 | 13.5 | 9.4 | 8.7 | 11.5 | 9.6 | 0.5 | 6.8 | 1.3 | 7.0 | −0.8 | 0.1 | 8.3 | 5.2 | 23 |
| | | (61) | (38) | (42) | (57) | (56) | (67) | (46) | (52) | (45) | (49) | (16) | (45) | (26) | (30) | (15) | (30) | (51) | (41) | |
| 24 | New Zealand | 28.9 | 2.9 | 1.0 | 4.7 | 4.2 | 10.3 | 4.7 | 4.3 | 4.8 | 4.4 | 1.6 | 4.3 | 2.7 | 3.8 | −1.1 | −0.5 | 5.3 | 4.5 | 24 |
| | | (74) | (65) | (98) | (18) | (20) | (42) | (14) | (19) | (9) | (12) | (44) | (26) | (54) | (15) | (11) | (25) | (16) | (20) | |
| 25 | South Africa | 2.9 | 1.4 | 0.3 | 6.4 | 5.2 | 14.3 | 6.4 | 9.3 | 10.9 | 9.7 | 0.8 | 5.1 | 1.3 | 7.8 | −0.4 | 2.6 | 9.0 | 6.0 | 25 |
| | | (1) | (25) | (21) | (31) | (31) | (70) | (26) | (59) | (40) | (52) | (24) | (32) | (28) | (35) | (22) | (56) | (61) | (59) | |
| 26 | Argentina | 47.8 | 5.6 | 1.0 | 5.4 | 4.7 | 9.6 | 5.4 | 3.1 | 12.1 | 4.9 | 1.0 | 6.7 | −0.2 | −0.3 | 1.2 | −6.5 | 8.0 | 4.3 | 26 |
| | | (93) | (84) | (88) | (24) | (23) | (32) | (20) | (12) | (53) | (16) | (30) | (44) | (10) | (3) | (57) | (1) | (47) | (16) | |
| 27 | Bolivia | 28.8 | 2.4 | 0.9 | 12.9 | 13.0 | 13.6 | 12.9 | 9.7 | 12.2 | 10.4 | 5.8 | 4.3 | | | | | 10.8 | 5.8 | 27 |
| | | (72) | (52) | (73) | (93) | (94) | (69) | (73) | (62) | (54) | (57) | (74) | (25) | | | | | (81) | (54) | |
| 28 | Brazil | 33.2 | 22.3 | 0.8 | 7.4 | 7.1 | 9.7 | 7.4 | 7.1 | 17.9 | 7.3 | 0.6 | 3.9 | 1.7 | 0.6 | −1.1 | −3.2 | 11.8 | 5.8 | 28 |
| | | (78) | (90) | (59) | (40) | (47) | (33) | (32) | (42) | (74) | (26) | (18) | (21) | (35) | (4) | (10) | (5) | (89) | (55) | |
| 29 | Chile | 40.3 | 7.2 | 0.8 | 10.3 | 10.3 | 10.8 | 10.3 | 6.7 | 11.2 | 7.8 | 4.9 | 4.2 | −1.3 | 9.7 | 6.4 | 5.4 | 6.1 | 4.6 | 29 |
| | | (89) | (88) | (61) | (68) | (71) | (47) | (54) | (35) | (41) | (29) | (71) | (24) | (2) | (49) | (63) | (62) | (24) | (24) | |
| 30 | Colombia | 34.5 | 5.1 | 0.5 | 4.8 | 4.0 | 8.1 | 4.8 | 4.2 | 11.2 | 6.5 | 0.4 | 0.3 | −0.7 | 0.8 | 0.1 | 0.8 | 5.0 | 5.0 | 30 |
| | | (80) | (81) | (36) | (20) | (17) | (25) | (16) | (17) | (42) | (22) | (14) | (5) | (4) | (6) | (28) | (42) | (15) | (35) | |
| 31 | Costa Rica | 17.2 | 1.3 | 0.3 | 10.1 | 10.1 | 9.8 | 10.1 | 11.0 | 11.8 | 11.2 | −0.7 | 8.0 | 2.0 | 8.9 | −2.5 | 0.9 | 7.4 | | 31 |
| | | (43) | (17) | (11) | (65) | (69) | (36) | (52) | (83) | (49) | (62) | (1) | (54) | (43) | (43) | (4) | (48) | (40) | | |
| 32 | Dominican Rep. | 27.8 | 2.6 | 0.2 | 4.3 | 3.2 | 11.1 | 4.3 | 9.8 | 9.6 | 9.7 | 3.5 | 0.3 | | | | | 6.4 | 3.1 | 32 |
| | | (67) | (57) | (4) | (17) | (10) | (51) | (13) | (64) | (32) | (51) | (66) | (6) | | | | | (27) | (9) | |
| 33 | Ecuador | 13.1 | 1.5 | 0.3 | 5.2 | 5.0 | 8.4 | 5.2 | 10.2 | 8.0 | 9.4 | 0.9 | 3.0 | | | | | 6.6 | 5.3 | 33 |
| | | (34) | (28) | (13) | (22) | (25) | (28) | (18) | (75) | (22) | (43) | (27) | (17) | | | | | (31) | (44) | |
| 34 | El Salvador | 10.0 | 1.3 | 0.7 | 7.1 | 7.0 | 8.0 | 7.1 | 6.5 | 12.3 | 7.8 | 1.7 | 5.6 | 1.5 | 5.4 | 0.2 | −0.2 | 6.1 | 6.1 | 34 |
| | | (23) | (18) | (56) | (39) | (46) | (24) | (30) | (33) | (55) | (30) | (46) | (36) | (30) | (21) | (35) | (28) | (25) | (61) | |
| 35 | Guatemala | 8.3 | 1.2 | 0.9 | 10.2 | 9.9 | 12.0 | 10.2 | 8.4 | 12.3 | 9.3 | | | 1.9 | | | | 5.9 | 5.5 | 35 |
| | | (12) | (14) | (76) | (66) | (63) | (58) | (53) | (51) | (56) | (40) | | | (41) | | | | (21) | (49) | |

*Table A.2b cont.*

| | Country, etc. | 120 | 121 | 122 | 200 | 201 | 202 | 203 | 204 | 205 | 206 | 207 | 208 | 209 | 210 | 211 | 212 | 213 | 214 | |
|---|---|---|---|---|---|---|---|---|---|---|---|---|---|---|---|---|---|---|---|---|
| 36 | Haiti | 37.5 | 3.0 | 0.8 | 1.0 | 1.9 | −0.9 | 1.0 | 1.3 | 5.6 | 2.4 | 1.2 | −0.8 | | | | | | | 36 |
| | | (86) | (66) | (63) | (6) | (7) | (5) | (4) | (8) | (12) | (6) | (38) | (3) | | | | | | | |
| 37 | Honduras | 15.5 | 1.2 | 0.2 | 10.8 | 10.7 | 12.8 | 10.8 | 11.4 | 21.1 | 13.0 | 1.0 | 8.5 | 0.6 | 13.3 | 0.3 | 3.8 | 6.4 | 5.2 | 37 |
| | | (38) | (15) | (6) | (78) | (78) | (64) | (62) | (88) | (82) | (72) | (31) | (56) | (16) | (60) | (38) | (58) | (28) | (42) | |
| 38 | Mexico | 7.7 | 1.4 | 0.2 | 8.4 | 6.1 | 11.0 | 8.4 | 7.8 | 13.0 | 9.6 | | | | | | | 10.6 | 8.3 | 38 |
| | | (9) | (23) | (10) | (49) | (35) | (49) | (39) | (48) | (61) | (50) | | | | | | | (80) | (78) | |
| 39 | Nicaragua | 20.1 | 1.7 | 0.4 | 10.4 | 10.4 | 10.5 | 10.4 | 12.3 | 10.0 | 11.5 | 0.9 | 9.1 | 1.8 | 8.4 | −0.8 | −0.6 | 8.6 | 6.7 | 39 |
| | | (53) | (34) | (30) | (71) | (74) | (44) | (56) | (93) | (33) | (65) | (28) | (61) | (37) | (39) | (16) | (24) | (58) | (68) | |
| 40 | Panama | 32.3 | 0.8 | 0.6 | 10.4 | 9.0 | 11.5 | 10.4 | 9.9 | 10.6 | 10.1 | 1.6 | 12.0 | 2.0 | 8.8 | −0.4 | −2.8 | 9.4 | 7.7 | 40 |
| | | (76) | (4) | (47) | (72) | (59) | (54) | (57) | (70) | (37) | (55) | (45) | (73) | (44) | (42) | (21) | (7) | (66) | (73) | |
| 41 | Paraguay | 26.4 | 4.4 | 0.4 | 6.9 | 5.0 | 15.1 | 6.9 | 7.2 | 11.5 | 8.4 | | 3.7 | | | | | 8.0 | 4.5 | 41 |
| | | (65) | (79) | (31) | (37) | (27) | (72) | (31) | (44) | (46) | (35) | | (20) | | | | | (48) | (21) | |
| 42 | Peru | 22.1 | 3.1 | 1.0 | 8.9 | 8.3 | 12.8 | 8.9 | 8.2 | 10.6 | 9.0 | 5.0 | 4.4 | 1.8 | 5.7 | 3.1 | 1.2 | 11.4 | 5.1 | 42 |
| | | (58) | (70) | (100) | (53) | (53) | (65) | (42) | (50) | (38) | (38) | (73) | (27) | (39) | (24) | (61) | (50) | (85) | (39) | |
| 43 | Uruguay | 9.7 | 25.8 | 0.9 | 4.0 | 4.1 | 3.9 | 4.0 | −0.2 | 7.1 | 2.0 | 0.7 | | | | | | 4.1 | 1.1 | 43 |
| | | (21) | (91) | (86) | (16) | (19) | (11) | (12) | (4) | (19) | (5) | (22) | | | | | | (8) | (1) | |
| 44 | Venezuela | 8.1 | 1.4 | 0.6 | 1.7 | 1.4 | 7.7 | 1.7 | 4.1 | 2.7 | 3.5 | 4.3 | 2.6 | 3.0 | 3.5 | 1.3 | 0.8 | 3.5 | 5.5 | 44 |
| | | (11) | (26) | (52) | (7) | (6) | (22) | (5) | (16) | (6) | (10) | (69) | (14) | (58) | (14) | (58) | (45) | (3) | (50) | |
| 45 | Jamaica | 9.7 | 3.1 | 0.3 | 8.0 | 7.6 | 8.9 | 8.0 | 9.2 | 9.4 | 9.3 | 1.5 | 4.1 | 3.7 | 6.2 | −2.2 | 2.1 | 7.1 | 5.0 | 45 |
| | | (19) | (69) | (14) | (45) | (49) | (30) | (36) | (57) | (31) | (41) | (41) | (23) | (60) | (27) | (6) | (53) | (36) | (36) | |
| 46 | Trinidad–Tobago | 12.2 | 1.5 | 0.9 | 4.7 | 5.1 | 2.8 | 4.7 | 5.1 | 3.4 | 4.7 | | | | | | | 6.1 | | 46 |
| | | (28) | (29) | (83) | (19) | (29) | (9) | (15) | (23) | (7) | (15) | | | | | | | (26) | | |
| 47 | Puerto Rico | | 0.9 | 0.1 | 10.8 | 10.6 | 11.4 | 10.8 | 11.1 | 14.4 | 12.0 | | | | | | | 11.2 | 6.1 | 47 |
| | | | (7) | (3) | (80) | (77) | (53) | (63) | (85) | (65) | (68) | | | | | | | (84) | (62) | |
| 48 | Iran | 15.8 | 1.8 | 0.7 | 12.4 | 12.5 | 11.6 | 12.4 | 13.3 | 12.8 | 13.1 | 0.7 | | 1.6 | | −1.0 | | 10.0 | | 48 |
| | | (40) | (35) | (57) | (90) | (91) | (56) | (71) | (99) | (59) | (73) | (20) | | (33) | | (12) | | (73) | | |

| | | | | | | | | | | | | | | | | | | | | |
|---|---|---|---|---|---|---|---|---|---|---|---|---|---|---|---|---|---|---|---|---|
| 49 | Iraq | 17.6 (45) | 2.9 (64) | 0.4 (26) | 6.9 (35) | 6.5 (40) | 11.2 (52) | 6.9 (29) | 4.0 (15) | 7.5 (20) | 5.8 (19) | 1.0 (32) | 5.5 (34) | | | | | 7.8 (45) | 8.8 (80) | 49 |
| 50 | Israel | 33.2 (77) | 2.6 (58) | 0.2 (7) | 16.1 (101) | 14.9 (102) | 18.1 (77) | 16.1 (79) | 11.1 (84) | 17.2 (73) | 13.7 (77) | 8.0 (76) | 12.7 (74) | 7.1 (65) | 10.2 (52) | 0.8 (50) | −2.3 (10) | 8.4 (55) | 6.6 (66) | 50 |
| 51 | Jordan | 20.0 (51) | 1.3 (20) | 0.5 (40) | 10.6 (75) | 12.9 (93) | 9.7 (35) | 10.6 (60) | 5.2 (24) | 18.5 (76) | 7.6 (27) | 1.6 (43) | 9.0 (60) | | | | | 8.3 (52) | 8.6 (79) | 51 |
| 52 | Kuwait | 9.7 (20) | | 0.6 (44) | 6.8 (34) | 6.8 (43) | 6.9 (20) | 6.8 (28) | 10.5 (77) | 12.9 (60) | 11.0 (61) | | | | | | | 6.4 (29) | | 52 |
| 53 | Lebanon | 7.3 (8) | 2.2 (48) | 0.6 (45) | 10.4 (70) | 10.3 (73) | 10.5 (43) | 10.4 (55) | 6.6 (34) | 18.9 (77) | 7.9 (31) | | | | | | | 5.9 (22) | | 53 |
| 54 | Saudi Arabia | 28.4 (70) | | 0.8 (67) | 11.4 (88) | 11.7 (90) | 6.1 (16) | 11.4 (69) | 15.0 (103) | 12.0 (52) | 13.2 (75) | | | | | | | 11.5 (87) | 9.8 (83) | 54 |
| 55 | Yemen, Peo. Dem. Rep. | 15.5 (39) | 2.0 (43) | 0.9 (87) | −2.4 (2) | −2.4 (2) | | | −0.4 (3) | | | | | | | | | | | 55 |
| 56 | Syria | 30.8 (75) | 2.1 (47) | 0.6 (49) | 5.6 (27) | 4.1 (18) | 8.3 (26) | 5.6 (23) | 6.3 (31) | 16.1 (71) | 6.9 (23) | 0.9 (29) | −5.5 (1) | 0.6 (19) | 2.6 (10) | 0.3 (39) | 8.7 (64) | 7.6 (42) | 5.3 (45) | 56 |
| 57 | Egypt | 8.5 (14) | 3.8 (74) | 0.4 (25) | 2.2 (8) | 4.9 (24) | −4.8 (3) | 2.2 (6) | 3.8 (14) | 2.5 (5) | 3.6 (11) | 3.9 (67) | −0.4 (4) | −1.7 (1) | −6.2 (1) | 5.8 (62) | −5.8 (2) | 5.9 (20) | 2.8 (8) | 57 |
| 58 | Afghanistan | 16.3 (41) | | 0.9 (72) | 11.4 (87) | 11.4 (87) | | | 12.8 (98) | | | | | | | | | | | 58 |
| 59 | Burma | 14.1 (36) | 5.2 (82) | 0.4 (23) | −7.3 (1) | −7.3 (1) | −7.0 (2) | −7.3 (1) | −4.2 (1) | −0.5 (1) | −3.5 (1) | 0.9 (26) | −4.9 (2) | | | | | 3.8 (5) | 2.6 (4) | 59 |
| 60 | Sri Lanka (Ceylon) | 13.9 (35) | 3.0 (68) | 1.0 (102) | −1.4 (3) | −1.3 (3) | −2.3 (4) | −1.4 (2) | 0.1 (5) | 0.9 (3) | 0.1 (2) | −0.2 (10) | 1.4 (8) | 5.5 (63) | −1.5 (2) | −5.3 (1) | −2.9 (6) | 4.3 (10) | 4.9 (33) | 60 |
| 61 | China, Nat. Rep. | 22.5 (59) | 3.4 (72) | 0.6 (43) | 24.2 (105) | 23.7 (105) | 25.2 (82) | 24.2 (82) | 17.0 (104) | 27.5 (83) | 18.6 (82) | −0.1 (11) | 15.1 (77) | 0.4 (13) | 15.9 (62) | −0.4 (20) | 0.6 (39) | 13.5 (92) | 10.0 (84) | 61 |
| 62 | Hong Kong | | 2.1 (46) | 1.0 (93) | 14.4 (98) | 14.4 (99) | | | 11.2 (87) | | | | | | | | | | | 62 |
| 63 | India | 28.5 (71) | 4.4 (78) | 1.0 (94) | 3.3 (12) | 3.7 (12) | 1.3 (6) | 3.3 (8) | 0.8 (6) | 8.7 (26) | 2.0 (4) | 5.8 (75) | 3.2 (18) | 5.2 (62) | 2.0 (8) | 0.5 (44) | −1.2 (18) | 4.7 (14) | 3.5 (10) | 63 |

*Table A.2b cont*

| | Country, etc. | 120 | 121 | 122 | 200 | 201 | 202 | 203 | 204 | 205 | 206 | 207 | 208 | 209 | 210 | 211 | 212 | 213 | 214 | |
|---|---|---|---|---|---|---|---|---|---|---|---|---|---|---|---|---|---|---|---|---|
| 64 | Indonesia | 35.3 | 97.6 | 1.0 | 2.7 | 3.4 | −22.6 | 2.7 | 3.6 | 0.4 | 2.6 | | 2.3 | | | | | −1.2 | 3.7 | 64 |
| | | (81) | (92) | (95) | (11) | (11) | (1) | (7) | (13) | (2) | (8) | | (9) | | | | | (1) | (11) | |
| 65 | Korea, Rep. of | 12.8 | 4.3 | 0.3 | 28.5 | 40.1 | 20.6 | 28.5 | 20.7 | 19.5 | 20.5 | 2.9 | 33.5 | 0.2 | 26.3 | 2.7 | −5.4 | 8.7 | 9.2 | 65 |
| | | (30) | (77) | (16) | (106) | (107) | (80) | (83) | (108) | (80) | (83) | (60) | (80) | (12) | (64) | (59) | (3) | (59) | (81) | |
| 66 | Malaysia | 5.2 | 1.1 | 0.8 | 5.2 | 5.2 | 4.6 | 5.2 | 4.2 | 6.3 | 4.6 | −0.4 | 4.0 | 0.6 | 4.6 | −0.1 | 1.3 | 6.9 | 6.1 | 66 |
| | | (3) | (12) | (65) | (23) | (30) | (13) | (19) | (18) | (17) | (13) | (6) | (22) | (18) | (18) | (25) | (51) | (35) | (63) | |
| 67 | Pakistan | 20.5 | 2.5 | 0.3 | 5.4 | 6.1 | 2.3 | 5.4 | 7.0 | 11.9 | 7.9 | 1.9 | 5.5 | 0.9 | 9.5 | 1.0 | 3.7 | 8.2 | 4.2 | 67 |
| | | (54) | (55) | (18) | (25) | (36) | (7) | (21) | (41) | (51) | (32) | (49) | (35) | (23) | (48) | (54) | (57) | (50) | (14) | |
| 68 | Philippines | 27.9 | 2.7 | 0.9 | 7.7 | 6.5 | 12.5 | 7.7 | 7.7 | 8.9 | 8.0 | 1.4 | 5.0 | 2.5 | 5.2 | −1.0 | 0.2 | 2.2 | 1.3 | 68 |
| | | (69) | (60) | (79) | (44) | (41) | (61) | (35) | (47) | (27) | (34) | (39) | (31) | (50) | (20) | (13) | (31) | (2) | (2) | |
| 69 | Singapore | 9.1 | 0.8 | 0.3 | 8.0 | 7.8 | 9.0 | 8.0 | 11.6 | 15.1 | 11.9 | | | | | | | 10.9 | | 69 |
| | | (17) | (5) | (20) | (46) | (50) | (31) | (37) | (90) | (68) | (67) | | | | | | | (82) | | |
| 70 | Thailand | 11.4 | 1.2 | 0.4 | 10.8 | 6.1 | 27.3 | 10.8 | 11.1 | 15.6 | 11.6 | −0.1 | 6.4 | −0.5 | 12.0 | 0.4 | 5.2 | 10.0 | 7.9 | 70 |
| | | (26) | (16) | (32) | (81) | (37) | (83) | (64) | (86) | (69) | (66) | (12) | (41) | (8) | (57) | (41) | (61) | (74) | (74) | |
| 71 | Algeria | 25.3 | | 0.5 | 5.6 | 5.1 | 3.5 | 5.6 | 7.7 | 6.2 | 7.2 | | | | | | | 7.7 | | 71 |
| | | (63) | | (33) | (26) | (28) | (10) | (22) | (46) | (15) | (24) | | | | | | | (43) | | |
| 72 | Burundi | 40.3 | 1.1 | 0.9 | 7.0 | 7.0 | | | 4.9 | | | | | | | | | | | 72 |
| | | (88) | (10) | (74) | (38) | (45) | | | (22) | | | | | | | | | | | |
| 73 | Cameroon | 17.1 | 2.1 | 0.7 | 8.7 | 8.7 | | | 10.8 | | | 1.1 | 2.9 | 6.4 | 3.9 | −5.0 | 0.9 | 9.1 | 5.9 | 73 |
| | | (42) | (44) | (55) | (51) | (57) | | | (81) | | | (35) | (15) | (64) | (16) | (2) | (47) | (62) | (56) | |
| 74 | Central African Rep. | 114.4 | 2.4 | 0.9 | 10.0 | 10.0 | | | 7.0 | | | | | | | | | | | 74 |
| | | (97) | (53) | (75) | (63) | (65) | | | (40) | | | | | | | | | | | |
| 75 | Chad | 82.4 | 1.6 | 0.5 | 6.4 | 6.4 | | | 9.8 | | | 0.5 | 7.0 | | | | | | | 75 |
| | | (94) | (30) | (35) | (30) | (38) | | | (63) | | | (17) | (48) | | | | | | | |
| 76 | Zaire | 40.4 | 10.5 | 0.8 | 13.9 | 13.1 | 29.4 | 13.9 | 12.3 | 11.7 | 12.1 | 10.5 | 2.4 | 2.9 | 1.1 | 7.4 | −1.3 | 5.6 | 9.5 | 76 |
| | | (90) | (89) | (71) | (97) | (95) | (84) | (76) | (94) | (48) | (69) | (77) | (11) | (57) | (7) | (64) | (17) | (19) | (82) | |

| | | | | | | | | | | | | | | | | | | | | |
|---|---|---|---|---|---|---|---|---|---|---|---|---|---|---|---|---|---|---|---|---|
| 77 | Dahomey | 18.2<br>(48) | | 0.1<br>(1) | 10.3<br>(69) | 10.3<br>(72) | | | 10.7<br>(78) | | | | | | | | | 4.4<br>(11) | | 77 |
| 78 | Ethiopia | 6.0<br>(6) | 2.1<br>(45) | 0.2<br>(5) | 7.7<br>(42) | 5.0<br>(26) | 15.3<br>(73) | 7.7<br>(33) | 6.9<br>(39) | 10.1<br>(34) | 8.0<br>(33) | 2.2<br>(55) | 4.5<br>(28) | 1.3<br>(27) | | 0.9<br>(51) | | 6.6<br>(32) | 4.9<br>(34) | 78 |
| 79 | Ghana | 20.1<br>(52) | 6.0<br>(86) | 1.0<br>(92) | 0.9<br>(5) | 0.6<br>(4) | 2.7<br>(8) | 0.9<br>(3) | −0.8<br>(2) | 4.2<br>(8) | 0.5<br>(3) | −0.5<br>(3) | 1.4<br>(7) | 1.4<br>(29) | 2.4<br>(9) | −0.7<br>(17) | 1.0<br>(49) | 6.5<br>(30) | 2.6<br>(5) | 79 |
| 80 | Ivory Coast | 11.5<br>(27) | 2.8<br>(62) | 0.9<br>(78) | 10.0<br>(64) | 10.0<br>(66) | 9.8<br>(37) | 10.0<br>(51) | 9.9<br>(68) | 11.8<br>(50) | 10.5<br>(58) | 4.9<br>(72) | 5.8<br>(38) | | | | | 10.1<br>(76) | 8.2<br>(77) | 80 |
| 81 | Kenya | 19.1<br>(49) | 1.1<br>(11) | 0.3<br>(15) | 6.7<br>(32) | 4.3<br>(22) | 10.0<br>(39) | 6.7<br>(27) | 9.8<br>(65) | 10.5<br>(36) | 10.1<br>(53) | −0.3<br>(8) | 7.7<br>(51) | 0.9<br>(22) | 6.1<br>(26) | −1.8<br>(7) | −1.5<br>(15) | 8.6<br>(57) | 6.6<br>(67) | 81 |
| 82 | Liberia | | | * | 10.8<br>(79) | 10.8<br>(82) | | | 14.5<br>(102) | | | | | | | | | | | 82 |
| 83 | Libya | 36.8<br>(85) | 1.3<br>(21) | 0.2<br>(8) | 40.1<br>(108) | 63.7<br>(109) | 7.3<br>(21) | 40.1<br>(84) | 18.6<br>(107) | 30.8<br>(84) | 23.6<br>(84) | | | | | | | 27.3<br>(95) | 24.3<br>(86) | 83 |
| 84 | Malagasy Rep. | 19.6<br>(50) | 1.0<br>(9) | 0.6<br>(46) | 6.9<br>(36) | 6.9<br>(44) | | | 6.8<br>(38) | | | 0.8<br>(23) | 4.8<br>(29) | 2.5<br>(49) | 2.9<br>(11) | −1.7<br>(9) | −1.7<br>(14) | 5.9<br>(23) | 5.2<br>(43) | 84 |
| 85 | Malawi | 11.3<br>(25) | | 0.2<br>(9) | 9.7<br>(59) | 9.0<br>(58) | 11.7<br>(57) | 9.7<br>(48) | 9.9<br>(69) | 10.4<br>(35) | 10.1<br>(54) | 3.9<br>(68) | 5.3<br>(33) | | | | | 10.2<br>(78) | 5.9<br>(67) | 85 |
| 86 | Mali | 83.5<br>(95) | | 1.0<br>(96) | 10.7<br>(76) | 9.4<br>(61) | 14.9<br>(71) | 10.7<br>(61) | 1.4<br>(9) | 6.2<br>(16) | 3.5<br>(9) | | | | | | | | | 86 |
| 87 | Mauritania | 46.1<br>(92) | 1.8<br>(36) | 0.4<br>(28) | 48.5<br>(109) | 48.5<br>(108) | | | 5.7<br>(28) | | | | | | | | | | | 87 |
| 88 | Morocco | 28.8<br>(73) | 2.7<br>(59) | 0.4<br>(29) | 3.8<br>(13) | 3.7<br>(13) | 4.4<br>(12) | 3.8<br>(9) | 5.3<br>(25) | 9.0<br>(28) | 6.3<br>(21) | 1.9<br>(48) | 2.3<br>(10) | 1.2<br>(25) | 4.1<br>(17) | 0.7<br>(49) | 1.7<br>(52) | 6.7<br>(33) | 4.3<br>(17) | 88 |
| 89 | Niger | 92.2<br>(96) | 2.2<br>(49) | 0.3<br>(17) | 10.7<br>(77) | 10.7<br>(80) | | | 10.7<br>(79) | | | | | | | | | 7.8<br>(46) | 4.5<br>(22) | 89 |
| 90 | Nigeria | 22.0<br>(57) | 5.0<br>(80) | 0.8<br>(66) | 9.7<br>(60) | 10.0<br>(67) | 6.2<br>(17) | 9.7<br>(49) | 5.3<br>(26) | 19.4<br>(79) | 8.9<br>(37) | −0.5<br>(4) | 6.8<br>(46) | 2.2<br>(47) | 3.2<br>(12) | −2.7<br>(3) | −3.4<br>(4) | 5.6<br>(18) | 5.0<br>(37) | 90 |
| 91 | Rwanda | 26.2<br>(64) | 0.6<br>(2) | 0.6<br>(48) | 31.0<br>(107) | 31.0<br>(106) | | | 32.9<br>(109) | | | 2.0<br>(51) | 6.5<br>(42) | | | | | | | 91 |

*Not calculated

*Table A.2b cont*

| | Country, etc. | 120 | 121 | 122 | 200 | 201 | 202 | 203 | 204 | 205 | 206 | 207 | 208 | 209 | 210 | 211 | 212 | 213 | 214 | |
|---|---|---|---|---|---|---|---|---|---|---|---|---|---|---|---|---|---|---|---|---|
| 92 | Senegal | 36.3 | 1.4 | 1.0 | 2.6 | 2.6 | | | 2.6 | | | | | | | | | 3.7 | 1.5 | 92 |
| | | (84) | (24) | (101) | (9) | (8) | | | (10) | | | | | | | | | (4) | (3) | |
| 93 | Sierra Leone | 10.2 | 2.3 | 0.9 | 3.9 | 3.7 | 5.0 | 3.9 | 2.8 | 1.7 | 2.5 | | | | | | | 4.5 | 5.6 | 93 |
| | | (24) | (51) | (81) | (14) | (14) | (14) | (10) | (11) | (4) | (7) | | | | | | | (12) | (51) | |
| 94 | Sudan | 12.8 | 2.7 | 0.9 | 4.0 | 3.8 | 5.7 | 4.0 | 4.6 | 5.3 | 4.7 | 1.5 | 2.6 | 2.6 | 0.7 | −1.0 | −1.8 | 4.2 | 4.3 | 94 |
| | | (31) | (61) | (82) | (15) | (15) | (15) | (11) | (21) | (11) | (14) | (42) | (13) | (52) | (5) | (14) | (13) | (9) | (18) | |
| 95 | Tanzania | 17.8 | 2.0 | 0.6 | 8.3 | 6.4 | 17.1 | 8.3 | 10.0 | 7.7 | 7.6 | 0.1 | 6.3 | 2.5 | 5.4 | −2.4 | −0.8 | 9.1 | 4.6 | 95 |
| | | (47) | (41) | (50) | (48) | (39) | (76) | (38) | (74) | (21) | (28) | (13) | (40) | (51) | (22) | (5) | (23) | (63) | (25) | |
| 96 | Togo | 8.4 | 2.5 | 0.8 | 12.8 | 12.8 | | | 9.9 | | | 2.5 | 11.8 | | | | | 16.6 | | 96 |
| | | (13) | (56) | (69) | (92) | (92) | | | (72) | | | (58) | (72) | | | | | (94) | | |
| 97 | Tunisia | 41.2 | 2.2 | 1.0 | 5.8 | 3.9 | 8.3 | 5.8 | 4.4 | 8.4 | 5.6 | 2.6 | 3.4 | 3.4 | 3.5 | −0.7 | 0.2 | 4.6 | 4.0 | 97 |
| | | (91) | (50) | (104) | (28) | (16) | (27) | (24) | (20) | (25) | (17) | (59) | (19) | (59) | (13) | (8) | (32) | (13) | (12) | |
| 98 | Uganda | 17.3 | 5.8 | 0.9 | 4.9 | 4.2 | 10.6 | 4.9 | 6.4 | 4.9 | 6.1 | 1.4 | 5.7 | 1.5 | 5.4 | −0.5 | −0.2 | 11.4 | 7.4 | 98 |
| | | (44) | (85) | (84) | (21) | (21) | (45) | (17) | (32) | (10) | (20) | (40) | (37) | (32) | (23) | (19) | (29) | (86) | (72) | |
| 99 | Upper Volta | 9.9 | 5.4 | 1.0 | 17.0 | 17.0 | | | 5.8 | | | | | | | | | 4.1 | | 99 |
| | | (22) | (83) | (106) | (103) | (103) | | | (29) | | | | | | | | | (7) | | |
| 100 | Zambia | 36.1 | 3.3 | 1.0 | 14.5 | 14.6 | 12.5 | 14.5 | 18.4 | 12.5 | 16.1 | 10.8 | 2.4 | | | | | 12.7 | 8.0 | 100 |
| | | (83) | (71) | (107) | (99) | (101) | (62) | (77) | (106) | (57) | (80) | (78) | (12) | | | | | (91) | (76) | |
| 101 | Bulgaria | | | 0.8 | 13.5 | 13.5 | | | 12.1 | | | | 15.6 | | 13.3 | | −2.1 | 8.4 | 7.9 | 101 |
| | | | | (60) | (95) | (97) | | | (91) | | | | (78) | | (59) | | (11) | (53) | (75) | |
| 102 | China, People's Rep. | | | * | 0.8 | 0.8 | | | 0.9 | | | | | | | | | | | 102 |
| | | | | | (4) | (5) | | | (7) | | | | | | | | | | | |
| 103 | Cuba | | | 0.4 | 2.7 | 2.7 | | | 6.2 | | | | | | | | | 7.8 | 2.6 | 103 |
| | | | | (24) | (10) | (9) | | | (30) | | | | | | | | | (44) | (6) | |
| 104 | Czechoslovakia | | | 1.0 | 6.8 | 6.8 | | | 7.2 | | | | 6.6 | | 7.1 | | 0.5 | 7.2 | 5.1 | 104 |
| | | | | (89) | (33) | (42) | | | (43) | | | | (43) | | (31) | | (38) | (38) | (40) | |

| | | | | | | | | | | | | | | | | | | | | |
|---|---|---|---|---|---|---|---|---|---|---|---|---|---|---|---|---|---|---|---|---|
| 105 | German Dem. | | | 1.0 | 7.6 | 7.6 | | | 8.0 | | | −0.7 | 8.0 | −0.8 | 7.1 | 0.1 | −0.9 | 4.0 | 5.0 | 105 |
| | Rep. | | | (90) | (41) | (48) | | | (49) | | | (2) | (55) | (3) | (32) | (30) | (21) | (6) | (38) | |
| 106 | Hungary | | | 0.9 | 9.8 | 9.8 | | | 9.9 | | | −0.3 | 10.3 | −0.7 | 9.5 | 0.5 | −0.8 | 6.8 | 5.6 | 106 |
| | | | | (77) | (62) | (62) | | | (67) | | | (7) | (70) | (5) | (47) | (43) | (22) | (34) | (52) | |
| 107 | Poland | | | 0.7 | 10.2 | 10.2 | | | 8.8 | | | −0.5 | 10.2 | −0.6 | 9.0 | 0.1 | −1.2 | 7.3 | 6.2 | 107 |
| | | | | (58) | (67) | (70) | | | (53) | | | (5) | (69) | (6) | (44) | (31) | (19) | (39) | (64) | |
| 108 | Romania | | | 0.9 | 10.9 | 10.9 | | | 9.2 | | | | | | | | | | | 108 |
| | | | | (80) | (83) | (84) | | | (58) | | | | | | | | | | | |
| 109 | USSR | | | 0.3 | 8.2 | 8.2 | | | 7.3 | | | | 9.1 | | 6.4 | | 7.0 | | 7.2 | 109 |
| | | | | (22) | (47) | (51) | | | (45) | | | | (62) | | (28) | | (63) | | (70) | |
| | Number of countries | 97 | 92 | 107 | 109 | 109 | 84 | 84 | 109 | 84 | 84 | 78 | 80 | 65 | 64 | 64 | 64 | 95 | 86 | |
| | Range | 2.9 to 114.4 | 0.5 to 97.6 | 0.1 to 1.0 | −7.3 to 48.5 | −7.3 to 63.7 | −22.6 to 29.4 | −7.3 to 40.1 | −4.2 to 32.9 | −0.5 to 30.8 | −3.5 to 23.6 | −0.7 to 10.8 | −5.5 to 33.5 | −1.7 to 7.1 | −6.2 to 26.3 | −5.3 to 7.4 | −6.5 to 8.7 | −1.2 to 27.3 | 1.1 to 24.3 | |
| | Median | 19.1 | 2.1 | 0.7 | 9.0 | 8.5 | 10.4 | 8.9 | 9.1 | 11.2 | 9.4 | 1.4 | 63.5 | 1.6 | 7.3 | 0.1 | 0.2 | 8.0 | 5.3 | |
| | Mean | 23.2 | 4.0 | 0.6 | 9.5 | 9.4 | 10.0 | 9.0 | 8.6 | 11.2 | 9.0 | 2.2 | 5.1 | 1.7 | 4.9 | 2.0 | 2.7 | 3.5 | 5.7 | |
| | Standard deviation | 18.4 | 10.5 | 0.3 | 7.1 | 8.7 | 7.1 | 6.0 | 4.9 | 5.6 | 4.5 | 2.2 | 5.1 | 1.7 | 4.9 | 2.0 | 2.7 | 3.5 | 2.8 | |
| | Coefficient of variation | 79 | 260 | 43 | 75 | 92 | 71 | 67 | 57 | 50 | 49 | 110 | 77 | 100 | 68 | 140 | 170 | 43 | 48 | |

## (c) Variables 215–305

| | Country, etc. | 215 | 217 | 218 | 220 | 221 | 222 | 300 | 301 | 302 | 303 | 304 | 305 | |
|---|---|---|---|---|---|---|---|---|---|---|---|---|---|---|
| 1 | United States | 10.1 | 2.1 | 3.0 | −11.9 | 2.7 | −245.7 | 43,137.1 | 28,090.2 | 15,046.9 | 43,137.1 | 24,839.7 | 12,998.1 | 1 |
| | | (73) | (73) | (41) | (9) | (26) | (1) | (109) | (109) | (84) | (84) | (109) | (84) | |
| 2 | United Kingdom | 5.7 | 0.7 | 2.1 | −3.5 | 4.0 | 176.7 | 21,913.2 | 13,997.4 | 7,915.8 | 21,913.2 | 14,492.5 | 6,685.5 | 2 |
| | | (23) | (45) | (26) | (41) | (55) | (105) | (107) | (107) | (83) | (82) | (107) | (83) | |
| 3 | Austria | 11.0 | 1.8 | 4.2 | −1.9 | 3.6 | −20.4 | 2,571.3 | 1,761.5 | 809.8 | 2,571.3 | 2,149.2 | 519.0 | 3 |
| | | (80) | (69) | (62) | (52) | (47) | (21) | (89) | (89) | (70) | (67) | (88) | (61) | |

*Table A.2c cont.*

| | Country, etc. | 215 | 217 | 218 | 220 | 221 | 222 | 300 | 301 | 302 | 303 | 304 | 305 | |
|---|---|---|---|---|---|---|---|---|---|---|---|---|---|---|
| 4 | Belgium–Luxembourg | 10.8 | 2.5 | 3.9 | –4.3 | 3.1 | 42.4 | 6,319.4 | 4,911.5 | 1,407.9 | 6,319.4 | 4,825.4 | 1,366.0 | 4 |
| | | (78) | (76) | (57) | (30) | (39) | (98) | (100) | (100) | (74) | (76) | (100) | (75) | |
| 5 | Denmark | 9.4 | –0.8 | 3.9 | –2.8 | 5.8 | –32.1 | 3,085.8 | 2,302.5 | 783.3 | 3,085.8 | 2,693.4 | 596.9 | 5 |
| | | (56) | (28) | (55) | (45) | (76) | (17) | (93) | (92) | (69) | (70) | (95) | (63) | |
| 6 | France | 14.1 | 3.9 | 4.6 | –5.0 | 4.0 | –15.5 | 14,151.0 | 10,276.4 | 3,874.6 | 14,151.0 | 10,106.4 | 3,645.5 | 6 |
| | | (101) | (85) | (64) | (25) | (54) | (26) | (106) | (106) | (81) | (81) | (106) | (81) | |
| 7 | Germany, West | 11.4 | 1.7 | 3.9 | –3.8 | 2.8 | 259.3 | 25,226.3 | 20,411.1 | 4,815.2 | 25,226.3 | 16,809.3 | 6,061.1 | 7 |
| | | (84) | (66) | (56) | (34) | (32) | (107) | (108) | (108) | (82) | (83) | (108) | (82) | |
| 8 | Italy | 12.8 | 2.9 | 5.0 | –5.3 | 3.9 | 193.4 | 11,346.4 | 7,670.0 | 3,676.4 | 11,346.4 | 7,759.2 | 2,603.1 | 8 |
| | | (94) | (81) | (67) | (22) | (52) | (106) | (103) | (102) | (80) | (78) | (102) | (78) | |
| 9 | Netherlands | 11.5 | 0.1 | 4.1 | –4.8 | 4.4 | –12.6 | 8,980.6 | 6,656.1 | 2,324.5 | 8,980.6 | 7,057.8 | 1,792.7 | 9 |
| | | (85) | (37) | (60) | (26) | (63) | (31) | (102) | (101) | (79) | (77) | (101) | (77) | |
| 10 | Norway | 9.2 | –0.1 | 4.0 | 2.7 | 4.3 | 0.8 | 3,119.2 | 1,549.4 | 1,569.8 | 3,119.2 | 2,304.2 | 938.5 | 10 |
| | | (52) | (36) | (58) | (78) | (61) | (76) | (95) | (86) | (75) | (72) | (89) | (70) | |
| 11 | Sweden | 9.5 | 0.3 | 3.4 | –5.1 | 4.2 | 6.2 | 5,316.7 | 4,207.2 | 1,109.5 | 5,316.7 | 4,371.5 | 943.7 | 11 |
| | | (62) | (40) | (48) | (24) | (58) | (84) | (99) | (99) | (72) | (75) | (99) | (71) | |
| 12 | Switzerland | 9.4 | 0.7 | 2.8 | –0.9 | 3.4 | 70.6 | 5,031.3 | 3,443.3 | 1,588.0 | 5,031.3 | 4,132.4 | 687.4 | 12 |
| | | (59) | (46) | (35) | (55) | (46) | (100) | (98) | (98) | (76) | (74) | (98) | (66) | |
| 13 | Canada | 9.5 | 1.7 | 3.4 | –2.3 | 2.8 | 115.7 | 12,191.8 | 9,998.9 | 2,192.9 | 12,191.8 | 9,249.2 | 3,402.2 | 13 |
| | | (60) | (67) | (50) | (49) | (34) | (104) | (105) | (105) | (78) | (80) | (105) | (80) | |
| 14 | Japan | 15.2 | –0.2 | 9.7 | –0.4 | 5.7 | 351.5 | 11,877.8 | 9,820.2 | 2,057.6 | 11,877.8 | 7,970.3 | 2,938.6 | 14 |
| | | (103) | (33) | (86) | (57) | (75) | (102) | (104) | (104) | (77) | (79) | (103) | (79) | |
| 15 | Finland | 9.4 | 1.5 | 4.1 | –3.7 | 5.2 | –14.8 | 1,806.1 | 1,467.9 | 338.2 | 1,806.1 | 1,621.6 | 295.0 | 15 |
| | | (58) | (60) | (61) | (36) | (71) | (28) | (83) | (83) | (58) | (63) | (85) | (49) | |
| 16 | Greece | 12.7 | 1.8 | 6.5 | –7.1 | 2.2 | –55.0 | 766.0 | 378.8 | 387.2 | 766.0 | 1,040.5 | 157.9 | 16 |
| | | (92) | (70) | (81) | (16) | (18) | (9) | (56) | (47) | (63) | (40) | (71) | (33) | |

| | | | | | | | | | | | | | | |
|---|---|---|---|---|---|---|---|---|---|---|---|---|---|---|
| 17 | Iceland | 8.7 | –1.1 | 3.0 | 2.6 | 11.1 | –3.1 | 165.0 | 103.6 | 61.4 | 165.0 | 118.9 | 60.1 | 17 |
| | | (48) | (21) | (39) | (75) | (83) | (48) | (27) | (19) | (25) | (12) | (17) | (17) | |
| 18 | Ireland | 9.5 | 1.3 | 3.8 | –1.0 | 4.6 | –17.2 | 1,070.1 | 710.2 | 359.9 | 1,070.1 | 1,059.6 | 175.5 | 18 |
| | | (61) | (57) | (54) | (54) | (65) | (24) | (67) | (63) | (60) | (51) | (73) | (37) | |
| 19 | Portugal | 13.1 | 2.8 | 5.3 | –2.3 | 4.7 | –37.0 | 1,083.7 | 685.9 | 397.8 | 1,083.7 | 1,020.1 | 244.0 | 19 |
| | | (97) | (80) | (74) | (48) | (67) | (14) | (68) | (60) | (65) | (52) | (70) | (46) | |
| 20 | Spain | 17.8 | 4.8 | 6.2 | –5.2 | 6.5 | –52.9 | 2,700.3 | 1,345.3 | 1,355.0 | 2,700.3 | 2,530.9 | 577.7 | 20 |
| | | (105) | (88) | (80) | (23) | (78) | (10) | (91) | (79) | (73) | (69) | (93) | (62) | |
| 21 | Turkey | 7.2 | –2.9 | 3.3 | –0.2 | 6.5 | 1.8 | 709.7 | 468.8 | 240.9 | 709.7 | 614.9 | 231.1 | 21 |
| | | (35) | (8) | (47) | (59) | (79) | (80) | (52) | (50) | (52) | (36) | (56) | (43) | |
| 22 | Yugoslavia | 13.5 | 1.6 | 5.0 | 5.4 | 12.6 | –12.4 | 1,612.7 | 1,064.2 | 548.5 | 1,612.7 | 1,570.5 | 250.7 | 22 |
| | | (99) | (63) | (66) | (84) | (85) | (33) | (80) | (71) | (67) | (60) | (81) | (47) | |
| 23 | Australia | 9.6 | 1.1 | 3.1 | –3.8 | 2.6 | –65.0 | 4,094.5 | 3,352.3 | 742.2 | 4,094.5 | 3,210.1 | 1,582.9 | 23 |
| | | (63) | (55) | (42) | (35) | (25) | (7) | (97) | (97) | (68) | (73) | (97) | (76) | |
| 24 | New Zealand | 4.4 | –0.7 | 2.7 | –6.2 | 3.9 | 3.1 | 1,111.8 | 1,017.5 | 94.3 | 1,111.8 | 820.5 | 316.0 | 24 |
| | | (15) | (29) | (34) | (19) | (51) | (82) | (70) | (69) | (31) | (54) | (63) | (52) | |
| 25 | South Africa | 9.7 | –0.8 | 2.9 | 0.1 | 2.8 | –116.2 | 3,116.7 | 2,657.1 | 459.6 | 3,116.7 | 2,369.2 | 969.3 | 25 |
| | | (66) | (27) | (36) | (62) | (35) | (2) | (94) | (94) | (66) | (71) | (90) | (73) | |
| 26 | Argentina | 4.9 | –3.3 | 2.4 | 3.1 | 22.9 | –0.8 | 1,641.0 | 1,388.9 | 252.1 | 1,641.0 | 1,296.5 | 414.2 | 26 |
| | | (19) | (6) | (29) | (80) | (88) | (69) | (81) | (81) | (55) | (61) | (76) | (56) | |
| 27 | Bolivia | 10.4 | 0.6 | 3.4 | 12.2 | 5.8 | –1.0 | 129.2 | 116.2 | 13.0 | 129.2 | 123.0 | 45.2 | 27 |
| | | (74) | (43) | (49) | (94) | (77) | (67) | (18) | (21) | (5) | (7) | (20) | (9) | |
| 28 | Brazil | 7.3 | –5.1 | 1.7 | 2.3 | 45.0 | –40.4 | 1,953.2 | 1,754.0 | 199.2 | 1,953.2 | 1,597.6 | 733.8 | 28 |
| | | (36) | (3) | (16) | (72) | (90) | (13) | (85) | (88) | (50) | (64) | (82) | (67) | |
| 29 | Chile | 7.8 | 2.7 | 2.0 | 2.1 | 26.6 | 9.5 | 753.1 | 658.7 | 94.4 | 753.1 | 645.1 | 234.8 | 29 |
| | | (40) | (79) | (25) | (70) | (89) | (89) | (55) | (58) | (32) | (39) | (57) | (44) | |
| 30 | Colombia | 6.5 | 0.4 | 1.7 | –4.0 | 11.3 | –22.2 | 727.9 | 575.0 | 152.9 | 727.9 | 571.4 | 319.2 | 30 |
| | | (29) | (41) | (17) | (32) | (84) | (20) | (53) | (54) | | (37) | (54) | (54) | |
| 31 | Costa Rica | 11.2 | 3.1 | | –3.6 | 2.1 | –7.0 | 164.1 | 135.1 | 29.0 | 164.1 | 165.0 | 50.4 | 31 |
| | | (82) | (83) | | (39) | (16) | (37) | (25) | (26) | (13) | (11) | (24) | (14) | |

*Table A.2c cont.*

| | Country, etc. | 215 | 217 | 218 | 220 | 221 | 222 | 300 | 301 | 302 | 303 | 304 | 305 | |
|---|---|---|---|---|---|---|---|---|---|---|---|---|---|---|
| 32 | Dominican Rep. | 9.7 | −1.1 | −0.5 | −3.7 | 1.8 | −13.4 | 195.9 | 167.5 | 28.4 | 195.9 | 170.0 | 78.9 | 32 |
| | | (65) | (22) | (2) | (38) | (9) | (30) | (30) | (31) | (12) | (15) | (27) | (22) | |
| 33 | Ecuador | 9.4 | 0.9 | 1.8 | −3.7 | 4.3 | −14.0 | 195.9 | 179.1 | 15.8 | 194.9 | 169.9 | 84.0 | 33 |
| | | (57) | (52) | (20) | (37) | (60) | (29) | (29) | (34) | (6) | (14) | (26) | (24) | |
| 34 | El Salvador | 7.8 | 1.3 | 2.4 | −0.1 | 0.7 | −2.5 | 193.2 | 173.7 | 19.5 | 193.2 | 170.6 | 46.5 | 34 |
| | | (41) | (58) | (30) | (60) | (2) | (56) | (28) | (33) | (10) | (13) | (28) | (10) | |
| 35 | Guatemala | 9.3 | 3.6 | 2.3 | −4.0 | 0.6 | −1.7 | 223.4 | 191.9 | 31.5 | 223.4 | 192.1 | 68.4 | 35 |
| | | (54) | (84) | (28) | (31) | (1) | (65) | (32) | (37) | (16) | (17) | (31) | (20) | |
| 36 | Haiti | 2.4 | | 0.8 | −0.3 | 2.9 | −0.8 | 48.5 | 36.9 | 11.6 | 48.5 | 42.8 | 20.5 | 36 |
| | | (8) | | (9) | (58) | (37) | (70) | (10) | (11) | (2) | (2) | (10) | (1) | |
| 37 | Honduras | 13.0 | 5.3 | 1.9 | −4.6 | 2.1 | −4.5 | 137.1 | 124.3 | 12.8 | 137.1 | 120.9 | 37.2 | 37 |
| | | (95) | (89) | (23) | (29) | (15) | (43) | (21) | (23) | (4) | (8) | (18) | (5) | |
| 38 | Mexico | 9.6 | −1.4 | 3.5 | −3.5 | 2.8 | −67.8 | 2,106.1 | 1,108.7 | 997.4 | 2,106.1 | 1,617.4 | 969.3 | 38 |
| | | (64) | (19) | (51) | (40) | (33) | (5) | (87) | (73) | (71) | (66) | (84) | (72) | |
| 39 | Nicaragua | 11.5 | 2.2 | 3.1 | 2.7 | 1.9 | −4.4 | 149.2 | 122.1 | 27.1 | 149.2 | 122.8 | 61.4 | 39 |
| | | (86) | (74) | (43) | (77) | (10) | (44) | (23) | (22) | (11) | (10) | (19) | (18) | |
| 40 | Panama | 10.1 | 0.8 | 4.6 | 10.0 | 1.2 | −3.2 | 255.3 | 93.3 | 162.0 | 255.3 | 207.9 | 81.4 | 40 |
| | | (72) | (49) | (63) | (91) | (6) | (47) | (37) | (16) | (47) | (22) | (34) | (23) | |
| 41 | Paraguay | 8.4 | −0.2 | 1.3 | 12.5 | 3.1 | −2.3 | 61.3 | 49.5 | 11.8 | 61.3 | 58.0 | 22.5 | 41 |
| | | (47) | (35) | (12) | (95) | (41) | (58) | (12) | (12) | (3) | (3) | (12) | (2) | |
| 42 | Peru | 9.0 | −2.2 | 1.9 | 0.8 | 10.0 | −3.0 | 800.7 | 686.5 | 114.2 | 800.7 | 576.2 | 297.6 | 42 |
| | | (51) | (13) | (22) | (65) | (82) | (50) | (58) | (61) | (37) | (42) | (55) | (50) | |
| 43 | Uruguay | 2.0 | −1.1 | 0.2 | −2.8 | 47.2 | 3.3 | 226.2 | 173.1 | 53.1 | 226.2 | 165.0 | 76.5 | 43 |
| | | (7) | (23) | (6) | (46) | (91) | (83) | (33) | (32) | (23) | (18) | (25) | (21) | |
| 44 | Venezuela | 3.5 | −0.9 | 1.8 | 2.4 | 1.2 | −41.3 | 2,687.3 | 2,532.8 | 154.5 | 2,687.3 | 1,391.5 | 1,107.0 | 44 |
| | | (13) | (25) | (19) | (74) | (4) | (12) | (90) | (93) | (44) | (68) | (78) | (74) | |

| | | | | | | | | | | | | | | |
|---|---|---|---|---|---|---|---|---|---|---|---|---|---|---|
| 45 | Jamaica | 9.3 | 1.5 | 3.2 | −2.2 | 3.8 | −12.4 | 378.6 | 237.0 | 141.6 | 378.6 | 281.8 | 176.1 | 45 |
| | | (55) | (61) | (46) | (50) | (49) | (34) | (41) | (42) | (40) | (26) | (40) | (38) | |
| 46 | Trinidad–Tobago | 4.7 | 0.9 | | 5.1 | 3.1 | −3.1 | 517.6 | 427.5 | 90.1 | 517.6 | 450.0 | 120.9 | 46 |
| | | (18) | (50) | | (83) | (40) | (49) | (46) | (49) | (30) | (31) | (50) | (30) | |
| 47 | Puerto Rico | 12.0 | 0.2 | 5.7 | | 2.8 | −95.9 | 1,480.9 | 1,088.2 | 392.7 | 1,480.9 | 1,530.4 | 610.7 | 47 |
| | | (89) | (39) | (77) | | (29) | (3) | (76) | (72) | (64) | (57) | (80) | (64) | |
| 48 | Iran | 13.1 | 1.5 | 5.8 | −6.4 | 2.0 | −27.9 | 1,663.0 | 1,543.0 | 120.0 | 1,663.0 | 1,057.9 | 759.7 | 48 |
| | | (96) | (62) | (79) | (18) | (12) | (18) | (82) | (85) | (38) | (62) | (72) | (68) | |
| 49 | Iraq | 5.8 | −2.2 | 3.2 | 1.9 | 2.0 | 14.6 | 987.7 | 891.7 | 96.0 | 987.7 | 433.9 | 483.8 | 49 |
| | | (24) | (12) | (44) | (69) | (14) | (96) | (65) | (68) | (33) | (49) | (48) | (60) | |
| 50 | Israel | 13.7 | 5.7 | 5.0 | −2.8 | 5.6 | −66.9 | 830.5 | 474.5 | 356.0 | 830.5 | 800.1 | 650.0 | 50 |
| | | (100) | (91) | (69) | (44) | (74) | (6) | (61) | (51) | (59) | (45) | (62) | (65) | |
| 51 | Jordan | 7.6 | 0.8 | | 11.9 | 5.2 | −6.7 | 87.4 | 25.3 | 62.1 | 87.4 | 153.4 | 37.5 | 51 |
| | | (38) | (48) | | (93) | (72) | (38) | (14) | (8) | (26) | (5) | (23) | (6) | |
| 52 | Kuwait | 11.0 | 0.9 | | 0.5 | | 45.7 | 1,452.9 | 1,293.5 | 159.4 | 1,452.9 | 436.4 | 108.2 | 52 |
| | | (81) | (51) | | (64) | | (99) | (74) | (78) | (46) | (55) | (49) | (26) | |
| 53 | Lebanon | 7.9 | 1.0 | | 3.0 | 1.9 | 6.9 | 510.9 | 186.2 | 324.7 | 510.9 | 482.2 | 95.1 | 53 |
| | | (42) | (53) | | (79) | (11) | (85) | (45) | (35) | (57) | (30) | (52) | (25) | |
| 54 | Saudi Arabia | 13.2 | 0.6 | 8.0 | 2.3 | | 18.2 | 1,581.2 | 1,439.5 | 141.7 | 1,581.2 | 501.7 | 807.4 | 54 |
| | | (98) | (44) | (85) | (73) | | (97) | (79) | (82) | (41) | (59) | (53) | (69) | |
| 55 | Yemen, Peo. Dem. Rep. | −0.4 | | | 11.1 | 4.2 | −2.0 | 164.5 | 164.5 | | | 233.4 | | 55 |
| | | (2) | | | (92) | (59) | (62) | (26) | (29) | | | (36) | | |
| 56 | Syria | 6.9 | −0.9 | 3.0 | 1.5 | 2.3 | −7.4 | 253.7 | 165.6 | 88.1 | 253.7 | 273.6 | 24.2 | 56 |
| | | (31) | (26) | (40) | (67) | (20) | (36) | (34) | (30) | (29) | (19) | (39) | (3) | |
| 57 | Egypt | 3.6 | −3.5 | 2.5 | −8.1 | 4.0 | −22.5 | 865.4 | 602.3 | 263.1 | 865.4 | 925.4 | 217.9 | 57 |
| | | (14) | (5) | (32) | (14) | (53) | (19) | (62) | (56) | (56) | (46) | (69) | (41) | |
| 58 | Afghanistan | 12.8 | | | −3.9 | | −2.6 | 113.6 | 113.6 | | | 207.5 | | 58 |
| | | (93) | | | (33) | | (54) | (17) | (20) | | | (33) | | |
| 59 | Burma | −3.5 | −8.6 | 0.5 | 6.6 | 2.5 | −6.3 | 209.5 | 191.6 | 17.9 | 209.5 | 190.5 | 49.7 | 59 |
| | | (1) | (1) | (8) | (85) | (23) | (39) | (31) | (36) | (9) | (16) | (30) | (13) | |

*Table A.2c cont.*

| | Country, etc. | 215 | 217 | 218 | 220 | 221 | 222 | 300 | 301 | 302 | 303 | 304 | 305 | |
|---|---|---|---|---|---|---|---|---|---|---|---|---|---|---|
| 60 | Sri Lanka | 0.1 | −4.8 | 2.5 | −8.4 | 2.6 | −1.8 | 400.6 | 356.0 | 44.6 | 400.6 | 406.2 | 48.2 | 60 |
| | (Ceylon) | (3) | (4) | (31) | (13) | (24) | (64) | (42) | (45) | (21) | (27) | (45) | (12) | |
| 61 | China, Nat. | 18.6 | 6.1 | 6.8 | −2.3 | 3.3 | 13.4 | 785.6 | 659.2 | 126.4 | 785.6 | 688.3 | 154.4 | 61 |
| | Rep. | (106) | (93) | (83) | (47) | (44) | (95) | (57) | (59) | (39) | (41) | (58) | (32) | |
| 62 | Hong Kong | 11.2 | | | | 1.5 | 2.2 | 1,374.2 | 1,374.2 | | | 1,754.7 | | 62 |
| | | (83) | | | | (7) | (81) | (73) | (80) | | | (87) | | |
| 63 | India | 2.0 | −1.6 | 1.4 | 1.9 | 6.6 | 11.1 | 2,004.5 | 1,637.7 | 366.8 | 2,004.5 | 2,445.8 | 473.4 | 63 |
| | | (6) | (17) | (13) | (68) | (80) | (93) | (88) | (87) | (61) | (65) | (92) | (58) | |
| 64 | Indonesia | 2.6 | 2.7 | 0.4 | −32.9 | 144.1 | −2.8 | 870.5 | 835.6 | 34.9 | 870.5 | 795.2 | 360.6 | 64 |
| | | (10) | (78) | (7) | (1) | (92) | (52) | (63) | (67) | (17) | (47) | (61) | (55) | |
| 65 | Korea, Rep. of | 20.5 | 13.1 | 6.6 | −5.3 | 13.5 | −63.6 | 567.9 | 323.8 | 244.1 | 567.9 | 860.2 | 161.5 | 65 |
| | | (107) | (96) | (82) | (21) | (86) | (8) | (47) | (44) | (54) | (32) | (67) | (34) | |
| 66 | Malaysia | 4.6 | −1.6 | 3.2 | 4.1 | 1.2 | 9.8 | 1,454.3 | 1,290.3 | 164.0 | 1,454.3 | 1,088.5 | 308.5 | 66 |
| | | (16) | (16) | (45) | (81) | (5) | (90) | (75) | (77) | (48) | (56) | (74) | (51) | |
| 67 | Pakistan | 7.9 | 0.6 | 2.3 | −10.6 | 3.9 | −44.2 | 633.5 | 521.5 | 112.0 | 633.5 | 873.2 | 236.6 | 67 |
| | | (43) | (42) | (27) | (10) | (50) | (11) | (51) | (52) | (35) | (35) | (68) | (45) | |
| 68 | Philippines | 8.0 | 6.0 | 1.8 | 2.7 | 5.4 | −14.9 | 996.7 | 763.8 | 232.9 | 996.7 | 846.0 | 269.7 | 68 |
| | | (46) | (92) | (21) | (76) | (73) | (27) | (66) | (65) | (51) | (50) | (65) | (48) | |
| 69 | Singapore | 11.9 | −2.0 | | −3.0 | 1.2 | −91.7 | 1,564.8 | 1,190.1 | 374.7 | 1,564.8 | 1,629.8 | 171.6 | 69 |
| | | (88) | (14) | | (43) | (3) | (4) | (78) | (74) | (62) | (58) | (86) | (35) | |
| 70 | Thailand | 11.6 | 1.1 | 4.8 | −1.6 | 2.0 | −19.3 | 818.3 | 575.0 | 243.3 | 818.3 | 825.1 | 109.2 | 70 |
| | | (87) | (56) | (65) | (53) | (13) | (22) | (59) | (55) | (53) | (43) | (64) | (27) | |
| 71 | Algeria | 7.2 | −2.9 | | 4.7 | | −32.8 | 934.2 | 783.4 | 150.8 | 934.2 | 734.7 | 434.5 | 71 |
| | | (33) | (9) | | (82) | | (16) | (64) | (66) | (42) | (48) | (60) | (57) | |
| 72 | Burundi | 4.9 | | | 7.6 | 2.7 | 0.5 | 17.8 | 17.8 | | | 24.5 | | 72 |
| | | (20) | | | (86) | (28) | (75) | (3) | (3) | | | (2) | | |

| | | | | | | | | | | | | | | |
|---|---|---|---|---|---|---|---|---|---|---|---|---|---|---|
| 73 | Cameroon | 10.8 | −0.2 | 3.5 | −2.1 | 3.2 | −2.5 | 152.2 | 152.2 | | | 152.5 | | 73 |
| | | (79) | (34) | (52) | (51) | (42) | (55) | (24) | (28) | | | (22) | | |
| 74 | Central African | 7.0 | | | −18.2 | 4.4 | 0.4 | 25.5 | 25.5 | | | 29.0 | | 74 |
| | Rep. | (32) | | | (5) | (62) | (74) | (7) | (9) | | | (3) | | |
| 75 | Chad | 9.8 | | | −22.0 | 4.9 | −2.2 | 24.7 | 24.7 | | | 38.6 | | 75 |
| | | (67) | | | (2) | (68) | (60) | (6) | (7) | | | (6) | | |
| 76 | Zaire | 12.1 | 9.0 | 5.2 | 31.2 | 20.9 | 7.9 | 569.6 | 539.1 | 30.5 | 569.6 | 337.4 | 224.2 | 76 |
| | | (91) | (95) | (73) | (97) | (87) | (87) | (48) | (53) | (15) | (33) | (44) | (42) | |
| 77 | Dahomey | 10.7 | −1.0 | | −4.7 | | −2.1 | 19.5 | 19.5 | | | 42.4 | | 77 |
| | | (76) | (24) | | (28) | | (61) | (4) | (4) | | | (9) | | |
| 78 | Ethiopia | 8.0 | 1.1 | 2.9 | −4.7 | 2.8 | −3.0 | 143.0 | 99.9 | 43.1 | 143.0 | 115.3 | 57.2 | 78 |
| | | (45) | (54) | (37) | (27) | (31) | (51) | (22) | (17) | (20) | (9) | (16) | (15) | |
| 79 | Ghana | 0.5 | −5.5 | −0.1 | −13.0 | 6.9 | 1.6 | 360.4 | 299.7 | 60.7 | 360.4 | 327.9 | 117.3 | 79 |
| | | (4) | (2) | (4) | (8) | (81) | (79) | (40) | (43) | (24) | (25) | (42) | (29) | |
| 80 | Ivory Coast | 10.5 | 1.7 | 5.1 | 1.2 | 3.2 | −3.3 | 490.9 | 377.9 | 113.0 | 490.9 | 319.3 | 174.8 | 80 |
| | | (75) | (68) | (70) | (66) | (43) | (46) | (44) | (46) | (36) | (29) | (41) | (36) | |
| 81 | Kenya | 10.1 | 0.1 | 3.5 | 19.5 | 2.1 | −17.6 | 417.7 | 346.1 | 181.6 | 417.7 | 336.8 | 128.3 | 81 |
| | | (70) | (38) | (53) | (96) | (17) | (23) | (43) | (41) | (49) | (28) | (43) | (31) | |
| 82 | Liberia | 14.5 | | | | | | 132.9 | 132.9 | | | 109.9 | | 82 |
| | | (102) | | | | | | (20) | (25) | | | (15) | | |
| 83 | Libya | 23.6 | −0.3 | 19.8 | 9.5 | 5.0 | 89.7 | 1,094.8 | 1,018.1 | 76.7 | 1,094.8 | 419.5 | 482.6 | 83 |
| | | (108) | (30) | (87) | (90) | (69) | (101) | (69) | (70) | (28) | (53) | (47) | (59) | |
| 84 | Malagasy Rep. | 6.8 | −1.2 | 3.0 | −10.2 | 2.7 | −2.4 | 103.4 | 103.4 | | | 147.3 | | 84 |
| | | (30) | (20) | (38) | (11) | (27) | (57) | (15) | (18) | | | (21) | | |
| 85 | Malawi | 10.1 | 2.3 | 1.6 | −3.1 | | −4.0 | 68.4 | 50.9 | 17.5 | 68.4 | 70.4 | 40.6 | 85 |
| | | (71) | (75) | (15) | (42) | | (45) | (13) | (14) | (8) | (4) | (13) | (8) | |
| 86 | Mali | 3.5 | | | 2.2 | | −0.2 | 27.4 | 20.6 | 6.8 | 27.4 | 41.5 | 36.5 | 86 |
| | | (12) | | | (71) | | (73) | (8) | (5) | (1) | (1) | (8) | (4) | |
| 87 | Mauritania | 5.7 | | | −18.4 | 4.5 | 7.8 | 49.6 | 49.6 | | | 32.7 | | 87 |
| | | (22) | | | (4) | (64) | (86) | (11) | (13) | | | (4) | | |
| 88 | Morocco | 6.3 | −1.5 | 1.4 | −8.5 | 2.3 | −16.2 | 575.5 | 416.4 | 159.1 | 575.5 | 458.9 | 178.6 | 88 |
| | | (28) | (18) | (14) | (12) | (19) | (25) | (49) | (48) | (45) | (34) | (51) | (39) | |

*Table A.2c* *cont.*

| | Country, etc. | 215 | 217 | 218 | 220 | 221 | 222 | 300 | 301 | 302 | 303 | 304 | 305 | |
|---|---|---|---|---|---|---|---|---|---|---|---|---|---|---|
| 89 | Niger | 10.7 | 5.5 | 1.7 | −0.1 | 3.7 | −1.9 | 24.2 | 24.2 | | | 34.9 | | 89 |
| | | (77) | (90) | (18) | (61) | (48) | (63) | (5) | (6) | | | (5) | | |
| 90 | Nigeria | 8.9 | 1.9 | 2.0 | −14.0 | 4.1 | −7.9 | 824.2 | 749.8 | 74.4 | 824.2 | 709.8 | 317.2 | 90 |
| | | (50) | (71) | (24) | (7) | (56) | (35) | (60) | (64) | (27) | (44) | (59) | (53) | |
| 91 | Rwanda | 32.9 | | | −6.2 | 1.7 | −1.3 | 14.2 | 14.2 | | | 21.1 | | 91 |
| | | (109) | | | (20) | (8) | (66) | (2) | (2) | | | (1) | | |
| 92 | Senegal | 2.6 | −2.4 | −0.7 | −17.5 | 2.4 | −1.0 | 129.7 | 129.7 | | | 175.8 | | 92 |
| | | (11) | (10) | (1) | (6) | (21) | (68) | (19) | (24) | | | (29) | | |
| 93 | Sierra Leone | 2.5 | −1.9 | 4.1 | 9.0 | 4.1 | 0.9 | 103.9 | 87.0 | 16.9 | 103.9 | 89.5 | 38.0 | 93 |
| | | (9) | (15) | (59) | (88) | (57) | (78) | (16) | (15) | (7) | (6) | (14) | (7) | |
| 94 | Sudan | 4.7 | −0.3 | 1.2 | −19.0 | 2.8 | −2.3 | 263.2 | 227.8 | 35.4 | 263.2 | 244.6 | 57.9 | 94 |
| | | (17) | (32) | (11) | (3) | (30) | (59) | (38) | (40) | (18) | (23) | (38) | (16) | |
| 95 | Tanzania | 7.6 | 2.0 | −0.1 | −7.6 | 2.5 | −5.1 | 268.5 | 219.1 | 49.4 | 268.5 | 232.7 | 46.9 | 95 |
| | | (39) | (72) | (3) | (15) | (22) | (41) | (39) | (38) | (22) | (24) | (35) | (11) | |
| 96 | Togo | 9.9 | 1.7 | | 8.0 | 3.3 | −0.4 | 31.7 | 31.7 | | | 43.8 | | 96 |
| | | (69) | (65) | | (87) | (45) | (71) | (9) | (10) | | | (11) | | |
| 97 | Tunisia | 5.6 | 1.5 | 1.1 | −7.1 | 3.0 | −2.6 | 254.1 | 145.2 | 108.9 | 254.1 | 237.2 | 110.0 | 97 |
| | | (21) | (59) | (10) | (17) | (38) | (53) | (36) | (27) | (34) | (21) | (37) | (28) | |
| 98 | Uganda | 6.1 | −2.3 | 2.5 | −0.5 | 4.6 | −4.5 | 254.1 | 223.8 | 30.3 | 254.1 | 204.5 | 62.4 | 98 |
| | | (26) | (11) | (33) | (56) | (66) | (42) | (35) | (39) | (14) | (20) | (32) | (19) | |
| 99 | Upper Volta | 5.8 | 6.8 | | 9.3 | 2.8 | −0.4 | 13.9 | 13.9 | | | 40.0 | | 99 |
| | | (25) | (94) | | (89) | (36) | (72) | (1) | (1) | | | (7) | | |
| 100 | Zambia | 16.1 | 4.2 | 5.0 | 0.3 | 5.1 | 10.3 | 731.6 | 694.2 | 37.4 | 731.6 | 412.8 | 197.4 | 100 |
| | | (104) | (87) | (68) | (63) | (70) | (91) | (54) | (62) | (19) | (38) | (46) | (40) | |

| | | | | | | | | | | | | | | |
|---|---|---|---|---|---|---|---|---|---|---|---|---|---|---|
| 101 | Bulgaria | 12.1 | 4.0 | 7.1 | | | 10.6 | 1,217.0 | 1,217.0 | | | 1,257.2 | | 101 |
| | | (90) | (86) | (84) | | | (92) | (72) | (76) | | | (75) | | |
| 102 | China, People's Rep. | 0.9 | | | | | | 1,871.4 | 1,871.4 | | | 1,439.8 | | 102 |
| | | (5) | | | | | | (84) | (90) | | | (79) | | |
| 103 | Cuba | 6.2 | −3.2 | 0.1 | | | −34.5 | 618.9 | 618.9 | | | 846.6 | | 103 |
| | | (27) | (7) | (5) | | | (15) | (50) | (57) | | | (66) | | |
| 104 | Czechoslovakia | 7.2 | −0.3 | 5.4 | | | 0.9 | 2,751.1 | 2,751.1 | | | 2,630.5 | | 104 |
| | | (34) | (31) | (76) | | | (77) | (92) | (95) | | | (94) | | |
| 105 | Germany, Dem. Rep. | 8.0 | 2.5 | 5.1 | | | −5.7 | 3,223.3 | 3,223.3 | | | 3,103.2 | | 105 |
| | | (44) | (77) | (71) | | | (40) | (96) | (96) | | | (96) | | |
| 106 | Hungary | 9.9 | 2.9 | 5.3 | | | −12.6 | 1,525.2 | 1,525.2 | | | 1,602.6 | | 106 |
| | | (68) | (82) | (75) | | | (32) | (77) | (84) | | | (83) | | |
| 107 | Poland | 8.8 | 1.6 | 5.2 | | | 12.7 | 2,302.5 | 2,302.5 | | | 2,440.4 | | 107 |
| | | (49) | (64) | (72) | | | (94) | (88) | (91) | | | (91) | | |
| 108 | Romania | 9.2 | | | | | 9.5 | 1,192.5 | 1,192.5 | | | 1,314.9 | | 108 |
| | | (53) | | | | | (88) | (71) | (75) | | | (77) | | |
| 109 | USSR | 7.3 | 0.7 | 5.8 | | | 114.2 | 8,811.7 | 8,811.7 | | | 8,172.5 | | 109 |
| | | (37) | (47) | (78) | | | (103) | (101) | (103) | | | (104) | | |
| | Number of countries | 109 | 96 | 87 | 97 | 92 | 107 | 109 | 109 | 84 | 84 | 109 | 84 | |
| | Range | −3.5 to 32.9 | −8.6 to 13.1 | −0.7 to 19.8 | −32.9 to 31.2 | 0.6 to 144.1 | −245.7 to 351.5 | 13.9 to 43,137.1 | 13.9 to 28,090.2 | 6.8 to 15,046.9 | 27.4 to 43,137.1 | 21.1 to 24,839.7 | 20.5 to 12,998.1 | |
| | Median | 9.3 | 0.8 | 3.2 | −2.3 | 3.5 | −2.6 | 753.1 | 575.0 | 151.9 | 804.5 | 576.2 | 227.7 | |
| | Mean | 9.0 | 0.8 | 3.5 | −1.7 | 7.0 | 0.3 | 2,275.6 | 1,811.3 | 737.2 | 2,779.2 | 1,773.4 | 761.0 | |
| | Standard deviation | 4.9 | 3.0 | 2.7 | 8.5 | 16.2 | 64.0 | 5,519.4 | 3,951.7 | 1,978.7 | 6,249.8 | 3,562.0 | 1,773.7 | |
| | Coefficient of | 54 | 380 | 76 | .051 | 230 | 20,000 | 240 | 220 | 270 | 220 | 200 | 230 | |

(d) Variables 306–347

| | Country, etc. | 306 | 315 | 307 | 308 | 310 | 316 | 320 | 321 | 325 | 330 | 331 | 345 | 346 | 347 | |
|---|---|---|---|---|---|---|---|---|---|---|---|---|---|---|---|---|
| 1 | United States | 37,837.8 (84) | 37,837.8 (109) | 65.1 (16) | 34.9 (69) | 45.1 (11) | 26.1 (11) | | 19.1 (40) | 32.2 (20) | 65.7 (14) | 34.3 (71) | 5,299.4 (109) | 10.9 (4) | 14.0 (101) | 1 |
| 2 | United Kingdom | 21,178.0 (82) | 21,178.0 (107) | 63.9 (15) | 36.1 (70) | 51.1 (21) | 19.0 (1) | 10.9 (61) | 20.5 (43) | 12.5 (7) | 68.4 (26) | 31.6 (59) | 735.2 (104) | 44.9 (51) | 33.2 (107) | 2 |
| 3 | Austria | 2,668.2 (68) | 2,668.2 (91) | 68.5 (23) | 31.5 (62) | 49.5 (19) | 32.2 (41) | 4.2 (31) | 45.6 (86) | 20.6 (11) | 80.6 (64) | 19.4 (21) | –96.9 (36) | 51.6 (61) | –3.6 (80) | 3 |
| 4 | Belgium–Luxembourg | 6,191.4 (76) | 6,191.4 (100) | 77.7 (39) | 22.3 (46) | 53.7 (26) | 36.3 (51) | 8.4 (51) | 62.3 (94) | 16.4 (9) | 77.9 (54) | 22.1 (31) | 138.7 (96) | 70.5 (78) | 2.2 (89) | 4 |
| 5 | Denmark | 783.3 (36) | 783.3 (51) | 74.6 (32) | 25.4 (53) | 52.5 (23) | 33.1 (43) | 8.1 (47) | 25.2 (55) | 56.1 (35) | 81.9 (70) | 18.1 (15) | –204.5 (20) | 61.8 (72) | –26.1 (23) | 5 |
| 6 | France | 13,751.9 (81) | 13,751.9 (106) | 72.6 (28) | 27.4 (57) | 43.2 (6) | 25.8 (8) | 5.7 (36) | 40.5 (83) | 26.3 (12) | 73.5 (45) | 26.5 (40) | 399.1 (101) | 25.9 (18) | 2.9 (90) | 6 |
| 7 | Germany, West | 22,870.4 (83) | 22,870.4 (108) | 80.9 (43) | 19.1 (42) | 53.5 (25) | 23.6 (4) | 8.2 (49) | 36.4 (75) | 9.4 (5) | 73.5 (44) | 26.5 (41) | 2,355.9 (108) | 38.8 (39) | 10.3 (100) | 7 |
| 8 | Italy | 10,362.3 (78) | 10,362.3 (103) | 67.6 (21) | 32.4 (64) | 44.9 (9) | 27.2 (15) | 9.2 (55) | 38.9 (79) | 20.1 (10) | 74.9 (48) | 25.1 (37) | 984.1 (107) | 33.9 (31) | 9.5 (99) | 8 |
| 9 | Netherlands | 8,850.5 (77) | 8,850.5 (102) | 74.1 (30) | 25.9 (55) | 40.5 (3) | 34.8 (48) | 4.2 (32) | 55.1 (91) | 40.9 (27) | 79.7 (61) | 20.3 (24) | 130.2 (95) | 87.4 (86) | 1.5 (88) | 9 |
| 10 | Norway | 3,242.8 (71) | 3,242.8 (95) | 49.7 (5) | 50.3 (80) | 47.0 (12) | 31.1 (35) | 8.9 (54) | 25.0 (54) | 31.9 (19) | 71.1 (32) | 28.9 (53) | –123.5 (30) | 84.0 (84) | –3.8 (79) | 10 |
| 11 | Sweden | 5,315.2 (75) | 5,315.2 (99) | 79.1 (41) | 20.9 (44) | 51.6 (22) | 26.8 (14) | 6.3 (40) | 30.2 (67) | 28.8 (13) | 82.2 (71) | 17.8 (14) | 1.5 (85) | 49.3 (57) | 0.1 (84) | 11 |
| 12 | Switzerland | 4,819.8 (74) | 4.819.8 (98) | 68.4 (22) | 31.6 (63) | 47.1 (13) | 25.2 (6) | 10.0 (57) | 39.3 (80) | 7.8 (4) | 85.7 (77) | 14.3 (8) | 211.5 (99) | 68.6 (76) | 4.4 (93) | 12 |
| 13 | Canada | 12,651.4 (80) | 12,651.4 (105) | 82.0 (49) | 18.0 (36) | 38.3 (1) | 60.8 (93) | 59.0 (102) | 6.6 (8) | 49.4 (31) | 73.1 (41) | 26.9 (44) | –499.8 (6) | 43.0 (48) | –4.0 (78) | 13 |
| 14 | Japan | 10,908.9 (79) | 10,908.9 (104) | 82.7 (53) | 17.3 (32) | 53.2 (24) | 31.8 (40) | 29.3 (84) | 5.7 (3) | 7.0 (3) | 73.1 (40) | 26.9 (45) | 968.9 (106) | 21.2 (14) | 8.9 (98) | 14 |

| | | | | | | | | | | | | | | | | |
|---|---|---|---|---|---|---|---|---|---|---|---|---|---|---|---|---|
| 15 | Finland | 1,916.6 | 1,916.6 | 81.3 | 18.7 | 57.7 | 31.6 | 5.9 | 27.7 | 39.2 | 84.6 | 15.4 | –110.5 | 48.3 | –5.8 | 15 |
| | | (63) | (84) | (44) | (41) | (33) | (39) | (37) | (60) | (25) | (76) | (9) | (34) | (56) | (73) | |
| 16 | Greece | 1,198.4 | 1,198.4 | 49.4 | 50.6 | 48.9 | 28.6 | 13.1 | 37.0 | 83.4 | 86.8 | 13.2 | –432.4 | 31.3 | –36.1 | 16 |
| | | (53) | (69) | (4) | (81) | (17) | (24) | (67) | (77) | (50) | (80) | (5) | (10) | (25) | (11) | |
| 17 | Iceland | 179.0 | 179.0 | 62.8 | 37.2 | 81.7 | 31.1 | 16.0 | 18.6 | 97.3 | 66.4 | 33.6 | –14.0 | 87.7 | –7.8 | 17 |
| | | (9) | (22) | (13) | (72) | (80) | (36) | (70) | (38) | (87) | (16) | (69) | (75) | (87) | (69) | |
| 18 | Ireland | 1,235.1 | 1,235.1 | 66.4 | 33.6 | 58.0 | 75.9 | 6.4 | 10.3 | 66.1 | 85.8 | 14.2 | –165.0 | 82.2 | –13.4 | 18 |
| | | (54) | (70) | (20) | (65) | (34) | (103) | (42) | (20) | (40) | (78) | (7) | (23) | (83) | (50) | |
| 19 | Portugal | 1,264.1 | 1,264.1 | 63.3 | 36.7 | 48.5 | 29.1 | 10.8 | 19.6 | 36.7 | 80.7 | 19.3 | –180.4 | 55.5 | –14.3 | 19 |
| | | (55) | (73) | (14) | (71) | (14) | (30) | (60) | (41) | (22) | (65) | (20) | (22) | (64) | (49) | |
| 20 | Spain | 3,108.6 | 3,108.6 | 49.8 | 50.2 | 45.0 | 26.7 | 12.1 | 35.3 | 57.7 | 81.4 | 18.6 | –685.2 | 26.0 | –22.0 | 20 |
| | | (70) | (94) | (6) | (79) | (10) | (13) | (64) | (74) | (36) | (68) | (17) | (4) | (19) | (30) | |
| 21 | Turkey | 846.0 | 846.0 | 66.1 | 33.9 | 54.4 | 28.7 | 16.8 | 34.7 | 94.2 | 72.7 | 27.3 | –136.3 | 16.1 | –16.1 | 21 |
| | | (38) | (53) | (19) | (66) | (27) | (27) | (72) | (72) | (72) | (39) | (46) | (29) | (7) | (44) | |
| 22 | Yugoslavia | 1,821.2 | 1,821.2 | 66.0 | 34.0 | 42.0 | 27.6 | 6.0 | 28.7 | 37.8 | 86.2 | 13.8 | –208.5 | 40.3 | –11.4 | 22 |
| | | (62) | (83) | (18) | (67) | (4) | (19) | (38) | (63) | (23) | (79) | (6) | (19) | (42) | (60) | |
| 23 | Australia | 4,793.0 | 4,793.0 | 81.9 | 18.1 | 49.4 | 30.3 | 11.3 | 13.9 | 80.3 | 67.0 | 33.0 | –698.5 | 35.5 | –14.6 | 23 |
| | | (73) | (97) | (48) | (37) | (18) | (34) | (64) | (24) | (46) | (20) | (65) | (3) | (32) | (47) | |
| 24 | New Zealand | 1,136.5 | 1,136.5 | 91.5 | 8.5 | 66.9 | 52.3 | 14.8 | 15.0 | 94.4 | 72.2 | 27.8 | –24.7 | 45.2 | –2.2 | 24 |
| | | (49) | (65) | (77) | (8) | (56) | (82) | (68) | (30) | (73) | (37) | (48) | (67) | (54) | (82) | |
| 25 | South Africa | 3,338.5 | 3,338.5 | 85.3 | 14.7 | 48.9 | 43.4 | 9.2 | 18.7 | 58.8 | 71.0 | 29.0 | –221.8 | 55.6 | –6.6 | 25 |
| | | (72) | (96) | (59) | (26) | (16) | (67) | (56) | (39) | (37) | (31) | (54) | (18) | (65) | (71) | |
| 26 | Argentina | 1,710.7 | 1,710.7 | 84.6 | 15.4 | 74.2 | 27.5 | 8.1 | 40.9 | 93.2 | 75.8 | 24.2 | –69.8 | 20.4 | –4.1 | 26 |
| | | (59) | (79) | (58) | (27) | (72) | (18) | (46) | (84) | (67) | (50) | (35) | (42) | (12) | (76) | |
| 27 | Bolivia | 168.2 | 168.2 | 89.7 | 10.1 | | 59.9 | 38.4 | 9.0 | 97.2 | 73.2 | 26.8 | –39.0 | 45.1 | –23.2 | 27 |
| | | (7) | (19) | (69) | (16) | | (92) | (92) | (16) | (86) | (42) | (43) | (60) | (53) | (29) | |
| 28 | Brazil | 2,331.4 | 2,331.4 | 89.8 | 10.2 | 68.1 | 37.4 | 33.2 | 26.3 | 91.9 | 68.5 | 31.5 | –378.2 | 19.9 | –16.2 | 28 |
| | | (65) | (86) | (70) | (15) | (61) | (55) | (85) | (59) | (61) | (27) | (58) | (12) | (10) | (43) | |
| 29 | Chile | 879.9 | 879.9 | 87.5 | 12.5 | | 37.4 | 28.0 | 31.4 | 28.9 | 73.3 | 26.7 | –137.3 | 31.8 | –15.6 | 29 |
| | | (40) | (56) | (64) | (21) | | (54) | (83) | (69) | (14) | (43) | (42) | (28) | (26) | (45) | |

*Table A.2d cont.*

| | Country, etc. | 306 | 315 | 307 | 308 | 310 | 316 | 320 | 321 | 325 | 330 | 331 | 345 | 346 | 347 | |
|---|---|---|---|---|---|---|---|---|---|---|---|---|---|---|---|---|
| 30 | Colombia | 890.6 | 890.6 | 79.0 | 21.0 | 74.9 | 50.9 | 47.5 | 22.1 | 92.9 | 77.9 | 22.1 | −162.8 | 28.4 | −18.3 | 30 |
| | | (41) | (57) | (40) | (45) | (74) | (79) | (97) | (48) | (63) | (56) | (29) | (24) | (21) | (40) | |
| 31 | Costa Rica | 215.4 | 215.4 | 82.3 | 17.7 | 81.4 | 53.5 | 50.4 | 22.9 | 83.1 | 76.6 | 23.4 | −51.4 | 56.4 | −23.9 | 31 |
| | | (12) | (26) | (50) | (35) | (79) | (84) | (98) | (50) | (49) | (52) | (33) | (51) | (66) | (26) | |
| 32 | Dominican Rep. | 248.9 | 248.9 | 85.5 | 14.5 | 82.2 | 82.1 | 79.2 | 8.3 | 97.4 | 68.3 | 31.7 | −53.1 | 40.9 | −21.3 | 32 |
| | | (16) | (31) | (60) | (25) | (81) | (106) | (105) | (13) | (88) | (25) | (60) | (50) | (43) | (32) | |
| 33 | Ecuador | 253.9 | 253.9 | 91.9 | 8.1 | 94.5 | 49.7 | 43.4 | 30.2 | 98.5 | 66.9 | 33.1 | −58.9 | 37.0 | −23.2 | 33 |
| | | (17) | (32) | (78) | (7) | (88) | (76) | (94) | (68) | (91) | (19) | (66) | (45) | (34) | (28) | |
| 34 | El Salvador | 217.1 | 217.1 | 89.9 | 10.1 | 63.1 | 41.7 | 25.7 | 27.7 | 79.1 | 78.6 | 21.4 | −23.9 | 51.1 | −11.0 | 34 |
| | | (13) | (27) | (71) | (14) | (50) | (61) | (80) | (61) | (44) | (57) | (28) | (68) | (60) | (61) | |
| 35 | Guatemala | 260.5 | 260.5 | 85.9 | 14.1 | 66.4 | 41.6 | 34.7 | 23.4 | 85.5 | 73.7 | 26.3 | −37.2 | 33.7 | −14.3 | 35 |
| | | (18) | (33) | (62) | (23) | (55) | (60) | (87) | (51) | (51) | (46) | (39) | (61) | (30) | (48) | |
| 36 | Haiti | 63.3 | 63.3 | 76.0 | 24.0 | | 56.2 | 50.9 | 32.6 | | 67.7 | 32.3 | −14.8 | | −23.4 | 36 |
| | | (1) | (10) | (34) | (51) | | (87) | (99) | (70) | | (22) | (63) | (74) | | (27) | |
| 37 | Honduras | 158.1 | 158.1 | 90.7 | 9.3 | 75.9 | 58.6 | 53.6 | 21.5 | 94.0 | 76.5 | 23.5 | −21.1 | 53.6 | −13.3 | 37 |
| | | (6) | (18) | (73) | (12) | (75) | (91) | (100) | (46) | (71) | (51) | (34) | (71) | (62) | (51) | |
| 38 | Mexico | 2,586.7 | 2,586.7 | 52.6 | 47.4 | 54.4 | 66.4 | 56.1 | 5.9 | 76.7 | 62.5 | 37.5 | −480.6 | 22.3 | −18.6 | 38 |
| | | (67) | (89) | (7) | (78) | (28) | (97) | (101) | (4) | (43) | (10) | (75) | (8) | (15) | (38) | |
| 39 | Nicaragua | 184.2 | 184.2 | 81.9 | 18.1 | 67.3 | 43.2 | 27.9 | 22.6 | 93.5 | 66.6 | 33.4 | −35.1 | 54.3 | −19.1 | 39 |
| | | (10) | (23) | (47) | (38) | (58) | (66) | (82) | (49) | (68) | (17) | (68) | (62) | (63) | (35) | |
| 40 | Panama | 289.1 | 289.1 | 36.5 | 63.5 | 73.9 | 70.0 | 66.7 | 6.3 | 99.1 | 71.9 | 28.1 | −33.8 | 76.5 | −11.7 | 40 |
| | | (21) | (36) | (3) | (82) | (71) | (99) | (103) | (6) | (97) | (34) | (51) | (63) | (80) | (58) | |
| 41 | Paraguay | 80.5 | 80.5 | 80.8 | 19.2 | | 44.9 | 24.1 | 14.8 | 96.1 | 72.1 | 27.9 | −19.2 | 32.4 | −23.9 | 41 |
| | | (3) | (12) | (42) | (43) | | (70) | (78) | (28) | (80) | (36) | (49) | (72) | (28) | (25) | |
| 42 | Peru | 873.8 | 873.8 | 85.7 | 14.3 | 55.2 | 42.6 | 37.4 | 29.7 | 93.1 | 65.9 | 34.1 | −73.1 | 42.7 | −8.4 | 42 |
| | | (39) | (55) | (61) | (24) | (31) | (64) | (91) | (65) | (65) | (15) | (70) | (41) | (47) | (68) | |

| | | | | | | | | | | | | | | | | |
|---|---|---|---|---|---|---|---|---|---|---|---|---|---|---|---|---|
| 43 | Uruguay | 241.5 (15) | 241.5 (30) | 76.5 (36) | 23.5 (49) | | 28.8 (28) | 11.5 (63) | 32.8 (71) | 80.0 (45) | 68.3 (28) | 31.7 (57) | −15.2 (73) | 31.8 (27) | −6.3 (72) | 43 |
| 44 | Venezuela | 2,498.5 (66) | 2,498.5 (88) | 94.3 (81) | 5.7 (4) | 92.5 (87) | 42.9 (65) | 41.8 (93) | 9.1 (17) | 98.8 (94) | 55.7 (6) | 44.3 (79) | 188.8 (97) | 56.5 (67) | 7.6 (95) | 44 |
| 45 | Jamaica | 457.9 (28) | 457.9 (43) | 62.6 (12) | 37.4 (73) | 61.5 (45) | 51.6 (80) | 37.0 (89) | 2.2 (1) | 92.3 (62) | 61.5 (9) | 38.5 (76) | −79.3 (39) | 87.9 (88) | −17.3 (41) | 45 |
| 46 | Trinidad–Tobago | 570.9 (32) | 570.9 (47) | 82.6 (52) | 17.4 (33) | 82.4 (82) | 47.4 (74) | 33.7 (86) | 11.8 (22) | 91.2 (59) | 78.8 (59) | 21.2 (26) | −53.3 (49) | 135.5 (95) | −9.3 (65) | 46 |
| 47 | Puerto Rico | 2,141.1 (54) | 2,141.1 (85) | 73.5 (29) | 26.5 (56) | | 91.0 (107) | 90.5 (106) | | | 71.5 (33) | 28.5 (52) | −715.2 (2) | 112.1 (94) | −33.4 (13) | 47 |
| 48 | Iran | 1,817.6 (61) | 1,817.6 (82) | 92.8 (79) | 7.2 (6) | 88.6 (86) | 29.0 (29) | 5.1 (34) | 18.6 (37) | 96.3 (82) | 58.2 (7) | 41.8 (78) | −155.4 (25) | 45.1 (52) | −8.5 (67) | 48 |
| 49 | Iraq | 917.7 (43) | 917.7 (59) | 90.3 (72) | 9.7 (13) | | 29.9 (32) | 1.4 (13) | 48.0 (88) | 98.1 (90) | 47.3 (3) | 52.7 (82) | 70.0 (91) | 78.6 (81) | 7.6 (96) | 49 |
| 50 | Israel | 1,450.1 (58) | 1,450.1 (77) | 57.1 (10) | 42.9 (75) | 58.7 (38) | 27.4 (17) | 14.9 (69) | 28.8 (64) | 30.4 (16) | 55.2 (5) | 44.8 (80) | −617.5 (5) | 60.5 (70) | −42.6 (9) | 50 |
| 51 | Jordan | 190.9 (11) | 190.9 (24) | 29.0 (1) | 71.0 (84) | 62.0 (47) | 34.5 (47) | 0.1 (1) | 4.3 (2) | 93.7 (70) | 80.4 (63) | 19.6 (22) | −103.5 (35) | 62.2 (73) | −54.2 (3) | 51 |
| 52 | Kuwait | 544.6 (30) | 544.6 (45) | 89.0 (68) | 11.0 (17) | 43.3 (7) | 37.3 (53) | 3.2 (27) | 44.3 (85) | 47.2 (29) | 80.1 (62) | 19.9 (23) | 908.2 (105) | 87.2 (85) | 166.8 (109) | 52 |
| 53 | Lebanon | 577.3 (33) | 577.3 (48) | 36.4 (2) | 63.6 (83) | | 25.9 (9) | 4.7 (33) | 15.0 (29) | 48.2 (30) | 83.5 (73) | 16.5 (12) | −66.4 (44) | 96.4 (90) | −11.5 (59) | 53 |
| 54 | Saudi Arabia | 1,309.1 (56) | 1,309.1 (74) | 91.0 (75) | 9.0 (10) | | 33.4 (44) | 6.2 (39) | 30.1 (66) | 99.7 (101) | 38.3 (1) | 61.7 (84) | 272.2 (100) | 97.0 (91) | 20.8 (104) | 54 |
| 55 | Yemen, Peo. Dem. Rep. | | 233.4 (28) | | | | 60.9 (94) | 0.3 (5) | 24.0 (52) | | | | −68.9 (43) | | −29.3 (18) | 55 |
| 56 | Syria | 297.9 (23) | 297.9 (37) | 65.3 (17) | 34.7 (68) | 64.4 (53) | 28.2 (22) | 1.6 (18) | 17.6 (35) | 89.2 (55) | 91.9 (84) | 8.1 (1) | −44.2 (55) | 43.1 (49) | −14.8 (46) | 56 |
| 57 | Egypt | 1,143.3 (50) | 1,143.3 (66) | 69.6 (24) | 30.4 (61) | 61.5 (44) | 28.6 (25) | 3.1 (26) | 14.0 (25) | 53.5 (34) | 80.9 (66) | 19.1 (19) | −241.0 (15) | 38.7 (38) | −21.1 (33) | 57 |

*Table A.2d cont.*

| | Country, etc. | 306 | 315 | 307 | 308 | 310 | 316 | 320 | 321 | 325 | 330 | 331 | 345 | 346 | 347 | |
|---|---|---|---|---|---|---|---|---|---|---|---|---|---|---|---|---|
| 58 | Afghanistan | | 207.5<br>(25) | | | 63.5<br>(52) | 41.7<br>(62) | 12.5<br>(65) | 9.2<br>(18) | 88.2<br>(53) | | | –93.8<br>(37) | | –45.2<br>(5) | 58 |
| 59 | Burma | 240.2<br>(14) | 240.2<br>(29) | 91.4<br>(76) | 8.6<br>(9) | 78.6<br>(76) | 27.3<br>(16) | 0.4<br>(6) | 7.5<br>(10) | 97.1<br>(84) | 79.3<br>(60) | 20.7<br>(25) | –30.8<br>(64) | 30.4<br>(24) | –12.8<br>(54) | 59 |
| 60 | Sri Lanka<br>(Ceylon) | 454.4<br>(27) | 454.4<br>(42) | 88.9<br>(67) | 11.1<br>(18) | 73.6<br>(70) | 37.4<br>(56) | 8.1<br>(48) | 8.3<br>(12) | 99.0<br>(96) | 89.4<br>(82) | 10.6<br>(3) | –53.8<br>(48) | 51.2<br>(59) | –11.8<br>(57) | 60 |
| 61 | China, Nat. Rep. | 842.7<br>(37) | 842.7<br>(52) | 83.9<br>(56) | 16.1<br>(29) | 54.5<br>(29) | 38.3<br>(57) | 22.0<br>(76) | 8.4<br>(14) | 51.2<br>(32) | 81.7<br>(69) | 18.3<br>(16) | –57.1<br>(46) | 42.3<br>(45) | –6.8<br>(70) | 61 |
| 62 | Hong Kong | | 1,754.7<br>(80) | | | 58.0<br>(35) | 33.4<br>(45) | 26.3<br>(81) | 8.8<br>(15) | 11.3<br>(6) | | | –380.5<br>(11) | | –21.7<br>(31) | 62 |
| 63 | India | 2,919.2<br>(69) | 2,919.2<br>(92) | 81.7<br>(46) | 18.3<br>(39) | 55.1<br>(30) | 31.4<br>(38) | 17.9<br>(74) | 7.3<br>(9) | 52.0<br>(33) | 83.8<br>(74) | 16.2<br>(11) | –914.7<br>(1) | 11.9<br>(5) | –31.3<br>(15) | 63 |
| 64 | Indonesia | 1,157.8<br>(51) | 1,157.8<br>(67) | 96.0<br>(84) | 4.0<br>(1) | 59.3<br>(40) | 36.8<br>(52) | 35.3<br>(88) | 37.8<br>(78) | 98.7<br>(93) | 68.8<br>(28) | 31.2<br>(57) | –285.3<br>(13) | 28.6<br>(22) | –24.6<br>(24) | 64 |
| 65 | Korea, Rep. of | 1,021.7<br>(45) | 1,021.7<br>(61) | 57.0<br>(9) | 43.0<br>(76) | 48.7<br>(15) | 49.2<br>(75) | 37.3<br>(90) | 6.2<br>(5) | 38.2<br>(24) | 84.2<br>(75) | 15.8<br>(10) | –453.8<br>(9) | 29.9<br>(23) | –44.4<br>(6) | 65 |
| 66 | Malaysia | 1,396.9<br>(57) | 1,396.9<br>(75) | 88.7<br>(66) | 11.3<br>(19) | 61.8<br>(46) | 29.3<br>(31) | 12.9<br>(66) | 10.5<br>(21) | 71.3<br>(41) | 77.9<br>(55) | 22.1<br>(30) | 57.4<br>(90) | 93.7<br>(89) | 4.1<br>(92) | 66 |
| 67 | Pakistan | 1,109.8<br>(47) | 1,109.8<br>(63) | 82.3<br>(51) | 17.7<br>(34) | 60.2<br>(41) | 22.7<br>(3) | 8.9<br>(53) | 14.7<br>(26) | 59.6<br>(38) | 78.7<br>(58) | 21.3<br>(27) | –483.9<br>(7) | 15.5<br>(6) | –43.6<br>(7) | 67 |
| 68 | Philippines | 1,115.7<br>(48) | 1,115.7<br>(64) | 76.6<br>(37) | 23.4<br>(48) | 61.5<br>(43) | 54.5<br>(85) | 44.3<br>(95) | 15.6<br>(31) | 90.3<br>(58) | 75.8<br>(49) | 24.2<br>(36) | –119.0<br>(32) | 32.6<br>(29) | –10.7<br>(62) | 68 |
| 69 | Singapore | 1,801.4<br>(60) | 1,801.4<br>(81) | 76.1<br>(35) | 23.9<br>(50) | 39.8<br>(2) | 28.3<br>(23) | 5.5<br>(35) | 6.5<br>(7) | 61.7<br>(39) | 90.5<br>(83) | 9.5<br>(2) | –236.6<br>(16) | 181.0<br>(96) | –13.1<br>(52) | 69 |
| 70 | Thailand | 934.3<br>(44) | 934.3<br>(60) | 70.3<br>(26) | 29.7<br>(59) | 65.2<br>(54) | 28.1<br>(21) | 8.0<br>(45) | 12.2<br>(23) | 90.2<br>(57) | 88.3<br>(81) | 11.7<br>(4) | –116.0<br>(33) | 36.6<br>(33) | –12.4<br>(55) | 70 |

| | | | | | | | | | | | | | | | | |
|---|---|---|---|---|---|---|---|---|---|---|---|---|---|---|---|---|
| 71 | Algeria | 1,169.2 (52) | 1,169.2 (68) | 83.9 (57) | 16.1 (28) | 68.8 (63) | 72.3 (101) | 0.5 (8) | 86.2 (106) | 93.1 (66) | 62.8 (11) | 37.2 (74) | −222.4 (17) | 63.3 (75) | −19.0 (37) | 71 |
| 72 | Burundi | | 24.5 (2) | | | | 77.0 (104) | 74.1 (104) | 16.8 (32) | | | | −6.7 (81) | | −27.3 (21) | 72 |
| 73 | Cameroon | | 152.5 (17) | | | 63.3 (51) | 55.2 (86) | 10.5 (59) | 76.3 (101) | 80.4 (47) | | | −0.2 (84) | 38.5 (36) | −0.2 (83) | 73 |
| 74 | Central African Rep. | | 29.0 (3) | | | 78.6 (77) | 53.0 (83) | 19.2 (75) | 51.3 (89) | 99.6 (100) | | | −3.5 (82) | | −12.1 (56) | 74 |
| 75 | Chad | | 38.6 (6) | | | 84.2 (83) | 62.1 (95) | 0.1 (2) | 62.4 (95) | 97.1 (85) | | | −13.9 (76) | | −36.0 (12) | 75 |
| 76 | Zaire | 561.6 (31) | 561.6 (46) | 94.7 (82) | 5.3 (3) | 71.1 (66) | 51.8 (81) | 10.3 (58) | 75.3 (100) | 31.0 (17) | 60.1 (8) | 39.9 (77) | 8.0 (87) | 73.2 (79) | 1.4 (86) | 76 |
| 77 | Dahomey | | 42.4 (8) | | | 58.9 (39) | 56.5 (88) | 6.6 (43) | 76.5 (102) | 93.5 (69) | | | −22.9 (70) | 26.8 (20) | −54.0 (4) | 77 |
| 78 | Ethiopia | 172.5 (8) | 172.5 (20) | 69.9 (25) | 30.1 (60) | 80.2 (78) | 50.1 (77) | 46.2 (96) | 18.5 (36) | 98.8 (95) | 66.8 (18) | 33.2 (67) | −29.5 (65) | 24.9 (16) | −17.1 (42) | 78 |
| 79 | Ghana | 445.2 (26) | 445.2 (41) | 83.2 (54) | 16.8 (31) | 74.9 (73) | 34.9 (49) | 16.8 (73) | 25.6 (56) | 96.1 (81) | 73.7 (47) | 26.3 (38) | −84.8 (38) | 44.2 (50) | −19.0 (36) | 79 |
| 80 | Ivory Coast | 394.1 (25) | 394.1 (40) | 77.0 (38) | 23.0 (47) | 71.5 (68) | 46.7 (73) | 16.1 (71) | 63.2 (96) | 95.3 (76) | 64.6 (13) | 35.4 (72) | −3.2 (83) | 81.9 (82) | 0.8 (85) | 80 |
| 81 | Kenya | 465.1 (29) | 465.1 (44) | 56.5 (8) | 43.5 (77) | 62.5 (49) | 32.5 (42) | 7.2 (44) | 21.9 (47) | 89.1 (54) | 72.4 (38) | 27.6 (47) | −47.3 (53) | 69.2 (77) | −10.2 (63) | 81 |
| 82 | Liberia | | 109.9 (13) | | | | | | | | | | 23.0 (89) | | 21.8 (106) | 82 |
| 83 | Libya | 902.1 (42) | 902.1 (58) | 93.0 (80) | 7.0 (5) | 99.5 (91) | 41.1 (58) | 4.0 (29) | 67.9 (98) | 99.9 (103) | 46.5 (2) | 53.5 (83) | 192.7 (98) | 111.3 (93) | 21.4 (105) | 83 |
| 84 | Malagasy Rep. | | 147.3 (16) | | | 73.2 (69) | 56.9 (88) | 22.3 (77) | 53.5 (90) | 94.4 (74) | | | −43.8 (56) | 20.1 (11) | −29.7 (17) | 84 |
| 85 | Malawi | 111.0 (4) | 111.0 (14) | 74.4 (31) | 25.6 (54) | 58.1 (36) | 66.5 (98) | 2.9 (23) | 10.0 (19) | 98.6 (92) | 63.4 (12) | 36.6 (73) | −42.6 (57) | 62.6 (74) | −38.4 (10) | 85 |

*Table A.2d cont.*

| | Country, etc. | 306 | 315 | 307 | 308 | 310 | 316 | 320 | 321 | 325 | 330 | 331 | 345 | 346 | 347 | |
|---|---|---|---|---|---|---|---|---|---|---|---|---|---|---|---|---|
| 86 | Mali | 78.0 | 78.0 | 75.1 | 24.9 | 67.4 | 44.3 | 2.0 | 8.1 | 97.6 | 53.2 | 46.8 | −50.6 | | −64.9 | 86 |
| | | (2) | (11) | (33) | (52) | (59) | (69) | (21) | (11) | (89) | (4) | (81) | (52) | | (2) | |
| 87 | Mauritania | | 32.7 | | | 95.0 | 41.5 | 1.7 | 68.3 | 99.2 | | | 16.9 | | 51.7 | 87 |
| | | | (4) | | | (89) | (59) | (19) | (99) | (98) | | | (88) | | (108) | |
| 88 | Morocco | 637.5 | 637.5 | 72.4 | 27.6 | 62.1 | 45.5 | 1.8 | 61.2 | 92.9 | 72.0 | 28.0 | −54.0 | 48.2 | −8.5 | 88 |
| | | (35) | (50) | (27) | (78) | (48) | (72) | (20) | (93) | (64) | (35) | (50) | (47) | (55) | (66) | |
| 89 | Niger | | 34.9 | | | 67.1 | 72.1 | 0.5 | 66.2 | 95.8 | | | −10.7 | 10.8 | −30.7 | 89 |
| | | | (5) | | | (57) | (100) | (7) | (97) | (79) | | | (79) | (3) | (16) | |
| 90 | Nigeria | 1,027.0 | 1,027.0 | 91.0 | 9.0 | 50.8 | 42.2 | 8.3 | 36.8 | 91.7 | 69.1 | 30.9 | −202.8 | 37.1 | −19.7 | 90 |
| | | (46) | (62) | (74) | (11) | (20) | (63) | (50) | (76) | (60) | (29) | (56) | (21) | (35) | (34) | |
| 91 | Rwanda | | 21.1 | | | 71.1 | 65.8 | 3.0 | 82.5 | 99.5 | | | −6.9 | | −32.7 | 91 |
| | | | (1) | | | (67) | (96) | (25) | (104) | (99) | | | (80) | | (14) | |
| 92 | Senegal | | 175.8 | | | 58.1 | 81.7 | 0.2 | 82.7 | 95.4 | | | −46.1 | 41.7 | −26.2 | 92 |
| | | | (21) | | | (37) | (105) | (4) | (105) | (77) | | | (54) | (44) | (22) | |
| 93 | Sierra Leone | 127.5 | 127.5 | 83.7 | 16.3 | 70.1 | 75.7 | 1.4 | 19.9 | 36.2 | 70.2 | 29.8 | −23.7 | 60.7 | −18.6 | 93 |
| | | (5) | (15) | (55) | (30) | (64) | (102) | (14) | (42) | (21) | (30) | (55) | (69) | (71) | (39) | |
| 94 | Sudan | 302.5 | 302.5 | 86.5 | 13.5 | 87.2 | 26.1 | 3.8 | 35.0 | 99.9 | 80.9 | 19.1 | −39.3 | 38.6 | −13.0 | 94 |
| | | (22) | (38) | (63) | (22) | (84) | (12) | (28) | (73) | (102) | (67) | (18) | (59) | (37) | (53) | |
| 95 | Tanzania | 279.6 | 279.6 | 81.6 | 18.4 | 60.2 | 35.4 | 6.4 | 17.6 | 86.0 | 83.2 | 16.8 | −11.1 | 56.9 | −4.0 | 95 |
| | | (20) | (35) | (45) | (40) | (42) | (50) | (41) | (34) | (52) | (72) | (13) | (78) | (68) | (77) | |
| 96 | Togo | | 43.8 | | | 67.5 | 50.8 | 4.0 | 76.8 | 95.5 | | | −12.1 | 40.2 | −27.6 | 96 |
| | | | (9) | | | (60) | (78) | (30) | (103) | (78) | | | (77) | (41) | (20) | |
| 97 | Tunisia | 347.2 | 347.2 | 57.1 | 42.9 | 42.8 | 45.4 | 1.5 | 58.4 | 81.4 | 68.3 | 31.7 | −148.5 | 57.5 | −42.8 | 97 |
| | | (24) | (39) | (11) | (74) | (5) | (71) | (17) | (92) | (48) | (24) | (61) | (26) | (69) | (8) | |
| 98 | Uganda | 266.9 | 266.9 | 88.1 | 11.9 | 68.1 | 34.1 | 24.3 | 14.7 | 89.7 | 76.6 | 23.4 | 4.0 | 49.8 | 1.5 | 98 |
| | | (14) | (34) | (65) | (20) | (62) | (46) | (79) | (27) | (56) | (53) | (32) | (86) | (58) | (87) | |
| 99 | Upper Volta | | 40.0 | | | 70.4 | 58.1 | 3.0 | 20.8 | 95.0 | | | −26.1 | 20.8 | −65.3 | 99 |
| | | | (7) | | | (65) | (90) | (24) | (45) | (75) | | | (66) | (13) | (1) | |

| | | | | | | | | | | | | | | | | |
|---|---|---|---|---|---|---|---|---|---|---|---|---|---|---|---|---|
| 100 | Zambia | 610.2 (34) | 610.2 (49) | 94.9 (83) | 5.1 (2) | 96.5 (90) | 43.7 (68) | 1.1 (12) | 25.0 (53) | 3.3 (2) | 67.6 (21) | 32.4 (64) | 121.4 (94) | 103.4 (92) | 19.9 (103) | 100 |
| 101 | Bulgaria | | 1,257.2 (71) | | | | 28.7 (26) | 0.9 (11) | 40.2 (82) | 31.8 (18) | | | –40.2 (58) | 39.8 (40) | –3.2 (81) | 101 |
| 102 | China, People's Rep. | | 1,439.8 (76) | | | | | | | | | | 432.6 (102) | | 15.7 (102) | 102 |
| 103 | Cuba | | 846.6 (54) | | | 88.1 (85) | 31.2 (37) | 0.1 (3) | 16.9 (33) | 96.8 (83) | | | –245.9 (14) | 42.5 (46) | –29.0 (19) | 103 |
| 104 | Czechoslovakia | | 2,630.5 (90) | | | 57.1 (32) | 21.7 (2) | 2.8 (32) | 25.8 (57) | 15.0 (8) | | | 120.5 (93) | 18.4 (8) | 4.6 (94) | 104 |
| 105 | Germany, Dem. Rep. | | 3,103.2 (93) | | | | 23.9 (5) | 1.5 (15) | 20.6 (44) | 0.0 (1) | | | 112.4 (92) | 25.7 (17) | 3.6 (91) | 105 |
| 106 | Hungary | | 1,602.6 (78) | | | 44.4 (8) | 27.6 (20) | 0.7 (9) | 39.8 (81) | 29.2 (15) | | | –77.5 (40) | 18.5 (9) | –4.8 (75) | 106 |
| 107 | Poland | | 2,440.4 (87) | | | | 25.7 (7) | 8.5 (52) | 25.9 (58) | 39.6 (26) | | | –137.8 (27) | 3.3 (1) | –5.6 (74) | 107 |
| 108 | Romania | | 1,314.9 (74) | | | | 29.9 (33) | 0.8 (10) | 46.7 (87) | 75.8 (42) | | | –122.3 (31) | | –9.3 (64) | 108 |
| 109 | USSR | | 8,172.5 (101) | | | | 26.1 (10) | 1.5 (16) | 28.2 (62) | 42.4 (28) | | | 639.2 (103) | 7.4 (2) | 7.8 (97) | 109 |
| | Variable number | 306 | 315 | 307 | 308 | 310 | 316 | 320 | 321 | 325 | 330 | 330 | 345 | 346 | 347 | |
| | Number of countries | 84 | 109 | 84 | 84 | 91 | 107 | 106 | 106 | 103 | 84 | 84 | 109 | 96 | 109 | |
| | Range | 63.3 to 37,837.8 | 21.1 to 37,837.8 | 29.0 to 96.0 | 4.0 to 71.0 | 38.3 to 99.5 | 19.0 to 91.0 | 0.1 to 90.5 | 2.2 to 86.2 | 3.3 to 99.9 | 38.3 to 91.9 | 8.1 to 61.7 | –914.7 to 5,299.4 | 3.3 to 181.0 | –65.3 to 166.8 | |
| | Median | 909.9 | 873.8 | 80.9 | 19.2 | 61.8 | 37.4 | 8.9 | 25.0 | 86.0 | 73.3 | 26.8 | –44.2 | 43.1 | –12.4 | |
| | Mean | 2,723.0 | 2,336.0 | 76.3 | 23.7 | 63.4 | 42.0 | 17.1 | 29.8 | 70.5 | 73.0 | 27.0 | 16.0 | 49.9 | –11.3 | |
| | Standard deviation | 5,666.2 | 5,086.3 | 14.4 | 14.4 | 14.5 | 15.9 | 19.4 | 20.8 | 30.4 | 10.1 | 10.1 | 629.9 | 29.2 | 25.6 | |
| | Coefficient of variation | 210 | 220 | 19 | 61 | 23 | 38 | 110 | 70 | 43 | 14 | 37 | 3,900 | 59 | .023 | |

(e) Variables 348–365

| | Country, etc. | 348 | 349 | 350 | 352 | 361 | 364 | 365 | |
|---|---|---|---|---|---|---|---|---|---|
| 1 | United States | 673,391.7 (97) | 3,461.5 (96) | 194.6 (106) | 81.4 (97) | 52.0 (91) | 3.5 (3) | 9,202.0 (108) | 1 |
| 2 | United Kingdom | 91,419.1 (93) | 1,682.4 (84) | 54.4 (99) | 81.9 (100) | 16.2 (21) | 3.5 (2) | 5,121.0 (104) | 2 |
| 3 | Austria | 8,775.1 (72) | 1,210.4 (80) | 7.3 (52) | 76.7 (77) | 51.1 (89) | 11.1 (23) | 2,631.0 (87) | 3 |
| 4 | Belgium–Luxembourg | 16,125.1 (81) | 1,706.4 (85) | 9.5 (65) | 84.9 (108) | 33.2 (69) | 6.3 (8) | 4,726.0 (103) | 4 |
| 5 | Denmark | 9,246.3 (74) | 1,942.5 (89) | 4.8 (44) | 79.1 (87) | 14.8 (14) | 14.3 (30) | 4,093.0 (99) | 5 |
| 6 | France | 94,693.5 (94) | 1,942.8 (90) | 48.8 (97) | 81.7 (98) | 38.9 (77) | 8.1 (14) | 2,968.0 (92) | 6 |
| 7 | Germany, West | 108,076.0 (95) | 1,902.7 (88) | 56.8 (100) | 82.2 (103) | 40.4 (79) | 4.4 (4) | 4,239.0 (100) | 7 |
| 8 | Italy | 53,801.9 (91) | 1,043.7 (76) | 51.6 (98) | 82.0 (101) | 50.3 (88) | 13.3 (28) | 1,783.0 (79) | 8 |
| 9 | Netherlands | 17,084.4 (82) | 1,390.1 (82) | 12.3 (72) | 80.8 (94) | 29.2 (64) | 8.3 (15) | 3,442.0 (93) | 9 |
| 10 | Norway | 6,445.4 (68) | 1,732.6 (86) | 3.7 (36) | 71.9 (65) | 16.0 (20) | 8.9 (18) | 3,553.0 (95) | 10 |
| 11 | Sweden | 18,993.3 (85) | 2,457.1 (94) | 7.7 (56) | 78.7 (85) | 16.3 (22) | 7.0 (11) | 4,458.0 (101) | 11 |
| 12 | Switzerland | 12,815.2 (78) | 2,161.1 (93) | 5.9 (49) | 72.4 (66) | 77.4 (95) | 6.0 (7) | 2,667.0 (88) | 12 |
| 13 | Canada | 49,644.3 (90) | 2,522.6 (95) | 19.7 (84) | 82.8 (104) | 24.7 (50) | 6.5 (9) | 7,593.0 (107) | 13 |
| 14 | Japan | 81,141.1 (92) | 828.8 (71) | 98.0 (103) | 73.1 (69) | 32.0 (68) | 11.8 (26) | 1,782.0 (78) | 14 |
| 15 | Finland | 6,916.9 (69) | 1,500.4 (83) | 4.6 (43) | 80.5 (92) | 17.8 (28) | 17.8 (36) | 2,719.0 (90) | 15 |
| 16 | Greece | 5,507.3 (65) | 644.1 (65) | 8.6 (59) | 49.9 (20) | 28.5 (61) | 25.1 (49) | 786.0 (67) | 16 |
| 17 | Iceland | 387.8 (7) | 2,019.6 (92) | 0.2 (1) | 76.5 (75) | 20.9 (34) | 16.0 (32) | 3,833.0 (98) | 17 |
| 18 | Ireland | 2,445.1 (45) | 851.9 (72) | 2.9 (26) | 77.1 (80) | 40.7 (80) | 21.1 (41) | 2,244.0 (83) | 18 |
| 19 | Portugal | 3,468.7 (56) | 377.0 (54) | 9.2 (62) | 72.4 (67) | 86.2 (97) | 21.2 (42) | 497.0 (59) | 19 |
| 20 | Spain | 17,945.5 (83) | 567.4 (63) | 31.6 (94) | 51.5 (23) | 46.3 (86) | 18.0 (37) | 1,038.0 (74) | 20 |
| 21 | Turkey | 8,539.4 (71) | 274.1 (45) | 31.2 (92) | 71.8 (64) | 26.0 (56) | 35.8 (73) | 350.0 (52) | 21 |
| 22 | Yugoslavia | 5,267.7 (62) | 270.0 (44) | 19.5 (83) | 79.1 (88) | 5.5 (2) | 28.0 (54) | 1,192.0 (76) | 22 |

*Table A.2e cont.*

| Country, etc. | 348 | 349 | 350 | 352 | 361 | 364 | 365 | |
|---|---|---|---|---|---|---|---|---|
| 23 Australia | 22,135.5 | 1,945.1 | 11.4 | 62.6 | 34.1 | 10.4 | 4,568.0 | 23 |
| | (86) | (91) | (68) | (45) | (72) | (22) | (102) | |
| 24 New Zealand | 4,972.2 | 1,890.6 | 2.6 | 70.2 | 13.9 | 12.5 | 2,551.0 | 24 |
| | (61) | (87) | (23) | (59) | (12) | (27) | (85) | |
| 25 South Africa | 10,299.1 | 576.3 | 17.9 | 71.4 | 23.6 | 9.9 | 2,695.0 | 25 |
| | (75) | (64) | (80) | (63) | (46) | (19) | (89) | |
| 26 Argentina | 11,696.7 | 518.7 | 22.5 | 59.6 | 24.6 | 16.7 | 1,331.0 | 26 |
| | (77) | (61) | (85) | (35) | (49) | (33) | (77) | |
| 27 Bolivia | 527.3 | 121.8 | 3.7 | 61.4 | 14.5 | 22.7 | 176.0 | 27 |
| | (11) | (20) | (34) | (41) | (13) | (46) | (39) | |
| 28 Brazil | 5,862.9 | 72.1 | 81.3 | 78.6 | 20.9 | 29.6 | 364.0 | 28 |
| | (66) | (5) | (102) | (84) | (35) | (60) | (53) | |
| 29 Chile | 2,822.2 | 324.0 | 8.7 | 42.1 | 16.4 | 10.4 | 1,048.0 | 29 |
| | (49) | (52) | (60) | (10) | (23) | (21) | (75) | |
| 30 Colombia | 4,161.8 | 230.4 | 18.0 | 82.9 | 16.8 | 31.1 | 527.0 | 30 |
| | (58) | (37) | (81) | (105) | (25) | (62) | (61) | |
| 31 Costa Rica | 576.7 | 387.0 | 1.5 | 77.0 | 8.7 | 26.9 | 296.0 | 31 |
| | (14) | (55) | (9) | (78) | (6) | (53) | (47) | |
| 32 Dominican Rep. | 1,032.4 | 285.2 | 3.6 | 69.6 | 15.6 | 26.0 | 158.0 | 32 |
| | (29) | (47) | (32) | (58) | (18) | (51) | (35) | |
| 33 Ecuador | 1,078.9 | 209.5 | 5.2 | 75.7 | 23.0 | 33.9 | 214.0 | 33 |
| | (30) | (29) | (47) | (74) | (44) | (69) | (42) | |
| 34 El Salvador | 783.1 | 267.3 | 2.9 | 70.5 | 22.8 | 29.1 | 170.0 | 34 |
| | (21) | (43) | (25) | (61) | (43) | (58) | (37) | |
| 35 Guatemala | 1,343.1 | 302.5 | 4.4 | 78.5 | 25.6 | 28.7 | 201.0 | 35 |
| | (34) | (49) | (41) | (83) | (54) | (57) | (40) | |
| 36 Haiti | | | 4.4 | 79.9 | 6.1 | 35.3 | 34.0 | 36 |
| | | | (39) | (91) | (3) | (72) | (11) | |
| 37 Honduras | 474.7 | 217.8 | 2.2 | 83.6 | 13.6 | 41.4 | 164.0 | 37 |
| | (10) | (34) | (17) | (106) | (10) | (78) | (36) | |
| 38 Mexico | 18,804.7 | 440.5 | 42.7 | 66.9 | 23.6 | 17.4 | 962.0 | 38 |
| | (84) | (57) | (96) | (50) | (45) | (35) | (70) | |
| 39 Nicaragua | 547.0 | 329.5 | 1.7 | 61.2 | 19.1 | 36.4 | 230.0 | 39 |
| | (12) | (53) | (12) | (40) | (31) | (75) | (44) | |
| 40 Panama | 642.7 | 518.3 | 1.2 | 50.2 | 31.6 | 23.7 | 1,030.0 | 40 |
| | (15) | (60) | (7) | (21) | (65) | (48) | (72) | |
| 41 Paraguay | 418.5 | 206.1 | 2.0 | 70.5 | 9.7 | 36.4 | 128.0 | 41 |
| | (8) | (28) | (16) | (60) | (7) | (74) | (31) | |
| 42 Peru | 3,397.9 | 291.7 | 11.6 | 80.8 | 17.3 | 20.2 | 546.0 | 42 |
| | (55) | (48) | (69) | (93) | (26) | (40) | (62) | |
| 43 Uruguay | 656.0 | 241.2 | 2.7 | 56.7 | 77.1 | 15.5 | 883.0 | 43 |
| | (17) | (39) | (24) | (29) | (94) | (31) | (68) | |
| 44 Venezuela | 8,051.1 | 923.3 | 8.7 | 51.3 | 33.3 | 7.6 | 2,544.0 | 44 |
| | (70) | (74) | (61) | (22) | (70) | (12) | (84) | |

*Table A.2e cont.*

| Country, etc. | 348 | 349 | 350 | 352 | 361 | 364 | 365 | |
|---|---|---|---|---|---|---|---|---|
| 45 Jamaica | 879.1 | 491.1 | 1.8 | 75.0 | 22.5 | 11.6 | 896.0 | 45 |
| | (24) | (59) | (13) | (72) | (41) | (24) | (69) | |
| 46 Trinidad–Tobago | 729.3 | 749.5 | 1.0 | 49.0 | 6.2 | 8.6 | 3,666.0 | 46 |
| | (19) | (68) | (4) | (17) | (4) | (16) | (97) | |
| 47 Puerto Rico | 3,032.3 | 1,153.5 | 2.6 | 79.2 | | 6.6 | 2,046.0 | 47 |
| | (53) | (78) | (21) | (89) | | (10) | (81) | |
| 48 Iran | 6,179.8 | 249.1 | 24.8 | 51.7 | 16.6 | 25.6 | 383.0 | 48 |
| | (67) | (41) | (88) | (24) | (24) | (50) | (55) | |
| 49 Iraq | 2,480.6 | 304.4 | 8.1 | 39.8 | 36.8 | 19.8 | 504.0 | 49 |
| | (46) | (51) | (57) | (7) | (74) | (38) | (60) | |
| 50 Israel | 3,018.4 | 1,183.7 | 2.6 | 65.9 | 36.5 | 8.6 | 2,237.0 | 50 |
| | (52) | (79) | (22) | (48) | (73) | (17) | (82) | |
| 51 Jordan | 469.0 | 245.5 | 1.9 | 21.5 | 71.9 | 22.6 | 301.0 | 51 |
| | (9) | (40) | (14) | (1) | (93) | (45) | (48) | |
| 52 Kuwait | 2,103.0 | 4,427.4 | 0.5 | 31.4 | 26.2 | 0.5 | 13,943.0 | 52 |
| | (41) | (97) | (2) | (4) | (57) | (1) | (109) | |
| 53 Lebanon | 1,094.7 | 456.1 | 2.4 | 25.4 | 45.2 | 11.6 | 611.0 | 53 |
| | (31) | (58) | (20) | (2) | (85) | (25) | (63) | |
| 54 Saudi Arabia | 2,653.0 | 393.0 | 6.7 | 38.6 | 44.0 | 7.7 | 366.0 | 54 |
| | (47) | (56) | (51) | (6) | (83) | (13) | (54) | |
| 55 Yemen, Peo. Dem. Rep. | | | 1.1 | 49.3 | 28.8 | | 9.0 | 55 |
| | | | (5) | (18) | (62) | | (3) | |
| 56 Syria | 1,152.7 | 220.0 | 5.2 | 59.9 | 15.7 | 32.1 | 348.0 | 56 |
| | (32) | (35) | (46) | (38) | (19) | (66) | (51) | |
| 57 Egypt | 4,643.0 | 158.0 | 29.4 | 64.3 | 18.5 | 28.6 | 307.0 | 57 |
| | (60) | (25) | (90) | (46) | (30) | (55) | (49) | |
| 58 Afghanistan | | | 15.1 | 66.0 | 22.4 | | 23.0 | 58 |
| | | | (77) | (49) | (40) | | (9) | |
| 59 Burma | 1,753.0 | 70.9 | 24.7 | 53.5 | 63.9 | 31.8 | 48.0 | 59 |
| | (39) | (4) | (87) | (25) | (92) | (63) | (18) | |
| 60 Sri Lanka (Ceylon) | 1,654.7 | 148.3 | 11.2 | 68.0 | 15.3 | 42.0 | 108.0 | 60 |
| | (37) | (24) | (67) | (55) | (15) | (81) | (27) | |
| 61 China, Nat. Rep. | 2,818.5 | 226.6 | 12.4 | 56.9 | 40.9 | 26.0 | 653.0 | 61 |
| | (48) | (36) | (73) | (30) | (81) | (52) | (66) | |
| 62 Hong Kong | | | 3.7 | 56.2 | | | 625.0 | 62 |
| | | | (33) | (28) | | | (64) | |
| 63 India | 37,638.6 | 77.5 | 486.6 | 67.5 | 25.5 | 47.5 | 171.0 | 63 |
| | (89) | (9) | (108) | (53) | (53) | (83) | (38) | |
| 64 Indonesia | 3,066.3 | 100.0 | 104.9 | 67.2 | 5.4 | 57.0 | 113.0 | 64 |
| | (54) | (13) | (105) | (52) | (1) | (91) | (28) | |
| 65 Korea, Rep. of | 2,257.5 | 117.0 | 28.4 | 40.7 | 33.5 | 41.3 | 447.0 | 65 |
| | (43) | (19) | (89) | (9) | (71) | (77) | (56) | |

*Table A.2e cont.*

| | Country, etc. | 348 | 349 | 350 | 352 | 361 | 364 | 365 | |
|---|---|---|---|---|---|---|---|---|---|
| 66 | Malaysia | 2,862.5 | 303.5 | 9.4 | 68.5 | 36.9 | 28.6 | 1,031.0 | 66 |
| | | (51) | (50) | (64) | (56) | (75) | (56) | (73) | |
| 67 | Pakistan | 10,425.6 | 101.3 | 102.9 | 49.3 | 25.3 | 47.0 | 88.0 | 67 |
| | | (76) | (14) | (104) | (19) | (51) | (82) | (25) | |
| 68 | Philippines | 5,327.0 | 164.6 | 32.3 | 81.1 | 12.0 | 32.0 | 205.0 | 68 |
| | | (63) | (26) | (95) | (96) | (8) | (64) | (41) | |
| 69 | Singapore | 966.3 | 519.5 | 1.9 | 79.1 | 13.5 | 4.9 | 639.0 | 69 |
| | | (27) | (62) | (15) | (86) | (9) | (5) | (65) | |
| 70 | Thailand | 3,956.1 | 128.7 | 30.7 | 53.6 | 79.2 | 32.1 | 128.0 | 70 |
| | | (57) | (22) | (91) | (26) | (96) | (65) | (30) | |
| 71 | Algeria | 2,856.0 | 239.6 | 11.9 | 87.1 | 27.7 | 41.9 | 320.0 | 71 |
| | | (50) | (38) | (71) | (109) | (58) | (80) | (50) | |
| 72 | Burundi | | | 3.2 | 36.7 | 37.9 | | 7.0 | 72 |
| | | | | (28) | (5) | (76) | | (1) | |
| 73 | Cameroon | 675.7 | 128.0 | 5.3 | 75.2 | 22.6 | 53.8 | 70.0 | 73 |
| | | (18) | (21) | (48) | (73) | (42) | (86) | (22) | |
| 74 | Central African Rep. | | | 1.4 | 62.3 | 15.4 | | 37.0 | 74 |
| | | | | (8) | (44) | (16) | | (13) | |
| 75 | Chad | | | 3.3 | 67.2 | 24.3 | | 15.0 | 75 |
| | | | | (29) | (51) | (48) | | (7) | |
| 76 | Zaire | 1,843.0 | 115.2 | 15.6 | 59.9 | 15.6 | 22.2 | 85.0 | 76 |
| | | (40) | (18) | (78) | (37) | (17) | (43) | (24) | |
| 77 | Dahomey | 188.0 | 79.7 | 2.4 | 54.9 | 26.0 | 48.6 | 31.0 | 77 |
| | | (2) | (10) | (18) | (27) | (55) | (84) | (10) | |
| 78 | Ethiopia | 1,358.0 | 59.8 | 22.7 | 45.0 | 39.0 | 65.4 | 12.0 | 78 |
| | | (35) | (2) | (86) | (14) | (78) | (94) | (6) | |
| 79 | Ghana | 1,662.9 | 214.9 | 7.7 | 78.0 | 31.6 | | 100.0 | 79 |
| | | (38) | (32) | (55) | (82) | (66) | | (26) | |
| 80 | Ivory Coast | 957.2 | 249.9 | 3.8 | 73.2 | 13.7 | 41.9 | 143.0 | 80 |
| | | (26) | (42) | (37) | (70) | (11) | (79) | (32) | |
| 81 | Kenya | 1,006.9 | 107.6 | 9.4 | 59.2 | 24.1 | 34.2 | 123.0 | 81 |
| | | (28) | (17) | (63) | (33) | (47) | (71) | (29) | |
| 82 | Liberia | | | 1.1 | 44.5 | | | 258.0 | 82 |
| | | | | (6) | (12) | | | (45) | |
| 83 | Libya | 1,329.3 | 820.5 | 1.6 | 45.9 | 50.1 | 4.9 | 280.0 | 83 |
| | | (33) | (70) | (11) | (15) | (87) | (6) | (46) | |
| 84 | Malagasy Rep. | 654.6 | 105.6 | 6.2 | 59.7 | 28.3 | | 43.0 | 84 |
| | | (16) | (15) | (50) | (36) | (60) | | (16) | |
| 85 | Malawi | 253.0 | 64.7 | 3.9 | 59.4 | 21.4 | 55.8 | 36.0 | 85 |
| | | (4) | (3) | (38) | (34) | (36) | (90) | (12) | |
| 86 | Mali | | | 4.5 | 29.3 | 6.4 | | 21.0 | 86 |
| | | | | (42) | (3) | (5) | | (8) | |

*Table A.2e cont.*

| | Country, etc. | 348 | 349 | 350 | 352 | 361 | 364 | 365 | |
|---|---|---|---|---|---|---|---|---|---|
| 87 | Mauritania | | | 1.0 | 43.4 | 28.0 | | 48.0 | 87 |
| | | | | (3) | (11) | (59) | | (19) | |
| 88 | Morocco | 2,384.3 | 178.9 | 13.3 | 81.1 | 21.5 | 32.5 | 157.0 | 88 |
| | | (44) | (27) | (74) | (95) | (38) | (67) | (34) | |
| 89 | Niger | 300.0 | 85.5 | 3.5 | 65.6 | 22.4 | 64.7 | 12.0 | 89 |
| | | (5) | (11) | (30) | (47) | (39) | (93) | (5) | |
| 90 | Nigeria | 4,295.3 | 73.4 | 58.5 | 74.5 | 31.8 | 54.9 | 44.0 | 90 |
| | | (59) | (7) | (101) | (71) | (67) | (89) | (17) | |
| 91 | Rwanda | | | 3.1 | 44.6 | 25.5 | | 8.0 | 91 |
| | | | | (27) | (13) | (52) | | (2) | |
| 92 | Senegal | 735.9 | 210.9 | 3.5 | 77.1 | 21.5 | | 148.0 | 92 |
| | | (20) | (30) | (31) | (81) | (37) | | (33) | |
| 93 | Sierra Leone | 309.9 | 131.3 | 2.4 | 61.5 | 19.5 | 30.8 | 62.0 | 93 |
| | | (6) | (23) | (19) | (42) | (32) | (61) | (21) | |
| 94 | Sudan | 1,372.2 | 100.0 | 13.7 | 72.5 | 31.4 | 39.8 | 81.0 | 94 |
| | | (36) | (12) | (75) | (68) | (64) | (76) | (23) | |
| 95 | Tanzania | 841.7 | 73.2 | 11.7 | 69.0 | 20.3 | 54.1 | 49.0 | 95 |
| | | (23) | (6) | (70) | (57) | (33) | (87) | (20) | |
| 96 | Togo | 176.0 | 107.3 | 1.6 | 67.8 | 43.4 | 49.8 | 41.0 | 96 |
| | | (1) | (16) | (10) | (54) | (82) | (85) | (14) | |
| 97 | Tunisia | 943.4 | 212.0 | 4.4 | 62.0 | 18.2 | 33.1 | 226.0 | 97 |
| | | (25) | (31) | (40) | (43) | (29) | (68) | (43) | |
| 98 | Uganda | 560.0 | 74.2 | 7.5 | 58.7 | 17.6 | 59.4 | 42.0 | 98 |
| | | (13) | (8) | (53) | (32) | (27) | (92) | (15) | |
| 99 | Upper Volta | 225.7 | 46.4 | 4.9 | 46.4 | 51.4 | 54.3 | 10.0 | 99 |
| | | (3) | (1) | (45) | (16) | (90) | (88) | (4) | |
| 100 | Zambia | 797.5 | 215.0 | 3.7 | 40.5 | 44.1 | 16.9 | 490.0 | 100 |
| | | (22) | (33) | (35) | (8) | (84) | (34) | (58) | |
| 101 | Bulgaria | 5,478.0 | 668.0 | 8.2 | 71.3 | | 34.0 | 2,573.0 | 101 |
| | | (64) | (66) | (58) | (62) | | (70) | (86) | |
| 102 | China, People's Rep. | | | 705.0 | 57.0 | | | 460.0 | 102 |
| | | | | (109) | (31) | | | (57) | |
| 103 | Cuba | 2,128.0 | 280.0 | 7.6 | 60.8 | | 74.3 | 1,005.0 | 103 |
| | | (42) | (46) | (54) | (39) | | (95) | (71) | |
| 104 | Czechoslovakia | 15,691.0 | 1,105.0 | 14.2 | 82.1 | | 9.9 | 5,664.0 | 104 |
| | | (80) | (77) | (76) | (102) | | (20) | (106) | |
| 105 | German Dem. Rep. | 22,160.0 | 1,385.0 | 16.0 | 81.9 | | 13.5 | 5,453.0 | 105 |
| | | (87) | (81) | (79) | (99) | | (29) | (105) | |
| 106 | Hungary | 9,078.0 | 890.0 | 10.2 | 79.6 | | 20.0 | 2,819.0 | 106 |
| | | (73) | (73) | (66) | (90) | | (39) | (91) | |
| 107 | Poland | 23,972.0 | 761.0 | 31.5 | 84.4 | | 22.7 | 3,508.0 | 107 |
| | | (88) | (69) | (93) | (107) | | (47) | (94) | |

*Table A.2e cont.*

| Country, etc. | 348 | 349 | 350 | 352 | 361 | 364 | 365 | |
|---|---|---|---|---|---|---|---|---|
| 108 Romania | 12,863.0 | 677.0 | 19.0 | 76.6 | | 29.3 | 1,981.0 | 108 |
| | (79) | (67) | (82) | (76) | | (59) | (80) | |
| 109 USSR | 220,247.0 | 955.0 | 230.6 | 77.0 | | 22.5 | 3,597.0 | 109 |
| | (96) | (75) | (107) | (79) | | (44) | (96) | |
| Number of countries | 97 | 97 | 109 | 109 | 97 | 95 | 109 | |
| Range | 176.0 | 46.4 | 0.2 | 21.5 | 5.4 | 0.5 | 7.0 | |
| | to | to | to | to | to | to | to | |
| | 673,391.7 | 4,427.4 | 705.0 | 87.1 | 86.2 | 74.3 | 13,943.0 | |
| Median | 2,822.2 | 302.5 | 7.7 | 68.0 | 24.6 | 23.7 | 383.0 | |
| Mean | 18,875.5 | 672.1 | 29.1 | 65.1 | 28.7 | 26.6 | 1,275.3 | |
| Standard deviation | 73,226.1 | 793.8 | 86.1 | 15.0 | 16.7 | 16.9 | 1,773.1 | |
| Coefficient of variation | 390 | 120 | 300 | 23 | 58 | 64 | 140 | |

Table A.3

Percentage contribution to world trade instability and related variables, for 83 countries, 1946–58 (country rankings, in ascending order, are as shown in parentheses)

| | Country | Percentage of world trade instability | | | | Percentage of total world trade | | | |
|---|---|---|---|---|---|---|---|---|---|
| | | Exports and imports (1) | Exports (2) | Imports (3) | Trade instability index (4) | Exports and imports (5) | Exports (6) | Imports (7) | |
| 1 | United States | 12.20 (83) | 16.58 (83) | 7.83 (82) | 8.51 (14) | 16.40 (83) | 20.0 (83) | 12.8 (83) | 1 |
| 2 | United Kingdom | 8.27 (82) | 8.11 (82) | 8.44 (83) | 9.97 (22) | 9.76 (82) | 9.3 (82) | 10.2 (82) | 2 |
| 3 | Austria | 1.51 (65) | 0.99 (59) | 2.04 (67) | 13.33 (50) | 0.95 (59) | 0.9 (60) | 1.0 (58) | 3 |
| 4 | Belgium | 2.57 (73) | 2.79 (76) | 2.36 (71) | 8.74 (16) | 3.03 (75) | 3.0 (77) | 3.0 (74) | 4 |
| 5 | Denmark | 0.61 (50) | 0.56 (52) | 0.67 (46) | 11.54 (37) | 1.15 (63) | 1.1 (63) | 1.2 (63) | 5 |
| 6 | France | 5.26 (79) | 5.05 (79) | 5.47 (80) | 13.77 (53) | 5.16 (79) | 4.8 (79) | 5.5 (79) | 6 |
| 7 | Germany, West | 6.20 (81) | 7.87 (81) | 4.54 (79) | 14.21 (57) | 7.40 (81) | 8.1 (81) | 6.7 (81) | 7 |
| 8 | Italy | 2.51 (72) | 2.59 (74) | 2.43 (72) | 12.03 (42) | 2.84 (74) | 2.4 (74) | 3.2 (75) | 8 |
| 9 | Netherlands | 3.53 (77) | 3.14 (77) | 3.92 (77) | 17.05 (62) | 3.28 (77) | 2.9 (76) | 3.6 (77) | 9 |
| 10 | Norway | 0.79 (54) | 0.64 (56) | 0.94 (58) | 9.23 (17) | 0.97 (60) | 0.8 (58) | 1.1 (61) | 10 |
| 11 | Sweden | 1.90 (67) | 1.53 (66) | 2.27 (70) | 10.31 (26) | 2.08 (73) | 2.0 (70) | 2.1 (73) | 11 |
| 12 | Switzerland | 1.07 (59) | 0.46 (48) | 1.69 (65) | 7.43 (7) | 1.63 (68) | 1.5 (68) | 1.7 (70) | 12 |
| 13 | Canada | 2.85 (76) | 1.94 (70) | 3.76 (76) | 5.77 (3) | 5.43 (80) | 5.2 (80) | 5.6 (80) | 13 |
| 14 | Japan | 5.10 (78) | 4.19 (78) | 6.02 (81) | 29.73 (79) | 3.26 (76) | 2.7 (75) | 3.8 (78) | 14 |

| | | | | | | | | |
|---|---|---|---|---|---|---|---|---|
| 15 Finland | 1.22 (63) | 1.21 (62) | 1.24 (61) | 18.61 (65) | 0.80 (56) | 0.8 (57) | 0.8 (57) | 15 |
| 16 Greece | 0.26 (28) | 0.19 (29) | 0.34 (31) | 13.27 (49) | 0.33 (34) | 0.2 (28) | 0.4 (45) | 16 |
| 17 Iceland | 0.06 (10) | 0.06 (13) | 0.07 (9) | 14.20 (56) | 0.09 (12) | 0.1 (18) | 0.1 (10) | 17 |
| 18 Ireland | 0.31 (31) | 0.11 (20) | 0.51 (39) | 9.37 (18) | 0.38 (40) | 0.3 (32) | 0.4 (44) | 18 |
| 19 Portugal | 0.26 (26) | 0.21 (30) | 0.31 (27) | 10.56 (29) | 0.37 (39) | 0.3 (37) | 0.4 (43) | 19 |
| 20 Spain | 0.41 (42) | 0.25 (35) | 0.58 (44) | 9.77 (19) | 0.58 (52) | 0.4 (47) | 0.7 (55) | 20 |
| 21 Turkey | 0.54 (48) | 0.32 (40) | 0.77 (52) | 23.57 (75) | 0.32 (31) | 0.3 (39) | 0.3 (30) | 21 |
| 22 Yugoslavia | 0.80 (55) | 0.86 (57) | 0.74 (49) | 16.09 (60) | 0.49 (48) | 0.4 (48) | 0.5 (50) | 22 |
| 23 Australia | 2.84 (75) | 2.56 (72) | 3.13 (74) | 18.64 (66) | 1.92 (70) | 2.1 (71) | 1.7 (69) | 23 |
| 24 New Zealand | 0.77 (53) | 0.54 (51) | 1.00 (59) | 11.89 (41) | 0.72 (54) | 0.7 (55) | 0.7 (54) | 24 |
| 25 South Africa | 0.97 (57) | 0.63 (54) | 1.32 (62) | 7.45 (8) | 1.35 (66) | 1.2 (64) | 1.5 (67) | 25 |
| 26 Argentina | 2.05 (70) | 1.90 (69) | 2.21 (68) | 15.63 (59) | 1.03 (62) | 0.9 (59) | 1.1 (62) | 26 |
| 27 Bolivia | 0.10 (15) | 0.09 (16) | 0.11 (16) | 12.61 (46) | 0.09 (11) | 0.1 (10) | 0.1 (9) | 27 |
| 28 Brazil | 1.69 (66) | 0.91 (58) | 2.47 (73) | 11.37 (36) | 1.31 (65) | 1.3 (65) | 1.3 (65) | 28 |
| 29 Chile | 0.38 (39) | 0.43 (46) | 0.33 (29) | 9.81 (20) | 0.39 (43) | 0.4 (42) | 0.3 (38) | 29 |
| 30 Colombia | 0.38 (40) | 0.32 (39) | 0.44 (36) | 13.36 (51) | 0.46 (46) | 0.5 (49) | 0.4 (42) | 30 |
| 31 Costa Rica | 0.06 (8) | 0.06 (11) | 0.06 (6) | 11.16 (35) | 0.09 (13) | 0.1 (12) | 0.1 (12) | 31 |
| 32 Dominican Rep. | 0.15 (18) | 0.13 (23) | 0.18 (18) | 11.10 (34) | 0.16 (22) | 0.2 (26) | 0.1 (16) | 32 |
| 33 Ecuador | 0.13 (16) | 0.16 (28) | 0.10 (14) | 10.32 (27) | 0.10 (14) | 0.1 (13) | 0.1 (13) | 33 |
| 34 El Salvador | 0.09 (14) | 0.09 (17) | 0.09 (13) | 10.69 (31) | 0.10 (15) | 0.1 (14) | 0.1 (14) | 34 |
| 35 Guatemala | 0.08 (13) | 0.06 (12) | 0.10 (15) | 8.20 (13) | 0.11 (16) | 0.1 (16) | 0.1 (17) | 35 |
| 36 Haiti | 0.04 (3) | 0.04 (5) | 0.04 (2) | 12.48 (45) | 0.03 (2) | 0.03 (4) | 0.1 (3) | 36 |
| 37 Honduras | 0.05 (7) | 0.05 (8) | 0.06 (7) | 9.92 (21) | 0.08 (9) | 0.1 (17) | 0.1 (6) | 37 |
| 38 Mexico | 0.58 (49) | 0.38 (44) | 0.78 (53) | 7.91 (11) | 0.86 (58) | 0.7 (54) | 1.0 (59) | 38 |
| 39 Nicaragua | 0.04 (5) | 0.04 (7) | 0.05 (5) | 8.66 (15) | 0.08 (10) | 0.1 (20) | 0.1 (8) | 39 |
| 40 Panama | 0.04 (6) | 0.02 (3) | 0.07 (11) | 5.02 (1) | 0.06 (7) | 0.03 (5) | 0.1 (15) | 40 |

*Table A.3 cont.*

| Country | (1) | (2) | (3) | (4) | (5) | (6) | (7) | |
|---|---|---|---|---|---|---|---|---|
| 41 Paraguay | 0.02 (2) | 0.02 (4) | 0.03 (1) | 7.38 (6) | 0.03 (1) | 0.03 (6) | 0.1 (2) | 41 |
| 42 Peru | 0.33 (33) | 0.15 (26) | 0.51 (40) | 7.97 (12) | 0.33 (32) | 0.3 (36) | 0.3 (31) | 42 |
| 43 Uruguay | 0.22 (22) | 0.12 (22) | 0.33 (30) | 15.01 (58) | 0.15 (21) | 0.1 (23) | 0.2 (22) | 43 |
| 44 Venezuela | 2.01 (68) | 1.80 (68) | 2.22 (69) | 10.43 (28) | 1.93 (71) | 2.2 (73) | 1.6 (68) | 44 |
| 45 Puerto Rico | 0.29 (29) | 0.21 (36) | 0.37 (32) | 5.16 (2) | 0.52 (50) | 0.4 (44) | 0.6 (52) | 45 |
| 46 Iran | 1.19 (62) | 1.76 (67) | 0.63 (45) | 48.42 (83) | 0.43 (44) | 0.5 (52) | 0.3 (33) | 46 |
| 47 Iraq | 0.35 (36) | 0.46 (47) | 0.25 (25) | 16.94 (61) | 0.30 (29) | 0.3 (31) | 0.3 (28) | 47 |
| 48 Israel | 0.48 (45) | 0.08 (15) | 0.88 (56) | 7.83 (10) | 0.24 (28) | 0.1 (19) | 0.3 (39) | 48 |
| 49 Jordan | 0.02 (1) | 0.01 (1) | 0.04 (3) | 7.18 (5) | 0.05 (6) | 0.02 (21) | 0.1 (11) | 49 |
| 50 Lebanon | 0.31 (32) | 0.05 (9) | 0.58 (43) | 12.18 (43) | 0.13 (17) | 0.04 (7) | 0.2 (23) | 50 |
| 51 Syria | 0.13 (17) | 0.12 (21) | 0.15 (17) | 11.59 (38) | 0.17 (23) | 0.2 (29) | 0.1 (18) | 51 |
| 52 Egypt | 0.47 (43) | 0.47 (49) | 0.48 (38) | 18.35 (64) | 0.49 (47) | 0.5 (50) | 0.4 (46) | 52 |
| 53 Burma | 0.36 (37) | 0.16 (27) | 0.56 (42) | 12.83 (47) | 0.23 (27) | 0.2 (25) | 0.2 (26) | 53 |
| 54 Cambodia | 0.07 (11) | 0.06 (10) | 0.08 (12) | 10.76 (33) | 0.05 (5) | 0.05 (9) | 0.1 (4) | 54 |
| 55 Ceylon (Sri Lanka) | 0.23 (23) | 0.22 (32) | 0.24 (24) | 10.27 (25) | 0.32 (30) | 0.3 (30) | 0.3 (29) | 55 |
| 56 China, Nat. Rep. | 0.16 (19) | 0.11 (19) | 0.22 (21) | 7.71 (9) | 0.14 (20) | 0.1 (11) | 0.1 (21) | 56 |
| 57 India | 1.14 (61) | 1.06 (61) | 1.22 (60) | 11.74 (40) | 1.65 (69) | 1.3 (67) | 2.0 (72) | 57 |
| 58 Indonesia | 2.02 (69) | 2.62 (75) | 1.42 (63) | 40.52 (82) | 0.81 (57) | 0.9 (61) | 0.7 (53) | 58 |
| 59 Korea, Rep. of | 0.37 (38) | 0.04 (6) | 0.70 (48) | 19.25 (68) | 0.21 (25) | 0.02 (3) | 0.4 (41) | 59 |
| 60 Malaya | 1.08 (60) | 1.41 (65) | 0.76 (50) | 24.34 (77) | 0.61 (53) | 0.7 (53) | 0.5 (48) | 60 |
| 61 Pakistan | 0.69 (52) | 0.62 (53) | 0.77 (51) | 22.31 (70) | 0.34 (37) | 0.3 (35) | 0.3 (40) | 61 |

| | | | | | | | | |
|---|---|---|---|---|---|---|---|---|
| 62 Philippines | 0.64 (51) | 0.37 (43) | 0.92 (57) | 10.64 (30) | 0.52 (49) | 0.4 (43) | 0.6 (51) | 62 |
| 63 Thailand | 0.50 (46) | 0.63 (55) | 0.38 (33) | 27.27 (78) | 0.33 (33) | 0.3 (38) | 0.3 (32) | 63 |
| 64 Vietnam, South | 0.26 (27) | 0.14 (25) | 0.38 (34) | 23.30 (72) | 0.18 (24) | 0.1 (24) | 0.2 (25) | 64 |
| 65 Belgian Congo (Zaire) | 0.38 (41) | 0.24 (34) | 0.53 (41) | 10.71 (32) | 0.39 (42) | 0.4 (40) | 0.3 (37) | 65 |
| 66 Ethiopia | 0.08 (12) | 0.09 (18) | 0.07 (8) | 11.62 (39) | 0.08 (8) | 0.1 (15) | 0.1 (5) | 66 |
| 67 Ghana | 0.30 (30) | 0.35 (41) | 0.26 (26) | 23.44 (73) | 0.22 (26) | 0.2 (27) | 0.2 (24) | 67 |
| 68 Liberia | 0.06 (9) | 0.07 (14) | 0.05 (4) | 17.89 (63) | 0.03 (3) | 0.04 (8) | 0.1 (1) | 68 |
| 69 Libya | 0.04 (4) | 0.02 (2) | 0.07 (10) | 10.24 (24) | 0.04 (4) | 0.01 (1) | 0.1 (7) | 69 |
| 70 Morocco | 0.54 (47) | 0.40 (45) | 0.68 (47) | 33.55 (80) | 0.33 (35) | 0.3 (33) | 0.3 (34) | 70 |
| 71 Nigeria | 0.33 (35) | 0.35 (42) | 0.32 (28) | 18.74 (67) | 0.34 (36) | 0.3 (34) | 0.3 (36) | 71 |
| 72 Rhodesia | 0.33 (34) | 0.26 (36) | 0.40 (35) | 13.99 (55) | 0.45 (45) | 0.4 (45) | 0.5 (47) | 72 |
| 73 Sudan | 0.25 (25) | 0.28 (37) | 0.22 (22) | 21.59 (69) | 0.13 (19) | 0.1 (21) | 0.1 (20) | 73 |
| 74 Tunisia | 0.21 (21) | 0.23 (33) | 0.20 (20) | 33.96 (81) | 0.13 (18) | 0.1 (22) | 0.1 (19) | 74 |
| 75 Bulgaria | 0.24 (24) | 0.29 (38) | 0.20 (19) | 24.22 (76) | 0.35 (38) | 0.4 (41) | 0.3 (27) | 75 |
| 76 China, People's Rep. | 2.81 (74) | 2.29 (71) | 3.34 (75) | 12.23 (44) | 2.05 (72) | 2.2 (72) | 1.9 (71) | 76 |
| 77 Cuba | 0.95 (56) | 1.04 (60) | 0.87 (55) | 13.55 (52) | 0.80 (55) | 0.8 (56) | 0.8 (56) | 77 |
| 78 Czechoslovakia | 1.07 (58) | 1.32 (64) | 0.83 (54) | 13.12 (48) | 1.27 (64) | 1.3 (66) | 1.2 (64) | 78 |
| 79 German Dem. Rep. | 2.21 (71) | 2.59 (73) | 1.83 (66) | 13.98 (54) | 1.57 (67) | 1.7 (69) | 1.4 (66) | 79 |
| 80 Hungary | 0.47 (44) | 0.48 (50) | 0.47 (37) | 22.97 (71) | 0.54 (51) | 0.5 (51) | 0.5 (49) | 80 |
| 81 Poland | 1.44 (64) | 1.31 (63) | 1.58 (64) | 23.57 (74) | 1.01 (61) | 0.9 (62) | 1.1 (60) | 81 |
| 82 Romania | 0.18 (20) | 0.14 (24) | 0.23 (23) | 6.80 (4) | 0.38 (41) | 0.4 (46) | 0.3 (35) | 82 |
| 83 USSR | 5.87 (80) | 7.50 (80) | 4.25 (78) | 9.98 (23) | 3.86 (78) | 4.2 (78) | 3.5 (76) | 83 |
| Total | 100.00 | 100.00 | 100.00 | | 100.00 | 100.0 | 100.0 | |

Table A.4

Percentage contribution to world trade instability and related variables, for 109 countries, 1959–71 (country rankings, in ascending order, are as shown in parentheses)

| | Country | Percentage of world trade instability | | | | Percentage of total world trade | | | |
|---|---|---|---|---|---|---|---|---|---|
| | | Exports and imports (1) | Exports (2) | Imports (3) | Trade instability index (4) | Exports and imports (5) | Exports (6) | Imports (7) | |
| 1 | United States | 12.2 (109) | 7.4 (107) | 17.0 (109) | 4.1 (20) | 16.1 (109) | 17.4 (109) | 14.9 (109) | 1 |
| 2 | United Kingdom | 5.6 (107) | 7.5 (108) | 3.8 (105) | 1.3 (1) | 8.5 (107) | 8.8 (107) | 8.3 (107) | 2 |
| 3 | Austria | 0.9 (81) | 1.0 (88) | 0.8 (80) | 4.5 (26) | 1.0 (90) | 1.0 (90) | 1.0 (91) | 3 |
| 4 | Belgium | 1.8 (95) | 2.4 (101) | 1.3 (88) | 3.4 (15) | 2.4 (100) | 2.5 (101) | 5.4 (106) | 4 |
| 5 | Denmark | 0.5 (67) | 0.9 (81) | 0.2 (35) | 2.8 (5) | 0.7 (85) | 1.2 (94) | 0.3 (51) | 5 |
| 6 | France | 3.6 (105) | 4.3 (105) | 3.0 (103) | 3.1 (9) | 5.5 (106) | 5.7 (106) | 5.4 (106) | 6 |
| 7 | Germany, West | 9.3 (108) | 11.5 (109) | 7.1 (108) | 4.5 (27) | 9.6 (108) | 10.2 (108) | 9.0 (108) | 7 |
| 8 | Italy | 3.5 (104) | 2.6 (102) | 4.5 (106) | 4.3 (25) | 4.3 (104) | 4.6 (104) | 4.1 (103) | 8 |
| 9 | Netherlands | 3.2 (103) | 4.2 (104) | 2.3 (99) | 4.2 (24) | 3.5 (103) | 3.6 (103) | 3.5 (102) | 9 |
| 10 | Norway | 0.8 (78) | 0.8 (77) | 0.8 (78) | 3.0 (7) | 1.3 (95) | 1.3 (96) | 1.3 (95) | 10 |
| 11 | Sweden | 1.5 (93) | 1.7 (97) | 1.3 (89) | 2.2 (13) | 2.1 (100) | 2.1 (100) | 2.1 (99) | 11 |
| 12 | Switzerland | 1.8 (96) | 1.3 (92) | 2.4 (100) | 4.9 (35) | 1.9 (98) | 2.0 (99) | 1.9 (98) | 12 |
| 13 | Canada | 3.1 (102) | 0.7 (74) | 5.5 (107) | 5.8 (41) | 2.7 (73) | 0.5 (73) | 5.0 (105) | 13 |
| 14 | Japan | 4.8 (106) | 6.6 (106) | 3.1 (104) | 4.8 (33) | 4.5 (105) | 4.8 (105) | 4.3 (104) | 14 |
| 15 | Finland | 0.8 (77) | 0.6 (69) | 1.0 (84) | 5.6 (40) | 0.7 (81) | 0.6 (77) | 0.8 (84) | 15 |
| 16 | Greece | 0.2 (43) | 0.2 (36) | 0.3 (52) | 3.1 (10) | 0.4 (61) | 0.3 (56) | 0.5 (69) | 16 |
| 17 | Iceland | 0.2 (37) | 0.2 (41) | 0.2 (41) | 10.7 (89) | 0.1 (29) | 0.1 (27) | 0.1 (22) | 17 |
| 18 | Ireland | 0.3 (48) | 0.3 (49) | 0.3 (51) | 3.3 (12) | 0.4 (69) | 0.4 (67) | 0.5 (70) | 18 |
| 19 | Portugal | 0.4 (60) | 0.6 (68) | 0.3 (54) | 4.6 (29) | 0.4 (71) | 0.4 (68) | 0.5 (72) | 19 |
| 20 | Spain | 2.1 (99) | 1.6 (96) | 2.6 (101) | 9.1 (81) | 1.1 (93) | 1.1 (92) | 1.2 (94) | 20 |

| | | | | | | | | |
|---|---|---|---|---|---|---|---|---|
| 21 Turkey | 0.4 (61) | 0.5 (59) | 0.4 (58) | 6.7 (59) | 0.3 (56) | 0.3 (52) | 0.3 (53) | 21 |
| 22 Yugoslavia | 0.7 (76) | 0.7 (73) | 0.8 (77) | 5.1 (37) | 0.7 (84) | 0.7 (82) | 0.7 (83) | 22 |
| 23 Australia | 1.5 (94) | 1.3 (91) | 1.8 (95) | 4.2 (22) | 1.8 (97) | 1.7 (98) | 1.9 (97) | 23 |
| 24 New Zealand | 0.5 (70) | 0.5 (66) | 0.6 (68) | 6.7 (58) | 0.4 (65) | 0.4 (70) | 0.4 (65) | 24 |
| 25 South Africa | 1.0 (86) | 0.8 (79) | 1.3 (90) | 4.1 (21) | 1.3 (96) | 1.3 (95) | 1.3 (96) | 25 |
| 26 Argentina | 1.1 (88) | 0.7 (75) | 1.6 (94) | 8.6 (76) | 0.7 (79) | 0.7 (83) | 0.7 (79) | 26 |
| 27 Bolivia | 0.1 (22) | 0.2 (35) | 0.1 (19) | 7.0 (62) | 0.1 (19) | 0.1 (18) | 0.1 (19) | 27 |
| 28 Brazil | 2.4 (101) | 2.2 (99) | 2.7 (102) | 14.0 (98) | 0.8 (86) | 0.8 (86) | 0.9 (86) | 28 |
| 29 Chile | 0.4 (55) | 0.5 (63) | 0.4 (57) | 6.7 (56) | 0.3 (51) | 0.3 (55) | 0.3 (56) | 29 |
| 30 Colombia | 0.4 (56) | 0.5 (65) | 0.4 (61) | 7.6 (68) | 0.3 (53) | 0.3 (53) | 0.3 (57) | 30 |
| 31 Costa Rica | 0.1 (17) | 0.1 (22) | 0.1 (22) | 6.1 (44) | 0.1 (22) | 0.1 (25) | 0.1 (26) | 31 |
| 32 Dominican Rep. | 0.3 (47) | 0.3 (45) | 0.3 (47) | 13.2 (96) | 0.1 (23) | 0.1 (30) | 0.1 (31) | 32 |
| 33 Ecuador | 0.1 (24) | 0.1 (19) | 0.2 (36) | 6.2 (45) | 0.1 (24) | 0.1 (29) | 0.1 (32) | 33 |
| 34 El Salvador | 0.2 (35) | 0.2 (29) | 0.2 (37) | 7.8 (70) | 0.1 (25) | 0.1 (28) | 0.1 (27) | 34 |
| 35 Guatemala | 0.1 (25) | 0.2 (30) | 0.1 (21) | 6.4 (49) | 0.1 (27) | 0.1 (32) | 0.1 (35) | 35 |
| 36 Haiti | – (5) | – (6) | – (5) | 12.3 (92) | – (5) | – (10) | – (10) | 36 |
| 37 Honduras | 0.2 (36) | 0.2 (38) | 0.2 (38) | 8.9 (79) | 0.1 (28) | 0.1 (21) | 0.1 (18) | 37 |
| 38 Mexico | 0.5 (69) | 0.5 (60) | 0.6 (72) | 2.9 (6) | 0.9 (87) | 0.8 (88) | 1.0 (89) | 38 |
| 39 Nicaragua | 0.2 (44) | 0.3 (43) | 0.2 (39) | 10.4 (87) | 0.1 (30) | 0.1 (23) | 0.1 (23) | 39 |
| 40 Panama | 0.1 (29) | 0.2 (27) | 0.1 (18) | 6.0 (42) | 0.1 (31) | 0.1 (37) | 0.1 (36) | 40 |
| 41 Paraguay | – (9) | – (13) | – (10) | 6.6 (51) | – (9) | – (12) | – (12) | 41 |
| 42 Peru | 0.5 (64) | 0.4 (57) | 0.6 (70) | 8.3 (72) | 0.3 (55) | 0.3 (58) | 0.3 (55) | 42 |
| 43 Uruguay | 0.2 (41) | 0.2 (32) | 0.2 (42) | 9.6 (84) | 0.1 (38) | 0.1 (33) | 0.1 (30) | 43 |
| 44 Venezuela | 1.1 (87) | 1.0 (87) | 1.2 (86) | 5.1 (36) | 1.0 (92) | 1.1 (91) | 1.0 (88) | 44 |
| 45 Jamaica | 0.1 (26) | 0.2 (34) | 0.1 (32) | 4.0 (18) | 0.2 (42) | 0.2 (41) | 0.2 (43) | 45 |
| 46 Trinidad–Tobago | 0.1 (33) | 0.1 (20) | 0.2 (34) | 3.3 (14) | 0.2 (45) | 0.2 (46) | 0.2 (47) | 46 |
| 47 Puerto Rico | 0.2 (45) | 0.3 (50) | 0.2 (44) | 1.9 (2) | 0.7 (83) | 0.6 (78) | 0.8 (85) | 47 |
| 48 Iran | 1.4 (91) | 1.4 (93) | 1.4 (92) | 9.8 (85) | 0.7 (82) | 0.7 (84) | 0.7 (82) | 48 |
| 49 Iraq | 0.5 (68) | 0.5 (62) | 0.6 (67) | 6.4 (48) | 0.4 (62) | 0.4 (65) | 0.4 (59) | 49 |
| 50 Israel | 0.4 (58) | 0.3 (42) | 0.6 (75) | 4.7 (30) | 0.4 (70) | 0.3 (61) | 0.6 (77) | 50 |
| 51 Jordan | 0.0 (13) | – (7) | 0.1 (27) | 11.8 (90) | 0.0 (14) | – (14) | 0.1 (24) | 51 |

*Table A.4 cont.*

| | Country | (1) | (2) | (3) | (4) | (5) | (6) | (7) | |
|---|---|---|---|---|---|---|---|---|---|
| 52 | Kuwait | 0.6 (71) | 0.9 (85) | 0.3 (53) | 7.4 (66) | 0.4 (63) | 0.6 (75) | 0.2 (45) | 52 |
| 53 | Lebanon | 0.3 (49) | 0.4 (53) | 0.2 (45) | 7.2 (64) | 0.2 (44) | 0.2 (45) | 0.2 (48) | 53 |
| 54 | Saudi Arabia | 0.8 (80) | 1.2 (90) | 0.5 (64) | 6.6 (54) | 0.5 (75) | 0.6 (81) | 0.5 (73) | 54 |
| 55 | Yemen, Peo. Dem. Rep. | 0.2 (46) | 0.3 (46) | 0.2 (43) | 12.1 (91) | 0.1 (39) | 0.1 (26) | 0.1 (28) | 55 |
| 56 | Syria | 0.1 (32) | 0.2 (26) | 0.1 (26) | 6.6 (52) | 0.1 (34) | 0.1 (34) | 0.1 (37) | 56 |
| 57 | Egypt | 0.5 (62) | 0.5 (61) | 0.5 (62) | 6.5 (50) | 0.3 (37) | 0.3 (62) | 0.4 (66) | 57 |
| 58 | Afghanistan | 0.1 (21) | – (1) | 0.3 (50) | 13.0 (95) | 0.0 (13) | – (17) | 0.1 (25) | 58 |
| 59 | Burma | 0.2 (34) | 0.3 (52) | 0.1 (29) | 10.7 (88) | 0.1 (20) | 0.1 (31) | 0.1 (29) | 59 |
| 60 | Sri Lanka (Ceylon) | 0.1 (31) | 0.2 (31) | 0.1 (31) | 3.0 (8) | 0.2 (49) | 0.3 (42) | 0.2 (42) | 60 |
| 61 | China, Nat. Rep. | 0.5 (66) | 0.5 (64) | 0.6 (71) | 9.1 (82) | 0.3 (52) | 0.3 (57) | 0.3 (52) | 61 |
| 62 | Hong Kong | 0.6 (72) | 0.8 (76) | 0.5 (63) | 4.6 (28) | 0.6 (77) | 0.6 (74) | 0.7 (80) | 62 |
| 63 | India | 1.4 (90) | 0.9 (80) | 1.9 (97) | 7.0 (61) | 0.9 (88) | 0.8 (87) | 1.1 (92) | 63 |
| 64 | Indonesia | 1.5 (92) | 1.4 (95) | 1.6 (93) | 16.2 (103) | 0.4 (68) | 0.4 (63) | 0.5 (67) | 64 |
| 65 | Korea, Rep. of | 0.9 (82) | 0.6 (72) | 1.2 (87) | 15.2 (102) | 0.3 (54) | 0.2 (47) | 0.4 (61) | 65 |
| 66 | Malaysia | 0.4 (59) | 0.6 (71) | 0.3 (48) | 3.5 (16) | 0.5 (74) | 0.6 (76) | 0.5 (75) | 66 |
| 67 | Pakistan | 0.4 (52) | 0.2 (39) | 0.6 (76) | 6.1 (43) | 0.3 (59) | 0.3 (51) | 0.4 (63) | 67 |
| 68 | Philippines | 0.6 (73) | 0.8 (78) | 0.5 (65) | 7.4 (67) | 0.4 (66) | 0.4 (66) | 0.4 (64) | 68 |
| 69 | Singapore | 1.1 (89) | 0.9 (82) | 1.4 (91) | 8.4 (74) | 0.6 (78) | 0.6 (80) | 0.7 (81) | 69 |
| 70 | Thailand | 0.4 (53) | 0.5 (58) | 0.3 (55) | 5.3 (39) | 0.3 (60) | 0.3 (59) | 0.4 (60) | 70 |
| 71 | Algeria | 0.8 (79) | 0.9 (86) | 0.8 (79) | 9.5 (83) | 0.4 (67) | 0.4 (64) | 0.5 (68) | 71 |
| 72 | Burundi | – (1) | – (2) | – (1) | 12.4 (93) | – (1) | – (3) | – (2) | 72 |
| 73 | Cameroon | 0.1 (23) | 0.2 (37) | 0.1 (15) | 6.7 (55) | 0.1 (21) | 0.1 (24) | 0.1 (17) | 73 |
| 74 | Central African Rep. | – (2) | – (3) | – (2) | 8.7 (77) | – (2) | – (7) | – (3) | 74 |
| 75 | Chad | – (3) | – (4) | – (3) | 10.0 (86) | – (3) | – (6) | – (6) | 75 |
| 76 | Zaire | 0.3 (51) | 0.3 (47) | 0.3 (46) | 6.7 (60) | 0.2 (46) | 0.2 (48) | 0.2 (46) | 76 |
| 77 | Dahomey | – (4) | – (5) | – (4) | 18.9 (105) | – (4) | – (4) | – (8) | 77 |
| 78 | Ethiopia | 0.1 (18) | 0.1 (23) | 0.1 (23) | 6.3 (47) | 0.1 (26) | 0.1 (22) | 0.1 (20) | 78 |
| 79 | Ghana | 0.2 (42) | 0.2 (24) | 0.3 (56) | 7.7 (69) | 0.1 (40) | 0.1 (40) | 0.2 (41) | 79 |

| | | | | | | | | |
|---|---|---|---|---|---|---|---|---|
| 80 Ivory Coast | 0.2 (38) | 0.3 (48) | 0.1 (24) | 4.8 (32) | 0.2 (41) | 0.2 (44) | 0.2 (40) | 80 |
| 81 Kenya | 0.1 (27) | 0.2 (33) | 0.1 (28) | 3.7 (17) | 0.2 (43) | 0.2 (43) | 0.2 (44) | 81 |
| 82 Liberia | 0.1 (28) | 0.3 (44) | – (6) | 12.6 (94) | 0.0 (15) | 0.1 (20) | – (13) | 82 |
| 83 Libya | 2.1 (98) | 3.3 (103) | 0.9 (83) | 22.6 (107) | 0.4 (64) | 0.4 (69) | 0.4 (58) | 83 |
| 84 Malagasy Rep. | 0.0 (14) | – (8) | 0.1 (17) | 6.7 (57) | 0.0 (16) | – (15) | 0.1 (16) | 84 |
| 85 Malawi | 0.0 (15) | – (9) | 0.1 (30) | 7.8 (71) | 0.0 (17) | – (13) | 0.1 (14) | 85 |
| 86 Mali | – (6) | – (10) | – (7) | 19.4 (106) | – (6) | – (8) | – (11) | 86 |
| 87 Mauritania | – (7) | – (11) | – (8) | 46.4 (109) | – (7) | – (11) | – (4) | 87 |
| 88 Morocco | 0.3 (50) | 0.2 (40) | 0.4 (59) | 6.2 (46) | 0.2 (48) | 0.2 (49) | 0.3 (50) | 88 |
| 89 Niger | – (8) | – (12) | – (9) | 15.1 (101) | – (8) | – (5) | – (5) | 89 |
| 90 Nigeria | 0.9 (83) | 1.1 (89) | 0.8 (81) | 13.2 (97) | 0.3 (58) | 0.3 (60) | 0.4 (62) | 90 |
| 91 Rwanda | – (10) | – (14) | – (11) | 26.4 (108) | – (10) | – (2) | – (1) | 91 |
| 92 Senegal | 0.1 (30) | 0.2 (28) | 0.1 (33) | 7.2 (63) | 0.1 (32) | 0.1 (19) | 0.1 (21) | 92 |
| 93 Sierra Leone | 0.0 (16) | – (15) | 0.1 (25) | 7.2 (65) | 0.1 (18) | – (16) | 0.1 (15) | 93 |
| 94 Sudan | 0.2 (39) | 0.2 (25) | 0.2 (40) | 8.5 (75) | 0.1 (33) | 0.1 (38) | 0.1 (38) | 94 |
| 95 Tanzania | 0.1 (19) | 0.1 (21) | 0.1 (16) | 5.2 (38) | 0.1 (35) | 0.1 (39) | 0.1 (35) | 95 |
| 96 Togo | – (11) | – (16) | – (12) | 8.8 (78) | – (11) | – (9) | – (9) | 96 |
| 97 Tunisia | 0.2 (40) | 0.3 (51) | 0.1 (14) | 9.0 (80) | 0.1 (36) | 0.1 (36) | 0.1 (39) | 97 |
| 98 Uganda | 0.1 (20) | 0.1 (18) | 0.1 (20) | 4.8 (34) | 0.1 (37) | 0.1 (35) | 0.1 (34) | 98 |
| 99 Upper Volta | – (12) | – (17) | – (13) | 14.3 (99) | – (12) | – (1) | – (7) | 99 |
| 100 Zambia | 1.0 (85) | 1.4 (94) | 0.6 (74) | 18.3 (104) | 0.2 (50) | 0.3 (54) | 0.2 (49) | 100 |
| 101 Bulgaria | 0.4 (54) | 0.4 (55) | 0.5 (66) | 4.7 (31) | 0.5 (72) | 0.5 (72) | 0.5 (71) | 101 |
| 102 China, People's Rep. | 2.1 (100) | 2.3 (100) | 2.0 (98) | 14.9 (100) | 0.7 (80) | 0.8 (85) | 0.6 (76) | 102 |
| 103 Cuba | 0.4 (57) | 0.6 (70) | 0.3 (49) | 8.4 (73) | 0.2 (47) | 0.2 (50) | 0.3 (54) | 103 |
| 104 Czechoslovakia | 0.7 (75) | 0.9 (83) | 0.6 (69) | 3.3 (11) | 1.0 (91) | 1.1 (93) | 1.0 (90) | 104 |
| 105 German Dem. Rep. | 1.0 (84) | 0.9 (84) | 1.1 (85) | 4.0 (19) | 1.2 (94) | 1.3 (97) | 1.2 (93) | 105 |
| 106 Hungary | 0.5 (63) | 0.4 (54) | 0.6 (73) | 4.2 (23) | 0.6 (76) | 0.6 (79) | 0.6 (78) | 106 |
| 107 Poland | 0.5 (65) | 0.6 (67) | 0.4 (60) | 2.4 (3) | 0.9 (89) | 0.9 (89) | 1.0 (87) | 107 |
| 108 Romania | 0.6 (74) | 0.4 (56) | 0.9 (82) | 6.6 (53) | 0.5 (73) | 0.5 (71) | 0.5 (74) | 108 |
| 109 USSR | 2.0 (97) | 2.1 (98) | 1.9 (96) | 2.8 (4) | 3.4 (102) | 3.6 (102) | 3.2 (101) | 109 |
| Total | 100.0 | 100.0 | 100.0 | | 100.0 | 100.0 | 100.0 | |

## Table A.5

Regression equations and correlation coefficients with export value instability as the dependent variable

| Regression equation (ranked by number of independent variable) | $r^2$ (uncorrected) | $r$ (uncorrected) | $r^2$ (corrected) | $r$ (corrected) | No. of countries | Level of significance |
|---|---|---|---|---|---|---|
| $Y = 6.402 + 0.005 X_{107}$ (12.12) (0.11) | .000 | .000 | .013 | .114 | 79 | NS |
| $Y = 3.203 + 0.542 X_{108}$ (4.01) (4.72) | .220 | .469 | .210 | .458 | 81 | .01 |
| $Y = 5.124 + 0.114 X_{109}$ (7.88) (0.64) | .006 | .077 | – | – | 65 | NS |
| $Y = 3.280 + 0.302 X_{110}$ (4.6) (3.1) | .138 | .371 | .124 | .352 | 64 | .01 |
| $Y = 4.283 + 0.290 X_{111}$ (7.21) (2.41) | .086 | .293 | .071 | .266 | 64 | .05 |
| $Y = 3.532 + 0.223 X_{112}$ (4.84) (2.78) | .113 | .336 | .098 | .313 | 63 | .01 |
| $Y = 5.334 + 0.317 X_{113}$ (7.82) (3.27) | .102 | .319 | .093 | .305 | 96 | .01 |
| $Y = 2.525 + 1.578 X_{114}$ (3.26) (5.83) | .289 | .538 | .280 | .529 | 86 | .01 |
| $Y = -0.690 + 1.089 X_{115}$ (−0.55) (8.10) | .380 | .617 | .374 | .612 | 109 | .01 |
| $Y = 4.100 + 0.492 X_{117}$ (4.95) (4.10) | .152 | .390 | .143 | .378 | 96 | .01 |
| $Y = 1.913 + 2.000 X_{118}$ (2.58) (7.07) | .370 | .608 | .363 | .602 | 87 | .01 |
| $Y = 4.998 + 0.148 X_{120}$ (3.77) (3.30) | .103 | .321 | .094 | .307 | 97 | .01 |
| $Y = 7.704 + 0.066 X_{121}$ (8.23) (0.79) | .007 | .084 | – | – | 92 | NS |
| $Y = 9.519 - 2.303 X_{122}$ (4.74) (0.81) | .006 | −.077 | – | – | 107 | NS |
| $Y = 1.607 + 0.683 X_{200}$ (1.52) (7.66) | .354 | .595 | .348 | .590 | 109 | .01 |
| $Y = 2.889 + 0.550 X_{201}$ (3.06) (7.45) | .342 | .585 | .336 | .580 | 109 | .01 |
| $Y = 7.678 - 0.089 X_{202}$ (8.23) (1.16) | .016 | −.126 | .004 | −.063 | 84 | NS |
| $Y = 4.137 + 0.295 X_{203}$ (4.54) (3.49) | .130 | .361 | .119 | .345 | 84 | .01 |
| $Y = 7.350 + 0.110 X_{204}$ (4.51) (0.69) | .004 | .063 | – | – | 109 | NS |

*Table A.5 cont.*

| Regression equation | $r^2$ (uncorrected) | $r$ (uncorrected) | $r^2$ (corrected) | $r$ (corrected) | No. of countries | Level of significance |
|---|---|---|---|---|---|---|
| $Y = 4.335 + 0.220\,X_{205}$ (3.67) (2.33) | .062 | .249 | .050 | .224 | 84 | .05 |
| $Y = 5.400 + 0.154\,X_{206}$ (1.21) (0.12) | .020 | .141 | .008 | .089 | 84 | NS |
| $Y = 5.837 + 0.326\,X_{207}$ (9.44) (1.55) | .030 | .173 | .017 | .130 | 78 | NS |
| $Y = 7.016 - 0.092\,X_{208}$ (9.03) (0.99) | .012 | −.110 | – | – | 80 | NS |
| $Y = 5.463 + 0.008\,X_{209}$ (11.23) (0.037) | .000 | .000 | – | – | 65 | NS |
| $Y = 5.284 + 0.001\,X_{210}$ (8.24) (0.005) | .000 | .000 | – | – | 64 | NS |
| $Y = 5.463 - 0.035\,X_{211}$ (15.35) (0.20) | .001 | −.032 | – | – | 64 | NS |
| $Y = 5.301 - 0.124\,X_{212}$ (14.89) (0.95) | .014 | −.118 | – | – | 64 | NS |
| $Y = 4.751 + 0.265\,X_{213}$ (3.58) (1.77) | .032 | .179 | .022 | .148 | 95 | .05 |
| $Y = 2.249 + 0.717\,X_{214}$ (2.23) (4.52) | .196 | .443 | .186 | .431 | 86 | .01 |
| $Y = 6.730 + 0.150\,X_{215}$ (4.07) (0.926) | .008 | .089 | – | – | 109 | NS |
| $Y = 6.786 + 0.099\,X_{217}$ (12.54) (0.57) | .003 | .055 | – | – | 96 | NS |
| $Y = 4.842 + 0.447\,X_{218}$ (6.25) (2.52) | .070 | .265 | .059 | .243 | 87 | .01 |
| $Y = 8.280 - 0.097\,X_{220}$ (9.42) (0.95) | .009 | −.095 | – | – | 97 | NS |
| $Y = 7.684 + 0.041\,X_{221}$ (0.95) (0.05) | .006 | .078 | – | – | 92 | NS |
| $Y = 8.024 + 0.005\,X_{222}$ (10.05) (0.39) | .001 | .032 | – | – | 107 | NS |
| $Y = 8.773 - 0.001\,X_{300}$ (10.55) (2.18) | .043 | −.207 | .034 | −.184 | 109 | .05 |
| $Y = 8.890 - 0.001\,X_{301}$ (10.54) (2.30) | .047 | −.217 | .038 | −.195 | 109 | .05 |
| $Y = 7.248 - 0.001\,X_{302}$ (12.98) (2.31) | .061 | −.247 | .050 | −.224 | 84 | .05 |
| $Y = 7.336 - 0.000\,X_{303}$ (12.81) (2.31) | .061 | −.247 | .050 | −.224 | 84 | .05 |
| $Y = 9.058 - 0.001\,X_{304}$ (10.64) (2.57) | .058 | −.241 | .050 | −.224 | 109 | .01 |

*Table A.5 cont.*

| Regression equation | $r^2$ (uncorrected) | $r$ (uncorrected) | $r^2$ (corrected) | $r$ (corrected) | No. of countries | Level of significance |
|---|---|---|---|---|---|---|
| $Y = 7.270 - 0.001\ X_{305}$ (12.70) (2.10) | .051 | −.226 | .039 | −.197 | 84 | .05 |
| $Y = 7.401 - 0.000\ X_{306}$ (12.78) (2.41) | .066 | −.257 | .055 | −.235 | 84 | .01 |
| $Y = 3.272 + 0.046\ X_{307}$ (1.13) (1.23) | .018 | .134 | .006 | .077 | 84 | NS |
| $Y = 7.890 - 0.046\ X_{308}$ (7.61) (1.23) | .018 | −.134 | .006 | −.077 | 84 | NS |
| $Y = -7.440 + 0.248\ X_{310}$ (−0.192) (4.27) | .170 | .412 | .160 | .400 | 91 | .01 |
| $Y = 8.905 - 0.000\ X_{315}$ (10.56) (2.34) | .049 | −.221 | .040 | −.200 | 109 | .01 |
| $Y = 3.416 + 0.110\ X_{316}$ (1.54) (2.23) | .045 | .212 | .036 | .190 | 107 | .05 |
| $Y = 8.800 - 0.042\ X_{320}$ (8.22) (1.00) | .010 | −.100 | – | – | 106 | NS |
| $Y = 4.589 + 0.117\ X_{321}$ (3.41) (3.16) | .087 | .295 | .079 | .281 | 106 | .01 |
| $Y = 2.007 + 0.085\ X_{325}$ (1.01) (3.25) | .096 | .310 | .087 | .395 | 102 | .01 |
| $Y = 19.037 - 0.168\ X_{330}$ (5.10) (3.31) | .118 | −.344 | .107 | −.327 | 84 | .01 |
| $Y = 2.270 + 0.168\ X_{331}$ (1.56) (3.31) | .118 | .344 | .107 | .327 | 84 | .01 |
| $Y = 8.090 - 0.001\ X_{345}$ (10.32) (0.59) | .003 | −.055 | – | – | 109 | NS |
| $Y = 6.318 + 0.011\ X_{346}$ (6.09) (0.61) | .004 | .063 | – | – | 96 | NS |
| $Y = 8.067 - 0.001\ X_{347}$ (9.40) (0.03) | .000 | .000 | – | – | 109 | NS |
| $Y = 7.078 - 0.000\ X_{348}$ (13.43) (1.89) | .037 | −.192 | .026 | −.161 | 97 | .05 |
| $Y = 8.176 - 0.002\ X_{349}$ (12.61) (3.21) | .098 | −.313 | .088 | −.297 | 97 | .01 |
| $Y = 8.233 - 0.005\ X_{350}$ (9.95) (0.58) | .003 | −.055 | – | – | 109 | NS |
| $Y = 23.139 - 0.231\ X_{352}$ (7.28) (4.86) | .181 | −.425 | .173 | −.416 | 109 | .01 |
| $Y = 7.721 + 0.025\ X_{361}$ (4.48) (0.48) | .002 | .045 | – | – | 97 | NS |
| $Y = 4.337 + 0.095\ X_{364}$ (4.70) (3.24) | .100 | .316 | .090 | .300 | 97 | .01 |

*Table A.5 cont.*

| Regression equation | $r^2$ (uncorrected) | $r$ (uncorrected) | $r^2$ (corrected) | $r$ (corrected) | No. of countries | Level of significance |
|---|---|---|---|---|---|---|
| $Y = 10.118 - 0.002\ X_{365}$ (11.03) (3.77) | .118 | −.344 | .110 | −.332 | 108 | .01 |

Note: Definitions of variables are given in Table A.1. $Y$ is the 'normal' export instability index value; $r^2$, the coefficient of determination; $r$, the coefficient of correlation. 'NS' means not significant at the 0.05 level. $t$ values are given in parentheses under the regression equations. $X_{100}$ is the dependent variable. For multiple regression equations with this as the dependent variable, see Chapter 4, part (B).

## Table A.6

### Regression equations and correlation coefficients with import value instability as the dependent variable

| Regression equation (ranked by number of independent variable) | $r^2$ (uncorrected) | $r$ (uncorrected) | $r^2$ (corrected) | $r$ (corrected) | No. of countries | Level of significance |
|---|---|---|---|---|---|---|
| $Y = 5.232 + 0.349\ X_{100}$ (10.60) (8.10) | .380 | .616 | .374 | .612 | 109 | .01 |
| $Y = 5.716 + 0.399\ X_{107}$ (6.59) (2.50) | .076 | .276 | .064 | .253 | 78 | .01 |
| $Y = 5.179 + 0.390\ X_{108}$ (5.80) (3.04) | .105 | .324 | .093 | .305 | 81 | .01 |
| $Y = 6.681 + 0.045\ X_{109}$ (8.72) (0.21) | .001 | .032 | — | — | 65 | NS |
| $Y = 1.682 + 0.739\ X_{110}$ (2.80) (9.23) | .579 | .761 | .572 | .756 | 64 | .01 |
| $Y = 5.473 + 0.335\ X_{111}$ (7.82) (2.36) | .082 | .286 | .068 | .261 | 64 | .05 |
| $Y = 2.792 + 0.483\ X_{112}$ (3.95) (6.21) | .388 | .623 | .378 | .615 | 63 | .01 |
| $Y = 5.262 + 0.418\ X_{113}$ (12.35) (6.93) | .338 | .581 | .331 | .575 | 96 | .01 |
| $Y = 3.986 + 1.327\ X_{114}$ (5.95) (5.68) | .278 | .527 | .269 | .519 | 86 | .01 |
| $Y = 3.908 + 0.602\ X_{117}$ (7.93) (8.45) | .432 | .657 | .426 | .653 | 96 | .01 |
| $Y = 3.838 + 1.541\ X_{118}$ (5.59) (5.58) | .289 | .538 | .281 | .530 | 87 | .01 |

*Table A.6 cont.*

| Regression equation | $r^2$ (uncorrected) | $r$ (uncorrected) | $r^2$ (corrected) | $r$ (corrected) | No. of countries | Level of significance |
|---|---|---|---|---|---|---|
| $Y = 6.319 + 0.082\,X_{120}$ (8.93) (3.43) | .110 | .332 | .101 | .318 | 97 | .01 |
| $Y = 7.424 + 0.130\,X_{121}$ (15.05) (2.96) | .089 | .298 | .078 | .279 | 92 | .01 |
| $Y = 7.592 + 0.464\,X_{122}$ (6.89) (0.30) | .001 | .032 | – | – | 107 | NS |
| $Y = 6.088 + 0.207\,X_{200}$ (8.65) (3.48) | .102 | .319 | .093 | .305 | 109 | .01 |
| $Y = 6.424 + 0.173\,X_{201}$ (10.31) (3.54) | .105 | .324 | .097 | .311 | 109 | .01 |
| $Y = 8.397 - 0.082\,X_{202}$ (11.69) (1.40) | .023 | −.152 | .011 | −.105 | 84 | NS |
| $Y = 6.938 + 0.070\,X_{203}$ (9.24) (1.01) | .012 | .110 | – | – | 84 | NS |
| $Y = 6.648 + 0.164\,X_{204}$ (7.52) (1.83) | .030 | .173 | .021 | .145 | 109 | .05 |
| $Y = 6.731 + 0.075\,X_{205}$ (7.19) (1.00) | .012 | .110 | – | – | 84 | NS |
| $Y = 7.371 + 0.022\,X_{206}$ (7.80) (0.24) | .001 | .032 | – | – | 84 | NS |
| $Y = 6.931 + 0.321\,X_{207}$ (10.97) (1.49) | .028 | .167 | .016 | .126 | 78 | NS |
| $Y = 7.620 - 0.026\,X_{208}$ (9.52) (0.27) | .001 | −.032 | – | – | 80 | NS |
| $Y = 6.989 - 0.106\,X_{209}$ (12.26) (0.43) | .003 | −.055 | | – | 65 | NS |
| $Y = 6.271 + 0.050\,X_{210}$ (8.40) (0.57) | .005 | .071 | – | – | 64 | NS |
| $Y = 6.793 + 0.239\,X_{211}$ (16.42) (1.17) | .022 | .148 | .006 | .078 | 64 | NS |
| $Y = 6.663 - 0.228\,X_{212}$ (16.22) (1.50) | .035 | −.187 | .020 | −.141 | 64 | NS |
| $Y = 7.370 - 0.004\,X_{213}$ (7.53) (0.04) | .000 | .000 | – | – | 95 | NS |
| $Y = 6.636 + 0.100\,X_{214}$ (6.90) (0.66) | .005 | .071 | – | – | 86 | NS |
| $Y = 6.511 + 0.171\,X_{215}$ (7.04) (1.89) | .032 | .179 | .023 | .152 | 109 | .05 |
| $Y = 7.172 + 0.150\,X_{217}$ (18.37) (1.20) | .015 | .122 | .005 | .071 | 96 | NS |
| $Y = 7.924 - 0.180\,X_{218}$ (11.41) (1.13) | .015 | −.122 | .003 | −.055 | 87 | NS |

*Table A.6 cont.*

| Regression equation | $r^2$ (uncorrected) | $r$ (uncorrected) | $r^2$ (corrected) | $r$ (corrected) | No. of countries | Level of significance |
|---|---|---|---|---|---|---|
| $Y = 8.051 - 0.106\ X_{220}$ (17.38) (1.97) | .039 | −.197 | .029 | −.170 | 97 | NS |
| $Y = 7.322 + 0.090\ X_{221}$ (14.72) (3.19) | .101 | .318 | .091 | .302 | 92 | .01 |
| $Y = 7.895 - 0.006\ X_{222}$ (18.13) (0.91) | .008 | −.089 | – | – | 107 | NS |
| $Y = 8.479 - 0.000\ X_{300}$ (18.09) (2.38) | .050 | −.224 | .041 | −.202 | 109 | .01 |
| $Y = 8.558 - 0.000\ X_{301}$ (18.02) (2.55) | .057 | −.239 | .048 | −.219 | 109 | .01 |
| $Y = 7.882 - 0.000\ X_{302}$ (18.12) (2.03) | .048 | −.219 | .036 | −.190 | 84 | .05 |
| $Y = 7.966 - 0.000\ X_{303}$ (17.92) (2.17) | .054 | −.232 | .043 | −.207 | 84 | .05 |
| $Y = 8.656 - 0.000\ X_{304}$ (18.05) (2.81) | .069 | −.263 | .060 | −.245 | 109 | .01 |
| $Y = 7.913 - 0.000\ X_{305}$ (17.8) (1.93) | .044 | −.210 | .032 | −.179 | 84 | .05 |
| $Y = 8.003 - 0.000\ X_{306}$ (17.77) (2.20) | .056 | −.237 | .044 | −.210 | 109 | .05 |
| $Y = 1.749 + 0.076\ X_{307}$ (0.81) (2.73) | .083 | .288 | .072 | .268 | 84 | .01 |
| $Y = 9.383 - 0.076\ X_{308}$ (12.11) (3.41) | .083 | −.288 | .072 | −.268 | 84 | .01 |
| $Y = 1.123 + 0.109\ X_{310}$ (0.54) (3.41) | .116 | .341 | .106 | .326 | 91 | .01 |
| $Y = 8.554 - 0.000\ X_{315}$ (17.99) (2.52) | .056 | −.237 | .048 | −.219 | 109 | .01 |
| $Y = 5.637 + 0.054\ X_{316}$ (4.63) (1.98) | .036 | .190 | .027 | .164 | 107 | .05 |
| $Y = 8.009 - 0.006\ X_{320}$ (13.59) (0.26) | .001 | −.032 | – | – | 106 | NS |
| $Y = 6.558 + 0.047\ X_{321}$ (8.76) (2.27) | .047 | .217 | .038 | .195 | 106 | .05 |
| $Y = 4.656 + 0.046\ X_{325}$ (4.32) (3.26) | .096 | .310 | .087 | .295 | 102 | .01 |
| $Y = 12.444 - 0.067\ X_{330}$ (4.11) (1.62) | .031 | −.176 | .019 | −.138 | 84 | NS |
| $Y = 5.773 + 0.067\ X_{331}$ (4.89) (1.62) | .031 | .176 | .019 | .138 | 84 | NS |
| $Y = 8.061 - 0.000\ X_{345}$ (18.19) (0.93) | .006 | −.077 | – | – | 107 | NS |

*Table A.6 cont.*

| Regression equation | $r^2$ (uncorrected) | $r$ (uncorrected) | $r^2$ (corrected) | $r$ (corrected) | No. of countries | Level of significance |
|---|---|---|---|---|---|---|
| $Y = 7.897 - 0.012\, X_{346}$ (10.51) (0.93) | .009 | −.095 | – | – | 96 | NS |
| $Y = 7.933 - 0.011\, X_{347}$ (16.35) (0.61) | .003 | −.055 | – | – | 109 | NS |
| $Y = 7.436 - 0.000\, X_{348}$ (19.22) (1.21) | .015 | −.122 | .005 | −.071 | 97 | NS |
| $Y = 8.183 - 0.001\, X_{349}$ (17.18) (2.80) | .076 | −.276 | .067 | −.259 | 97 | .01 |
| $Y = 7.789 + 0.009\, X_{350}$ (16.84) (1.77) | .028 | .167 | .019 | .138 | 109 | .05 |
| $Y = 14.468 - 0.098\, X_{352}$ (7.68) (3.49) | .102 | −.319 | .094 | −.307 | 109 | .01 |
| $Y = 8.914 - 0.024\, X_{361}$ (9.67) (0.86) | .008 | −.089 | – | – | 97 | NS |
| $Y = 5.731 - 0.062\, X_{364}$ (8.31) (2.84) | .078 | .279 | .069 | .263 | 97 | .01 |
| $Y = 9.319 - 0.001\, X_{365}$ (18.21) (4.24) | .145 | −.381 | .137 | −.370 | 108 | .01 |

Note: Definitions of variables are given in Table A.1. $Y$ is the 'normal' import instability index value; $r^2$, the coefficient of determination; $r$, the coefficient of correlation. 'NS' means not significant at the 0.05 level. $t$ values are given in parentheses under the regression equations. $X_{115}$ is the dependent variable. For multiple regression equations with this as the dependent variable, see Chapter 5, part (B).

## Table A.7

### Receipts from exports and outlays on imports, for 83 countries, by year, 1946–58 (millions of currency units, except where otherwise specified)

| Country/currency unit | | 1946 | 1947 | 1948 | 1949 | 1950 | 1951 | 1952 | 1953 | 1954 | 1955 | 1956 | 1957 | 1958 | |
|---|---|---|---|---|---|---|---|---|---|---|---|---|---|---|---|
| 1 Argentina | X | 1,256 | 1,689 | 1,698 | 730 | 1,190 | 1,399 | 866 | 1,240 | 1,161 | 1,071 | 1,169 | 1,148 | 1,106 | 1 |
| (US $) | M | 839 | 1,722 | 1,539 | 1,116 | 1,074 | 1,610 | 1,258 | 884 | 1,075 | 1,310 | 1,228 | 1,415 | 1,349 | |
| 2 Australia | X | 279 | 326 | 466 | 581 | 647 | 1,038 | 755 | 946 | 918 | 879 | 897 | 1,125 | 889 | 2 |
| (Australian £) | M | 306 | 326 | 453 | 540 | 708 | 964 | 1,339 | 745 | 926 | 1,130 | 1,124 | 1,073 | 1,131 | |
| 3 Austria | X | n.a. | 111 | 229 | 329 | 385 | 532 | 606 | 676 | 794 | 878 | 1,166 | 1,275 | 1,252 | 3 |
| (US $) | M | n.a. | 316 | 496 | 625 | 510 | 700 | 705 | 602 | 725 | 1,000 | 1,085 | 1,250 | 1,202 | |
| 4 Belgium–Luxembourg | X | 48 | 77 | 89 | 95 | 102 | 159 | 149 | 139 | 146 | 175 | 204 | 211 | 204 | 4 |
| (Belgian franc)† | M | 66 | 93 | 96 | 93 | 112 | 145 | 140 | 136 | 145 | 160 | 185 | 196 | 183 | |
| 5 Bolivia | X | 78 | 77 | 104 | 93 | 81 | 126 | 98 | 67 | 75 | 87 | 86 | 79 | 57 | 5 |
| (US $) | M | n.a. | 88 | 109 | 105 | 82 | 123 | 107 | 92 | 93 | 108 | 107 | 111 | 93 | |
| 6 Brazil | X | n.a. | 1,226 | 1,250 | 1,165 | 1,403 | 1,833 | 1,485 | 1,654 | 1,662 | 1,542 | 1,635 | 1,591 | 1,410 | 6 |
| (US $) | M | n.a. | 1,370 | 1,286 | 1,282 | 1,295 | 2,302 | 2,193 | 1,624 | 1,892 | 1,569 | 1,615 | 1,876 | 1,674 | |
| 7 Bulgaria | X* | n.a. | n.a. | n.a. | n.a. | 124 | 128 | 171 | 206 | 233 | 230 | 339 | 500 | 506 | 7 |
| (US $) | M* | 595 | 728 | 1,283 | 1,002 | 721 | 440 | 158 | 200 | 196 | 250 | 251 | 332 | 367 | |
| 8 Burma | X | n.a. | n.a. | n.a. | n.a. | 765 | 1,001 | 1,261 | 1,265 | 1,184 | 1,179 | 1,165 | 1,238 | 1,036 | 8 |
| (kyat) | M | n.a. | n.a. | n.a. | n.a. | 637 | 782 | 950 | 1,170 | 1,364 | 1,158 | 1,150 | 1,774 | 1,097 | |
| 9 Cambodia | X* | n.a. | n.a. | n.a. | 968 | 1,316 | 1,602 | 1,778 | 1,937 | 2,188 | 1,402 | 1,282 | 1,811 | 1,852 | 9 |
| (riel) | M* | n.a. | n.a. | n.a. | n.a. | n.a. | n.a. | n.a. | 1,492 | 1,750 | 1,665 | 1,980 | 2,043 | 2,570 | |
| 10 Canada | X | 3,268 | 3,678 | 4,067 | 4,005 | 4,183 | 5,089 | 5,571 | 5,397 | 5,145 | 5,764 | 6,365 | 6,394 | 6,332 | 10 |
| (Canadian $) | M | 2,841 | 3,576 | 3,602 | 3,828 | 4,484 | 5,583 | 5,360 | 5,792 | 5,528 | 6,374 | 7,639 | 7,733 | 7,319 | |
| 11 Chile | X | 266 | 329 | 384 | 300 | 331 | 419 | 512 | 382 | 446 | 537 | 535 | 457 | 401 | 11 |
| (US $) | M | 295 | 365 | 383 | 385 | 343 | 464 | 496 | 442 | 445 | 513 | 550 | 580 | 534 | |
| 12 China, People's Rep. | X* | n.a. | 418 | 488 | 426 | 535 | 525 | 368 | 433 | 380 | 487 | 641 | 652 | 751 | 12 |
| (US $) | M* | n.a. | n.a. | n.a. | n.a. | n.a. | n.a. | n.a. | n.a. | n.a. | 1,306 | 1,500 | 2,140 | 1,800 | |
| 13 China, Nat. Rep. | X | n.a. | n.a. | n.a. | n.a. | 100 | 101 | 125 | 134 | 105 | 137 | 141 | 174 | 185 | 13 |
| (US $) | M | n.a. | n.a. | n.a. | n.a. | 189 | 155 | 225 | 215 | 236 | 208 | 248 | 271 | 311 | |
| 14 Colombia | X | 216 | 286 | 323 | 359 | 432 | 506 | 523 | 666 | 716 | 634 | 727 | 678 | 609 | 14 |
| (US $) | M | 271 | 413 | 375 | 347 | 445 | 515 | 492 | 650 | 757 | 770 | 747 | 607 | 560 | |

*Table A.7 cont.*

| Country | | 1946 | 1947 | 1948 | 1949 | 1950 | 1951 | 1952 | 1953 | 1954 | 1955 | 1956 | 1957 | 1958 | |
|---|---|---|---|---|---|---|---|---|---|---|---|---|---|---|---|
| 15 Costa Rica | X | 26 | 37 | 49 | 52 | 67 | 72 | 83 | 92 | 98 | 95 | 81 | 99 | 110 | 15 |
| (US $) | M | 38 | 57 | 52 | 64 | 65 | 71 | 89 | 93 | 99 | 103 | 101 | 119 | 119 | |
| 16 Cuba | X | 411 | 820 | 785 | 644 | 714 | 852 | 730 | 715 | 614 | 674 | 780 | 947 | 860 | 16 |
| (US $) | M | 411 | 693 | 691 | 561 | 722 | 873 | 854 | 676 | 687 | 728 | 823 | 1,026 | 1,001 | |
| 17 Czechoslovakia | X* | 287 | 573 | 753 | 806 | 779 | 845 | 874 | 994 | 1,005 | 1,176 | 1,387 | 1,358 | 1,513 | 17 |
| (US $) | M* | 196 | 549 | 677 | 713 | 635 | 870 | 874 | 879 | 933 | 1,053 | 1,186 | 1,387 | 1,357 | |
| 18 Denmark | X | 2,300 | 3,133 | 3,594 | 4,536 | 5,875 | 7,634 | 7,807 | 8,072 | 8,633 | 9,535 | 10,315 | 11,207 | 11,675 | 18 |
| (Danish krone) | M | 3,064 | 3,436 | 3,882 | 4,804 | 6,704 | 7,907 | 7,654 | 7,974 | 9,156 | 9,368 | 10,431 | 10,914 | 10,796 | |
| 19 Dominican Rep. | X | 71 | 89 | 87 | 78 | 90 | 131 | 128 | 119 | 132 | 130 | 140 | 182 | 155 | 19 |
| (US $) | M | 52 | 85 | 94 | 71 | 70 | 124 | 132 | 115 | 109 | 139 | 145 | 158 | 165 | |
| 20 Ecuador | X | 45 | 49 | 56 | 46 | 86 | 77 | 115 | 107 | 140 | 127 | 130 | 148 | 154 | 20 |
| (US $) | M | 46 | 61 | 70 | 72 | 66 | 78 | 96 | 108 | 157 | 148 | 153 | 154 | 159 | |
| 21 Egypt | X | 90 | 109 | 184 | 211 | 269 | 291 | 219 | 215 | 222 | 227 | 219 | 237 | 250 | 21 |
| (£) | M | 118 | 129 | 198 | 207 | 279 | 307 | 272 | 223 | 220 | 272 | 269 | 271 | 270 | |
| 22 El Salvador | X | 70 | 111 | 123 | 154 | 186 | 225 | 235 | 252 | 281 | 288 | 332 | 349 | 320 | 22 |
| (colon) | M | 62 | 105 | 120 | 121 | 152 | 204 | 214 | 231 | 260 | 285 | 321 | 346 | 318 | |
| 23 Ethiopia–Eritrea | X | 63 | 94 | 89 | 83 | 83 | 129 | 120 | 188 | 184 | 193 | 177 | 220 | 182 | 23 |
| (Ethiopian $) | M | 67 | 90 | 94 | 87 | 74 | 105 | 122 | 155 | 176 | 194 | 184 | 210 | 235 | |
| 24 Finland | X | 35 | 64 | 79 | 93 | 107 | 226 | 195 | 157 | 184 | 197 | 197 | 271 | 290 | 24 |
| (markka)† | M | 28 | 53 | 74 | 80 | 105 | 181 | 209 | 145 | 172 | 202 | 232 | 262 | 269 | |
| 25 France | X | 789 | 1,484 | 1,522 | 2,109 | 2,461 | 3,157 | 2,872 | 3,196 | 3,827 | 4,646 | 4,701 | 4,594 | 4,460 | 25 |
| (US $) | M | 3,175 | 3,162 | 3,173 | 2,812 | 2,677 | 4,202 | 3,520 | 3,414 | 3,634 | 4,658 | 6,020 | 6,517 | 5,508 | |
| 26 German Dem. Rep. | X* | n.a. | n.a. | n.a. | n.a. | 1.6 | 2.9 | 3.0 | 3.9 | 2.8 | 2.8 | 3.1 | 4.5 | 4.7 | 26 |
| (rouble)† | M* | n.a. | n.a. | n.a. | n.a. | 2.1 | 3.6 | 4.6 | 3.9 | 4.4 | 4.7 | 5.3 | 6.5 | 6.7 | |
| 27 Germany, West | X | n.a. | n.a. | 796 | 1,424 | 2,153 | 3,875 | 4,691 | 5,323 | 6,471 | 7,676 | 9,272 | 11,118 | 11,658 | 27 |
| (US $) | M | n.a. | 1,001 | 1,825 | 2,300 | 2,807 | 3,707 | 4,144 | 4,340 | 5,523 | 7,031 | 8,029 | 9,401 | 9,700 | |
| 28 Ghana | X* | 15 | 23 | 50 | 43 | 68 | 83 | 77 | 80 | 105 | 91 | 78 | 84 | 97 | 28 |
| (£) | M* | 13 | 23 | 31 | 45 | 48 | 64 | 67 | 74 | 71 | 88 | 89 | 97 | 85 | |
| 29 Greece | X | 64 | 116 | 134 | 119 | 129 | 154 | 180 | 201 | 241 | 322 | 345 | 402 | 392 | 29 |
| (US $) | M | 409 | 327 | 419 | 395 | 448 | 474 | 316 | 277 | 363 | 419 | 526 | 575 | 578 | |
| 30 Guatemala | X | 53 | 69 | 72 | 67 | 84 | 88 | 94 | 98 | 105 | 110 | 133 | 128 | 123 | 30 |
| (US $) | M | 47 | 63 | 80 | 81 | 84 | 93 | 81 | 87 | 104 | 116 | 157 | 170 | 173 | |

| | | | | | | | | | | | | | | | |
|---|---|---|---|---|---|---|---|---|---|---|---|---|---|---|---|
| 31 Haiti | X | 126 | 175 | 169 | 171 | 211 | 270 | 287 | 220 | 313 | 228 | 300 | 220 | 261 | 31 |
| (gourde) | M | n.a. | n.a. | n.a. | n.a. | 220 | 267 | 296 | 283 | 284 | 313 | 312 | 235 | 253 | |
| 32 Honduras | X | 37 | 49 | 55 | 62 | 64 | 72 | 70 | 75 | 60 | 58 | 81 | 71 | 77 | 32 |
| (US $) | M | n.a. | 61 | 62 | 63 | 62 | 74 | 79 | 80 | 60 | 65 | 86 | 88 | 87 | |
| 33 Hungary | X* | n.a. | n.a. | 165 | 280 | 329 | 396 | 443 | 503 | 525 | 609 | 493 | 488 | 680 | 33 |
| (US $) | M* | 31 | 123 | 166 | 284 | 311 | 389 | 437 | 488 | 532 | 554 | 481 | 683 | 631 | |
| 34 Iceland | X | 45 | 58 | 79 | 58 | 42 | 52 | 55 | 72 | 80 | 83 | 92 | 85 | 98 | 34 |
| (US $) | M | 85 | 94 | 86 | 75 | 47 | 64 | 63 | 77 | 81 | 92 | 103 | 95 | 100 | |
| 35 India | X | 4,654 | 5,371 | 5,101 | 4,982 | 6,586 | 8,783 | 7,895 | 6,702 | 6,835 | 7,796 | 7,621 | 8,334 | 6,904 | 35 |
| (rupee) | M | 4,922 | 6,573 | 6,332 | 7,176 | 6,147 | 9,699 | 8,453 | 6,602 | 7,083 | 8,261 | 10,838 | 13,240 | 11,415 | |
| 36 Indonesia | X | 58 | 129 | 372 | 353 | 831 | 1,326 | 956 | 712 | 813 | 923 | 896 | 899 | 695 | 36 |
| (US $) | M | 203 | 296 | 577 | 831 | 655 | 1,196 | 1,213 | 832 | 842 | 826 | 1,061 | 996 | 760 | |
| 37 Iran | X | 333 | 371 | 592 | 519 | 757 | 761 | 309 | 91 | 111 | 217 | 351 | 504 | 764 | 37 |
| (US $) | M | 321 | 389 | 578 | 580 | 775 | 368 | 127 | 189 | 297 | 439 | 638 | 759 | 942 | |
| 38 Iraq | X | 38 | 40 | 30 | 36 | 64 | 83 | 115 | 159 | 192 | 209 | 195 | 157 | 227 | 38 |
| (dinar) | M | 43 | 55 | 55 | 51 | 66 | 78 | 109 | 136 | 158 | 191 | 204 | 203 | 211 | |
| 39 Ireland | X | 82 | 95 | 109 | 115 | 126 | 140 | 168 | 181 | 184 | 183 | 180 | 201 | 204 | 39 |
| (£) | M | 83 | 143 | 148 | 142 | 172 | 217 | 196 | 207 | 205 | 232 | 209 | 208 | 221 | |
| 40 Israel | X | n.a. | n.a. | n.a. | 43 | 46 | 55 | 86 | 102 | 133 | 144 | 178 | 223 | 239 | 40 |
| (US $) | M | n.a. | n.a. | n.a. | 261 | 326 | 409 | 393 | 365 | 369 | 428 | 534 | 557 | 551 | |
| 41 Italy | X | 432 | 773 | 1,357 | 1,411 | 1,602 | 2,121 | 1,958 | 2,289 | 2,439 | 2,776 | 3,208 | 3,910 | 3,998 | 41 |
| (US $) | M | 1,038 | 1,540 | 1,710 | 1,679 | 1,652 | 2,341 | 2,559 | 2,704 | 2,656 | 2,964 | 3,479 | 4,085 | 3,737 | |
| 42 Japan | X | 105 | 184 | 287 | 601 | 1,054 | 2,139 | 2,192 | 2,192 | 2,372 | 2,720 | 3,304 | 3,719 | 3,662 | 42 |
| (US $) | M | 322 | 543 | 674 | 908 | 982 | 1,981 | 2,002 | 2,418 | 2,452 | 2,515 | 3,663 | 4,310 | 3,204 | |
| 43 Jordan | X | n.a. | n.a. | n.a. | n.a. | 4 | 4 | 5 | 6 | 8 | 10 | 10 | 13 | 12 | 43 |
| (dinar) | M | n.a. | n.a. | n.a. | n.a. | 15 | 18 | 19 | 20 | 20 | 27 | 27 | 37 | 37 | |
| 44 Korea, Rep. of | X | n.a. | n.a. | n.a. | n.a. | 47 | 81 | 124 | 72 | 65 | 71 | 60 | 76 | 86 | 44 |
| (US $) | M | n.a. | n.a. | n.a. | n.a. | 83 | 133 | 216 | 352 | 245 | 351 | 394 | 465 | 404 | |
| 45 Lebanon | X | n.a. | n.a. | n.a. | n.a. | 52 | 90 | 77 | 88 | 93 | 108 | 130 | 133 | 101 | 45 |
| (£) | M | n.a. | n.a. | n.a. | n.a. | n.a. | 384 | 436 | 371 | 510 | 627 | 590 | 675 | 477 | |
| 46 Liberia | X* | 12 | 13 | 16 | 16 | 28 | 52 | 37 | 31 | 26 | 43 | 45 | 40 | 57 | 46 |
| (US $) | M* | 5 | 9 | 9 | 8 | 11 | 17 | 18 | 19 | 23 | 26 | 27 | 38 | 28 | |
| 47 Libya | X | 2.2 | 1.9 | 2.9 | 2.7 | 3.6 | 4.7 | 4.6 | 3.5 | 3.8 | 4.6 | 4.2 | 5.4 | 5.1 | 47 |
| (£) | M | n.a. | n.a. | n.a. | n.a. | 8 | 12 | 14 | 14 | 17 | 22 | 27 | 35 | 42 | |
| 48 Malaysia | X* | 720 | 1,323 | 1,764 | 1,721 | 4,014 | 6,074 | 3,917 | 3,020 | 3,105 | 4,156 | 4,166 | 4,171 | 3,726 | 48 |
| (dollar) | M* | n.a. | 610 | 847 | 927 | 1,311 | 1,869 | 1,660 | 1,451 | 1,319 | 1,543 | 1,751 | 1,814 | 1,657 | |
| 49 Mexico | X | 531 | 672 | 699 | 647 | 803 | 981 | 974 | 938 | 1,055 | 1,304 | 1,388 | 1,386 | 1,374 | 49 |
| (US $) | M | 718 | 887 | 788 | 649 | 771 | 1,106 | 1,078 | 1,060 | 1,079 | 1,179 | 1,441 | 1,558 | 1,548 | |

*Table A.7 cont.*

| Country | | 1946 | 1947 | 1948 | 1949 | 1950 | 1951 | 1952 | 1953 | 1954 | 1955 | 1956 | 1957 | 1958 | |
|---|---|---|---|---|---|---|---|---|---|---|---|---|---|---|---|
| 50 Morocco | X* | 10 | 18 | 38 | 54 | 66 | 88 | 96 | 94 | 100 | 115 | 119 | 118 | 147 | 50 |
| (French franc)† | M* | 18 | 33 | 75 | 103 | 115 | 160 | 180 | 171 | 168 | 174 | 161 | 148 | 167 | |
| 51 Netherlands | X | 1.4 | 3 | 4 | 5 | 7 | 9 | 10 | 11 | 12 | 13 | 13 | 14 | 16 | 51 |
| (guilder) | M | 2.7 | 4.6 | 5.2 | 5.6 | 8.0 | 9.4 | 8.5 | 9.3 | 11.5 | 12.6 | 14.9 | 16.1 | 14.5 | |
| 52 New Zealand | X | 148 | 164 | 136 | 151 | 206 | 270 | 266 | 257 | 234 | 266 | 296 | 301 | 293 | 52 |
| (£) | M | n.a. | 98 | 138 | 153 | 187 | 299 | 270 | 239 | 295 | 303 | 296 | 342 | 321 | |
| 53 Nicaragua | X | 20 | 25 | 31 | 28 | 38 | 50 | 55 | 59 | 67 | 87 | 81 | 89 | 86 | 53 |
| (US $) | M | 23 | 30 | 35 | 32 | 38 | 44 | 55 | 62 | 80 | 91 | 88 | 99 | 101 | |
| 54 Nigeria | X* | 25 | 44 | 62 | 81 | 90 | 120 | 130 | 124 | 150 | 132 | 135 | 128 | 136 | 54 |
| (£) | M* | 20 | 33 | 42 | 58 | 62 | 85 | 113 | 108 | 114 | 136 | 153 | 152 | 167 | |
| 55 Norway | X | 2.5 | 3.5 | 4.4 | 4.6 | 5.8 | 8.7 | 8.7 | 7.9 | 8.6 | 9.8 | 12.0 | 13.0 | 11.8 | 55 |
| (Norwegian krone)† | M | 3.1 | 5.1 | 5.3 | 6.0 | 6.7 | 8.6 | 8.8 | 9.0 | 9.9 | 10.8 | 12.0 | 13.0 | 13.0 | |
| 56 Pakistan | X | n.a. | n.a. | 0.8 | 1.0 | 1.3 | 2.8 | 1.9 | 1.5 | 1.3 | 1.7 | 1.9 | 2.0 | 1.8 | 56 |
| (rupee)† | M | n.a. | n.a. | 0.7 | 1.5 | 1.5 | 2.3 | 2.7 | 1.7 | 1.5 | 1.7 | 2.8 | 2.8 | 2.8 | |
| 57 Panama | X | 71 | 67 | 85 | 90 | 82 | 84 | 96 | 103 | 124 | 139 | 141 | 145 | 158 | 57 |
| (US $) | M | n.a. | n.a. | n.a. | n.a. | 93 | 102 | 118 | 115 | 135 | 141 | 153 | 173 | 164 | |
| 58 Paraguay | X | 28 | 23 | 31 | 30 | 35 | 44 | 37 | 34 | 40 | 40 | 38 | 41 | 43 | 58 |
| (US $) | M | n.a. | n.a. | 36 | 32 | 27 | 36 | 44 | 39 | 45 | 43 | 46 | 51 | 55 | |
| 59 Peru | X | 153 | 178 | 185 | 187 | 210 | 274 | 282 | 268 | 287 | 317 | 359 | 374 | 332 | 59 |
| (US $) | M | 173 | 198 | 196 | 185 | 218 | 312 | 338 | 338 | 308 | 363 | 462 | 531 | 459 | |
| 60 Philippines | X | 390 | 568 | 630 | 444 | 477 | 581 | 523 | 594 | 562 | 568 | 619 | 611 | 629 | 60 |
| (US $) | M | 468 | 768 | 729 | 731 | 464 | 627 | 560 | 621 | 644 | 728 | 688 | 824 | 722 | |
| 61 Poland | X* | 127 | 248 | 533 | 619 | 630 | 762 | 776 | 831 | 869 | 913 | 975 | 975 | 1,060 | 61 |
| (US $) | M* | 146 | 320 | 516 | 632 | 668 | 925 | 863 | 774 | 904 | 932 | 1,022 | 1,251 | 1,227 | |
| 62 Portugal | X | n.a. | n.a. | 5.7 | 5.7 | 8.0 | 11.1 | 10.0 | 10.9 | 11.7 | 12.0 | 14.8 | 15.2 | 14.8 | 62 |
| (escudo)† | M | n.a. | n.a. | 11.8 | 10.1 | 9.0 | 10.4 | 10.7 | 10.5 | 11.2 | 13.0 | 14.5 | 16.4 | 15.5 | |
| 63 Puerto Rico | X | 373 | 352 | 357 | 372 | 330 | 387 | 434 | 537 | 552 | 559 | 618 | 687 | 696 | 63 |
| (US $) | M | 311 | 393 | 441 | 429 | 437 | 538 | 567 | 629 | 675 | 739 | 815 | 920 | 951 | |
| 64 Rhodesia-Nyasaland | X | n.a. | 55 | 70 | 84 | 103 | 129 | 146 | 156 | 177 | 203 | 211 | 189 | 168 | 64 |
| (£) | M | 46 | 74 | 92 | 116 | 134 | 182 | 192 | 182 | 190 | 235 | 272 | 286 | 254 | |
| 65 Romania | X* | n.a. | n.a. | n.a. | n.a. | 207 | 259 | 298 | 341 | 350 | 391 | 395 | 390 | 430 | 65 |
| (US $) | M* | n.a. | n.a. | n.a. | n.a. | n.a. | n.a. | n.a. | 385 | 338 | 384 | 352 | 415 | 482 | |
| 66 South Africa | X | 227 | 226 | 265 | 290 | 393 | 478 | 478 | 492 | 537 | 603 | 678 | 734 | 671 | 66 |
| (£) | M | 277 | 382 | 441 | 404 | 395 | 583 | 537 | 551 | 568 | 656 | 674 | 746 | 751 | |

| | | | | | | | | | | | | | | | |
|---|---|---|---|---|---|---|---|---|---|---|---|---|---|---|---|
| 67 Spain | X* | 734 | 886 | 1,141 | 1,234 | 1,192 | 1,476 | 1,402 | 1,476 | 1,422 | 1,366 | 1,353 | 1,457 | 1,487 | 67 |
| (peseta) | M* | 897 | 1,163 | 1,475 | 1,426 | 1,191 | 1,298 | 1,751 | 1,824 | 1,879 | 1,931 | 2,332 | 2,179 | 2,446 | |
| 68 Sri Lanka (Ceylon) | X | 958 | 967 | 1,167 | 1,217 | 1,584 | 1,934 | 1,584 | 1,726 | 1,940 | 2,125 | 2,007 | 1,916 | 1,946 | 68 |
| (rupee) | M | 833 | 1,117 | 1,082 | 1,189 | 1,378 | 1,768 | 1,926 | 1,840 | 1,591 | 1,741 | 1,870 | 2,072 | 2,002 | |
| 69 Sudan | X | 10 | 17 | 29 | 33 | 38 | 83 | 51 | 48 | 44 | 54 | 71 | 61 | 54 | 69 |
| (£) | M | n.a. | 19 | 26 | 28 | 33 | 46 | 65 | 57 | 55 | 62 | 58 | 81 | 65 | |
| 70 Sweden | X | 4.0 | 4.7 | 5.5 | 5.8 | 7.4 | 11.8 | 10.9 | 10.4 | 11.2 | 12.2 | 13.9 | 15.7 | 15.2 | 70 |
| (krona)† | M | 4 | 6 | 6 | 5 | 7 | 11 | 11 | 10 | 11 | 12 | 14 | 15 | 15 | |
| 71 Switzerland | X* | 2,676 | 3,268 | 3,435 | 3,457 | 3,911 | 4,690 | 4,748 | 5,163 | 5,264 | 5,616 | 6,195 | 6,702 | 6,615 | 71 |
| (Swiss franc) | M* | 3,423 | 4,820 | 4,999 | 3,791 | 4,536 | 5,911 | 5,193 | 5,054 | 5,587 | 6,397 | 7,590 | 8,442 | 7,330 | |
| 72 Syria | X | n.a. | n.a. | n.a. | n.a. | 93 | 109 | 120 | 142 | 192 | 201 | 221 | 206 | 167 | 72 |
| (US $) | M | n.a. | n.a. | n.a. | n.a. | 118 | 140 | 149 | 153 | 223 | 226 | 228 | 204 | 205 | |
| 73 Thailand | X | 45 | 87 | 218 | 274 | 308 | 376 | 345 | 336 | 291 | 359 | 388 | 430 | 349 | 73 |
| (US $) | M | 59 | 139 | 151 | 231 | 249 | 324 | 362 | 390 | 353 | 375 | 404 | 463 | 427 | |
| 74 Tunisia | X* | 3.9 | 6.5 | 12.7 | 27.2 | 40.0 | 37.5 | 40.1 | 38.8 | 44.2 | 37.2 | 39.1 | 54.0 | 64.4 | 74 |
| (French franc)† | M* | 11 | 17 | 34 | 42 | 52 | 64 | 65 | 60 | 59 | 63 | 68 | 63 | 65 | |
| 75 Turkey | X | 159 | 240 | 215 | 267 | 282 | 350 | 405 | 431 | 365 | 396 | 456 | 455 | 349 | 75 |
| (US $) | M | 96 | 263 | 368 | 378 | 324 | 435 | 588 | 573 | 524 | 526 | 482 | 490 | 424 | |
| 76 United Kingdom | X | 5.8 | 6.8 | 9.2 | 10.4 | 9.0 | 10.7 | 10.8 | 10.5 | 11.2 | 12.0 | 13.4 | 13.8 | 13.4 | 76 |
| (US $)† | M | 6.4 | 8.6 | 9.2 | 9.3 | 8.1 | 11.8 | 10.3 | 10.1 | 10.6 | 12.2 | 12.5 | 12.9 | 12.2 | |
| 77 United States | X | 14.7 | 19.7 | 16.8 | 15.9 | 13.9 | 18.9 | 18.1 | 17.1 | 17.9 | 20.0 | 23.5 | 26.5 | 23.1 | 77 |
| (US $)† | M | 7.3 | 8.3 | 10.5 | 9.9 | 12.3 | 15.4 | 16.0 | 16.9 | 16.3 | 18.2 | 20.1 | 21.2 | 21.3 | |
| 78 Uruguay | X | 192 | 210 | 226 | 229 | 296 | 276 | 239 | 297 | 279 | 210 | 228 | 157 | 170 | 78 |
| (US $) | M | 179 | 248 | 239 | 220 | 247 | 353 | 273 | 227 | 312 | 250 | 234 | 279 | 172 | |
| 79 USSR | X* | n.a. | 274 | 494 | 281 | 252 | 391 | 468 | 382 | 501 | 633 | 812 | 1,043 | 1,036 | 79 |
| (US $) | M* | n.a. | n.a. | n.a. | n.a. | n.a. | n.a. | n.a. | n.a. | n.a. | 3,061 | 3,613 | 3,938 | 4,350 | |
| 80 Venezuela | X | 530 | 715 | 1,126 | 997 | 1,198 | 1,386 | 1,501 | 1,570 | 1,728 | 1,970 | 2,308 | 2,857 | 2,610 | 80 |
| (US $) | M | 534 | 905 | 1,275 | 1,189 | 1,171 | 1,314 | 1,442 | 1,533 | 1,711 | 1,899 | 2,353 | 3,395 | 2,691 | |
| 81 Vietnam | X* | n.a. | n.a. | 1.1 | 1.1 | 1.6 | 2.5 | 2.0 | 1.9 | 2.0 | 2.4 | 1.6 | 2.8 | 1.9 | 81 |
| (piastre)† | M* | n.a. | n.a. | 2.3 | 3.8 | 4.2 | 6.1 | 9.0 | 10.6 | 11.4 | 9.2 | 7.6 | 10.1 | 8.1 | |
| 82 Yugoslavia | X | 62 | 179 | 348 | 226 | 191 | 230 | 296 | 231 | 296 | 336 | 423 | 514 | 532 | 82 |
| (US $) | M | 277 | 288 | 399 | 356 | 310 | 466 | 425 | 459 | 408 | 513 | 545 | 727 | 759 | |
| 83 Zaire (Belgian Congo) | X | n.a. | n.a. | 14.5 | 14.7 | 17.6 | 22.8 | 25.3 | 25.0 | 27.1 | 30.2 | 33.6 | 30.9 | 28.9 | 83 |
| (Belgian franc)† | M | n.a. | n.a. | 12 | 14 | 14 | 21 | 27 | 26 | 28 | 32 | 36 | 37 | 33 | |

X = exports; M = imports.

* For goods only; otherwise, figures are for goods and services.

† '000,000,000.

# Table A.8

## Receipts from exports and outlays on imports, for 109 countries, by year, 1959–71 (US $ million)

| | Country | | 1959 | 1960 | 1961 | 1962 | 1963 | 1964 | 1965 | 1966 | 1967 | 1968 | 1969 | 1970 | 1971 | |
|---|---|---|---|---|---|---|---|---|---|---|---|---|---|---|---|---|
| 1 | Afghanistan | X* | 136 | 98 | 111 | 148 | 77 | 92 | 112 | 108 | 112 | 119 | 137 | n.a. | n.a. | 1 |
| | | M* | 183 | 170 | 206 | 292 | 140 | 185 | 209 | 250 | 232 | 206 | 209 | n.a. | n.a. | |
| 2 | Algeria | X | n.a. | n.a. | n.a. | n.a. | 897 | 859 | 753 | 734 | 899 | 1,002 | 1,037 | 1,293 | n.a. | 2 |
| | | M | n.a. | n.a. | n.a. | n.a. | 1,011 | 1,042 | 994 | 947 | 984 | 1,277 | 1,480 | 1,618 | n.a. | |
| 3 | Argentina | X | 1,148 | 1,270 | 1,195 | 1,379 | 1,502 | 1,564 | 1,662 | 1,795 | 1,707 | 1,778 | 2,039 | 2,220 | 2,074 | 3 |
| | | M | 1,134 | 1,467 | 1,768 | 1,649 | 1,270 | 1,528 | 1,438 | 1,535 | 1,523 | 1,793 | 2,258 | 2,355 | 2,522 | |
| 4 | Australia | X | 2,326 | 2,327 | 2,770 | 2,827 | 3,297 | 3,615 | 4,021 | 4,227 | 4,642 | 4,797 | 5,594 | 6,383 | 6,403 | 4 |
| | | M | 2,644 | 3,168 | 2,933 | 3,133 | 3,423 | 4,030 | 5,196 | 4,913 | 5,571 | 6,253 | 6,535 | 7,222 | 7,288 | |
| 5 | Austria | X | 1,356 | 1,509 | 1,638 | 1,755 | 1,923 | 2,137 | 2,359 | 2,521 | 2,667 | 2,965 | 3,547 | 4,284 | 4,766 | 5 |
| | | M | 1,308 | 1,599 | 1,674 | 1,738 | 1,926 | 2,177 | 2,457 | 2,773 | 2,848 | 3,102 | 3,495 | 4,328 | 5,262 | |
| 6 | Belgium | X | 3,666 | 4,186 | 4,482 | 4,808 | 5,242 | 6,086 | 6,718 | 7,206 | 7,786 | 8,700 | 10,480 | 12,782 | n.a. | 6 |
| | | M | 3,646 | 4,094 | 4,446 | 4,740 | 5,334 | 6,100 | 6,568 | 7,264 | 7,520 | 8,600 | 10,280 | 11,896 | n.a. | |
| 7 | Bolivia | X | 64 | 58 | 68 | 71 | 82 | 109 | 127 | 146 | 170 | 172 | 192 | 213 | 207 | 7 |
| | | M | 89 | 89 | 97 | 120 | 131 | 142 | 166 | 179 | 212 | 228 | 244 | 237 | 252 | |
| 8 | Brazil | X | 1,435 | 1,463 | 1,540 | 1,299 | 1,502 | 1,548 | 1,757 | 1,882 | 1,839 | 2,086 | 2,601 | 3,117 | 3,322 | 8 |
| | | M | 1,772 | 1,984 | 1,816 | 1,790 | 1,716 | 1,522 | 1,549 | 1,992 | 2,192 | 2,634 | 2,968 | 3,699 | 4,674 | |
| 9 | Bulgaria | X* | 470 | 572 | 663 | 770 | 834 | 980 | 1,176 | 1,305 | 1,458 | 1,615 | 1,794 | 2,004 | 2,180 | 9 |
| | | M* | 581 | 633 | 666 | 780 | 933 | 1,062 | 1,178 | 1,478 | 1,572 | 1,782 | 1,749 | 1,831 | 2,099 | |
| 10 | Burma | X | 258 | 262 | 250 | 283 | 287 | 248 | 256 | 208 | 143 | 122 | 139 | 134 | 134 | 10 |
| | | M | 268 | 286 | 254 | 268 | 276 | 286 | 274 | 228 | 174 | 214 | 187 | 211 | 197 | |
| 11 | Burundi | X* | n.a. | n.a. | n.a. | 19 | 14 | 32 | 13 | 14 | 16 | 15 | 12 | 24 | 19 | 11 |
| | | M* | n.a. | n.a. | n.a. | 32 | 31 | 30 | 18 | 19 | 19 | 23 | 21 | 22 | 30 | |
| 12 | Cameroon | X* | 108 | 97 | 98 | 103 | 135 | 140 | 139 | 145 | 158 | 189 | 211 | 232 | 224 | 12 |
| | | M* | 82 | 84 | 96 | 102 | 128 | 133 | 151 | 146 | 188 | 187 | 191 | 242 | 252 | |
| 13 | Canada | X | 7,034 | 7,012 | 7,293 | 7,637 | 8,403 | 9,814 | 10,381 | 12,107 | 13,563 | 15,516 | 17,330 | 20,217 | 22,186 | 13 |
| | | M | 8,327 | 8,045 | 8,042 | 8,306 | 8,750 | 10,055 | 11,285 | 13,029 | 13,890 | 15,593 | 18,129 | 19,092 | 21,925 | |
| 14 | Central African Rep. | X* | 15 | 14 | 14 | 15 | 22 | 28 | 26 | 31 | 29 | 36 | 33 | 31 | 37 | 14 |
| | | M* | 17 | 20 | 22 | 25 | 26 | 28 | 27 | 31 | 40 | 36 | 33 | 34 | 38 | |

| | | | | | | | | | | | | | | | |
|---|---|---|---|---|---|---|---|---|---|---|---|---|---|---|---|
| 15 | Chad | X* | n.a. | 13 | 21 | 17 | 23 | 27 | 27 | 24 | 27 | 28 | 29 | 30 | 30 | 15 |
| | | M* | n.a. | 25 | 25 | 29 | 29 | 35 | 31 | 32 | 40 | 38 | 50 | 62 | 67 | |
| 16 | Chile | X | 488 | 551 | 521 | 567 | 564 | 683 | 793 | 978 | 996 | 1,032 | 1,314 | 1,303 | n.a | 16 |
| | | M | 530 | 728 | 823 | 793 | 772 | 826 | 845 | 1,086 | 1,098 | 1,212 | 1,308 | 1,417 | n.a. | |
| 17 | China, People's Rep. | X* | 2,248 | 2,017 | 1,456 | 1,562 | 1,595 | 1,788 | 1.958 | 2,172 | 1,939 | 1,979 | n.a. | n.a. | n.a. | 17 |
| | | M* | 2,026 | 1,953 | 1,382 | 1,085 | 1,165 | 1,390 | 1,801 | 1,905 | 1,824 | 1,753 | n.a. | n.a. | n.a. | |
| 18 | China, Nat. Rep. | X | 177 | 195 | 234 | 253 | 388 | 492 | 529 | 660 | 799 | 1,042 | 1,326 | 1,730 | 2,388 | 18 |
| | | M | 300 | 325 | 365 | 379 | 402 | 483 | 624 | 687 | 869 | 1,175 | 1,375 | 1,742 | 2,229 | |
| 19 | Colombia | X | 610 | 592 | 578 | 571 | 590 | 749 | 709 | 663 | 713 | 791 | 880 | 1,019 | 997 | 19 |
| | | M | 550 | 676 | 721 | 747 | 736 | 892 | 732 | 953 | 802 | 982 | 1,093 | 1,348 | 1,346 | |
| 20 | Costa Rica | X | 94 | 105 | 102 | 113 | 115 | 136 | 137 | 164 | 174 | 208 | 229 | 281 | 275 | 20 |
| | | M | 119 | 125 | 122 | 135 | 149 | 168 | 214 | 217 | 233 | 259 | 289 | 361 | 410 | |
| 21 | Cuba | X* | 675 | 618 | 625 | 521 | 544 | 714 | 686 | 593 | 711 | 651 | 664 | 1,043 | n.a. | 21 |
| | | M* | 673 | 638 | 703 | 759 | 867 | 1,019 | 866 | 926 | 998 | 1,089 | 1,168 | 1,300 | n.a. | |
| 22 | Czechoslovakia | X* | 1,785 | 1,930 | 2,046 | 2,194 | 2,462 | 2,576 | 2,689 | 2,745 | 2,864 | 3,005 | 3,319 | 3,792 | 4,357 | 22 |
| | | M* | 1,602 | 1,816 | 2,024 | 2,070 | 2,160 | 2,429 | 2,673 | 2,736 | 2,680 | 3,007 | 3,294 | 3,696 | 4,010 | |
| 23 | Dahomey | X* | n.a. | 18 | 15 | 11 | 13 | 13 | 14 | 10 | 15 | 22 | 24 | 33 | 46 | 23 |
| | | M* | n.a. | 31 | 25 | 27 | 33 | 31 | 34 | 33 | 48 | 49 | 51 | 64 | 83 | |
| 24 | Denmark | X | 1,822 | 1,965 | 2,021 | 2,178 | 2,461 | 2,765 | 3,050 | 3,259 | 3,404 | 3,558 | 4,019 | 4,549 | 5,065 | 24 |
| | | M | 1,820 | 2,027 | 2,131 | 2,419 | 2,431 | 2,959 | 3,225 | 3,456 | 3,678 | 3,780 | 4,399 | 5,050 | 5,399 | |
| 25 | Dominican Rep. | X | 150 | 173 | 152 | 190 | 197 | 204 | 145 | 161 | 186 | 201 | 228 | 263 | 296 | 25 |
| | | M | 153 | 128 | 117 | 205 | 247 | 284 | 177 | 235 | 260 | 286 | 321 | 379 | 444 | |
| 26 | Ecuador | X | 152 | 155 | 142 | 159 | 165 | 178 | 197 | 203 | 218 | 226 | 220 | 256 | 263 | 26 |
| | | M | 157 | 175 | 170 | 170 | 174 | 209 | 226 | 226 | 259 | 306 | 359 | 395 | 474 | |
| 27 | Egypt | X | 743 | 866 | 735 | 709 | 837 | 859 | 926 | 990 | 862 | 810 | 890 | 991 | 1,032 | 27 |
| | | M | 875 | 958 | 912 | 1,090 | 1,129 | 1,153 | 1,188 | 1,175 | 1,160 | 1,058 | 1,194 | 1,453 | 1,518 | |
| 28 | El Salvador | X | 124 | 117 | 131 | 151 | 166 | 193 | 214 | 212 | 231 | 237 | 227 | 254 | 255 | 28 |
| | | M | 123 | 146 | 134 | 153 | 183 | 225 | 240 | 262 | 266 | 261 | 260 | 266 | 304 | |
| 29 | Ethiopia | X | 79 | 92 | 99 | 112 | 118 | 141 | 160 | 164 | 155 | 175 | 182 | 187 | 195 | 29 |
| | | M | 100 | 104 | 113 | 137 | 144 | 159 | 190 | 208 | 193 | 218 | 202 | 226 | 249 | |
| 30 | Finland | X | 992 | 1,169 | 1,260 | 1,331 | 1,402 | 1,566 | 1,735 | 1,834 | 1,872 | 1,994 | 2,428 | 2,883 | 3,013 | 30 |
| | | M | 965 | 1,215 | 1,330 | 1,433 | 1,426 | 1,742 | 1,924 | 2,029 | 2,013 | 1,929 | 2,425 | 3,117 | 3,368 | |
| 31 | France | X | 5,933 | 7,033 | 7,983 | 8,667 | 9,933 | 11,445 | 12,882 | 12,936 | 16,929 | 17,491 | 20,615 | 24,346 | 27,770 | 31 |
| | | M | 5,314 | 6,476 | 7,128 | 8,055 | 9,679 | 11,497 | 12,486 | 12,782 | 16,248 | 17,598 | 21,376 | 23,709 | 26,427 | |
| 32 | Germany, Dem. Rep. | X* | 2,121 | 2,191 | 2,261 | 2,353 | 2,713 | 2,932 | 3,070 | 3,205 | 3,456 | 3,791 | 4,153 | 4,581 | 5,076 | 32 |
| | | M* | 1,992 | 2,170 | 2,216 | 2,372 | 2,331 | 2,634 | 2,810 | 3,215 | 3,279 | 3,393 | 4,123 | 4,847 | 4,960 | |

*Table A.8 cont.*

| | Country | | 1959 | 1960 | 1961 | 1962 | 1963 | 1964 | 1965 | 1966 | 1967 | 1968 | 1969 | 1970 | 1971 | |
|---|---|---|---|---|---|---|---|---|---|---|---|---|---|---|---|---|
| 33 | Germany, West | X | 12,840 | 14,341 | 15,743 | 16,533 | 18,045 | 20,085 | 22,202 | 24,920 | 27,018 | 30,467 | 35,486 | 41,722 | 48,540 | 33 |
| | | M | 11,132 | 12,411 | 13,903 | 15,776 | 16,562 | 18,708 | 22,223 | 23,329 | 23,053 | 25,913 | 31,706 | 38,497 | 44,102 | |
| 34 | Ghana | X | 350 | 364 | 362 | 348 | 340 | 354 | 359 | 315 | 315 | 356 | 390 | 467 | 365 | 34 |
| | | M | 369 | 459 | 494 | 411 | 448 | 429 | 571 | 433 | 384 | 396 | 426 | 482 | 485 | |
| 35 | Greece | X | 378 | 396 | 460 | 503 | 582 | 610 | 672 | 815 | 890 | 954 | 1,049 | 1,217 | 1,432 | 35 |
| | | M | 519 | 584 | 659 | 776 | 842 | 1,005 | 1,164 | 1,313 | 1,351 | 1,448 | 1,678 | 1,975 | 2,265 | |
| 36 | Guatemala | X | 120 | 132 | 129 | 136 | 181 | 201 | 229 | 264 | 234 | 269 | 306 | 355 | 348 | 36 |
| | | M | 160 | 158 | 153 | 159 | 202 | 247 | 271 | 285 | 306 | 327 | 333 | 373 | 413 | |
| 37 | Haiti | X | 40 | 54 | 45 | 54 | 53 | 45 | 45 | 42 | 41 | 48 | 49 | 53 | 61 | 37 |
| | | M | 38 | 62 | 70 | 68 | 60 | 60 | 37 | 66 | 59 | 58 | 64 | 73 | 78 | |
| 38 | Honduras | X | 77 | 72 | 80 | 88 | 91 | 104 | 140 | 159 | 172 | 199 | 190 | 199 | 211 | 38 |
| | | M | 79 | 69 | 79 | 91 | 108 | 121 | 151 | 183 | 206 | 229 | 228 | 269 | 243 | |
| 39 | Hong Kong | X* | 574 | 689 | 688 | 763 | 873 | 1,012 | 1,143 | 1,324 | 1,527 | 1,744 | 2,177 | 2,514 | 2,832 | 39 |
| | | M* | 866 | 1,026 | 1,045 | 1,165 | 1,297 | 1,496 | 1,569 | 1,767 | 1,818 | 2,058 | 2,457 | 2,905 | 3,342 | |
| 40 | Hungary | X* | 770 | 874 | 1,029 | 1,099 | 1,206 | 1,352 | 1,510 | 1,594 | 1,702 | 1,790 | 2,084 | 2,317 | 2,500 | 40 |
| | | M* | 793 | 976 | 1,026 | 1,149 | 1,306 | 1,495 | 1,521 | 1,566 | 1,776 | 1,803 | 1,928 | 2,506 | 2,989 | |
| 41 | Iceland | X | 96 | 100 | 107 | 130 | 142 | 163 | 193 | 211 | 179 | 155 | 183 | 240 | 246 | 41 |
| | | M | 109 | 108 | 101 | 121 | 147 | 171 | 188 | 218 | 232 | 201 | 178 | 232 | 321 | |
| 42 | India | X | 1,620 | 1,668 | 1,704 | 1,749 | 2,027 | 2,144 | 2,034 | 1,916 | 1,999 | 2,145 | 2,160 | 2,403 | 2,489 | 42 |
| | | M | 2,148 | 2,547 | 2,496 | 2,694 | 2,917 | 3,408 | 3,507 | 3,279 | 3,303 | 2,985 | 2,778 | 2,750 | 3,137 | |
| 43 | Indonesia | X | 857 | 947 | 823 | 764 | 705 | 707 | 680 | 743 | 773 | 882 | 1,006 | 1,173 | 1,256 | 43 |
| | | M | 832 | 1,152 | 1,624 | 1,133 | 926 | 936 | 927 | 866 | 1,056 | 1,133 | 1,367 | 1,553 | 1,520 | |
| 44 | Iran | X | 851 | 901 | 947 | 1,052 | 1,128 | 1,193 | 1,358 | 1,492 | 1,792 | 1,939 | 2,347 | 2,613 | 3,956 | 44 |
| | | M | 961 | 1,037 | 1,004 | 1,015 | 1,061 | 1,160 | 1,465 | 1,623 | 1,928 | 2,408 | 2,390 | 3,124 | 3,953 | |
| 45 | Iraq | X | 661 | 715 | 719 | 743 | 830 | 921 | 975 | 1,032 | 930 | 1,169 | 1,203 | 1,248 | 1,694 | 45 |
| | | M | 627 | 731 | 754 | 713 | 718 | 883 | 948 | 1,018 | 866 | 990 | 1,028 | 1,149 | 1,505 | |
| 46 | Ireland | X | 577 | 650 | 740 | 737 | 820 | 975 | 1,046 | 1,150 | 1,269 | 1,269 | 1,388 | 1,559 | 1,731 | 46 |
| | | M | 658 | 711 | 825 | 874 | 983 | 1,155 | 1,244 | 1,297 | 1,325 | 1,420 | 1,672 | 1,849 | 2,043 | |
| 47 | Israel | X | 272 | 336 | 398 | 472 | 577 | 619 | 711 | 832 | 909 | 1,147 | 1,288 | 1,397 | 1,849 | 47 |
| | | M | 576 | 673 | 835 | 955 | 1,019 | 1,184 | 1,224 | 1,272 | 1,440 | 1,865 | 2,157 | 2,631 | 3,020 | |
| 48 | Italy | X | 4,463 | 5,459 | 6,249 | 6,999 | 7,642 | 8,795 | 10,579 | 11,887 | 12,783 | 14,639 | 16,957 | 18,918 | 22,133 | 48 |
| | | M | 3,895 | 5,342 | 6,005 | 6,979 | 8,704 | 8,468 | 8,696 | 10,108 | 11,510 | 12,303 | 14,944 | 18,239 | 19,517 | |

| | | | | | | | | | | | | | | | | |
|---|---|---|---|---|---|---|---|---|---|---|---|---|---|---|---|---|
| 49 | Ivory Coast | X | n.a. | n.a. | n.a. | n.a. | 305 | 406 | 373 | 422 | 441 | 559 | 611 | 649 | 652 | 49 |
| | | M | n.a. | n.a. | n.a. | n.a. | 303 | 393 | 380 | 433 | 463 | 523 | 574 | 672 | 706 | |
| 50 | Jamaica | X | 202 | 259 | 279 | 287 | 315 | 335 | 362 | 437 | 440 | 427 | 481 | 538 | 560 | 50 |
| | | M | 267 | 302 | 303 | 314 | 325 | 397 | 410 | 494 | 517 | 543 | 619 | 713 | 749 | |
| 51 | Japan | X | 4,256 | 4,927 | 5,166 | 5,949 | 6,526 | 8,026 | 9,895 | 11,572 | 12,413 | 15,358 | 18,940 | 22,978 | 28,406 | 51 |
| | | M | 3,872 | 4,759 | 6,107 | 5,967 | 7,259 | 8,434 | 8,878 | 10,183 | 12,425 | 14,135 | 16,640 | 20,800 | 22,357 | |
| 52 | Jordan | X | 25 | 48 | 58 | 67 | 71 | 92 | 104 | 116 | 103 | 104 | 129 | 122 | 97 | 52 |
| | | M | 123 | 128 | 129 | 142 | 172 | 160 | 179 | 216 | 181 | 228 | 306 | 254 | 263 | |
| 53 | Kenya | X | n.a. | n.a. | n.a. | n.a. | 322 | 351 | 348 | 405 | 383 | 418 | 465 | 526 | 542 | 53 |
| | | M | n.a. | n.a. | n.a. | n.a. | 316 | 335 | 363 | 433 | 446 | 483 | 496 | 598 | 716 | |
| 54 | Korea, Rep. of | X | 104 | 117 | 146 | 163 | 176 | 211 | 290 | 455 | 643 | 880 | 1,150 | 1,379 | 1,669 | 54 |
| | | M | 331 | 379 | 344 | 455 | 578 | 432 | 484 | 778 | 1,060 | 1,547 | 1,945 | 2,182 | 2,767 | |
| 55 | Kuwait | X | 932 | 1,076 | 1,059 | 1,182 | 1,243 | 1,344 | 1,414 | 1,472 | 1,474 | 1,562 | 1,658 | 1,775 | 2,696 | 55 |
| | | M | 313 | 294 | 303 | 342 | 395 | 395 | 493 | 582 | 745 | 768 | 812 | 786 | 852 | |
| 56 | Lebanon | X | 227 | 275 | 404 | 383 | 364 | 437 | 485 | 539 | 540 | 642 | 660 | 722 | 964 | 56 |
| | | M | 302 | 373 | 483 | 455 | 436 | 519 | 599 | 667 | 605 | 699 | 699 | 762 | 906 | |
| 57 | Liberia | X* | 67 | 82 | 62 | 68 | 81 | 126 | 135 | 150 | 159 | 168 | 195 | 213 | 222 | 57 |
| | | M* | 43 | 69 | 91 | 132 | 108 | 111 | 105 | 112 | 125 | 107 | 114 | 150 | 162 | |
| 58 | Libya | X | 129 | 58 | 67 | 191 | 375 | 664 | 851 | 1,055 | 1,232 | 1,942 | 2,270 | 2,533 | 2,865 | 58 |
| | | M | 151 | 257 | 286 | 357 | 387 | 685 | 735 | 910 | 1,067 | 1,563 | 1,780 | 1,640 | 1,909 | |
| 59 | Malagasy Rep. | X* | n.a. | 75 | 78 | 94 | 82 | 92 | 92 | 98 | 104 | 116 | 105 | 145 | 160 | 59 |
| | | M* | n.a. | 111 | 103 | 122 | 127 | 136 | 138 | 142 | 145 | 170 | 170 | 171 | 232 | |
| 60 | Malawi | X | n.a. | n.a. | n.a. | n.a. | n.a. | 44 | 53 | 65 | 73 | 64 | 71 | 78 | 99 | 60 |
| | | M | n.a. | n.a. | n.a. | n.a. | n.a. | 67 | 88 | 111 | 109 | 109 | 119 | 128 | 157 | |
| 61 | Malaysia | X | n.a. | n.a. | 1,166 | 1,181 | 1,212 | 1,248 | 1,408 | 1,422 | 1,381 | 1,517 | 1,806 | 1,851 | 1,805 | 61 |
| | | M | n.a. | n.a. | 1,098 | 1,171 | 1,232 | 1,273 | 1,350 | 1,375 | 1,338 | 1,439 | 1,532 | 1,750 | 1,808 | |
| 62 | Mali | X | n.a. | n.a. | 18 | 13 | 14 | 35 | 24 | 26 | 24 | 26 | 22 | 46 | 53 | 62 |
| | | M | n.a. | n.a. | 62 | 80 | 59 | 84 | 82 | 75 | 65 | 63 | 72 | 95 | 121 | |
| 63 | Mauritania | X* | n.a. | n.a. | 2 | 3 | 16 | 46 | 57 | 69 | 72 | 72 | 70 | 89 | n.a. | 63 |
| | | M* | n.a. | n.a. | 31 | 36 | 30 | 16 | 24 | 23 | 37 | 35 | 39 | 56 | n.a. | |
| 64 | Mexico | X | 1,305 | 1,354 | 1,436 | 1,564 | 1,699 | 1,824 | 1,965 | 2,200 | 2,246 | 2,486 | 2,948 | 3,053 | 3,299 | 64 |
| | | M | 1,466 | 1,673 | 1,664 | 1,731 | 1,900 | 2,236 | 2,363 | 2,591 | 2,881 | 3,243 | 3,557 | 4,110 | 4,212 | |
| 65 | Morocco | X | 456 | 521 | 479 | 470 | 519 | 586 | 580 | 556 | 559 | 612 | 679 | 713 | 751 | 65 |
| | | M | 349 | 486 | 571 | 545 | 604 | 590 | 556 | 617 | 664 | 716 | 761 | 910 | 919 | |
| 66 | Netherlands | X | 4,687 | 5,298 | 5,571 | 5,926 | 6,468 | 7,445 | 8,222 | 8,730 | 9,393 | 10,516 | 12,430 | 14,723 | 17,339 | 66 |
| | | M | 4,204 | 4,955 | 5,371 | 5,751 | 6,393 | 7,604 | 8,161 | 8,866 | 9,388 | 10,385 | 12,369 | 15,127 | 16,482 | |

*Table A.8 cont.*

| | Country | | 1959 | 1960 | 1961 | 1962 | 1963 | 1964 | 1965 | 1966 | 1967 | 1968 | 1969 | 1970 | 1971 | |
|---|---|---|---|---|---|---|---|---|---|---|---|---|---|---|---|---|
| 67 | New Zealand | X | 879 | 879 | 859 | 890 | 1,020 | 1,138 | 1,120 | 1,196 | 1,046 | 1,133 | 1,322 | 1,392 | 1,579 | 67 |
| | | M | 777 | 943 | 1,004 | 881 | 1,045 | 1,136 | 1,248 | 1,311 | 1,183 | 1,054 | 1,211 | 1,425 | 1,556 | |
| 68 | Nicaragua | X | 84 | 72 | 77 | 98 | 121 | 143 | 170 | 170 | 181 | 191 | 191 | 216 | 225 | 68 |
| | | M | 86 | 90 | 92 | 119 | 137 | 164 | 204 | 231 | 255 | 241 | 236 | 264 | 276 | |
| 69 | Niger | X* | 12 | 13 | 15 | 14 | 22 | 21 | 25 | 35 | 33 | 29 | 23 | 32 | 41 | 69 |
| | | M* | 7 | 13 | 19 | 27 | 24 | 33 | 38 | 45 | 46 | 41 | 45 | 58 | 58 | |
| 70 | Nigeria | X | 503 | 510 | 542 | 529 | 584 | 656 | 819 | 867 | 739 | 660 | 964 | 1,345 | 1,997 | 70 |
| | | M | 597 | 699 | 708 | 675 | 732 | 911 | 1,077 | 1,131 | 993 | 944 | 1,145 | 1,478 | 2,261 | |
| 71 | Norway | X | 1,784 | 1,914 | 2,015 | 2,106 | 2,304 | 2,639 | 2,907 | 3,164 | 3,539 | 3,903 | 4,250 | 4,811 | 5,214 | 71 |
| | | M | 1,862 | 2,041 | 2,215 | 2,293 | 2,495 | 2,721 | 3,016 | 3,318 | 3,744 | 3,764 | 4,087 | 4,974 | 5,626 | |
| 72 | Pakistan | X | 411 | 494 | 499 | 534 | 565 | 621 | 641 | 671 | 689 | 751 | 779 | 805 | 776 | 72 |
| | | M | 521 | 734 | 787 | 869 | 965 | 1,148 | 1,239 | 1,113 | 1,401 | 1,271 | 1,303 | 1,591 | 1,431 | |
| 73 | Panama | X | 175 | 125 | 142 | 176 | 195 | 203 | 229 | 253 | 298 | 327 | 361 | 397 | 438 | 73 |
| | | M | 189 | 157 | 170 | 197 | 221 | 224 | 262 | 295 | 327 | 342 | 395 | 462 | 517 | |
| 74 | Paraguay | X | 42 | 43 | 50 | 46 | 45 | 51 | 67 | 64 | 63 | 68 | 78 | 90 | 90 | 74 |
| | | M | 48 | 56 | 63 | 55 | 56 | 62 | 76 | 87 | 92 | 104 | 116 | 111 | 120 | |
| 75 | Peru | X | 376 | 503 | 571 | 622 | 628 | 767 | 776 | 914 | 887 | 1,003 | 1,057 | 1,213 | 1,092 | 75 |
| | | M | 414 | 481 | 588 | 668 | 721 | 762 | 940 | 1,167 | 1,206 | 1,062 | 1,087 | 1,103 | 1,160 | |
| 76 | Philippines | X | 612 | 643 | 613 | 716 | 892 | 942 | 1,092 | 1,187 | 1,222 | 1,166 | 1,123 | 1,341 | 1,408 | 76 |
| | | M | 687 | 787 | 787 | 778 | 789 | 966 | 1,054 | 1,122 | 1,433 | 1,551 | 1,552 | 1,489 | 1,509 | |
| 77 | Poland | X* | 1,145 | 1,326 | 1,504 | 1,646 | 1,770 | 2,096 | 2,228 | 2,272 | 2,527 | 2,858 | 3,142 | 3,547 | 3,872 | 77 |
| | | M* | 1,419 | 1,495 | 1,687 | 1,885 | 1,979 | 2,072 | 2,340 | 2,494 | 2,645 | 2,853 | 3,210 | 3,608 | 4,038 | |
| 78 | Portugal | X | 489 | 536 | 568 | 671 | 728 | 961 | 1,064 | 1,241 | 1,352 | 1,392 | 1,435 | 1,686 | 1,965 | 78 |
| | | M | 536 | 605 | 757 | 761 | 822 | 1,023 | 1,210 | 1,362 | 1,448 | 1,612 | 1,777 | 2,109 | 2,411 | |
| 79 | Puerto Rico | X | 878 | 949 | 1,038 | 1,161 | 1,283 | 1,363 | 1,583 | 1,826 | 2,016 | 2,238 | 2,398 | 2,519 | n.a. | 79 |
| | | M | 1,196 | 1,254 | 1,456 | 1,568 | 1,832 | 2,072 | 2,299 | 2,518 | 2,796 | 3,209 | 3,594 | 4,040 | n.a. | |
| 80 | Romania | X* | 523 | 717 | 793 | 818 | 915 | 1,000 | 1,102 | 1,186 | 1,395 | 1,469 | 1,633 | 1,851 | 2,101 | 80 |
| | | M* | 502 | 976 | 1,026 | 1,149 | 1,022 | 1,168 | 1,077 | 1,213 | 1,546 | 1,609 | 1,741 | 1,961 | 2,103 | |
| 81 | Rwanda | X* | n.a. | n.a. | n.a. | n.a. | 4 | 12 | 11 | 11 | 14 | 15 | 14 | 25 | 22 | 81 |
| | | M* | n.a. | n.a. | n.a. | n.a. | 5 | 12 | 17 | 18 | 20 | 22 | 34 | 29 | 33 | |
| 82 | Saudi Arabia | X | 824 | 899 | 970 | 1,055 | 1,122 | 1,130 | 1,297 | 1,648 | 1,700 | 1,938 | 2,020 | 2,370 | 3,583 | 82 |
| | | M | 605 | 641 | 710 | 837 | 896 | 919 | 1,059 | 1,411 | 1,459 | 1,803 | 1,868 | 2,057 | 2,753 | |

| | | | | | | | | | | | | | | | | |
|---|---|---|---|---|---|---|---|---|---|---|---|---|---|---|---|---|
| 83 | Senegal | X* | 116 | 113 | 124 | 124 | 111 | 123 | 130 | 150 | 139 | 153 | 115 | 152 | 136 | 83 |
| | | M* | 178 | 172 | 155 | 155 | 168 | 172 | 163 | 160 | 165 | 186 | 181 | 193 | 237 | |
| 84 | Sierra Leone | X | n.a. | n.a. | n.a. | n.a. | 87 | 103 | 98 | 91 | 85 | 109 | 124 | 124 | 114 | |
| | | M | n.a. | n.a. | n.a. | n.a. | 107 | 127 | 137 | 122 | 115 | 115 | 138 | 147 | 140 | 84 |
| 85 | Singapore | X | n.a. | n.a. | n.a. | n.a. | 1,323 | 1,124 | 1,241 | 1,388 | 1,433 | 1,578 | 1,808 | 1,942 | 2,246 | 85 |
| | | M | n.a. | n.a. | n.a. | n.a. | 1,421 | 1,154 | 1,274 | 1,372 | 1,495 | 1,720 | 2,114 | 2,556 | 3,106 | |
| 86 | South Africa | X | 2,151 | 2,204 | 2,337 | 2,468 | 2,643 | 2,843 | 2,901 | 3,269 | 3,543 | 3,875 | 3,982 | 3,972 | 4,329 | |
| | | M | 1,940 | 2,159 | 2,045 | 2,058 | 2,468 | 2,965 | 3,366 | 3,315 | 3,854 | 3,871 | 4,411 | 5,198 | 5,751 | 86 |
| 87 | Spain | X | 804 | 1,180 | 1,303 | 1,523 | 1,684 | 2,175 | 2,424 | 2,920 | 2,977 | 3,358 | 3,906 | 4,900 | 5,950 | 87 |
| | | M | 913 | 885 | 1,246 | 1,702 | 2,137 | 2,455 | 3,248 | 3,875 | 3,852 | 4,020 | 4,799 | 5,448 | 5,832 | |
| 88 | Sri Lanka (Ceylon) | X | 432 | 431 | 407 | 420 | 404 | 409 | 443 | 394 | 383 | 374 | 363 | 379 | 369 | 88 |
| | | M | 473 | 482 | 429 | 421 | 442 | 451 | 439 | 463 | 447 | 436 | 504 | 449 | 442 | |
| 89 | Sudan | X | 210 | 213 | 205 | 260 | 274 | 231 | 239 | 273 | 254 | 287 | 292 | 327 | 357 | 89 |
| | | M | 167 | 215 | 269 | 319 | 349 | 316 | 279 | 291 | 303 | 338 | 320 | 370 | 397 | |
| 90 | Sweden | X | 2,937 | 3,356 | 3,515 | 3,734 | 4,044 | 4,600 | 5,004 | 5,362 | 5,709 | 6,166 | 7,096 | 8,408 | 9,186 | 90 |
| | | M | 2,932 | 3,461 | 3,462 | 3,704 | 4,008 | 4,539 | 5,137 | 5,454 | 5,675 | 6,179 | 7,148 | 8,568 | 8,831 | |
| 91 | Switzerland | X | 2,610 | 2,917 | 3,200 | 3,496 | 3,797 | 4,194 | 4,533 | 5,027 | 5,392 | 6,153 | 7,075 | 8,010 | 9,003 | 91 |
| | | M | 2,435 | 2,823 | 3,412 | 3,834 | 4,157 | 4,325 | 4,346 | 4,641 | 4,902 | 5,350 | 6,245 | 7,608 | 8,579 | |
| 92 | Syria | X | 175 | 188 | 163 | 239 | 258 | 247 | 247 | 259 | 249 | 291 | 333 | 326 | 323 | 92 |
| | | M | 195 | 237 | 209 | 245 | 257 | 258 | 242 | 315 | 287 | 332 | 403 | 406 | 486 | |
| 93 | Tanzania | X | n.a. | n.a. | 171 | 172 | 210 | 240 | 229 | 297 | 291 | 299 | 314 | 340 | 391 | 93 |
| | | M | n.a. | n.a. | 177 | 185 | 198 | 212 | 235 | 302 | 300 | 315 | 302 | 387 | 463 | |
| 94 | Thailand | X | 395 | 454 | 536 | 532 | 549 | 695 | 766 | 962 | 1,069 | 1,081 | 1,154 | 1,172 | 1,273 | 94 |
| | | M | 465 | 494 | 534 | 602 | 666 | 754 | 819 | 980 | 1,177 | 1,295 | 1,394 | 1,470 | 1,496 | |
| 95 | Togo | X* | n.a. | 14 | 19 | 17 | 18 | 30 | 27 | 36 | 32 | 39 | 44 | 55 | 49 | 95 |
| | | M | n.a. | 26 | 26 | 27 | 29 | 42 | 45 | 47 | 45 | 47 | 56 | 65 | 70 | |
| 96 | Trinidad–Tobago | X | n.a. | n.a. | 416 | 416 | 427 | 489 | 496 | 525 | 517 | 562 | 595 | 597 | 654 | 96 |
| | | M | n.a. | n.a. | 453 | 471 | 485 | 539 | 576 | 561 | 535 | 563 | 636 | 689 | 772 | |
| 97 | Tunisia | X | 242 | 209 | 191 | 179 | 202 | 206 | 197 | 232 | 241 | 276 | 316 | 355 | 458 | 97 |
| | | M | 226 | 271 | 277 | 279 | 309 | 330 | 377 | 364 | 385 | 351 | 404 | 452 | 489 | |
| 98 | Turkey | X | 447 | 439 | 484 | 519 | 522 | 576 | 681 | 756 | 765 | 766 | 857 | 1,049 | 1,365 | 98 |
| | | M | 564 | 556 | 607 | 754 | 780 | 665 | 711 | 865 | 852 | 994 | 1,036 | 1,181 | 1,433 | |
| 99 | Uganda | X | n.a | n.a. | n.a. | n.a. | n.a. | n.a. | n.a. | 228 | 235 | 237 | 255 | 297 | 273 | 99 |
| | | M | n.a. | n.a. | n.a. | n.a. | n.a. | n.a. | n.a. | 244 | 245 | 240 | 259 | 271 | 342 | |
| 100 | United Kingdom | X | 15,442 | 16,304 | 16,951 | 17,562 | 18,626 | 19,625 | 21,087 | 22,403 | 22,647 | 23,774 | 26,830 | 30,151 | 33,470 | 100 |
| | | M | 14,798 | 16,805 | 16,643 | 16,856 | 17,883 | 20,149 | 20,695 | 21,574 | 22,734 | 23,861 | 25,176 | 28,203 | 29,937 | |

*Table A.8 cont.*

| | Country | | 1959 | 1960 | 1961 | 1962 | 1963 | 1964 | 1965 | 1966 | 1967 | 1968 | 1969 | 1970 | 1971 | |
|---|---|---|---|---|---|---|---|---|---|---|---|---|---|---|---|---|
| 101 | United States | X | 24,563 | 28,509 | 29,617 | 31,548 | 33,939 | 38,701 | 40,938 | 45,117 | 47,825 | 52,798 | 58,204 | 62,891 | 66,133 | 101 |
| | | M | 23,462 | 23,238 | 22,987 | 25,347 | 26,702 | 28,798 | 32,411 | 38,130 | 41,141 | 48,281 | 53,673 | 60,783 | 66,938 | |
| 102 | Upper Volta | X | n.a. | n.a. | 3 | 7 | 8 | 11 | 15 | 16 | 18 | 21 | 19 | 18 | 17 | 102 |
| | | M | n.a. | n.a. | 28 | 35 | 37 | 40 | 37 | 38 | 36 | 41 | 46 | 47 | 55 | |
| 103 | Uruguay | X | 151 | 171 | 221 | 197 | 208 | 231 | 253 | 248 | 219 | 238 | 264 | 282 | 258 | 103 |
| | | M | 201 | 246 | 244 | 269 | 212 | 237 | 184 | 199 | 235 | 221 | 270 | 324 | 297 | |
| 104 | USSR | X* | 5,441 | 5,562 | 5,998 | 7,033 | 7,272 | 7,683 | 8,175 | 8.841 | 9,652 | 10,634 | 11,655 | 12,800 | 13,806 | 104 |
| | | M* | 5,073 | 5,628 | 5,832 | 6,455 | 7,059 | 7,736 | 8,058 | 7,913 | 8,537 | 9,410 | 10,327 | 11,739 | 12,476 | |
| 105 | Venezuela | X | 2,467 | 2,529 | 2,562 | 2,627 | 2,552 | 2,580 | 2,609 | 2,547 | 2,700 | 2,736 | 2,759 | 2,892 | 3,375 | 105 |
| | | M | 2,537 | 2,024 | 2,005 | 2,165 | 1,997 | 2,304 | 2,504 | 2,440 | 2,456 | 2,886 | 2,876 | 2,916 | 3,371 | |
| 106 | Yemen, P.D.R. | X* | 171 | 171 | 185 | 188 | 196 | 207 | 188 | 190 | 138 | 110 | 144 | 146 | 105 | 106 |
| | | M* | 204 | 218 | 235 | 241 | 272 | 297 | 302 | 286 | 198 | 202 | 218 | 202 | 159 | |
| 107 | Yugoslavia | X | 603 | 712 | 750 | 909 | 1,073 | 1,223 | 1,494 | 1,731 | 1,831 | 1,934 | 2,350 | 2,911 | 3,444 | 107 |
| | | M | 775 | 925 | 1,036 | 1,026 | 1,217 | 1,508 | 1,509 | 1,844 | 1,988 | 2,109 | 2,493 | 3,363 | 3,883 | |
| 108 | Zaire | X | n.a. | n.a. | n.a. | n.a. | n.a. | 412 | 385 | 505 | 494 | 614 | 724 | 853 | n.a. | 108 |
| | | M | n.a. | n.a. | n.a. | n.a. | n.a. | 414 | 427 | 517 | 479 | 555 | 670 | 869 | n.a. | |
| 109 | Zambia | X | n.a. | n.a. | n.a. | n.a. | n.a. | 369 | 390 | 663 | 704 | 772 | 1,231 | 994 | 730 | 109 |
| | | M | n.a. | n.a. | n.a. | n.a. | n.a. | 287 | 309 | 579 | 690 | 741 | 684 | 752 | 840 | |

*For goods only; otherwise figures are for goods and services.

# Index

# The author

Professor Coppock, who holds degrees from Swarthmore College and Columbia University, has taught economics at a number of universities and colleges, most recently at the American University of Beirut, and is the author of several books, mainly in international economics. For thirteen years he was a US Government economist, most of the time in the US Department of State. He is now Professor Emeritus of the Pennsylvania State University.